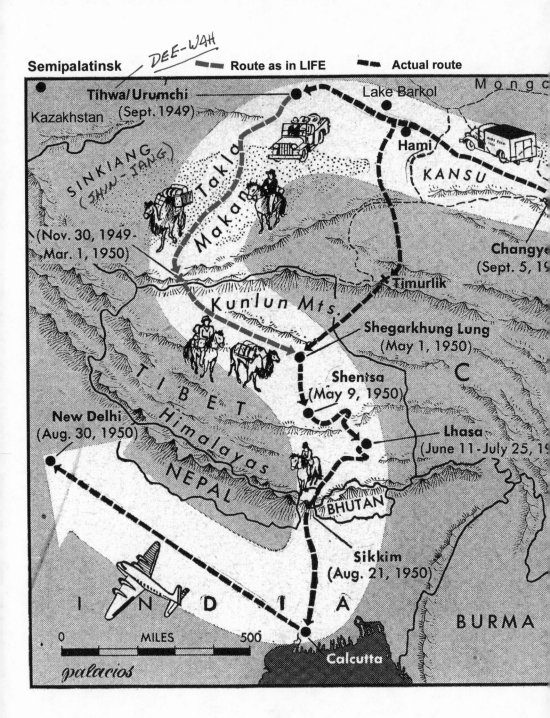

Map from *Life* magazine, November 1950, edited to show actual journey

The Great Wall

INNER MONGOLIA

Peking

Yellow Sea

Shan

Lanchow

Tzehu\ Dingyuanying
(Aug. 20, 1949)

Sian

Nanking

Shanghai

H

I

N

Hankow

A

Chengtu

Chungking

Kweiyang

Kunming

Hong Kong

South
China Sea

Semipalatinsk

Kazakhstan

Mongolia

Koktogai

Alma Ata

Kulja

Eastern Turkistan Republic

(ETR)

Chingil River Ford

Peitaishan

Tihwa/ Urumchi

China Sinkiang

INTO TIBET

THE CIA'S FIRST ATOMIC SPY
AND HIS SECRET EXPEDITION TO LHASA

THOMAS LAIRD

GROVE PRESS • NEW YORK

Published simultaneously in Canada
Printed in the United States of America

FIRST GROVE PRESS PAPERBACK EDITION

Library of Congress Cataloging-in-Publication Data

Laird, Thomas.
    Into Tibet : The CIA's first atomic spy and his secret expedition to Lhasa / by Thomas Laird.
    p. cm.
    ISBN 0-8021-3999-X (pbk.)
    1. United States—Relations—China—Tibet.   2. Tibet (China)—Relations—United States.   3. Espionage, American—China—Tibet.   I. Title: America's secret expedition to Lhasa.   II. Title.
E183.8.T55 L35 2002
303.48'2730515—dc21   2001058459

DESIGN BY LAURA HAMMOND HOUGH

Grove Press
841 Broadway
New York, NY 10003

03   04   05   06   07   10   9   8   7   6   5   4   3   2   1

TO JANN FENNER

AND MY PARENTS,

LOIS WILSON AND TOMMY LAIRD

CONTENTS

AUTHOR'S NOTE

DURING SIX YEARS of research, I tracked down thousands of pages of U.S. government documents, dozens of letters, two diaries, and the survivors of these events. Several of the government documents quoted in this story were obtained only through Freedom of Information Act requests that took several years to bear fruit. Every assertion of fact in this book is based on these documents, published sources, or interviews with specialists, eyewitnesses, and the survivors of the journey. When you see a conversation in quotation marks in this book, they indicate that a person who was at that location at that time recalls those words being said. Or the quotations were recorded in writing at the time or shortly afterward. The tense of these quotations has sometimes been altered to fit them into the narrative. If conversations are not in quotes, it indicates that after exhaustive research I believe that this is what was said.

Occasionally, recalling events of fifty years ago, survivors' recollections fail, or are at odds with others' memories; when this is so I indicate that in the source notes and tell you what happened to the best of my understanding. Descriptions of places and weather and clothes are based on testimony from the survivors, published accounts, and my own experiences in Tibet.

I have given myself more leeway with descriptive passages. I have occasionally conflated events or conversations, which did occur, into one time and place; these few instances are also noted in the source notes. A few names have been changed, but only for minor characters. For the ease of the average reader I have chosen to use the standard spellings for place and people names that were current in America at the time when the events in this book took place. Thus today's Xinjiang is Sinkiang, Xian is Sian, Beijing is Peking, and Osman Batur is Osman Bator.

It is important that the reader understand that when I believe there is doubt about what happened, or what was said, I alert you to that doubt—if not in the text, then in the source notes. For fifty years great pains were taken, and even now continue to be taken, to conceal what truly happened before, during, and after this expedition.

PREFACE

INTO TIBET TELLS the story of a secret American expedition to Tibet in 1949 and 1950 that has never before been told. Only two of the five men who set out survived. Theirs was a two-thousand-mile, one-year trek, and it is one of the most remarkable adventure stories of the twentieth century. The two survivors are the only Americans alive today who have walked across Tibet. However, their story is more than just an adventure tale. The survivors are the last Americans ever to meet the Dalai Lama in independent Tibet. China invaded Tibet six weeks after they left the country. Yet today these men and their journey are not part of history. The primary purpose of this book is to tell as much about their remarkable journey as we are allowed to know.

The facts remained hidden behind a cover story for fifty years. The moment I stumbled upon the first hints of this adventure in the dusty files of the National Archives in Washington, D.C., I felt great sympathy with the men who had trekked through the Himalayas half a century ago. Although I am an American, at forty-eight I have spent more of my life in the Himalayas than in the United States. I first arrived in Nepal in 1972, a nineteen-year-old kid, traveling alone overland from Europe. I have been based in Nepal since, and have made more than fifty treks in the Himalayas. In 1991 I became the *Asiaweek* reporter for Nepal.

For much of 1991 and 1992 I lived in Mustang, a remote Buddhist barony within Nepal that juts up through the Himalayas onto the Tibetan Plateau. The people, their culture, and their language are essentially Tibetan, though Nepal has ruled the area since about 1770. The feudal serfs of Mustang were liberated from their noble masters only in 1956. Incredible fourteenth-century Tibetan Buddhist murals have survived in Mustang, while the Chinese have destroyed 90 percent of such art in Tibet. Mustang became a time capsule of preinvasion Tibet—made more alluring by the fact that it was a forbidden land. The Nepalese government forbade foreigners to visit Mustang during the thirty years before my one-year permit was issued. Nepal and China had not forgotten the covert Central Intelligence Agency support for a Tibetan guerrilla movement based in Mustang after the Chinese invasion of Tibet in 1950. When the United States halted support to the Tibetans in the 1970s, China and Nepal agreed to disarm the guerrillas. Nepalese sensitivities to this Cold War history—and, some said, Chinese pressure—kept Mustang closed to all non-Nepalese during the 1970s and 1980s even as tourism became Nepal's major industry. Mustang became the most coveted travel destination in Nepal.

In 1990 Nepal erupted into revolution. My photography of violent clashes in front of the Royal Palace in Kathmandu was published in many international news magazines. The new government that came to power felt I had risked my life getting pictures out to the world. The new prime minister asked me if there was something I wanted in Nepal, after having lived there for twenty years. I said I wanted to go to Mustang. So in 1991 the government issued me the first (and only) one-year travel permit for Mustang. I spent most of my time there shooting 50,000 photographs, working on a book that Peter Matthiessen and I eventually published, titled *East of Lo Monthang: In the Land of Mustang*.

At the end of my year in Mustang I was eager to fly to the National Archives in Washington, D.C. A number of searing experiences drove me there.

Weapons air-dropped into Mustang by the CIA have never been properly removed from the area. While I was there two teenagers each had blown off a hand with an old CIA-supplied grenade. They found a grenade abandoned beside a trail and tried to break it open. Another young man was killed in 1999 in a similar incident. Seeing the mangled bodies of the children of Mustang made America's hidden history plain: it saddened and angered me.

I spoke with an old Tibetan guerrilla after I came out of Mustang. During one of his raids from Mustang into Tibet, he had acquired intelligence that gave the CIA six months' advance warning of China's first atomic test explosion. When I met him, he was ill, without family, living on charity from other Tibetans. CIA sources say that his atomic intelligence was, dollar for dollar, some of the most valuable intelligence of the entire Cold War. This hero remains unknown, though his eyes still shine with affection for his CIA trainers and love for American ideals.

The maimed boys and the abandoned intelligence hero became symbols to me. Back in the 1960s CIA operatives assured the Tibetan guerrillas that the United States wanted to help the Tibetans drive the Chinese out of Tibet. In fact the guerrillas served U.S. interests, not Tibetan ones. That was made obvious when the United States abruptly established diplomatic relations with China in the 1970s. Covert support to the Tibetans was cut off the next day. Hundreds of guerrillas died as a result of that U.S. abandonment. The weapons of that secret war were left in Mustang to kill innocent children. Its heroes were left without pensions. All of this was collateral damage of American actions, which America now denies ever happened. This cynical manipulation of people and history enraged me.

The fate of the maimed boys in Mustang was before me as I entered the National Archives in 1994 looking for declassified records about the CIA's involvement in Mustang during the 1960s. I discovered in two hours that this U.S. history is still hidden—nearly all the government documents remained classified TOP SECRET. Yet during those same two hours I committed myself to an exploration that would ultimately last six years.

Instead of information about Tibetan guerrillas in Mustang, I found scattered declassified State Department documents about a vice consul named Douglas Mackiernan, Fulbright scholar Frank Bessac, White Russian refugee Vasili Zvansov, and their trip to Tibet in 1949 and 1950. The story of the Mackiernan party gripped me at once. Although most of the State Department documents about it were classified, and the CIA had released none of its documents, from the first moment I started reading the crinkling onion-skin letters, sent to the United States from China and India fifty years earlier, I was hooked.

I copied a few hundred pages of documents and flew home. By 1994 the computer revolution was starting to hit Kathmandu. One day, I ran Bessac's name through a CD-ROM that had every telephone listing in the United States. On my third call from Kathmandu, I suddenly found myself talking to Frank Bessac—ex-CIA as well as Fulbright—in the United States. I was surprised when he told me that he had written about his experience for *Life* magazine in 1950. He warned me cryptically, "Henry Luce turned it into a Cold War yarn." My mother-in-law, back in Los Angeles, had the magazine with Bessac's story in my hands within weeks.

I audiotaped, and videotaped, dozens of hours of interviews with Bessac and then transcribed them. I eventually found seven surviving participants. Each document and each person led me to more people and more documents. I traveled from New Jersey to Dharamsala, India, to interview people. The story still eluded me. After five years of work, I discovered that the survivors did not understand the whole story. At the last moment, a previously unknown diary turned up. It took years for the story, as I now understand it, to take shape in my mind. It is not the same story that *Life* published in 1950. Nor is this just the story that the survivors themselves recall. Despite six years of work, there remain many mysteries here.

The Dalai Lama worried aloud to me when I interviewed him for this book. He wondered if revealing the covert American presence in Tibet in 1950 would give the Chinese some excuse for their invasion. After all, when China invaded Tibet in 1950 it said that its motivating reason was to halt the imperialist plots of American agents in Tibet. At the time, America denied that there were any American agents in Tibet prior to the invasion. Until now that denial has stood unchallenged. This book proves, for the first time, not only that there were Americans in Tibet, but that several agents, in and out of Tibet, worked actively to send military aid to the Tibetans prior to the Chinese invasion. It proves that the highest levels of the U.S. government were involved in that planning—despite government denials ever since. Tibetans were led to believe that the United States would help them if China invaded. This book shows, for the first time, why Tibetans felt betrayed by America after the Chinese invasion— and how American actions may have hastened the Chinese invasion of Tibet—tragically even while Americans on the ground tried to help the country.

There are many reasons why the CIA documents, which would reveal every detail about the story that is told here, remain secret even now, fifty years later. The Dalai Lama's concern may be one of them. In addition, the United States prefers to blame China alone for the invasion, rather than to dilute Chinese guilt with any hint of U.S. involvement. But one reason stands out from all others. I believe that the CIA realizes it indirectly involved Tibet in the one of America's first atomic intelligence operations led by Douglas Mackiernan back in 1950, at the birth of the Cold War, an operation that benefited the United States but that may have helped destroy Tibet. Nothing about American atomic intelligence operations in foreign countries has ever been declassified by the CIA. This may be the primary reason why this Tibetan chapter of U.S. history has remained hidden. It is not covert U.S. operations in Tibet that are being hidden, but the U.S. atomic secrets to which they are linked. And yet while the CIA operations revealed here were intended to be covert, at the time of these events the Chinese knew almost everything you are about to read. The failure to keep these operations secret may have helped precipitate the Chinese invasion of Tibet in 1950—though precipitating the invasion of Tibet was the opposite of America's avowed intentions. The CIA seems to be hiding its own tragic mistakes behind the veil of national security.

Every CIA director, since 1950, as well as current director George Tenet, has known that these secret operations claimed the life of the first CIA undercover agent ever killed in the line of duty. He is honored by the CIA for his contributions and sacrifice. But the agency may not yet know precisely why that man died. Certainly, it has not linked his death to McCarthyism. A current employee of the CIA says that the administrators of the CIA believe that discussing the covert operation, in which that first agent died, would disrupt modern Sino-U.S. relations. Another CIA employee has written a letter that states there are practical national security reasons why the story behind his death cannot be revealed to the public. In the CIA foyer, near the wall where the CIA honors agents who have died in service to the United States, a line from Christian scripture is inscribed: "And ye shall know the truth, and the truth shall make you free." I agree with these sentiments entirely, though now, more than ever, I am unsure if anyone ever knows the full truth, certainly with regard to these events.

Despite all that, readers will want to know if this is a true story. Many facts and many chapters of history are condensed and brought to life in this book, but much is also left out. I have not tried to write an academic history of Tibet. Rather, my aim is to penetrate to the furious, chaotic heart of Tibet's fight for freedom at the moment when that freedom was lost. I try to reveal the essence of what happened, not through a recitation of every fact but by an understanding of what the Americans who lived through these events did and felt, and what motivated them.

My final answer is still the same: Yes, this is a true story.

—Thomas Laird
laird100@yahoo.com
www.intotibet.info

Washington, D.C.; Coral Gables, Florida; New Haven, Connecticut; Hackettstown, New Jersey; Missoula, Montana; Kona, Hawaii; Boston, Massachusetts; New York City; Manhattan Beach, Albany, Berkeley, Santa Rosa, and Palo Alto, California; Gauhati, New Delhi, and Dharamsala, India; Lhasa, Tibet; Kathmandu, Nepal
August 1994–November 2001

PART ONE

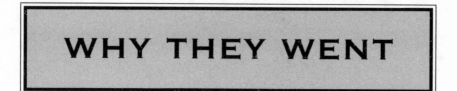

WHY THEY WENT

"The only new thing in the world is the history you don't know."

—PRESIDENT HARRY S. TRUMAN

SHEGAR-HUNGLUNG
THE TIBET-SINKIANG BORDER
33.40 NORTH, 87.20 WEST
2PM, APRIL 29, 1950

The first gunshot was as loud inside the yak-wool tent as it was outside on the Tibetan Plateau. Frank Bessac spilled his wooden cup of salt and butter tea as he raced over to peer out of the tent flap. The two young Tibetan women busy serving tea only moments before crowded up behind him and looked over his shoulder toward his camp.

A hundred yards away a knot of horses and men circled Bessac's canvas tent. Puffs of smoke raced off on the wind as several shooters on their horses lowered their rifles. A dozen short-legged Tibetan ponies pranced around on the treeless plain, silhouetted against the vast sky. One horseman climbed off his horse and advanced on the tent, shouting, with his gun drawn. In the distance, Bessac could see two horsemen approaching his tent from behind. The expedition was surrounded, and apparently everyone was in the tent as someone shouted back at the Tibetans.

Bessac cursed softly to himself.

"Damn! Travel for eight months and the first Tibetans we see start shooting."

Bessac turned back to his hosts and for the fifth time tried his Mongolian and Chinese on the two Tibetan girls. In their fright, they clung to each other but looked at him just as blankly as they had before. The old man, who had slowly warmed to him as tea was made and served, now got up off his carpet by the dung-fueled fire and walked to the tent door.

Without ceremony, the old man started to push him out of the tent. Bessac grabbed the wool robe of the Tibetan, and tried to pull him toward his own tent, pleading. The old man quickly brushed off

Bessac's hands, but he paused and listened, as Bessac shouted desperately in English.

"Look, you're Tibetan. You could talk to them. We're Americans. We're going to Lhasa! Meet the Dalai Lama. The government knows we are coming. Dalai Lama. Lhasa!"

When Bessac finished pleading, the eyes of the old man remained flat, seemingly devoid of any understanding. They could not understand him in English, Chinese, or Mongolian, and now clearly they were not even going to let him back inside their tent.

At sixteen thousand feet on the treeless Changthang Plateau, Bessac had only two options. Their tent or his. There was not even a rock to hide behind. The Tibetans were the first humans the expedition had met in two months. When Bessac turned back toward his camp and the swirling horses and men surrounding it, the rest of his party began to emerge from the canvas tent.

At a hundred yards, it was impossible to tell who was holding up the white flag. Doug Mackiernan and the three Russians were all dressed, like Bessac, in crudely sewn Kazak sheepskin robes. It was obvious to Frank that these were his friends, and not another party of Tibetans or Kazak, only because they had trekked together for so long.

When he saw them walk out of the tent, Frank started running back. He grabbed his glasses, trying to keep them on his head as he ran, because without them he would be virtually blind. The Tibetans gathered in front of the tent with their raised guns. Three men were in front, with the feeble-looking white flag advancing toward the guns. Behind them, someone crouched back, as if not sure he should advance unarmed on the Tibetans.

The Tibetans were startled—perhaps by the flag or by the fact that the foreigners walked confidently toward them with no weapons in their hands. Some of the Tibetans remained mounted, their horses shifting under them. Others stood on the ground. Yet they all kept their guns keenly focused on Bessac's friends. Suddenly, one of the Tibetans in the front rank of gunmen stepped back, and Bessac stopped running.

"Don't shoot," Bessac said softly.

The Tibetan, who had retreated a step, fired first. A puff of white smoke rose into the wind. Then almost at once, all the other Tibetans fired, and a wave of smoke rose above their heads. The sound of the volley reached Bessac as he started running again toward his friends.

When the guns fired, the man who had held back dropped low and began to dodge between the bullets. Bessac's heart leapt as he saw him make for the tent. Was it Mackiernan?

At the same moment, the other three men moved in an entirely different way. They twisted in midair, the way bodies do when bullets hit them. And then they went down hard, and at such unnatural angles.

Running as fast as he could at sixteen thousand feet, Bessac shouted at the gunmen in English.

"Don't shoot. Dalai Lama! Dalai Lama! Lhasa!"

Bessac was now close enough to see the amazement on the Tibetans' faces. As they turned around and saw him running toward them, they began to fire at him. The earth six feet to his left burst in a small fountain of dust. Another blast of dust flared three feet to his right.

His instincts, drilled into him at the Outfit's camp on Catalina Island, took over—Bessac found himself kissing the earth behind a tiny hillock that he had not till now known was there. A bullet kicked up the dirt just above his hat. He waited, listening for the next bullet. The sweat that had broken out all over his body turned cold as he lay there. A minute passed, where he could hear only the wind.

He raised his head just enough so that his eyeglasses peeked over the earth at the gunmen. One of them pointed at Bessac, and then began to trace circles around his own eyes. Again, he pointed at Bessac and shouted at his friends. Seeing this, Bessac realized that he was the only person in his party wearing glasses and wondered what that meant to the Tibetans.

Shouting erupted among the Tibetans. Bessac listened, watched, and then stood up. No one pointed a gun at him. He held his ground and removed his glasses to wipe off the dirt, pondering his next move. The Tibetans watched intently as he cleaned his glasses. When he started walking slowly toward them, they were still watching him with their guns lowered.

At twenty yards, Bessac again started shouting in English, then Chinese, and then Mongolian, repeatedly.

"Lhasa! Dalai Lama! Lhasa!"

At five yards, the Tibetans raised their guns again. Bessac stopped walking, locked his eyes on them, and continued his mantra, softly now.

"Dalai Lama. Lhasa."

The doubt in the eyes of the Tibetans grew, and they looked back and forth at one another, the barrels of their guns sinking ever closer toward the earth. Then the man who had retreated and fired first raised his gun and shook it at Bessac as he shouted, "Kowtow! Kowtow!"

He pointed his gun at the earth and shook it again as he yelled once more, "Kowtow!"

A Chinese phrase that Frank knew well. Bow down. Get on your knees. Submit to me. Show me your subservience.

Frank didn't think; he spoke, in English, not loudly at first but his voice rose louder into the wind as his anger increased.

"I damn well won't kowtow to you. You come up here shooting people, people invited by the Dalai Lama to come to Lhasa—and you want me to kowtow? I will not kowtow. No goddamned kowtow! You are going to kowtow to me when the Dalai Lama finds out what you have done! Americans don't kowtow to anybody!"

The Tibetans watched blankly as Frank spoke. When he took off his glasses and waved them at the Tibetans, emphasizing his refusal to kowtow, some of the men smiled.

The grim-faced leader did not smile but only stared sternly at Bessac. When his men laughed, he leveled his gun barrel at Bessac, now at point-blank range. One of the laughing Tibetans behind the leader jerked up his head quickly to catch Bessac's eye. He then cocked his head toward the ground, and raised a free hand as if firing his gun.

Bessac saw the mimed gestures. He could see the look of almost mock concern on the one Tibetan's face as he again violently cocked his head toward the ground.

What the hell, he thought to himself as he let his pride go and sank to his knees.

A ripple of words erupted from the head Tibetan, his gun dropping back down toward the earth.

"La, la, la. Nyingje."

The Tibetan who had mimed for him slung his rifle over his shoulder, stepped out of the group, and walked toward Bessac, pulling a goat-hair rope out of his robe. Bessac kept his eyes locked on the ground and did not move. The mime pulled Bessac's hands behind his back and bound them. Bessac glanced up and saw the rest of the Tibetans rush over to the expedition's camel loads, which sat outside the tent on the ground. Then the man who had bound his hands took off Bessac's glasses, and his world three feet away immediately turned to a gray blur.

He listened to the Tibetans as they cracked open the crate with the machine guns. He could hear their startled shouts of surprise and glee when they found the gold bars. He heard the clicking of a Geiger counter as it was flicked on and off, and then what sounded like a rock smashing into Mackiernan's machine. Bessac only hoped they would not play with the grenades.

Those were all smaller, distant things. Most of his attention was focused on a human foot, which lay quite near him in the dirt. It belonged to one of his friends. A crudely sewn sheepskin covered the leg. Five feet away, the face that belonged to the foot was a complete blur. As his world shrank, Bessac knew he should try to get closer so he could see the face and check if he was alive. Instead, he looked at the foot and the robe and remembered when the Kazak sold them the sheepskins. He thought about how they measured one another and cut the skins. He remembered sitting in the Kazak yurt turning the fleece in and the leather out, stitching up the robes as the snow fell outside.

"Warm enough to get you to Tibet, doesn't matter what they look like. And I guess the Tibetans won't be expecting diplomats in tuxedos."

Who said that? Who was that lying in front of him, in such an odd and uncomfortable position, lying so still?

AN ATOMIC MONOPOLY, AN ATOMIC PEACE
PRELUDE TO COLD WAR
1945 TO 1949

The Americans who walked into Tibet—and the resulting fatal shoot-out on the Tibetan border in 1950—took the first steps of that journey by traveling to China during World War II, and by surviving the war. Neither Frank Bessac nor Douglas Mackiernan went to China as an average soldier. Both men worked with the Office of Strategic Services, in their own different ways. The OSS was disbanded at war's end, broken into different pieces. Many of these fragments were eventually reforged into America's first peacetime intelligence outfit: the Central Intelligence Agency. Both men began their time in China as, in common parlance, spies.

In 1945 atomic intelligence was the crown jewel of the American intelligence community. The astounding value of atomic bombs, and the consequential value of any intelligence about uranium, was personal for Bessac, though unlike Mackiernan he had no involvement with American atomic intelligence in China. In the final days of World War II Bessac was scheduled for what was billed as a suicidal intelligence mission behind Japanese lines, in southern China, when the atomic explosions at Hiroshima and Nagasaki abruptly ended the war. The value of the bomb for Bessac, as for so many American soldiers in the Pacific, was simple: "It saved my life." It is estimated that more than 250,000 American lives would have been lost in any invasion of Japan. Atomic bombs saved those lives—in seconds—just as surely as they vaporized hundreds of thousands of Japanese.

In 1946 no nation could ignore the fact that the United States was the sole possessor of atomic bombs, a monopoly that made America the world's first superpower. Nothing was of greater national concern to America than how long its atomic monopoly would last. President

Truman, his generals, and his diplomats all assumed that it would last longer than it did. This assumption, based on a misleading interpretation of atomic intelligence, and a misguided faith in a particular covert operation, was one of the greatest policy, and intelligence, failures of the postwar period. Promises were made based on the assumption of invincibility; policy was created, particularly in Asia, as if America would forever be the world's sole atomic power. In fact, the period of America's atomic monopoly lasted only from the summer of 1945 to the summer of 1949. It took just these four short years for Russia to steal America's bomb design and find the scarce uranium with which to make one—despite a massive American effort to prevent it.

From 1945 to 1949 little else in the world was more feared, despised, desired, or more secret than atomic bombs and their key ingredient, uranium. An ounce of that dull gray metal was now worth ten thousand times an ounce of gold—but none was for sale. America had the bomb: that was no longer a secret in 1946. After Hiroshima the greatest atomic secret was that America was fighting to maintain a global monopoly on the supply of uranium. The chief aim of that secret battle was to keep uranium out of Russia's hands.

With Pearl Harbor as their defining moment, and Hiroshima still ringing in their ears, America's postwar leaders knew that they had to collect military intelligence from all over the world, more effectively and more thoroughly than ever before. Not only was an American monopoly on uranium essential, but it was just as important for America to know, in advance, if any nation were to secretly build an atomic bomb. Such goals demanded that intelligence material from around the world be collected, centralized, digested, and disseminated to all levels of the American government. The fear of failure for the U.S. intelligence community was unlike anything ever felt before the Atomic Age. Failure could mean annihilation of all Americans, and that driving fear was described by a simple phrase repeated many times: "An atomic Pearl Harbor." The newsreels of Hiroshima made it clear what an intelligence failure, which could allow an atomic Pearl Harbor in the United States, would mean.

As World War II turned into the Atomic Peace before the Cold War, individual Americans were thrust by an emerging global intelligence outfit into distant affairs in the most remote corners on earth. Americans were headed into places so remote that hardly any American had ever heard of them.

In this new era America needed intelligence about the Mongol, Kazak, and Tibetan peoples of Inner Asia. This was no longer an academic exercise—as remote as they are, these people were no longer unconnected to America. For a time, during the years of the American atomic monopoly, and just as it collapsed, some Americans wondered if the survival of America might not depend upon relations with these people, and intelligence about America's enemies that these people could supply.

America's emerging national security interests in Inner Asia were complicated by the Republic of China's insistence that all of these people, and all their land, where no Chinese lived, belonged to China. During the war the United States had blindly recognized and supported China's extravagant territorial claims, simply because China was America's only Asian ally. As the atomic peace settled over Asia, some Americans in China wondered at the wisdom of that course.

STRATEGIC SERVICES UNIT, HQ
PEKING, THE REPUBLIC OF CHINA
MARCH 5, 1946

"Fragrant Comes the Night," a Chinese dance melody, played on the tinny gramophone inside the nineteenth-century Mandarin mansion, which served as HQ. The music drifted through the formal garden that surrounded the minor palace of an old Manchu bureaucrat not far from the Forbidden City. The family who owned the house was happy to have the Americans renting it in the hard spring just after World War II.

Peking's literary and social elite, and their young daughters, milled about at a dinner party in honor of the Americans who had helped China defeat the Japanese invaders and colonialists. The eviction of millions of Japanese from China—some of whom had been there for decades before the war—was nearly complete. The few American military men who had stayed on in Peking were guests at a party to honor those who had helped China free herself from Japanese colonialism.

Frank Bagnall Bessac, twenty-four years old and fluent in Chinese, would be a civilian in weeks, but that night he was still in the U.S. Army.

At the outbreak of the war, Bessac enlisted. He was a twenty-year-old private scrambling through his last year at the College of the Pacific. Eager for war, he was irritated when the U.S. Army selected him for Chinese-language training at Cornell University. He was still railing against army delays when he was sent to Fort Riley, Kansas, for cavalry training—where the Office of Strategic Services (OSS) recruited him as a secret intelligence agent: OSS-SI. After training, he boarded a ship to India. From there he flew over the Himalayas and into the western sliver of China that Chiang Kai-shek had not lost to the invading Japanese.

By the summer of 1945 he was based in Kunming, ready to be dropped behind Japanese lines in occupied China as the intelligence officer on a Chinese paratrooper commando mission. It was a suicide mission. Despite the unexpected end of the war, brought on by Hiroshima, Bessac felt an obligation to put his training to work for his country, so he stayed on in postwar China. His sense of honor and his vision of the OSS as knights in shinning armor made him stay. Like many early CIA recruits he had special knowledge and a desire to serve.

The U.S. Army's Strategic Services Unit (SSU) at Peking had inherited the best secret intelligence agents in China from the OSS when it was disbanded after World War II. In 1946 Bessac's SSU intelligence reports on the Chinese Communist Eighth Route Army, and others, were studied by American diplomats in Washington and Moscow. He was one of only two American intelligence agents in Peking who spoke Chinese. Peking SSU was ranked as the outstanding intelligence unit of the United States military in China. But that night, America's agents in Peking had a night off.

Some of the young Chinese women were dressed in Western evening gowns while older women wore elegant Chinese silk robes.

A great Peking cook worked for days creating the endless stream of Chinese dishes the guests sampled during the banquet. Bessac's friend John Bottorff was going steady with a girl from one of the best families. Bottorff's girl had brought her younger sister, Mei-ling. Frank Bessac, or Pai Chih-jen as the Chinese called him, kept Mei-ling company that night.

After dinner Frank and Mei-ling danced inside the part-Western, part-Chinese mansion with the other couples. It was a strange night, as Peking's old Manchu elite tried to dress up for a world fresh out of war but not quite yet at peace. Mei-ling was also at an awkward stage, at the point between childhood and womanhood. Her schoolgirl's bob was growing out. She was alluring in her evening gown. When she glanced shyly up at Bessac, he remembered his younger sister, innocent and filled with promise. She was totally off limits, leaving the evening bittersweet.

Bessac, a strongly patriotic young Californian, felt honor bound to stay on in China after the war, but the pay wasn't great. His life contained many such dualities. The previous autumn he had fallen in love with a Chinese woman. He did not have enough money to marry her, and the direction of his life was still too uncertain to take on the responsibility of marriage.

He was also torn between U.S. government policy in China and his own conscience. Shortly after Hiroshima had ended the war, while he waited to go to Peking, the army had made him sign a pledge that he would not discuss what was called "the China question" with any Chinese. The end of World War II was the opening salvo for a Chinese civil war between the Nationalists, led by Chiang Kai-shek, and the Communists, led by Mao Tse-tung. The China question was simple: Who would rule? It was already creating deep divisions in America, though the American public was certain that Chiang would easily defeat Mao. It would be four more years before that assumption was proven false, causing the issue to boil over into McCarthyism and another Red Scare in America.

In a heated letter to his father, Bessac explained that his first six months in China (June to December 1945) proved to him that Generalissimo Chiang Kai-shek was a fascist dictator. Too many Chinese were getting shot or tortured for expressing their political opinions,

which made it clear that the Chinese people would ultimately re-
ject Chiang. Bessac was certain Mao would one day rule China, and
wondered why the United States was driving Mao into the arms of
the Russians. Bessac thought that it was already too late to change
sides. Russia would arm the Chinese Communists, and America
would arm the Nationalists. This served the interests of Russian
imperialism in China. He believed Russia wanted to see China at
war and the United States bogged down there. Bessac thought the
only way to avoid a war in China was for the United States to switch
its support to the Communists. Bessac wanted to serve his country.
He had volunteered for an OSS mission that was considered a suicide mission by many. His patriotism was unquestionable, and he
wanted what was best for the United States. So that spring he was
angry with a government in Washington that had no apparent understanding of the disaster developing in China. Washington was not
listening to what its own intelligence agents on the ground in China
were saying.

Bessac considered solving his problems by quitting the military and
securing a better-paying job as an investigator for the United Nations
Relief and Rehabilitation Administration (UNRRA). That plan was
nixed when his boss at SSU, Ben Smith, told Bessac that he was essential, and sent him off on another cloak-and-dagger trip. "Long
Live the OSS!" was Bessac's cynical salute that spring, though the OSS
had been dead for six months. He had the China Blues, as it was then
called.

After dancing, he and Mei-ling went out into the garden, where
the music faintly echoed. They walked through a moon gate and
looked at the early blooming plums. Then he took her back to the
party, said good night, and returned to his room in the back courtyard of the mansion. There he climbed into his bed and picked up
Owen Lattimore's *Inner Asian Frontiers of China*. Bessac had recently
discovered the grand old man of China studies. If he could not
surrender to romance, he could plunge into the ancient life of China.

> The general line of the Great Wall of China marks one of the most
> absolute frontiers in the world. . . . Agriculture teems in China, and
> mankind swarms. Beyond the Great Wall men are fewer and more

widely scattered. . . . Over thousands of miles . . . men neglect agriculture altogether. . . . The secret of the nomadic life is the control
of animals by men.

Many differences—including race, nationality, language, religion
. . . can be referred to the Great Wall line of cleavage. In China . . . in
spite of wide variations of dialect . . . all men speak the Chinese language . . . beyond the Wall such languages as . . . Manchu, Mongol
[Tibetan] and Central Asian Turkish . . . are not "dialects" of Chinese.

The Great Wall of China is a . . . boundary . . . distinguishing the
Chinese . . . from the barbarian. . . . It serves not only to keep the
outsiders from getting in but to prevent the insiders from getting out
. . . because in entering "un-Chinese" terrain [beyond the Wall] the
Chinese had to modify or abandon their Chinese economy, thus
weakening their attachment to other Chinese.

Bessac read on into the night about the thousand-year war, along
the Great Wall, between the nomads on the highland steppes of Inner
Asia and the farmers on the lowland river deltas of China.

The war along the Great Wall never went well for China. It is a
bitter reality that Chinese try to ignore or deny. The Chinese turned
the murderous Mongol conquest of China—from 1215 to 1368—
into what they call the Yuan Dynasty. The Manchu conquest lasted
from 1644 to 1912 and many Chinese still view this as a Chinese
dynasty. In both cases Chinese today attempt through a jujitsu-like
use of history to turn the facts on their heads. They claim all the
military victories of these foreign invaders as Chinese. They say that
both of these dynasties became Chinese dynasties. Or as China's
greatest works of philosophy say, the losers win, the strong are weak,
the weak rule. In fact, the losers lost, and the invading foreigners
crushed China. When Lattimore points to the history of the Great
Wall as the primary way to understand modern China, he is pointing to the center of Chinese history. Lattimore also dismissed China's
claims over the territory conquered by Mongols and Manchu, as early
as 1934.

the Mongols and Tibetans . . . regarded the fall of the Manchu
Empire as the destruction of a framework, which ought simply to

have allowed the original component parts of the Empire to resume their own national identities. Nor can there be any doubt that legally and historically they were right.

Bessac continued reading Lattimore long after the music and the laughter from the party had faded.

The twittering sparrows, nesting in the tiled roof of the mansion, woke Bessac before it was light enough to see the curling geometric wooden grills in the windows. He jogged out of the gated compound and ran along his lane. At last, he emerged from the densely packed alleys of ancient Peking into the cleared space behind the Tibetan lama temple and ran along the inner face of the vast outer walls of the city. In the early dawn light, they towered out of the mists. A group of elders, gathered in the clear space, moved slowly through the graceful forms of tai chi. Chittering clouds of sparrows flew in and out of their nests within the wall and left the soaring brick walls streaked white.

Construction of the fifty-foot-high walls began in 1266 at the order of an invading Mongol conqueror. It amazed Bessac to realize that the Chinese were ruled by invading foreigners during four hundred fifty of the past eight hundred years—and all of them ruled from within the walls of Peking.

These four centuries of Inner Asian rule, as much as European colonialism in China during the nineteenth and twentieth centuries, created the deep sense of national grievance that underlies modern Chinese nationalism. Perhaps for this reason Mao had Peking's ancient Mongol walls pulled down when he was victorious in 1949.

In 1946 the outer city walls of Peking stretched nearly fifteen miles, enclosing a maze of walled compounds, alleyways, and parklands: home to 1.5 million people. At the heart of the city was the massive pink inner wall surrounding the yellow glazed tile roofs of the Forbidden City, home to both foreign empires that had ruled China. Walls within walls within walls, and all of them had something to do with Mongols, Manchu, and the Great Wall.

A group of Mongols standing near the gate of their walled compound pointed at the American jogging by. Bessac waved at them and kept running. He dodged a coal seller, slipped by a noodle cart, and ran on. As he jogged through the chaos, he noticed the thick-chested Mongols laughing, out of the corner of his eye.

"How did I know they were Mongols and not Chinese?" he wondered to himself as he kept running. The large-framed men, with square heads and square shoulders, looked nothing like the frailer Chinese. Generations of free life on horseback had created a people quite different from those sprung from generations of settled farming life. Chinese are not Mongols.

Their faces, their hands, the stance of the body—all these images of Mongolia ran through Bessac's mind as he dodged nimbly in and out between the teeming crowds of Chinese within the walled city of Peking. One world inside the Great Wall; another outside it. One people within the Great Wall; others outside of it.

That spring the SSU sent Bessac north through the Great Wall to what Chinese called the province of Inner Mongolia, to report on a conference at Kalgan between the Mongols who were a majority there and the Communist Party, which controlled the territory along the border with Russia's ally, the Mongolian People's Republic. From Kalgan Bessac drove north a few more days. The Outfit then demonstrated its intense interest in Inner Mongolia, when it sent a twenty-four-seat Dakota to fly him and his translator further north, deep into the Gobi Desert. He landed in a hidden valley called Peitzemiao, and spent a week riding with the nomads on the vast treeless steppes of Inner Asia—in a land far beyond the control of any Chinese. The Communist Party hoped to convince Bessac that a Communist state would treat the "minority people" of Inner Mongolia differently than the Republic of China had since it overthrew the Manchu Empire in 1912.

In Peitzemiao Bessac developed a lifelong committment to the non-Chinese outside the Great Wall. Their free way of life appealed to his American sense of freedom. He came to China to defeat Japanese colonialism and now he saw no reason why America should support Chinese colonialism beyond the Great Wall. His first lesson beyond the Great Wall was simply that there were no Chinese there. Though Mao Tse-tung and Chiang Kai-shek were about to kill millions of Chinese in a civil war there was one thing the two men agreed upon. Inner Mongolia and Tibet—like all the lands conquered by the Mongol and Manchu invaders of China—were part of China.

Riding across the steppes with the Mongols of Inner Mongolia, Bessac learned that the people there did not share that view of history. The Mongols of the "province" of Inner Mongolia were not Chinese and never had been. Bessac saw that the ancient war along the Great Wall was finding a new expression in the twentieh century. He reported the message from Inner Mongolia to the SSU and his reports were sent to U.S. embassies around the world.

We are not Chinese. We are Mongol. We are nomads and the Chinese are farmers. Communist or Nationalist are the same to us. They are both Chinese and they want our land. Now they have trains and machine guns, and we are afraid.

The Mongols Bessac listened to that spring could just as well have been speaking for the Tibetans or the Kazaks—or any of the people just beyond the Great Wall whose lands the Chinese had coveted for millenia. Owen Lattimore was the man who introduced Frank Bessac to this basic lesson about China, and he never forgot it.

Lattimore, in his conclusion to *Inner Asian Frontiers of China,* said that the nomads and the farmers had fought along the Great Wall for two thousand years. During all that time, there was no victor.

"Neither could hold sway over the other, and yet neither could absorb or even permanently subdue the other."

Until now. By 1946, China had begun to inherit the industrial power of the West, technology the Inner Asians had not mastered. Technology that would allow Chinese farmers to thrive on the arid steppes. At that same moment, American intelligence agents were being sent into the heart of that thousand-year war—of which America was ignorant. America would see this war as one between Communism and anti-Communism. The ancient war along the Great Wall was about to spark new battles—in Tibet, Sinkiang, Korea, Vietnam, and America.

U.S. EMBASSY
NANKING, CAPITAL OF THE REPUBLIC
OF CHINA
MARCH 1946

The phonograph was not played at cocktails. Instead, the sound of twenty different conversations produced a steady hum, punctuated with laughter and the clink of ice in glasses. White-liveried Chinese servants circulated with drinks. Three single women from the code room in the U.S. embassy were having a cocktail party. The hostesses had already made their rounds and were now hovering in front of the man that American women in Nanking had quickly voted the handsomest man in town. Handsome, but difficult, that was the word.

They stood in a circle in front of U.S. Army Air Force Major Douglas Seymour Mackiernan, just in from China's far northwest province of Sinkiang (modern Xinjiang—both pronounced *shin-jang*). Thirty-three years old, he was at a cocktail party during an easy posting in the new postwar Chinese capital, Nanking. He was enjoying a brief period back in what he sardonically called "civilization."

The officer's short-cropped dark hair was slicked back. His dark, sleepy eyes glowed with an intense light, which the women found both a little frightening and appealing. He allowed himself to be inspected, but answered in monosyllables. Better their mindless chatter than that from men in the room who thought they knew something. Ponderous conversations about who would win the Chinese civil war—all of them spouting whatever they had read in the newspapers.

The women hovered around Mackiernan. Their black cocktail dresses flared out fashionably, though the Nanking tailors still cut them according to last fall's fashion in New York—well below the knee. The center of their attention shifted his always-present pipe as he answered their questions. One of the braver women reached out and touched Mackiernan on the shoulder, for emphasis. You were in Tihwa? Now that's an outpost. It must be the most remote U.S. consulate in China.

Mackiernan's uniform looked as if it had been pressed within the hour, and he stood tall in it. The young woman leaned closer to catch his soft-spoken reply, couched in a thick Boston accent. It was hard to get him talking. When Tihwa (pronounced *dee-wha,* modern Urumchi) came up, he launched into a long monologue.

Mackiernan talked about the camels crossing the dunes between the oasis towns; the long trains of animals in the desert; the yurt camps at night; the Silk Road that ran from Rome to Peking, and how Marco Polo passed along it to China. He said that the life that Marco Polo had seen was still alive in Tihwa. He joked about how Sinkiang was nominally Chinese, how it was actually run by non-Chinese Uighur and Kazak who made up 95 percent of the population. He frightened them with a tale of a dust storm. He talked about hunting in the desert on horseback.

Mackiernan knew Tihwa well. He had fallen in love with a young Russian during his long World War II posting to Sinkiang, and was married in the Russian Orthodox Church in Tihwa—a bigamous war marriage, when he was still married to Darrell, his first wife.

One of the rapt women asked him how he could stand to be in Nanking after having lived that life. Mackiernan reverted to curt replies. Officers went where they were sent. He expected soon to be sent back to Tihwa, as a clerk for the State Department.

One of the young women pointed out that he was an officer, and that he would lose a lot of Army Air Force rank to start as a clerk for the State Department. He brushed it off. It did not seem to matter to him: not nearly as much as getting back to Tihwa. Tihwa had become Mackiernan's obsession during the war.

Douglas Seymour Mackiernan was a twenty-nine-year-old research scientist at MIT when the war broke out in 1942, a man who had already set his course. Because of a childhood spent in Mexico and Brazil he spoke German and Spanish fluently. He was an avid radio hobbyist from the age of six. Despite obvious abilities he was expelled from MIT after his freshman year because of poor grades. He told his family he already knew the course work and didn't want to waste time studying what he already knew. There was substance beneath this arrogance. He was smart enough that MIT immediately hired him as a research assistant, despite his lack of a degree. In 1936 and 1937 he worked as a researcher for an advanced meteorology project jointly supported by MIT, the U.S. Weather Bureau, Pan American Airways, and the Cuban Weather Service. He worked on one of the first teams to send balloon-borne data detectors into the path of hurricanes, that were able to radio back weather data which enabled meteorologists to begin to predict the path of hurricanes. He was bold enough to walk in on the father of the American rocket, Robert Goddard, simply to pick his brains, and talented enough to begin testing his own rocket engines a few months later, as a hobby. By 1942, Mackiernan's lifelong involvement with meteorology and radios had taken him to the forefront of science. H.T. Stetson employed him at MIT's Cosmic Terrestrial Research Laboratory in Needham, just outside Boston—and even co-authored a substantial research paper with his young protégé in the same year. Many of the men at MIT that Mackiernan should have graduated with—and he seems to have had their respect for the work he did if not the degree—went on to build radar and America's first atomic bomb. He was running with a pack of young scientific brains that were about to change the world.

When war broke out, OSS did not select Mackiernan. Instead, he cut his own path into American intelligence. Family legend says that Mackiernan was able to receive encoded weather broadcasts from the Soviet Union on his ham station at home, WHTQ. It is more likely that he detected those broadcasts with the cutting-edge radio receivers at Stetson's lab in Needham. How he obtained the coded data soon became irrelevant. Mackiernan and his brother Angus broke the Russians' code while sitting around the family dinning room table one night. Within weeks Mackiernan informed the U.S. Army Air Forces of this breakthrough, which gave the U.S. access to weather data from all over the Soviet Union—data the Russians had encoded because they hoped not to share it with their new allies. This achievement apparently brought Mackiernan to the attention of high-ranking officers. By 1943 he was an army officer and had become chief of the U.S. Army Air Force's Cryptoanalysis Section in Washington. He left that desk job to set up a weather station in Alaska. From there he went on to Asia. That same year he drove from India to China through the Himalayas on the Burma Road. By war's end, he had established a vital weather collection base in China's far northwest province of Sinkiang, at Tihwa, hard up on the soft white Russian underbelly of Inner Asia. There he collected data with radio-equipped weather balloons. He also intercepted weather radio broadcasts from within the U.S.S.R. and decoded them. U.S. bombers over Tokyo— and Hiroshima—relied on his data in the closing days of the war. At some point during this journey, Mackiernan began to work closely with the OSS and other intelligence outfits.

Weeks after Hiroshima Mackiernan sent letters to his mother, Mary Mackiernan, saying that he had actually been sent on a "special assignment into Russian Territory." The nature of his assignment remains unknown—but few if any U.S.-born intelligence agents ever worked undercover inside the U.S.S.R. By November 1945 he was back in Tihwa—and by now he spoke Russian, French, Spanish, and German. Like Bessac, Mackiernan was a talented man with a strong desire to serve his country. Also, like Bessac, Mackiernan's intelligence work in China for the United States was becoming entangled with the Chinese civil war. He told his mother that his "mission would not be accomplished until the threat of Russian Intervention in the Chinese civil war has died out."

By spring of 1946 his letters said that his intelligence work was "very secret." His trip to Nanking and Shanghai that spring, when he dropped in on the diplomatic party at the embassy, was just a brief furlough from the Cold War that was already erupting in Inner Asia. By then Mackiernan had already begun to read Lattimore and his time with the peoples of Inner Asia had already convinced him that Chinese colonialism there was against U.S. strategic interests. But what would it take for the slumbering bureaucrats in Washington to awaken to the new threat that Lattimore, Bessac, and Mackiernan saw looming on the horizon?

ALPHABET SOUP
OSS TO SSU TO CIG TO CIA
1946–1947

After his trip to Inner Mongolia, Bessac was sent home to the United States, where he was discharged. Weeks later he was in Washington. When the OSS was disbanded and Bessac went into SSU some of his old friends had been sent to the State Department's new Research and Intelligence Department, and some went to the newly formed civilian intelligence operation called the Central Intelligence Group, or CIG. The old-boy network swept him along. Within months SSU was dead and he was reassigned to CIG's office in Peking, to the same Mandarin mansion he had just left.

Bessac describes the chaos of the period. "There was this whole alphabet soup period, when OSS became SSU, and then CIG and then finally CIA. But for me it was always just the Outfit. Nothing really changed for me, whether I was working with OSS or CIG. It was the same group of people."

Mackiernan's transition from OSS and Air Force Intelligence to the CIA was via another route. The State Department had adapted to the public presence of a military attaché in every embassy, but the new CIA agents had to be secret agents. The State Department debated how it could satisfy the cover needs of the newest member of the team.

> The facilities of the Department of State still offer some good covers for field agents, but . . . less emphasis should be placed on the more glamorous titles, and some of the run-of-the-mill designation should be used. Why not use a few "vice consuls" or "clerks"?

In November 1947 the State Department wrote marching orders for hundreds of new "clerks" and "vice consuls." One clerk was moving faster than all the rest.

On February 7, 1947, the U.S. ambassador to China, Stuart Leighton, telegraphed the secretary of state and asked for permission for U.S. Air Force Major Douglas Mackiernan to join the State Department. Mackiernan had volunteered to go to Tihwa and already knew the area from wartime service there.

CIG's name was changed to the CIA informally as early as May 1, 1947, though it would not be formalized until September. By May 5 Mackiernan had filled out his application for State. On May 12 he left the U.S. embassy in Nanking, driving a four-wheel-drive command car across China. His dream had come true. Mackiernan was heading back to the largest town in Sinkiang, Tihwa, to become a clerk. Tihwa certainly needed a clerk.

THE AMERICAN CONSULATE
TIHWA, SINKIANG
THE REPUBLIC OF CHINA
MARCH 25, 1946

Sinkiang. Twice the size of Texas. The far northwest corner of China. The Russian and Mongolian borders were only one hundred and fifty miles from Tihwa. Peking was two thousand miles and three time zones to the east. Although claimed by China, Chinese were fewer than 4 percent of the population. In 1946 there were one hundred and fifty Russians inside the Russian consular compound at Tihwa, and only one American was stationed in the U.S. consulate before Mackiernan arrived.

The northern part of Sinkiang had been overrun by the Russians, who were calling it the Eastern Turkestan Republic (ETR), but John Hall Paxton, the U.S. Consul, was so overworked maintaining the consulate's financial books that he hardly had time to do more than outline these events in his reports to Washington. There was no time to report on whether the nomadic Kazak in the Altai Mountains, on the Mongol-Russian border, would get along with their new sponsors.

Paxton noticed one strange telegram from the State Department in the summer of 1946. The United States was trying to maintain what it believed was a monopoly on uranium.

The Department instructs you to exercise extreme vigilance to insure that any transactions in, or offerings of, uranium or uranium bearing materials are observed discreetly and reported immediately in detail to the Department.

MURRAY HILL
1943–1950

The purpose of the Manhattan Engineering District was to create an atomic bomb; the purpose of Murray Hill was to corner the world's supply of uranium. The code name for the Manhattan Project was based on its location in New York, where some of the earliest offices for atomic research were located. Murray Hill, a distinct neighborhood in Manhattan, provided the code name for the secret within the secret. Murray Hill geologists searched the world for new uranium deposits. Murray Hill directives guided the State Department as it negotiated monopoly access treaties to all known uranium supplies. It was because of Murray Hill that every U.S. embassy and consulate in the world received the same communiqué that Paxton had received in Tihwa.

General Leslie R. Groves, who was in charge of everything to do with the construction of America's first atomic bomb, was particularly enthralled by Murray Hill, and he regularly overemphasized its impact. President Truman was an early convert to Groves's certainty about Murray Hill. A religious belief in Murray Hill caused America's top leaders to assume that Stalin was not the threat he seemed to the public. Men at the Manhattan Project believed, correctly, that uranium itself was the atomic secret, not the science of splitting the atom. And they intended to keep uranium scarce.

Despite this U.S. effort Stalin was prepared to go to any length to obtain the uranium required to build an atomic bomb. On January 25, 1946 Igor Kurchatov, father of the Russian bomb, was summoned by Stalin who told him in the strongest possible language that Russia, though poor, would pay any price to have an atomic bomb. It should be done as quickly as possible, without counting the cost. The first problem was to find enough uranium despite American efforts to prevent it.

KOKTOGAI
ALTAI MOUNTAINS
RUSSIAN-OCCUPIED SINKIANG
EASTERN TURKESTAN REPUBLIC
MAY 15, 1946

One hundred and twenty miles to the north of Tihwa, the Kazak migration from the desert valley to the new grass on the mountains above was under way. The foundation of the ETR had not changed an ancient way of life. For hundreds of years the Kazak had made this migration, ignoring all Chinese claims that they were part of China. Now they ignored the fact they were part of a Russian puppet state.

Twelve hundred Kazak families drifted slowly up the southern slopes of the Altai Mountains, hard up on the borders of Mongolia and Russia. Each family traveled with a long line of camels. On the lead camel, yurt poles swayed atop bundles of felt yurt coverings. One camel load was covered with a splash of color. The bright blue and red woolen carpets patterned with Kazak tribal motifs were visible from miles away. Other camel loads lashed between the two humps provided a cushioned perch for children and wives, the senior wife at the front of the caravan, the junior at the rear, with their children spread between them. The herds of goats and sheep were scattered out in a half-mile circle around the caravan, grazing and ambling along as the caravan made its way up into the mountains.

Here was the nomadic life beyond the Great Wall that had so impressed Owen Lattimore. America's greatest Inner Asian expert had walked through these same mountains in the 1920s while on his honeymoon, and it was this nomadic life he described in his books. This was also the life that Bessac first witnessed around Peitzemiao. Though the tribes were Kazak, not Mongol, and the location was two thousand miles west of Peitzemiao, nomadic life was similar throughout Inner Asia. The land itself demanded this way of life from the people. There was no other way to live on the steppe before industrialization arrived in the late twentieth century.

Each day they gained altitude as they followed the new grass up the wide flanks of the Altai Mountains. In a dozen places across the Altai, Kazak repeated this scene. The families never gathered in these desert mountains; no single place contained enough grass for their herds to congregate. Even spread out across the Altai, they remained one people: "the Kazak Horde of Osman Bator," as Mackiernan christened them.

The Kazak returning in the spring of 1946 to the valley of Koktogai did not find an empty valley awaiting them, as they always had before. The fresh grass was there, but so were three green trucks and a dozen tents with red Russian flags fluttering above them. The Russian army had sent in a mining expedition and had even built an airfield to support it. All over the Kazak's once pristine valley small holes had been dug in the turf.

Alerted to the presence of the Russians, Osman Bator rode over to see what they were doing. One of the Russian soldiers walked up to Osman as he dismounted to examine the rocks the Russians seemed to be collecting.

"We will pay you ten meters of cloth for forty pounds of this rock. And two or three meters of cloth for this rock. Have your people collect these rocks for us."

Osman listened to the Russian. When the Russian stopped speaking, Osman had nothing to say in reply and the ham-handed man nimbly mounted his horse and rode back up into the mountains above Koktogai.

In Osman's yurt that night, the elders tore the flat bread served by the women and ate the lamb that had been grilled over the dung fire. Only after tea was served to them, after the meal, did Osman speak.

The Chinese came to the Altai in the 1930s and mined gold, it seemed they were few, and so we let them come. By 1940, they tried to drive us off our grazing lands when they wanted to take even more gold. In 1945, we let the Russians come into our land, so that we could get the guns we needed to drive out the Chinese. The Chinese have been out of our mountains for a year now. Many of you were with me down in the Oasis towns of the desert, when we used the Russian machine guns to kill the Chinese by the hundreds. We did well and the infidels were thrown out from our land. The Russians said that if we declared we were not part of China, and were now this Eastern Turkestan Republic, that we could be independent, so we did that. But now the Russians have come to take another rock from beneath the grass. There are only a few Russians here now.

We must watch the Russians. For the time being, the people may sell them rocks, if they have the desire to do that, if they need cloth. But let us watch the Russians.

Osman watched for almost exactly one year.

AT THE CHINGIL RIVER FORD
ALTAI MOUNTAINS
SINO-RUSSIAN BORDER
APRIL 10, 1947

Osman looked down on a scene of devastation, a nomad's nightmare: two hundred and fifty families with a quarter of a million sheep penned up at the bottom of a mountain gorge, on the stony flood plain along the west bank of the Chingil River.

Osman rode up to his vantage on a hill above the river gorge, hoping to see that half the herds had crossed the Chingil. Instead, he found a herd of sheep three hundred yards thick stretched out for miles along the west bank of the Chingil. A thousand people on horse and camel, each threading his way through the herds trying to keep order among the maddened sheep. A tower of dust rose half a kilometer into the sky, above the milling animals, marking the spot for their enemies.

Their only hope for escape was across the Chingil, but even from up here on the hilltop above the traditional ford Osman could see that the river was running three feet higher than usual. It was wider, deeper, and rougher than it should have been at that time of year. This was why the frightened animals milled about on the flood plain.

Osman watched as a raft of two hundred sheep, led by a bold ram, broke free from the terrified flock and rushed into the river. They tried to swim, but the strong current swept them downstream. One by one their furry heads disappeared under the churning river only to reappear downstream, their lifeless bodies tumbling in the current.

Directly below him, the lone ferry loaded with twenty horses and camels set out for the ten-minute crossing. The long oars manned by three men each dipped into the river and the square flat-bottomed ferry moved off to the other shore.

The tribe could not stay on the riverbank: there was no grass for the herds on the sandy, boulder-strewn plain along the river. And they would be lucky if their enemies allowed them time to get the people across the river.

Turning back to the west, Osman saw something more danger-ous than the disaster at the ford below him. A convoy of Russian trucks followed slowly behind a party of mounted Kazak, obviously headed straight toward him. Making a quick calculation, he could see that they had no more than two hours to get across the Chingil. After running and fighting for fifteen days, with only brief stops to water and feed the animals, it all came down to the next two hours.

Osman mounted and rode downhill. The haunches of his short-legged pony dug into the slope of dust and gravel. Automatically one boy or man from each of the two hundred and fifty yurts threaded his way on horseback through the quarter of a million sheep and goats toward Osman.

As Osman reached the river plain at the bottom of the gorge, the two hundred and fifty messengers intercepted him. Despite the roar-ing wind in the gorge and a dust so thick it ringed the nostrils of men and horse alike, their mounts did not jib or rear. The men and their mounts drew in and circled Osman.

Though Osman had to shout to be heard above the roaring river, the bleating animals, and the scouring wind, his deep voice was calm as always. Every man and boy heard the words, offered with no explanation, that sealed their fate. Words a nomad never wants to hear.

Leave the herds to their fate, said Osman Bator. Get every women, child, man, and a mount for each of them, across the river first. Then take across the food, the yurts, carpets, and those rocks the Russians want. Take those, too. Get the other camels and horses across the river if you can. You have two hours to be on the other bank, with your guns, ready to fight. The women and animals that get across must take shelter up on the meadows above. If for some reason we are separated, go to the Chinese army camp at what they call Peitaishan—what we call Red Spring, underneath the mountain of Baitik Tagh. Cross the Chingil, sink the ferry, and keep the Russians on this side. Go.

THE WHITE HOUSE AND THE POTALA
MARCH 1947

That same spring, President Truman made the foreign policy statement for which he is most well known: "I believe that it must be the policy of the United States to support free peoples who are resisting attempted subjugation by armed minorities or by outside pressures."

Though the Truman Doctrine was designed for Europe, it had repercussions in Asia. Even the twelve-year-old Dalai Lama got the message. After a hard day of lessons, he used to listen to a radio in his tiny, cold quarters in the upper reaches of the Potala as he ate dinner with his caretakers. The distant foreign radio broadcasts whistled in and out of reception. He tried to pick out a word here and there. He pored over his copies of *Life* magazine, though he could only understand the pictures. Still, the message got through. America's new self-definitions reached out even as far as the young Tenzin Gyatso's unheated rooms in the Potala. "I had the impression of America as . . . oh, really . . . as the Champion of Freedom!" he would later say.

Frank Bessac trumpets this ethic when he tells us why he went to China to fight in World War II—the Truman Doctrine was an evolution of a policy established by President Franklin D. Roosevelt. "I went to destroy Japanese colonialism in China. Americans were ready to die for that. What right did they have to invade China? The French had come to help us throw out the British in 1776. Remember Lafayette. It's a grand tradition, America at its best."

Truman now said that America would champion free men everywhere. The UN would solve world disputes without force. The world listened in part because of the instant appeal of the ideal. It listened also because America had just defeated Japan with a new bomb. A bomb that no one else in the world could make.

OSMAN BATOR, DOUGLAS MACKIERNAN, AND URANIUM
MAY AND JUNE 1947

In May 1947, Douglas Mackiernan began his journey to Tihwa. The first leg of the trip was a two thousand, four hundred–mile journey across China from Nanking. Mackiernan made that trek with a Foreign Service buddy, Edwin Martin (later ambassador to Burma, 1971–73). As far as Martin knew, they were the only Americans ever to drive from Sian to Tihwa.

According to Martin, Mackiernan drove an Army 6x6 truck with a one-ton trailer attached, and Martin drove an old battered Jeep. First, they barged the vehicles across the Yangtze River from Nanking to Pukow and then loaded them onto flatbed railcars. They camped out on the open railcars and watched half of China speed by during the next ten days—through Suchow, Kaifeng, Chengchow, Loyang, and finally Sian (Xian). From there, the two-man caravan embarked on a seventeen-hundred-mile drive to Tihwa—a dirt road the entire way. The potted, rutted track saw more ox carts and camel caravans than automobiles. Martin said later that it was only because of "Mac's resourcefulness" that they made it through in good shape.

On June 5 and 7, only a few days before Mackiernan arrived back at Tihwa, skirmishes between Russian-backed Mongolian forces and the Kazak and Chinese forces at Peitaishan erupted. Osman had come to ground at Peitaishan after his flight from the ETR. Now he was aligned with the Chinese Nationalist forces in Sinkiang—the very men he had fought against earlier. Four Mongolian fighter planes attacked the camp at Peitaishan in daylight. The fighters, with red and gold sickles and hammers on their tail fins, ripped machine-gun fire through the Kazak-Chinese camp. Two Nationalist soldiers were killed, along with thirty horses. Perhaps Osman provoked these attacks by his guerrilla raids on Mongol troops patrolling the other side of the mountain. Perhaps the Russians sent their proxy Mongol troops and fighters after Osman because the Russians wanted Osman dead. We do not know the full details even now. The fighting was quickly dubbed the Peitaishan Incident. For a few days, American papers wrote headlines about the mysterious fighting in that remote area. It looked as if the Russians were about to take all of Sinkiang, after nibbling off the ETR. But then some suggested that Chiang Kai-shek was blowing a border skirmish out of proportion as he tried to convince the United States that it had to increase financial aid to the brave Chinese who were standing alone against a Communist invasion. One American journalist in Nanking linked the Peitaishan Incident to rumors that uranium had been discovered in northwest China. Since no independent observer had visited Peitaishan, no one was certain what was happening there.

Mackiernan had a few nights of rest at Tihwa after his long trip from Nanking before Osman's son, Cherezima, arrived in Tihwa, having ridden two hundred miles on horseback from Peitaishan. His silk warrior's bonnet, topped with owl feathers, gave him an unusual appearance. He brought the alarming news of the Peitaishan attack and a plea for reinforcements, arms, and ammunition.

The State Department ordered its newest vice consul to make an on-the-spot investigation at Peitaishan. Since Osman's camp was several days away by car, Mackiernan took the U.S. consulate mechanic and driver, Erwin Kontescheny, with him.

Erwin was born in 1918 in the town of Muglitz near the German-Czech border. The chaos of World War II drove him, his father, and his mother across Europe, Russia, and finally Russian Inner Asia into Chinese Sinkiang. He was living there when the ETR was created and Soviet troops appeared in Sinkiang. His father disappeared into a new Russian prison, never to return.

When John Paxton, the U.S. consul at Tihwa, made a brief tour through the ETR in 1947, Erwin climbed into the high-security compound where the ETR was housing the American consul and managed a covert midnight meeting with him. Kontescheny convinced Paxton that no one would be a more loyal or grateful employee for the Americans. Paxton, moved by the man's bravery and his horrible tale, smuggled Erwin out of the ETR and back to Tihwa. There, Kontescheny's magic hands with broken engines earned him a spot as the consulate's mechanic and driver.

When interviewed in 1999, Erwin Kontescheny was grateful to have survived World War II and the Cold War. His work for Consul Paxton finally rewarded him with American citizenship, and later a quiet retirement in New Jersey. He still remembers his drive more than fifty years earlier from Tihwa to Peitaishan with Douglas Mackiernan.

"Mr. Mackiernan liked his guns, and he was a very good shot. I was driving along through the desert. Mr. Mackiernan had a Colt .45 that he liked to shoot. So as I am driving along, he would pull that out. We were bumping up and down, and he would point out a rock off in the distance.

"'See that rock, Erwin? The one between the two thorn bushes over there.'

"'Yes, I am seeing it, Mr. Mackiernan,' I said to him.

"And then while we were driving along, that truck bumping up and down, he shot that .45 of his. *Bam! Bam!* He fired very quick, not looking like he took much effort to do it.

"And then, just like that. *Bam!* He hits the first rock right in the center. And *bam!* He hits the second rock that he pointed out, again, right in the center. He was a very good shot, Mr. Mackiernan."

The temperature soared over one hundred degrees during the two-day drive. At last, they began to rise out of the desert, and they spotted a party of Kazak horsemen waiting for them. They camouflaged the car and continued on horseback into the mountains above. Peitaishan was a cool inviting oasis with yurts scattered across the meadow.

Mackiernan was directed into the largest yurt in camp. A smoke hole was open in the top of the felted dome and a dung fire burned beneath it. Osman sat by the fire with his hooded hunter—a golden eagle—perched quietly in the shadows behind him. The women busily prepared dinner as the two men met for the first time. Mackiernan may have knelt before Osman and presented him with a traditional gift of gold. Certainly, the men had dinner and a long night of political discussions around the dung-fire hearth. Osman spoke about his fight with the Chinese and the Russians as his people fought for their independence. He showed Mackiernan the many weapons he had seized from the Mongols. At Peitaishan, Mackiernan even went out one night on a guerrilla raid against the Mongol lines with the Kazak. He noted with relish the Kazak ferocity in battle. When he asked the Kazak what they did with enemy battle casualties, they replied, "Feed them to the wolves of the forests."

Mackiernan later exhibited his detailed knowledge of all types of arms and weapons—U.S., German, and Russian—when he listed every type of weapon that Osman had captured. During the course of several days, Osman begged Mackiernan for minor support. Osman said that he could fight his way back into the ETR and retake his old homeland if Mackiernan could secure modest American assistance.

The Kazak leader also explained the mystery that surrounded the minerals at Koktogai. He told Mackiernan that at first he had simply watched the mining, as Russians had been mining in other parts of the Altai since 1944. Osman was grateful that the Russians had given the Kazak the arms with which to drive the Chinese out in 1945. So he tried to live with them. When Osman's tribe did not find enough rocks for the Russians, and when they refused to work in the mines the Russians had opened, the Russians began to show favor to another Kazak leader in the Altai Mountains, one who supported the mining.

In March 1947, the Russians gave one hundred rifles to Osman's rival. By April, his rival was openly supporting Russian mining. Osman declared that the Russian mines must be closed. Hundreds of laborers were brought into the mine area, and trucks began a daily trek back to Russia fully loaded with rocks.

Osman knew there was something special about the rocks, but he did not know what. He gave samples of them to Mackiernan and asked him to try to find out why the Russians wanted them so badly.

While at Peitaishan—and on other occasions—Kontescheny talked with the Kazak who worked with Osman. "I heard Osman was attacking the Russian trucks that were working at the Russian uranium mine," he remembered. The Russians had guards on top of the trucks, and the Kazak would kill them, and then throw all the stones back out of the truck. They took it off the truck and spread it out again. They did that whenever they had a chance."

It is possible Osman started attacking the Russian uranium mine at Koktogai before he met Douglas Mackiernan. Or perhaps he started those attacks only after he met the CIA's new secret agent. The chronology is unclear. When he left Peitaishan, Mackiernan took the rock samples back to Tihwa. During the next few weeks, he jury-rigged an electroscope. He dug out his copy of James Dwight Dana's *System of Mineralogy* and compared the weak indications of radioactivity in the samples to those of uranium and thorium. He rigged a scale within a tub of water and estimated the specific gravity of the samples. All the numbers pointed in one direction: radioactivity; either the samples contained a radioactive ore or they had been mined somewhere close to radioactive ores.

Paxton shared with Mackiernan the standing order from the State Department to report all transactions in uranium. He also told Mackiernan that Edmund O. Clubb, when he was consul at Tihwa back in 1943, had already reported to Washington the local suspicion that the U.S.S.R. was mining uranium in the Altai Mountains. Mackiernan made a full report on everything Osman Bator had told him and prepared the samples for shipment to Washington along with his own initial scientific analysis of them.

Consul Paxton had already telegraphed his own message to Washington about the possibility of uranium in Sinkiang.

> The USSR might be willing to make considerable temporary ideological compromise and even forego immediate political sovereignty, allowing the natives assemblage or the Independence they desire provided Russian extraction of ores is permitted to continue.

Osman's rocks were sent to the Atomic Energy Commission in Washington, D.C. This is intelligence—this is how the CIA and the State Department were supposed to work together. Mackiernan may have begun to think of more—covert action based on intelligence. Osman's attacks on the uranium mines started at about this time and it's possible that Mackiernan initiated them. Erwin Kontescheny remembers that Mackiernan kept in daily radio contact with at least two radio transmitters inside of the Soviet Union from the summer of 1947. Possibly he was still receiving data from agents he established when he was inside the U.S.S.R. in 1945, just as the war ended. Certainly Mackiernan was reporting on uranium by the summer of 1947, but he may already have started to search for intelligence about the building of Stalin's first atomic bomb. He may have been looking for ways to slow down the construction of that bomb.

PEGGE LYONS AND DOUGLAS MACKIERNAN
TIHWA, SINKIANG
JULY AND AUGUST 1947

In 1947 Sinkiang was still a scoop, but not one many journalists could land. Some journalists died trying to enter Sinkiang but most were simply turned back, jailed, or shot at. Visas were difficult to obtain, or impossible, and so were flights. Driving in over land took a month on dirt roads, or longer by camel and caravan routes. Those few who made and survived the trip published accounts of their adventures. Peter Fleming and Elia Maillard wrote a pair of classic travel books after they traveled together around the edge of Sinkiang during the 1930s. Owen Lattimore wrote about the area in a *National Geographic* cover story. Sinkiang was almost as remote and exotic as Tibet.

The scoop for a news journalist headed for Tihwa in 1947 was the "Soviet Occupied Zone" of Sinkiang, or the ETR. The fact that the Soviets had detached the northern part of the province, but that no journalist had been there and reported on conditions, made it a Holy Grail. The China-based journalist Walter Sullivan said that he'd have split a gut to go to the ETR. The only two journalists who finally did storm this never-never land were female, beautiful, and adventurous. Yet neither one of them, after breaching the mysterious ramparts that lured them to Sinkiang, ever published a story.

In early 1947, Barbara Stephens, a *Time* stringer, managed to convince the Uighur commissars of the Eastern Turkestan Republic, with whom she met in Tihwa, to give her a visa for the ETR to the north. She went, she saw, she wrote long diaries, and she shot many pictures. On her flight back, her plane crashed, and all on board died. Her diaries and film were lost. To add to the mystery, a Chinese general (wanted dead by several players) and the son of a British Member of Parliament were also on board that doomed flight.

The American journalist Margaret, or Pegge, Lyons, whose pen name was Pegge Parker, managed to survive her trip to Tihwa in the summer of 1947. Though this twenty-eight-year-old scribe gained entry to the ETR she never wrote a serious story about her trip, despite her hard charging credentials as a journalist. Born in 1919 in Harrisburg, Pennsylvania, she was writing a teen column for the *Harrisburg Telegraph* by the time she was eighteen-years-old. In 1942 at the outbreak of WWII she was already the women's editor at the *Washington Times Herald*. By 1943 she was doing features about what it felt like to jump with the paratroopers or ride as a gunner in a tank during battle training. Camel cigarettes saw her as a new American icon and created a full-page ad about her. "Give her a typewriter, a pack of Camels, and let those presses roll! Pegge Parker, ace war reporter, is an expert on G.I.'s, camps, and Camels." Before heading out to China after the war she stopped off in Fairbanks, Alaska where she was the only reporter for the *Fairbanks Daily News Miner*. Though she went to China as a freelance journalist, the U.S. Army in Shanghai soon hired her. She served in the Graves Registration Service as a PRO (press representation officer). Despite that official position, she filed her own stories to the *New York Daily News* and others. Her army connections were enough to get her into Tihwa. Her dual status as a freelancer and U.S. Army PRO irritated journalists who were unable to gain access to Sinkiang. While she was in Sinkiang in July and August 1947, a Shanghai-based journalist tried to have her court-martialed. Her army boss ordered her to stop filing reports once he discovered that his erstwhile charge was somehow off in Sinkiang. Lyons knew her business, though. Before she left for Sinkiang, she had known that Russia wanted to make the area into an "autonomous" region for reasons she summed up succinctly: ". . . Sinkiang, rich, rich Sinkiang with a heart of gold, oil in her veins and uranium in her pocket . . ."

Word that uranium might be behind the Peitaishan Incident that Mackiernan had been sent out to investigate was starting to leak into the press. Pegge Lyons was the first to react to the rumor. In tiny Tihwa she met Mackiernan as soon as she got off the plane, and apparently fell in love at first sight. He seemed to her like a piece of gold dropped into dusty Tihwa. "He was a prince among men," she would say much later. She turned to him on the day of her arrival as she tried to understand the rat's nest of Sinkiang-ETR-China-Russia politics. When she received an invitation to visit the ETR, she shared the letter with him and he helped her translate it. Mackiernan explained that people were being beaten to death in the streets of Tihwa, even in the middle of the day. When locals frightened by the encroaching U.S.S.R. gave her a letter on the street, again she went to Mackiernan. He insisted that she should not walk the streets alone anymore, and that he should always be with her when she went out. She had been in Tihwa only a few days when she realized that she wanted to marry Douglas Mackiernan.

Their affair began before she left for the ETR. Looking back today she says he was "handsomer than Henry Fonda." Though now officially working for the State Department he could not stop wearing his army-green wool pants and his blue officer's shirt—it was the uniform for his generation of the old-boy's network. His puffy lips and eyelids beneath thick eyebrows gave him a just-out-of-bed sleepy look. The two were a matched pair. Even in Tihwa, Pegge roughed it in a certain style. Her manicured and lacquered ruby red nails were in perfect form, and her dark hair formed a tight widow's peak above her perfect heart-shaped chin. He was handsome and she was beautiful. They both had some of that confidence that beautiful people have—who are used to getting what they want, if only with a smile. But there was a twist to their "red hot romance." Mackiernan instructed her to collect intelligence for him while she was in the ETR. Looking back, she believes that he encouraged her to head for a town in the ETR that was near the Russian border. He wanted specifics about the numbers of soldiers and their equipment, particularly their guns and weapons. He wanted to know whether the soldiers in the ETR were local Uighur and Kazak, or Russian. He also lent her his Leica camera.

"Now we are not taking Sunday school pictures or something," he told her. "I want detailed pictures . . . of any group of troops marching . . . or trucks . . . take the camera and play the giggly schoolgirl. Wear your bobby socks and a little cotton dress with your curls blowing in the wind so you look like some American student . . . who has gotten a free ride." When Mackiernan tells her to smile and bat her eyes and act innocent—to get the intelligence pictures he wants—he knew what it took to do that, and knew that she had it.

Perhaps he was looking for trucks carrying uranium. Mackiernan plainly instructed Lyons to look for the Bear's paw in everything she saw. Her diary makes it clear she knew that uranium existed in Sinkiang before she went, but she does not indicate when she learned more. Her few comments about anything atomic are linked to her brief meeting with Osman Bator. She and Mackiernan apparently rode out to his camp.

Fifty years later, she remembers the smell of people and clothes, rarely washed, sharp and pungent in the yurt. She remembers trying to speak with Osman to find a language they shared. She remembers her rising excitement as she caught a glimpse of Osman's link, somehow, to things atomic. Osman began to understand what she wanted to write about:

"His life and his people and what's to be the fate of these people along the Russian border not far from where the [Russian] atomic energy tests are done. Once I got that picture clear, there was no stopping me. I really wanted to know everything there was out there."

It is possible Lyons heard hints in 1947 that Stalin would test his bomb near Tihwa, but what is more likely is that Mackiernan said something about uranium.

She spent only a few days in the ETR but wrote thousands of words in her diary about the experience. She found that every house in an area that was nominally part of China had a picture of Stalin in it, and that Russian troops were plainly visible. In the flood of impressions Lyons recorded, one essential political statement stands out. The governor of the ETR she met in the town of Kulja, Hakim Bek Huja, made it clear why she had been invited and why the presence of the Russians in the ETR was merely a strategic accommodation:

"We believe big governments (American implied) will help us. The more they know of the true situation the less chance China has of disposing of us as she wants to."

Here was the governor of a Russian puppet state telling the journalist that the non-Chinese Uighur and Kazak of Sinkiang were fighting for independence from the colonial Chinese and would take help from either the Russians or the Americans. But America needed nothing from the ETR and so was willing to accept China's "right" to rule the area, as a gesture to a valued ally. Russia, on the other hand, was willing to grant the locals almost anything, perhaps because of uranium. In 1947 this was all classified information, as Lyons would soon discover. Meanwhile, she was in love, and after four days in Kulja she flew back to Tihwa, desperate to see Mackiernan after a brief but all-too-long separation.

Everything was cast in the rosy glow of their love. Lyons loved the intrigue, and she loved that both she and Mackiernan spoke Russian. Mackiernan was happy with her photos from the ETR: "Your first assignment was A-OK, you passed." She delighted in walking the streets of Tihwa at night with Mackiernan, knowing he had a .45 under his coat. When he seized her lion-tight and kissed her passionately the first time they brushed against one another in a midnight dark hallway, she nearly swooned. Her Jeep rides with him, when he drove across the mountainside as though the Willys was a Kazak stallion, were thrilling. Sitting in his abandoned weedy garden, neglected lovingly by his Uighur gardener, she sipped coffee, looking at the stars and talking with Mackiernan. Or she sat snug in a rattan chair with him listening to Rimsky-Korsakov on the BBC. Mackiernan could be so funny, acting out his stories in multiple accents. She took the first horseback ride of her life up into the snow-clad Tien Shan Mountains above the town, and sat on a boulder in a roaring mountain stream as Mackiernan belted out Mexican cowboy songs from his youth and told tales of how he first fell in love with radios as boy. Every evening they went out to the edge of town and watched the twenty-five-thousand-foot peaks of "their" Heavenly Mountains turn from gas-flame blue to scarlet.

She wanted to marry this man and build a mud-walled house on the outskirts of Tihwa facing the Heavenly Mountains. She talked about quitting the army and becoming his writer-wife in Tihwa, filing reports on the evolving political situation at the heart of Inner Asia.

Yet from the beginning Mackiernan made her understand that he was not free to marry her. She didn't want to know at first but he kept trying to tell her. Mackiernan was trying not to fall in love with her. He confessed that he was married to his first wife, Darrell, by whom he had already had a daughter. Initially he did not confess to Lyons that he had also made a bigamous marriage to a local Russian girl during the war. Nor did he tell her that no one in Tihwa knew he had married Darrell, his American wife, before World War II. His Russian wife was the only wife the Tihwa folk ever knew. Even the British consul had attended the wedding in the local Russian Orthodox Church in the last year of the war.

Eventually, Mackiernan confessed to Lyons his illegal, bigamous marriage to his wartime lover in Tihwa. He fell to his knees.

"I can't marry you . . . can't.

"So you know now. You had to know why our dreams are hopeless. I don't dare ask you to share this crucifixion. It would always be there and we'd both know it. I guess it was a tragedy from the start. God, how I tried to keep from loving you."

For a Catholic woman like Lyons, it was a nightmare revelation in the midst of a beautiful affair that she thought would culminate in marriage. But she forgave him and their affair continued. Mackiernan took her out again in the Jeep, and she found herself looking over at him repeatedly, thinking to herself.

"Is he REALLY the one? I take long thoughtful looks of dread and incredulity at him at times and think: Doug, forever and EVER? Jeepers!"

When it began to rain, the new couple—they called themselves Connivers Inc.—pitched a lean-to and lay down. The smell of the crushed green sage under their lean-to dampened by the falling rain would remain with Lyons for the rest of her life.

Pegge Lyons's diary:

July 14, 1947—TIHWA—Mark ye well the day of July 13 in the year of our lord 1947. I don't know whether to record this in language for posterity or merely to make note and await future developments. Maybe the latter for how can I be sure of something as drastic as marrying this darling love of my life Douglas Seymour Mackiernan. . . ."

. . . We decided to remember the date of our "proposal" plans made in a dry riverbed in the middle of no man's land in the Republic of China on the day of July 13, Sunday, 1947.

CIA HEADQUARTERS
Q BUILDING
WASHINGTON, D.C.
JULY 1947

Q building—where Frank Bessac had joined OSS in 1943—was unchanged. It was still an ivy-covered brick building down near the Potomac, where the Watergate let water into the river. It looked like an overgrown brick schoolhouse outside, and the hallways inside were government green. No sign at the door told you what went on inside. Bessac signed in and found his way to the office of his old friend and handler, Marge Kennedy. Once her office door was closed she chanted her half of the mantra.

"The OSS is dead . . ."

Frank finished it for her: "Long live the OSS."

They laughed. Then they talked about the old OSS days, about things in China, and about how the transition from OSS to SSU to CIG had gone. Afterward, Kennedy debriefed Bessac on his intelligence trips in China. She listened and took notes.

Kennedy then explained that there were some changes taking place at the Outfit. She told Bessac that he would be returning to China, but that they wanted him to go undercover. Times were changing in China. It was no longer like Peitzemiao when the Communists had been eager to show China to the Americans.

They agreed that in the fall of 1947 Frank would be a student at Peking's Fujen University, and that would also be his cover. The Outfit would pay his return to China and keep him on the payroll. Finally, she got around to codes.

"Your code for your undercover work is Oregon. Your reply is the letter D. This is your recognition code. Anyone who uses it on you is an employee of the Central Intelligence Agency, and they know you are too."

"Central Intelligence Agency?"

"Yeah, that's what they are calling the Outfit now."

"So when they say 'Oregon,' I say 'D'."

"That's right, Frank. Unless you aren't working for the Outfit. As before, failure to reply correctly would mean the agent could not contact you, or work with you. Nothing about how the recognition codes are used has changed. Failure to reply correctly, for whatever reason, means no contact."

THE ATOMIC ENERGY COMMISSION AND THE ARMED FORCES SPECIAL WEAPONS PROJECT
WASHINGTON, D.C.
JULY 1947

On July 14, 1947, the Joint Chiefs of Staff commanded the creation of a monitoring net that could detect any atomic explosion, anywhere on earth.

> The Soviets will continue atomic research and will produce atomic weapons as soon as possible. In consequence, the United States should exhaust every practicable means of gaining factual information concerning the development of atomic . . . weapons within the USSR.

The Armed Forces Special Weapons Project (AFSWP), within the Air Force, was assigned this task, but it took two years to set up the atomic explosion detection net because no one at the top was pushing—everyone in the know assumed that Murray Hill would make it impossible for the U.S.S.R. to build a bomb. The Atomic Energy Commission, a civilian body, had assumed responsibility for nearly all things atomic in the United States in January. The military, which had run the Manhattan Project, kept the Foreign Atomic Intelligence Unit to itself—not even the CIA was given the lead on that subject.

The atomic detection project, originally called AFSWP, was soon renamed AFOAT-1 (Air Force, deputy chief of staff for Operations, Atomic Energy Office, Section One). None of the modern equipment that today details atomic explosions from satellites, or triangulates their precise location with the help of a global seismographic net, existed in 1947. These technical means were being born, but they were, and are, controlled by the military, not civilians. Somehow, Douglas

43

Mackiernan would work directly with military *and* civilian intelligence
—the Air Force and the CIA—most likely because of his old wartime
friendships. Many of the technicians and scientific contractors for
AFOAT-1 were old MIT boys, like Mackiernan—and many of them
were class of '35 or '36, just as Mackiernan should have been.

PEGGE AND DOUG
SHANGHAI AND TIHWA
SEPTEMBER 1947

One of Mackiernan's buddies at the U.S. embassy in Nanking,
W. Walton Butterworth, second to the ambassador, was intrigued by
the uranium reports from Tihwa. In July Butterworth initiated negotiations for a Murray Hill–inspired treaty with China that would
have given the United States a monopoly on any uranium found in
China. It is possible Mackiernan's uranium samples inspired that
treaty work. As August turned to September, it also appears that
Mackiernan began an involvement with AFOAT-1 at the Air Force,
but the details of that remain mysterious.

After he fought to get to Tihwa, Mackiernan stayed there for only
two months before he asked the State Department to grant him leave
without pay. He did not return until the fall of 1948. His affair with
Lyons may have been the cause of this change of heart. Alternatively,
he may have left Tihwa and returned to the United States because
he was being drawn into atomic intelligence projects that would be
carried out in Tihwa.

Lyons's motivations and movements are clearer than Mackiernan's.
She was forced to return to Shanghai by her irate army boss after he
saw her byline on Associated Press (AP) pieces being published in
American papers. Once she got back to Shanghai, Lyons began to
receive the first of a stream of messages from Mackiernan. She replied
to his love notes in kind: "Life without you impossible." By September
Mackiernan had taken leave without pay and flown to Shanghai.

After a passionate reunion that left them both with shaky knees, they were inseparable for the next few days. Whatever doubts Pegge had about Doug vanished when she was in his arms. There she could not imagine ever being alone. He would always shield her and protect her, forever. She wore fancy hats, high heels, and "sniff-swooning" perfumes for him in Shanghai. It was a thrilling counterpoint to roughing it when they had first met in Tihwa. But it wasn't all bliss.

A letter from her mother arrived saying that even if he got a divorce and she married Mackiernan in a civil ceremony they would still be unmarried in the eyes of the Church. Her mother was horror-stricken at the idea, and she didn't even know about the Russian wife. When Pegge was out of Doug's sight for even a few hours, these worries surfaced, and she would begin to look for something false or untrue in him and anything he said. Lyons's set in Shanghai was composed of writers and journalists. It included journalists such as Robert Sharrod of *Time,* Walter Logan of United Press, and Tom Masterson at AP as well as the pro-Chinese Communist writer Jack Beldon. Within this gang she was only an aspiring stringer. Worse, as a PRO, she was a tainted stringer requesting treatment that would have seemed strange to a working journalist.

Though Lyons had gotten her political scoop, she begged Masterson not to print it. So far, AP had just printed her pieces about making up the wives of the Red Commissars in the ETR with U.S. cosmetics. Her army boss made it clear to her that while she was not going to be court-martialed for her escapades in Sinkiang, she would certainly lose her job if her political ETR story was published. Masterson sneered at her.

Still he let her off the hook—he didn't run her political piece. And then Jack Beldon managed to get her a commission with *Collier's* magazine to write a longer piece on the politics of the ETR. She thought she would work on that once she was out of the army. Her situation took a turn for the better. Even with Mackiernan.

One night, he said the words she had been waiting for. There was little he could do about his bigamous Russian wife, but he could, at least, divorce his legal wife, Darrell.

Lyons flew into OPERATION PRONTO. She raced around for visas and shots, and they began the search for reservations on a ship to the United States, via India and Europe.

THE U.S. ARMY ADVISORY GROUP HQ
NANKING, CHINA
SEPTEMBER 25, 1947

Mackiernan flew up to Nanking before leaving China. There he ran into an old friend, a U.S. pilot, Colonel William Hopson. Hopson had just come back from Okinawa where Air Force Major General Albert F. Hegenberger had given him a job that required Mackiernan's input.

Hegenberger first made a name for himself in 1927, as a young lieutenant in the Army Air Corps. He was the navigator on board the first plane to fly from the U.S. mainland to Honolulu. Maitland Field in Oakland is named after the pilot of the "Bird of Paradise"—Lt. Lester J. Maitland—and the road that leads to it is named for Maitland's navigator.

During the closing days of World War II, Hegenberger, by then a major general, was named Commanding General of the Tenth Air Force. He oversaw the transfer of the planes and men of the Tenth over the Himalayas from a rear base in India to a forward base in Kunming, China. U.S. Army Air Corps fliers in China relied on weather forecasts coming out of Air Weather Station 233 run by Mackiernan at Tihwa. Hegenberger may have first heard of Mackiernan during the war—or perhaps earlier, since they both had been born in the Boston area and had attended MIT.

In 1947 Hegenberger asked Hopson to investigate sites for a U.S. bomber base in western China. Hegenberger was making contingency plans to attack Russia's industrial heartland in Inner Asia, in case World War Three broke out, and it was starting to look as if it might. He would have to refuel his Okinawa-based bombers in northwest China if he wanted to attack Russia.

Hopson was glad to meet Mackiernan in Nanking, and Hopson's report makes it clear why.

Mr. Douglas S. Mackiernan, American vice-consul at Tihwa . . .
passed through Nanking on 25 September 1947. . . .

Mr. Mackiernan has spent many years in Western China and has
a thorough knowledge of the climate, geography, sociology and ide-
ologies of the area. He suggested the area near Chia Yu Kwan . . . as
a location meeting the various requirements for an advanced fighter-
bomber base."

Hopson's trust in Mackiernan was absolute. Mackiernan's sug-
gestions for base sites were the only ones offered to Hegenberger.
In November 1947, a team of seven U.S. Army Air Force officers
flew out to Tihwa and inspected the sites during a stopover en route.
American plans for a bombing campaign against the Soviet Union
went forward based on the intelligence given by Mackiernan. Was
this the CIA at work? Not really, just old friends. Yet the CIA was
founded upon this old-boy military network—as was AFOAT-1.

In December 1947 Air Force General Hegenberger was named
director of AFOAT-1. When he began searching for places to set up
the atomic explosion detection equipment in China he knew exactly
where to look: Tihwa. Though it might have appeared as if it were the
least important outpost on earth—and it certainly was the most deso-
late U.S. outpost in China—Mackiernan and Hegenberger knew that
Tihwa was a front-row seat for the birth of the Cold War.

SHANGHAI TO PEKING
THE REPUBLIC OF CHINA
SEPTEMBER 25–29, 1947

As Mackiernan prepared to leave China, Bessac was just returning.
Every step of the way he learned more about what being undercover
meant. He took a ship back to China, rather than flying—the government could not fly him back in military transport since that would
break his cover. When he arrived in Shanghai, Bessac realized that

his new budget as a student would not allow him to fly up to Peking as he had always done when working openly with the Outfit. But there was another side to his new situation.

He met three guys his age during the trip across the Pacific. Their first night in Shanghai, he took them out to Sun Ya's, one of the best Cantonese restaurants in town; then to Yar's, a White Russian restaurant, and even to Seventh Heaven, which Bessac thought was the best nightspot in town. At Seventh Heaven, he earned great respect from the new boys when he asked the beautiful young woman who was singing to perform his favorite Chinese song. His stock with his new friends rose even higher when he persuaded her, after her set, to join them at their table. Speaking Chinese as well as he did was useful for pursuits other than the collection of intelligence.

The coastal steamer from Shanghai to Tientsin, the port for Peking, took four days. The hot, cramped cabin on the steamer that he shared with his new friends seemed very small their first night out. Yet the trip was pleasant. The food was edible. They played a lot of pinochle. And the views of the coast of China from the upper deck were extraordinary.

The Chinese passengers down in steerage were sleeping and living on the deck and in cramped passageways. Most were seasick. It reminded Bessac of his 1945 voyage from Los Angeles to Calcutta in an overcrowded navy troop transport, sleeping in shifts in hot bunks. The sides of the ship, and the decks, reeked with GI vomit.

In 1947, as he returned to China, Bessac saw that life for the Chinese was terrible, and getting worse. Prices for everything had doubled in the past six months, press gangs roamed the countryside, and Nationalist corruption and profiteering were a crushing burden. Bessac felt that most Chinese were ready to accept a Chinese Communist victory in the civil war that continued to tear China apart.

Before he had traveled home to the United States in the summer of 1947, he had written his parents that the U.S. political offensive against the U.S.S.R. was not going to work in China. He said that the Chinese Communist revolution was part of a global agrarian revolution that he did not believe could be stopped by any amount of U.S. military aid to the Nationalist Chinese. He went on to say that the United States had to evolve an expression of its own culture that could be exported, as precisely as Communism was now being exported. He felt that America's focus on using other nations as military bases, and what he called American imperialism, was not a way to win friends in foreign nations. In closing, he said the United States would fail in its battle with the Communists unless Americans also became revolutionaries.

They were the brave words of a twenty-five-year-old to his parents, and Bessac looks back on the letter today as youthful ranting. Even so, perhaps those feelings had something to do with the discomfort that Frank Bessac felt growing within himself as he returned to take up an undercover position for the CIA in China.

UNITED STATES STEAMSHIP PRESIDENT POLK
OFF THE CHINA COAST
OCTOBER 4, 1947

Pegge Lyons sat on deck in a sun chair with green-striped cushions. Mackiernan was beside her again, and they were leaving China. Recorded music played over loudspeakers. Swimmers splashed in the nearby pool. Liveried waiters scurried back and forth with iced drinks. It was such a different venue for the lovers of Sinkiang.

Lyons wrote in her diary. Seated beside her, Mackiernan studied a Tibetan grammar book that someone in Shanghai had given him. She knew better than to ask questions about his work. In 1999, looking back, Pegge said that he "wanted to take a break and maybe he was working along the way to justify his time off from the CIA." She was not certain why he was on the ship, nor why he studied Tibetan every day.

All she knew was that he worked for the State Department and that they were going home so he could get a divorce, and then they would get married. Never to return to China. That was enough for her. Mackiernan already knew differently about many of those assumptions, but he talked to her about such things strictly on a need-to-know basis.

She knew about need-to-know. Her army boss in China had tried at the last minute to stop her from leaving the army. He said she had "secret information," and that she would be retained in the army until the ban on that information was lifted. It was probably the information about ETR that held her up—since this was the information the army insisted she never publish. Her old friend Fern Carrender assured her that he was only bluffing, and so it proved to be. She was out of the army and out of China. And though her political article on ETR was never published she did make a complete report to Mackiernan about every gun she saw in the ETR, and someone studied her photographs from the ETR back in Washington.

Sitting beside Mackiernan gliding down the China coast, Lyons wondered if she was out of her mind. She wondered if men ever thought of anything but their own pleasure. Still, she loved him and wanted to marry him. Except when she thought she was crazy to even consider the idea. Or when she wondered why she was leaving her career as a journalist to become a wife.

As Lyons and Mackiernan left China listening to their own hidden voices and the sound of canned music on the decks of the *President Polk,* Osman Bator was once again at war on the steppes of Inner Asia. Back in the Peitaishan Mountains of Sinkiang, the Chinese garrison commander had added weapons to those Osman had seized from the Mongols. Osman then invaded his old homeland, out of which the Russians had thrown him. He fought his way directly back to the Altai Mountains to the area called Koktogai, near the Russian uranium mine. There he engaged in a battle with troops, possibly Soviet, who were, perhaps, defending the mine. Details of the battle are still vague fifty years later. Only the outcome is known. Osman was defeated in his homeland and again withdrew to Chinese-controlled Sinkiang. Russian support for the ETR—for the Turkic people there who wanted independence from both China and Russia—continued so long as they had access to the strategic minerals in the ETR. For some unknown reason the only American journalist ever to make it into the ETR and out alive with her notes would never publish a story about what she had witnessed there.

Perhaps it was the uranium that had to be kept hidden. Maybe the secret was that the non-Chinese Inner Asians of the ETR would have taken U.S. support, instead of Russian, if only it had been offered. Maybe the two were somehow linked. Even now we do not know the full story.

BESSAC'S COVER
PEKING, CHINA
OCTOBER 15, 1947

The brown-and-white sparrows that infested the walled courtyards of Peking woke Bessac at dawn. Their loud chittering echoed off the brick walls. He stretched in his elegant four-poster Chinese bed and looked out into his courtyard. It was all gray brick with only a single plum tree in one corner; it resembled a Chinese painting. From within his walled courtyard all he could see of the outside world was the sky above. In 1947 Peking was still a city of closed courtyards encircled by its towering city walls, and Bessac had slipped back into that cloistered world as if he had never left it.

He no longer rose and jogged in his army clothes, to the amusement of the Chinese and Mongols, as he had in 1946. Instead, he awakened and put on a Chinese silk robe lined in lambskin now that the weather was turning cold. His cook gave him a cup of Chinese green tea that he sipped in his breakfast room, watching the sun filter into the courtyard through the morning haze. Then he walked out of his courtyard, past the old gateman who lived in a cubbyhole in the gate, and out into the alleyway. It was a dreamy gray world as the sun broke through the early haze. Gatekeepers swept the gateways along the alley. Clouds of sparrows soared above the buildings. A coal seller chanted his wares and water splashed loudly into the alleyway from a window above.

Bessac strolled along through this waking world until he came to the massive gate at the Mandarin's Examination Hall, with its tiled roof, wooden pillars, and granite paving stones. Walking through the impressive gate, he entered the ten-acre compound. Seventeenth-century buildings were scattered within the park. He pulled out one of the four Confucian classics—the very book that Manchu Dynasty civil servants were required to memorize. He walked among the courtyards and trees, over the moats, and along the temple porticos as he memorized the same Chinese text, word for word, that the Mandarins before him had learned by heart as they walked through this very place.

By 1947 Frank Bessac saw himself, half-jokingly, as a Mandarin scholar. He lived in an ancient Chinese house inside a courtyard in the heart of Peking. He was memorizing the Confucian classics in Chinese, and he could recite them to his teacher, exactly as the Mandarins a century before him had.

Upon his return from the United States, he slipped deeper into this role than ever before. He was, after all, a real student, even if he was using it for CIA cover as well.

Strolling through the Guoizen Temple, surrounded by such ancient Chinese beauty, he could not unfortunately escape thinking about the Outfit. It was not as though he disliked the Outfit. Rather, he did not like being under student cover. Today, Bessac looks back and says that he simply did not enjoy looking at China through the lens of government employment. He says he wanted to be free to see China as it was. Bessac's letters of the time indicate a general disapproval of U.S. policies in China. There are several possible reasons for the conflict between his undercover position and his own views of China. In mid-October 1947, as his mind wandered from his reading, he put the book back inside his robe and headed home.

THE CRAG HOTEL, COTTAGE NO. 8
PENANG, MALAYSIA
OCTOBER 21, 1947

There wasn't much privacy on board the USS *Polk*. They were both in dormitories. Lyons shared her stateroom, and its bathroom, with three other ladies. Mackiernan had similar accommodations. They spent all day together on the decks; the dining room was grand and the food was great.

The new couple was pleased to slip away from the ship for a few nights while it remained in port. Cottage No. 8 was a small house up on the mountain overlooking the port below. They had two airy bedrooms with snow-white sheets and fine woolen blankets to ward off the nighttime chill. The boy served tea on the veranda, and then afterward they sat in their own private garden above the port of Penang.

She never wanted to forget these moments. He was reading from his favorite author, Kipling. The wind fluttered the pages of the book in his hands and rippled his dark hair across his brow. Her heart resonated with every word that Mackiernan read.

> *I've taken my fun where I've found it*
> *I've rogued and I've ranged in my time.*
> *I've 'ad my pickin' o' sweet hearts.*

Mackiernan laughed as he read, with a wistful turn to his voice.

> *For to admire and for to see*
> *For to be'old this world so wide*
> *It never done no good to me*
> *But can't drop it if I tried.*

She wanted the moment to last forever until he began to read the haunting rhymes of "The 'Mary Gloster'." As she listened to those words, the mood changed. She wondered if Mackiernan heard what she heard as he read.

I've paid for your sickest fancies
I've humored your crackedest Whim . . .

For a man he must go with a woman.
Which women don't understand.

Hearing this at sunset from Mackiernan's lips, she peered into his eyes. Was he aware that these words made her think of the secret of Tihwa and her fears about his faithfulness to her? If so he gave no sign of it.

When the sky was dark blue with the last light of the tropics he put down the book, rose, and held out his arms to her.

"Come on, honeybunch. We'd better go for chow."

Next morning the boy served them tea in bed—the colonial tradition called bedtea—and delivered the morning papers on the same tray. She read aloud to him from *The Straits Echo:*

Chinese infiltration and grasp on the money granted, the Malays are indolent and like to live without making more than the necessary effort to support themselves and family, and the Chinese have worked through the heat like galley slaves to mass their Capital.

Mackiernan's comment stuck in her mind. He admitted Chinese colonialism in Malaysia. He said it was just like what he saw the Chinese doing in Inner Asia. "The Chinese are doing in Malaya what foreigners did in China," he said. "Carving out fortunes and never putting back into the country what they take out in mass capital. All the wealth made in Malaya goes back to China in some form or other."

FRANK BESSAC AND PRINCE DE
PEKING, CHINA
OCTOBER 1947

On the way home from his lessons at Fujen University, Bessac stopped at the Mongol Prince De's courtyard not far from his own *houtong*— as the gray-brick courtyards of old Peking were called. Prince De was a direct descendent, through thirty-one recorded generations, of Genghis Khan. Mongols say that from the enthronement of Genghis Khan in 1206 until the arrest of Prince De in 1950, the Golden Descendants of Genghis Khan always ruled the Mongol people. Sometimes the empire of those princes included Mongolia, China, and half of Europe, but political boundaries never defined the Mongols. Their nationalism centered on the Banner, or tribe, and the princes who led the Banners. Genghis Khan—and his descendants—were the only princes who ever unified all the Mongol Banners. Prince De was the last Mongol prince, and he led the Mongols of Inner Mongolia as they fought their last battle along the Great Wall.

Bessac met Prince De in 1946, shortly after he had returned to Peking from Inner Mongolia. The Outfit sent Bessac to interview the prince on many occasions, and the two men, working together as agent and source, slowly developed what Bessac believes was a friendship.

Prince De devoted his life to the national survival of the Mongolian people of southern Mongolia. At various times in his life, openly or secretly, he worked or negotiated with the Japanese army, American intelligence agents, and the Communist and Nationalist Chinese. In every case, he had only one goal—the national survival of the Mongolian people of southern or Inner Mongolia. He was willing to deal with anyone to achieve that goal.

Bessac says today that he visited Prince De occasionally in the fall of 1947 only to practice his Mongolian with an old friend. The prince greeted Bessac without pretensions and invited him to take tea. Dressed in his Western-style white shirt and black pants, he settled back in his old British sofa, and considered the young American in Chinese robes in front of him. The prince had a message for the American government, but Bessac was telling him he no longer worked for the Americans.

Bessac understood only about half of what the Prince said in Mongolian, and so he got the old man to repeat it for him in Chinese. After Bessac finished taking his notes, he sighed, and then replied in Chinese. "Prince De, I have quit the service of my government. I am just a student now. I worked for them before, but not now. I have told you this before. Now I am studying Mongolian. It is very good of you to help me study Mongolian with this conversation, but I have quit my work for the government."

Yes, as you say. Still you will tell them that we want real autonomy, won't you? You understand that, yes? Bessac looked out the window into the courtyard and said nothing as he listened. Prince De's gray-brick courtyard looked much like his. There was nothing to see except the brick walls and the same small slice of sky. They were so far away from the vast sky of the open steppe. Finally, Bessac spoke to the prince in Chinese, " I have seen Mongols who've built a beautiful brick courtyard, with high walls, and a nice house within the walls. However, they lived just outside the walls, on the open steppe, in a yurt. Have you seen that?"

Looking back on those days Frank Bessac now says that sometime during October 1947 he wrote a letter of resignation to the CIA. He is not sure what date he wrote it. Nor does he recall whether he mailed it to Washington, or gave it to the local office in Peking. He believes now that it was not because he disliked the CIA that he quit. The CIA will not confirm or deny that Frank Bessac ever worked for them. Bessac says that he quit simply because he no longer wanted to look at China through U.S. government lenses. His GI Bill gave him the economic freedom to stay in China without the CIA, and he disliked being undercover, so he quit.

Nevertheless two sources (one American and one Mongol) state that Frank Bessac did not quit the CIA in 1947. One of these sources, a former CIA agent, says that from what he knows of the CIA Bessac would not have been allowed to quit after being sent back to China as a contract undercover agent. Bessac further confuses what happened in the fall of 1947 when he says that, although he quit, he was still available for contract work with the Outfit, if the need ever presented itself.

THE GREEN LANTERN
STOUGHTON, MASSACHUSETTS
JANUARY TO AUGUST 1948

Just north of Boston snow covered the ground under the bare trees that stretched out around the isolated gas station. Colorless winter sunlight from a slate sky cast a shadowless illumination through the plate-glass windows into the Green Lantern's office. Douglas Mackiernan, Sr., listened with his mouth agape as his eldest son stood before him, explaining his future.

"I'm gonna set you up, Pop. But we gotta get this thing going. You gotta sell the gas station."

He had run the Green Lantern with his boys' help for more than fifteen years. It had been their only hope during the depression. Now Douglas, only a few days back from China, was telling him to dump it.

"My brothers are not gonna be pumping gas. They're not gonna have time to pump gas. You're gonna sell this friggin' place and we'll make a radio station here."

It fell on Mackiernan Senior like a bomb, but gazing at his wife behind the cash register he could tell by the look on her face that she and her eldest son had already made the decision. Douglas exuded confidence, and it was easy to trust him. He just hoped to hell the boy knew what he was talking about.

Does mary know her uncles?

"Right, Pop? Right! We're gonna do something."

Stuart Mackiernan looks back fifty years, and laughs in amazement at his elder brother's audacity. The radio equipment arrived at the Green Lantern, and Douglas Mackiernan ordered his brothers, Stuart, Duncan, Malcolm, and Angus to install it in one end of a seventy-foot-long former chicken shed that had been insulated and converted into the radio house. In a storm of work and excitement, Douglas was the calm center. He was, "always reasonable and calm. I never saw him blow his top. Angus did that all the time . . . but Dougie you could jab him in the rear end and he'd say, 'oh', but he's still thinking."

"Hey, look, World Weather was a good idea," says Stuart. "It made two thousand dollars the first year and two years later it made ninety thousand dollars. That was a lot of money back in those days. . . . The government paid good. . . . We thought it was great."

Duncan Mackiernan recalls, "Dougie decided what we were worth, and he just paid us that, and no one argued. Dougie was like that."

That spring Douglas had them setting up a sixty-foot-high tower from which they strung a massive antenna. And they put other antennae in the woods, some more than five hundred feet long. They could pick up signals from the other side of the earth, from Tihwa and from elsewhere deep inside the Soviet Union. Though his brothers would not know it for years, Douglas was building the radio receivers that would receive data from the covert atomic detection equipment that the United States was about to install inside the U.S.S.R. and at Tihwa.

Stuart made the trips down to Washington to sign the contracts.

"It was all set up, Doug did that. . . . He couldn't get the contract because he was working for the government." It would have been inappropriate for Douglas, as a government employee, to become a U.S. government contractor, but no one stopped him from arranging the contract with the government and then making sure his family received it. It was a deal that left Douglas Mackiernan secretly in charge, which is probably what was intended.

"We incorporated in May of '48 and our first contract started in June of '48. . . ." Stuart says. "The ruse, at least the story, the cover, was that we would set up World Weather because the world needed better weather forecasting, and the government was willing to pay for weather forecasting because the army was incapable of intercepting this stuff. Great incompetence, and we were wonderful and we would do it under contract.

"The object of the game was to intercept foreign weather, from our radio station . . . and transmit it by teletype down to Andrews Air Force Base. To SAC, Strategic Air Command. I did not have any reason to think the CIA was involved. Not at its infancy. Our contracts were with the Air Force. The party line was that the Air Force needed this weather information."

Angus was the only other trained meteorologist in the family besides Douglas. Naturally, the people at Andrews Air Force Base, the Air Weather folks at SAC, wanted to talk with Angus, not Malcolm and Stuart. But Angus wouldn't go down to Washington.

"I think he knew more than any of us knew . . . that it wasn't just weather. He was aware of the hanky-panky. Where most of the Mackiernan boys were very gung ho, my country right or wrong, Angus was not that way. He was definitely more critical, Parlor Pink . . . he probably voted Democratic." If he voted Democratic in the privacy of the polling booth, he was the only Mackiernan who did so. And if Angus was told that the "hanky-panky" meant receiving data from an atomic explosion detection net, he and Douglas never told the other brothers. It is probably not a coincidence that the Mackiernan contract was nailed down in the spring of 1948. Those were the exact months when all the early AFOAT-1 contracts were being signed. And just like many other AFOAT-1 contractors, World Weather was also a new technical start-up that sprang out of MIT.

Mackiernan brought his fiancée Pegge Lyons up to the Green Lantern once, just after she had arrived from Europe in January 1949. They had traveled together on the USS *Polk* as far as Genoa, and then spent a month together in Italy and Switzerland, before Mackiernan left her and headed home, theoretically to get divorced from his first wife, Darrell. In January, when Pegge showed up at Stoughton, the divorce was still not completed and Mom Mackiernan had her sleeping in the library. Pegge soon set off to New York in search of a job as a journalist, while anxiously awaiting Mackiernan's divorce.

Lyons was trying to be patient about the divorce, but it was hard—especially since by February she was pregnant. Her doubts about marrying Mackiernan were put firmly away. Despite many months of effort, she did not land a journalist job in New York. Eventually, Mackiernan got her a secretarial job in Washington, D.C., at the Russian Bureau of the State Department, where she worked as long as she could. Through it all, Mackiernan traveled incessantly—Lyons was told he was in Nevada trying to get the divorce processed.

She rushed through the marble halls of Union Station to see Mackiernan off to Las Vegas one spring day. He looked snappy in his ever-present trench coat and had a suitcase full of Russian-language LPs. His second suitcase was full of arcane books on Sinkiang. He kissed her and then puffed on a cigar as he stepped up into the Liberty Express. As the train pulled out, he leaned down and whispered hoarsely above the train, loud enough for her to hear, "I wish you were coming with me, babydoll."

During the spring and summer of 1948, Pegge says that Douglas went back and forth to Nevada several times, without concluding the divorce. These long disappearances may have provided cover opportunity for Mackiernan.

Lyons says that "he always had mysterious comings and goings. I knew better than to say, 'You'll be back at 5 P.M. and then we are going to dinner,' or something like that. I knew that he didn't know when he would be back."

Mackiernan may have participated in the tests of General Hegenberger's atomic explosion detection equipment during the U.S. atomic tests at Eniwetok Atoll in the South Pacific. By May 1948, World Weather was operational, and it could have received test signals from Hegenberger's equipment in the Pacific during the May 14 Zebra atomic test. The details of Mackiernan's work that spring remain unknown, but he had a lot on his plate, including a full social life.

According to Lyons, Owen Lattimore drove down from Johns Hopkins University in Baltimore to Washington one night specifically to have dinner with Mackiernan before he returned to Sinkiang. Mackiernan, like Bessac, had devoured *Inner Asian Frontiers of China* while living with the Inner Asians.

Lattimore and Mackiernan spent the night talking about the fate of the peoples of East Turkestan and the Tibetans, in light of the impending defeat of Chiang Kai-shek's Nationalist government.

Mackiernan complained that America had no idea what democracy really was, or of what its foreign policy toward the people of Inner Asia, or China, should be. This was compounded by the fact that even if it had understood these two things, it had no rational way to communicate that democracy, or American foreign policy, to anyone. He undoubtedly shared his views about the Kazak and Inner Asia in general, since they coincided precisely with those of Lattimore. Stuart remembers his brother's attitude clearly. The Kazak, "just had no use for the Chinese, any Chinese. Whether it was Mao or who in the hell it was. Whether they were Nationalist or Communist Chinese didn't matter. It was just get out of our country. Doug shared that feeling, absolutely, he was fighting for their independence. He wasn't a cold war anti-Communist."

Lyons did not record what Lattimore said to Mackiernan—the old man seemed too intellectual to her. Lattimore's view's on Inner Asia at this time are no secret; he was writing articles to promote them. Owen Lattimore was frustrated at the course American foreign policy was taking.

The U.S. government was under pressure to aid the Europeans as they tried to regain their colonies in Indonesia and Vietnam. Lattimore warned that if America did not support Asian nationalism against European colonialism, the Asians would turn—as the Mongols had done in their struggle against Chinese colonialism—to the only alternative source of support: Russia. The French in Vietnam and the Dutch in Indonesia argued that reassertion of their colonial rights was "sound" and that the arguments in favor of Vietnamese and Indonesian independence were "sentimental." FDR had wanted to oppose this postwar colonialism in Asia, but his successor, Truman, needed European support for American agendas in Europe.

Lattimore argued that support for colonialism—whether Chinese or French—in Asia ran against American ideals and that it would help the Communists. "In the Far East, we have got to hold up our end against Russia. We can't do it unless we stop pushing into Communism people whom the Russians themselves couldn't lead into Communism."

Lattimore's understanding of China was so impressive that President Roosevelt recommended him as an American adviser to Chiang

Kai-shek in 1942, and he had served Chiang well. When Roosevelt's vice president, Henry Wallace, decided to make a tour of Russian Siberia and Inner Asia near the end of World War II, Lattimore was again called upon as the obvious choice to guide the vice president during his journey. None of this experience impressed President Truman after FDR's death.

Truman did not bring Lattimore onto the China policy team at the State Department as many had advised and expected him to do. Like many Americans, Truman had little appreciation for the sparkling erudition that bubbled through every comment Lattimore ever made. No one doubted Lattimore's knowledge, but Pegge Lyons's pointed judgment of Lattimore helps explain why the makers of American foreign policy were ignoring him. A good ol' boy he was not. If he were too much of an intellectual for Lyons, few Americans would have seen it otherwise. The normally quiet Douglas Mackiernan, on the other hand, talked nonstop with the grand old man of China studies, throughout their dinner together.

That spring Mackiernan revealed to Lyons that World Weather was somehow involved with his work for the U.S. government. "His plans with the State Department are to set up an international weather station in Boston. His two brothers in charge. And to take me with him back . . . into Sinkiang, where Doug will hold the rank of Vice Consul."

Mackiernan said little more than that since he was always tight-lipped about his work. "What he could not say, he did not say," recalls Lyons. That's who he was. There was one hint in a conversation with his wife, which she still recalls. She asked him what a certain piece of equipment was, that she noticed him discussing on the phone.

"You're not to worry about things like that. That's my job." Then as if to indicate that she was also on the same team, he closed the conversation by saying, "It's a device to measure tremors in the earth." She deduced that the equipment, and his work, had something to do with uranium and the Russians.

When Mackiernan told his family that he planned to leave them in charge of the Green Lantern operation and return to China, they were shocked. Stuart remembers that the information fell like a bomb on Mackiernan Senior, immediately after he had closed the Green Lantern. By then the boys had a contract with the government and were very busy. In June the first check arrived, the first of what would become a flood. The Mackiernans were not too concerned with what World Weather was actually doing or for whom.

World Weather was neither part of the State Department, as Lyons was led to believe, nor was it only a contractor for the Air Force, as Stuart initially believed. Mackiernan deflected the curiosity of his wife and his brother by telling them exactly enough to keep them from asking more. He told each of them a different story, and they never compared notes. World Weather was probably a private contractor for AFOAT-1. It was part of a broader effort that linked the State Department and the Air Force with the CIA and the AEC. Just when Hegenberger approached Mackiernan to set up this intelligence operation is not clear; interestingly both Hegenberger and Mackiernan returned briefly to Washington, D.C., in December 1947, and Hegenberger took control of AFOAT-1 that month.

Mackiernan set up his part of AFOAT-1 so that his family would never know exactly what they were doing. They were receiving a coded data stream and then passing it on, still coded, to Andrews Air Force Base. The Mackiernan family had no need to know that their actions were part of a much larger operation, but they were.

Compartmentalize information so that none of your agents understand the full scope of what is going on. That's the prime directive for an intelligence agent managing an intelligence operation as well as for those above him managing the field agent, and so on up the chain. Use people to get the intelligence you need, but never let them know what they are obtaining for you. You get information. Give little or nothing in return.

Surely the CIA never intended that this directive would guide relations with one's own family. Of course an agent would keep his family ignorant of his work, that makes sense. Mackiernan actually involved his family in intelligence operations—to their and his financial benefit—but compartmentalized their knowledge so that they could not understand the purpose of the operation. He ran his family the same way he ran agents. In doing so he made a mistake that still haunts the CIA today—he confused what was good for him, or for American intelligence, with what was good for others, or for the foreign policy of the United States.

Seeing in retrospect how he used his family for intelligence operations, we would be blind not to see a rime of frost around his heart. A great agent, as one of his daughters would say—but a terrible father.

Mackiernan's actions speak of a supreme self-confidence. A man playing his game with such self-assurance that he is willing to bet the life of his wife and the livelihood of his brothers on the accuracy of his knowledge, his deft use of power and the ultimate success of his machinations. Mackiernan's pride and skill maps the innermost chambers of the CIA's own heart. Although he is an archetype, which retrospectively gives us insight, he was also just an agent, whose scientific intelligence was part of a much larger operation being run by Hegenberger.

In the spring of 1948, General Hegenberger ordered the commanding general of the Air Force Weather Service, Brig. Gen. Donald N. Yates, stationed at Andrews Air Force Base, to start building and installing the Air Force hardware for AFOAT-1. That military effort was linked to work being carried out by private AFOAT-1 contractors—like Mackiernan—that same spring. Yates was an old friend of Mackiernan's from his early days at Air Weather in Washington, before Mackiernan had left for China. While Mackiernan set up at the Green Lantern, Yates ordered the alteration of U.S. Air Force Air Weather planes in Alaska. He equipped them with air filter devices to detect radiation in the atmosphere, while Mackiernan established part of the land-based system.

Stuart Mackiernan had no idea who General Yates was because he had no need to know. He did meet with the general at Andrews Air Force Base, because Yates was his boss for the World Weather contracts. In August 1948 it came as no surprise when Yates, Colonel Taylor, and two other Air Force officers announced they would be pulling an inspection tour up at the Green Lantern. Douglas Mackiernan saw no need to be there during the inspection. He was off in Nevada trying to get his divorce finalized when the Air Force inspected their new covert atomic intelligence radio farm.

The Air Force officers walked through the New England forest out to the Radio House. Apparently, they liked the looks of the science, but one thing bothered them.

"What the hell is this about Doug going back to China?" asked Colonel Taylor. "Don't let him go."

At first Stuart could not understand what they were talking about. They indicated plainly that they did not think Douglas would come back alive. Once Angus understood this message, he snorted at them,

"Oh, blah!" he said and walked away.

The colonel was quite specific: "Don't let him go. He's crazy."

"Talk him out of it, do what ever the hell you can do to talk him out of it." When Stuart asked why his brother was in danger, the Air Force officers pointed their fingers at "Communists in the State Department."

General Yates was telling the brothers Mackiernan that Douglas was going to be betrayed by Communists in the State Department and might not return alive from China. This was six months before Senator Joseph McCarthy made "Communists in the State Department" a modern legend. It had already become a staple belief of many in the military, the FBI, and of anyone who hated FDR. The closer America came to "losing China," the more Americans became convinced that it was not Chiang's corruption that was losing the Chinese civil war. It had to be some cabal of Communists in the U.S. government who were secretly causing his defeat. Mackiernan brushed aside the Red Scare stories from his brother and mother without answering any questions about his real work.

"I'm going back to do meteorology and this kind of stuff, but I'll be back and we'll do some scientific stuff." Stuart got the impression that he had to hold the business together until his elder brother returned to run the show. The CIA seemed quite eager to have Mackiernan go to China, and then to have him return to the United States where his scientific skills could be put to further use.

Later that summer, shortly before Douglas Mackiernan left for China, Stuart walked in on his mother and older brother during one of their periodic "clandestine conventions." Douglas often got together with his mother to tell her more about what was going on. As Stuart explains, "Dougie wasn't close to pop; he wasn't his confidant like Mother was. Mother, if you told her something and told her to keep her mouth shut, she would keep her mouth shut. She didn't need to brag like pop. He would go to his brother."

"Well Dougie's over there looking at the Atom bomb, and what's your son doing?"

"My mother never needed to brag. Dougie was like mom; he didn't need to brag. If you have a spy you need someone who doesn't need to tell others. He doesn't need people patting him on the back; he is already so self-confident. That's the kind of man Doug was. He exuded self-confidence."

When Stuart barged into his mother's sewing room he could see Douglas's heavy trench coat spread out on the table beside the sewing machine. More than fifty gold bars were lined up on it.

"Mom was sewing these gold bars into Dougie's coat. She was putting them into little rows . . . in the jacket, all up and down. . . . They were these little biscuits, like sugar cubes, like a double sugar cube . . . kinda rough . . . though I didn't get a close look."

Douglas immediately threw his younger brother out of the room. This was one more of his secrets with his mother. "Mom and I are talking. Get outta here."

They both knew Stuart had seen the gold. Later, when he asked about it, Douglas was curt and brief. "That's for the characters," was all he would say.

Mother Mackiernan was just as brief and used exactly the same word. "He's taking it for the characters."

Duncan Mackiernan also heard about gold in the house that summer. He recalled that Douglas had "melted gold, and stashed it into the case of a worn-out B battery" of a type used for army field radios. From these and other hints, it appears that Mackiernan took between one hundred and three hundred ounces of gold bullion back to China in 1948. At modern rates of exchange the CIA gave him somewhere between forty thousand dollars and one hundred and twenty thousand dollars with which to influence events in Inner Asia.

Stuart felt that the gold was for the characters and that the "characters were White Russians, or people working in concert with the White Russians." People like Osman Bator, of whom Mackiernan spoke occasionally that summer.

In his conversations with Stuart, Douglas never directly linked Osman to the gold or to uranium. Yet other scientific endeavors in the Mackiernan household during the summer of 1948 do link the gold to Osman and to uranium. Douglas had not forgotten the Russian uranium mine in the Altai, nor that Osman could still send people back to it if required. Not only were the Mackiernan brothers building Douglas his radio reception net. He also found another contract for the family science business—an order to build a few Geiger counters. His brothers built them. Though most were sold to a scientific customer, a few Geiger counters went back with Douglas to China. When he returned to Sinkiang, he would not have to build a handmade electroscope to test rock samples for uranium.

Stuart says, "The only thing I know is that he was taking Geiger counters with him . . . the only reason you take one in those days is to look for uranium . . . and he said he was going to . . . look for uranium. And he said something about the Russians getting their uranium from Sinkiang."

All of this suggests that Douglas Mackiernan was taking the gold back for an operation that had something to do with the Russian uranium mine in the ETR.

In the meantime, he and Pegge Lyons bought a brand-new Willys Jeep in Washington, and he drove it out to Nevada; Lyons flew to the West Coast. On August 29, 1948—exactly one year before Russia would test its first atomic bomb—Doug finally secured his divorce from Darrell in Las Vegas. And at long last, on September 2, Mackiernan married Lyons in San Francisco.

None of this was easy for the women in his life. Gail Mackiernan, his daughter with his first wife, today a noted marine biologist, remembers a few brief childhood meetings with her father that summer. She describes her father this way: "He was a wonderful agent, but a dud as a husband and a father."

Mackiernan's marriage to Pegge Lyons does not alter this image. She had been waiting to marry him for a year. He married her as soon as he was legally able, at a judge's office downtown.

During the wedding, an out-of-tune American Legion marching band began to practice in the next building. The judge's assistants rushed to close the windows but the off-key racket continued throughout the ceremony.

Douglas and Pegge flew into Shanghai during the first week of September 1948. It was only in China that a doctor looked up at Pegge in surprise from his stethoscope and gave her the news: Two heartbeats. Not one. Two. On September 30, 1948, Mrs. Douglas

Mackiernan gave birth to Mike and Mary Mackiernan. Though they were born in China the twins lived there for only two months before they were evacuated.

By November the Chinese civil war was ending. Chiang Kai-shek's armies were turning over to the Communists without any resistance. In this way, as several U.S. generals testified, the more money the United States gave Chiang to fight Mao Tse-tung the better Mao was armed to fight Chiang. In the end, the U.S. generals wanted to stop giving Chiang any arms or money, because it seemed only to speed up the pace of Mao's victory drive. Later accusations of Communists in the State Department has obscured this fact: U.S. generals supported President Truman and Secretary of State Dean Acheson when they decided to pull the plug on Chiang. The corruption of Chiang was not a message that the U.S. media had pressed upon the American public.

As late as 1949, the U.S. press was still full of praise for Chiang, the brave democratic, Christian president of China—and anyone who said otherwise risked being branded a Communist. *Time,* owned by a China-born missionary's son, Henry Luce, pushed this propaganda so forcefully that Chiang was on its cover an unprecedented seven times. After a steady diet of pro-Chiang propaganda, Americans could not understand how the Christian president, after receiving so much U.S. aid, could be losing. The dark secret—that Chiang was corrupt and his armies had been left unpaid and starving while he and his cronies pocketed the U.S. aid—went underreported, at best, if not all together censored. For Mrs. Mackiernan, the collapse of Chiang was mostly a chaotic and colorful backdrop for her personal tragedy, as she recorded in her diary.

We were going to Kiangwan Airfield from whence Doug was to take off for Nanking and eventually Tihwa. And I am to stay in Shanghai to await shipment to San Francisco for the duration of China's political earthquake. We reached the separation decision simultaneously after working uphill for many anxious days. The babies' tender age decided us. We felt we couldn't expose them to unnecessary risk. How, where, and when we shall meet again we don't know.

At the airport, we stood in a whipping cold wind saying last things, practical details of financial affairs. I got back in the consulate car. Doug leaned in the doorway.

"Remember I love you extremely much my darling," he said and kissed me long and hard.

Pegge Mackiernan and her twin infants were aboard one of the first American evacuation flights from Shanghai. By mid-November, she was looking for a house in Fairfax, California. A single mom, with twins. A former journalist dependent upon her husband for all income. Officially, Mackiernan was making $209 a month from his State Department job; what was happening to his CIA salary, which was four times that, has never been discovered. Of this monthly salary, Mackiernan had to pay his first daughter, from his first wife, one hundred dollars a month. Thus, Pegge was forced to live with her twins on $109 a month, and unable to take a job because of her children.

After he left his new family, it took Mackiernan one month to drive across China. On December 10, 1948, he finally reached Tihwa with a truckload of equipment, which he drove directly into his own compound next door to the U.S. consulate.

DOUGLAS MACKIERNAN AND LONG-RANGE DETECTION OF ATOMIC EXPLOSIONS
1948 TO MARCH 10, 1949

Major General Albert Hegenberger's first step as head of AFOAT-1 was to run tests on potential detection equipment during U.S. atomic tests at Eniwetok Atoll in the South Pacific. In April and May 1948, the United States exploded several atomic bombs in the atmosphere there. Hegenberger tested many types of equipment. He sent planes equipped with filters through the radioactive clouds that drifted downwind from the blasts. He tried out optical flash detectors. Early versions of today's seismographic system that detects tremors from atomic blasts in the earth were also tested. Ground-based microphones were tested. Microphones were sent up in balloons to detect the sound of the blast even at very great distances. The Roswell, New Mexico, UFO mystery was likely created by AFOAT-1 security measures gone awry. A balloon carrying a sonic detector crashed, and the Air Force could hardly explain what all the secrecy was about as it whisked the balloon and its top-secret gear away.

After Hegenberger's tests, conclusions were reached about which equipment worked and which did not. Hegenberger disassembled his test equipment from installations all over the Pacific and began to install bits and pieces of it all over the world as an interim, experimental monitoring net. He turned over some of this work to old friends.

Some equipment was set up on military bases, and some was set up under cover inside such U.S. properties as embassies and consulates. For this global intelligence mission, the State Department, the CIA, and the Department of Defense worked as a team—and they worked closely with U.S. private enterprise and universities. This was the new intelligence community, working together, using high-tech means to protect America from a new menace.

Hegenberger had a problem with the sonic detector devices. These wonderfully sensitive microphones had to be placed within six hundred to twelve hundred miles of the atomic blast (depending on the bomb's strength) to be of any use. Once in range, they were some of his best equipment. They could tell the location of the explosion within a range of one hundred miles. Even better, they could determine precisely the size of the atomic explosion. None of the other information-collection systems Hegenberger tested at Eniwetok could give him that information. The nonsonic methods located a blast only within a few thousands miles, and timed it to within days—not very useful for fine-pointed decision making.

Only one American facility in the world was within six hundred to twelve hundred miles of the potential test sites in the remote areas of the Eurasian continent where the Russians were most likely to test their first bomb: the American consulate at Tihwa. Perhaps

Hegenberger thought of Mackiernan at once. A direct link between the two men is proven by one document.

On March 10, 1949, as Hegenberger's monitoring group started to install devices worldwide, Mackiernan sent a message from Tihwa to his old Nanking buddy, W. W. Butterworth, who had been promoted back to Washington and was now the newly appointed undersecretary for Far Eastern Affairs at the State Department.

TOP SECRET

Regarding Hegenberger Mission: all equipment on hand including spares for set, sent from Fairfield.

It has been more than fifty years since America's first atomic explosion monitoring system went on line. It is still considered so secret that this message is only one of two such from Mackiernan to Hegenberger—though dozens passed between them—that have been declassified. This message, and an eyewitness who helped Mackiernan bury the detectors outside of Tihwa, prove that he installed Hegenberger's sonic detectors in Tihwa during March 1949. By then Mackiernan's brothers had been on line in Massachusetts for months, picking up the data coming in from monitor stations, like Mackiernan's in Tihwa.

Mackiernan's achievements were remarkable. He designed the receiver station for the atomic detection units and secured for his family the contract to operate it. He installed at least one detection station in China. There is also evidence that Mackiernan set up detection stations at four locations inside the Soviet Union—perhaps utilizing the White Russians he met in Sinkiang. Even after fifty years, this is about as far as we can peer through the veil of secrecy.

By the spring of 1949, Stuart Mackiernan was collecting at the Green Lantern coded information streams from inside the Soviet Union. He says that one of the stations he was receiving was his brother's. The signals came bouncing off the ionosphere, pinging in from several locations inside Russia, as well as from Tihwa. All the information was coded. The brothers Mackiernan were paid well to receive this data and to pipe it straight on to Andrews Air Force Base. By the spring of 1949 they believed that it wasn't just coded weather data.

They had some exceptionally fine equipment, and after a time they thought it might have been nice to sell weather forecasts as their cover stated they were doing. When Stuart raised that idea with the Air Force, the request was refused. The Mackiernans were not to take their cover so seriously. Douglas Mackiernan's reception unit was going to have only one employer, and the brothers did not need to know who that was, nor what they were collecting, from where, or to whom they were sending the coded data streams.

Though Mackiernan's cover was working out well from an intelligence perspective, it is doubtful that he was very useful to the State Department as vice consul at the U.S. consulate in Tihwa. In the spring of 1949, months after he finally returned from his long unexplained "leave without pay," Consul Paxton filled out a Personnel Efficiency Report on Mackiernan.

Paxton officially rated him overall as a "very good" employee. He noted that Mackiernan was a competent cryptographer and an "Expert technician along many mechanical, electrical and scientific lines," but added that he had "no qualifications for clerical work other than limited interpreting in Russian."

He has seemed more content since his recent marriage, [but] he is now separated from his family and his personality is often mercurial. When he is in a good mood he can be almost irresistibly charming to people, but when "in the dumps" he often gives short answers and on occasion has seemed abrupt in dealing with people.

He has had good security training and is unquestionably loyal . . . and can be depended to carry out effectively any duties which he feels are properly within his field . . .

While he has remarkable ability in his special lines he seems disposed to make little effort to assist in any other paper work. Apparently due primarily to his abhorrence of writing anything not strictly technical . . .

[His] . . . services would be much more useful at this post, which has until recently been shortstaffed . . . if he were interested in other functions of the office. . . . He shows small interest in contacts with local officials. . . . Such assistance would have been particularly helpful in catching up the back-log of routine work which had accumulated . . .

when Mr. Mackiernan, absent fourteen months from the post on leave without pay, had left the principal officer to work unassisted.

Paxton was even more outspoken about his perceptions of Mackiernan when writing unofficially, to Robert Linden, who was soon supposed to replace Paxton.

> He often fails to carry out his promises . . . demonstrated unreliability . . . does not follow definite instructions . . . has been absent on leave without pay for over fourteen months and has not written me a line since he left . . . says that his pay-status is so complicated that he doesn't want to go back on the payroll until he gets back to his post . . .
>
> I believe you would be well advised to take what he *says* with a grain of salt and keep him under strict control if you decide it is worth the risk of having such an employee on your staff at all.

Despite this withering assessment of Mackiernan, Paxton knew there was more to the man than met the eye.

> He inspires confidence to a greater extent that seems justified by his actual conduct once he is out of sight. . . . You have, however, been put on guard and can make your own decision on the basis of the foregoing facts which may counterbalance the force of Doug's charm.

Office politics were strained, and one reason was Mackiernan's secret life. Worse, Mackiernan was not under Paxton's control, nor could he tell Paxton any details of who his actual employer was or the nature of his true job. Although Paxton knew Mackiernan was using the State Department for intelligence cover, security issues dictated that Paxton never know the extent of Mackiernan's commitments. His secret life was causing acrimony and resentment within the confines of the small, isolated consulate. Paxton could not know that during Mackiernan's fourteen months away from Tihwa he had been working, or that his pay status *was* complicated. To Paxton trapped in Tihwa, without any time off, Mackiernan's unexplained trip around the world could easily have caused resentment and misunderstanding.

Despite these conflicts in Tihwa, his intelligence work was of great national security interest that spring. The higher-ups in the State Department in Washington knew this, even if Paxton could not.

DEPARTMENT OF STATE
WASHINGTON, D.C.
APRIL 19, 1949

On April 15, the message archives at the State Department was combed for every report on file about uranium in Sinkiang. The undersecretary of state, the second most powerful man in the department, wanted all the reports in his office. That man was now Mackiernan's old friend from China, W. Walton Butterworth. Mackiernan's report of 1947 about the rocks Osman had given him was taken from the archives. Reports from as far back as 1943 were pulled about uranium in Sinkiang.

By April 15 dozens of documents covering reports of uranium in the Soviet-occupied zone of Sinkiang were assembled. A high-powered group of Washington bureaucrats gathered on April 19 to study them.

Mr. Trueheart, a representative from the Atomic Energy Commission, was summoned to the meeting; Gordon Arneson, the undersecretary's special assistant for intelligence matters, wrote the conversation memo on the meeting. The State Department's chief Chinese affairs specialist, Sprouse, told the assembled group the actual state of play and it went like this:

If the Russians are indeed mining uranium in Sinkiang, as Mackiernan reports, and if we went to Chiang Kai-shek's government and asked them to try to stop it, they would ask us for so much money in return that it would not be worth the effort. Mr. Sprouse was echoing President Truman's assessment of Chiang Kai-shek.

I discovered . . . that Chiang Kai-shek and the Madame and their families . . . were all thieves, every last one of them, the Madame and him included. And they stole seven hundred and fifty million dollars out of the thirty-five billion that we sent to Chiang. . . .

There was only one thing left for the United States to do in such a situation: covert action, special operations. The assembled consultants agreed upon what should be done, and who should do it. By 1949 the Outfit was legally authorized to carry out covert operations even during peacetime. Though CIA records about this operation remain classified, State Department records make it clear what was going on.

In order to acquire further intelligence on the reported uranium deposits, it was agreed to request Mr. Butterworth to convey to Mr. Mackiernan at Tihwa (through safe channels) the desire of the Atomic Energy Commission and the Department of State to secure some reliable samples from the alleged mines.

On April 22 Gordon Arneson drafted a message for Mackiernan's old friend Butterworth, now the undersecretary of state for Far Eastern Affairs, Secretary of State Acheson's most trusted adviser.

On April 23, Butterworth sent a message to Mackiernan, a message Paxton was not allowed to see, as the coding made clear.

TOP SECRET—EYES ALONE, MACKIERNAN
Dept and AEC strongly interested your obtaining soon such reliable samples from alleged Soviet uranium mining operations as are obtainable. Suggest they be brought out by Consul Paxton after arrival his relief. Your previous efforts in this connection appreciated. U.S. Govt. is not in a position to take effective action to prevent shipment of ores to USSR, but maximum intelligence regarding such facts as mineral composition, magnitude deposits, grade of ores, and rate of shipments, is considered important.

Perhaps some message from Mackiernan, or elsewhere, prompted this sudden policy review in relation to uranium in Sinkiang. It's probable that Mackiernan also received orders from the CIA, to amplify those from the AEC and the State Department. As is so often the case, the degree to which we are allowed to understand the directing forces behind Mackiernan's actions is intentionally limited. We run into the veil of classified material, and beyond that even the most time-consuming research cannot peer.

THE RAID ON THE U-2 MINE
SINKIANG AND THE ETR
APRIL OR MAY 1949

Sometime in late April or early May 1949, Douglas Mackiernan, responding to his instructions from the AEC and the State Department—and presumably the CIA—contacted five White Russian refugees living in Sinkiang. They were part of a group of one hundred and fifty to two hundred anti-Communists supported by the Nationalist government, whom Mackiernan occasionally drew upon for covert projects. He sought them out that April because he needed some uranium samples.

The command car came in the night. Douglas Mackiernan was driving, and he had brought his trusted assistant, Vasili Zvansov. The twenty-six-year-old Zvansov sported a white-blond crew cut, stood six feet tall, and weighed a muscular one hundred and ninety-five pounds. He knew these White Russians at Guichen, one hundred and fifty miles from Tihwa. He had been their quartermaster before he had been selected to work with Mackiernan.

In 1944 Zvansov had fled with them from the Altai Mountains of northern Sinkiang when the Russians invaded the area to aid the Kazak and Turkic peoples as they proclaimed the foundation of the ETR. Hundreds of White Russians who had fled Russia during the Communist Revolution there had taken refuge in Sinkiang, near the Soviet-Chinese border. The arrival of Soviet troops in the Altai forced these people to flee again. Some joined Osman Bator in the mountains. Some joined the Nationalist troops. In April 1949 about one hundred of these armed anti-Communist soldiers, supported by the Chinese Nationalists, were in Guichen, Sinkiang.

Half a dozen of these White Russians had been born in a little town called Semipalatinsk in what is today called Kazakhstan. In 1949 it was the Kazak Soviet Socialist Republic. "Semi" is where Stalin tested his first atomic bomb in the summer of 1949. A Russian we know now only as Ivan X—his last name is obscured by the sources who will talk about him—and four other Russians accepted Mackiernan's money and his orders. They rode their horses three hundred miles north to the Russian uranium mine inside the ETR at Koktogai in the Altai Mountains. They were sent to obtain the "reliable samples" that the AEC had requested. Only Ivan X returned alive: his four friends were killed. Ivan brought the rocks for which the four Russians had died and gave them to Mackiernan. There are rumors that Mackiernan went on the raid to the U-2 mine—yet to date they are unsubstantiated. Somehow Ivan passed through the U.S.S.R. on his way back from Koktogai, though that would have been four hundred miles out of his way.

Perhaps Ivan installed atomic explosion detection equipment near the Russian test site back in his old hometown of Semi. If Mackiernan needed a spy to send to Semi, no one would have been more loyal than a White Russian like Ivan X, who had suffered so much under Stalin. Many White Russians were political refugees, or deserters from the Red Army. They were wanted dead or alive by the Russians.

We know Ivan went to the mine and brought back the rocks, and that the U.S. government eventually resettled his wife in the United States for services rendered. We know Ivan was born in Semipalatinsk, and we know the bomb was tested there. If these facts suggest that Mackiernan was running agents inside the U.S.S.R., it remains only speculation.

Mackiernan did not forget his debt to Ivan X, though America's payment of it would be long delayed.

HAWAII

JUNE 1, 1996

Vasili Zvansov, Mackiernan's right-hand man during his time in Tihwa, is an old man today. The white-blond hair of his youth is now white with a hint of gold, brightly bleached by the Hawaiian sun. The massive forearms and bulging biceps of his youth have melted away. The alabaster skin that covered them is now leathered and dark from a youth in the sun of Inner Asia and his Hawaiian retirement.

He walks with a slight limp in his left leg. With Russian hospitality, he greets visitors in the driveway and escorts them into the neat retirement home he shares with his still beautiful wife. He speaks in American phrases, but his Russian accent covers it all.

"I was born in 1923 in Kazakhstan to Russian parents who had been forced there during the revolution and after. My father had fled to Sinkiang when Communists tried to kill him. I crossed the Russian border from Kazakhstan into Sinkiang when I was nineteen. The year was 1942. I was a deserter from Stalin's army. I had only been in that army three months, but I never agreed with the system, so I could not fight for such a system. So I ran. I was hired by one of Chiang Kai-shek's generals in Sinkiang, General Omar Ma, to work in a Russian brigade. I was the quartermaster receiving all the money and things from the Nationalist government. They gave us all guns and ammunitions, about one hundred and fifty or two hundred of us. I was just a young kid running for my life. I never wanted to fight. But I had to fight for Stalin's Red Army some few months—they would kill you if you didn't. But then I found the right time to run from them and I got to Sinkiang. Then in Sinkiang I had to fight for General Ma. We were in north Sinkiang when it became Russian puppet state—they called it Eastern Turkestan Republic, or ETR.

"The Russians organized a Red Brigade, a partisanship, against Nationalist to chase Chinese out of Sinkiang in 1944. The Russians said to the Kazak, Here, we give you weapons. You kill the Chinese. You drive them out of Sinkiang, because this belongs to you, and you are going to be the boss not anybody else. We ran. We fought. We left our homes, again. We fought then we surrendered. The big officers were shot, and then ETR was established, and for two months we were under the ETR. But then Osman Bator sent his army to liberate us, and we joined Osman Bator and then we stayed with him, and then more army came from ETR and they chased us again, and then we withdrew till we met up with General Ma's Nationalist army in Guichen. That's when I was with the group of Russians who were working against the Communists, that's all we knew. Including me. We don't want to obey the Communists. We called Eskadrone.

"Then Osman went back into the mountains—but I went to work with Mackiernan. That was in 1947. Eskadrone stayed with Nationalists.

"I was in Guichen not far from Tihwa, then I met General Ma. He was the big man, and I only met him then. He had contact with American consulate in Urumchi—what we called Tihwa in those times. Then one day he asked me if I wanted to go to work with the Americans in Urumchi. That General Ma, he had decided that Mao was going to take Sinkiang. He gave me a warning and said I should get near the Americans. It seemed like General Ma looked at all the Russians and hired me to work for the CIA. That is my thinking but I could be wrong.

"I said I be glad to. I thought it was the only way to get out of Sinkiang.

"So then in 1948, I started working with Mackiernan, and Doug trained me to operate the radio. But all I did was as a radio helper. But I knew all the local tribes and languages and customs and so on, so I said I would be glad to help.

"Doug worked for the CIA. He was looking all over; they keep an eye on everything. Maybe Doug knew about the uranium mining or other things, but he did not talk. He was not a big talker. He was talking very limited time.

"The year I was in Tihwa, before we went to Tibet, I stayed in a big mansion. Douglas had me stay at the mansion and watch the mansion and three horses. I had a room, and so did Doug but there were ten rooms with baths and everything. Once every week, I hired a woman to come clean. I studied the radio, but most I was busy with horses and house. The other Russians working with Osman Bator were in the country, but sometime they came to talk with me at the mansion. I was the translator.

"About that uranium mine, I heard only that there was many trucks going from the mine to Russia, and then they said this was being sold to England. I didn't know nothing about that Russian atomic bomb.

"There was one thing, however. I did not understand it at the time. In the spring of 1949, Douglas asked me to go out with him in the Jeep. He had me put some boxes from his private compound into the Jeep. He told me they were radios. We drove outside Tihwa, and we buried these boxes in the earth. I could not look in them, except one brief look through the cracks of the crate. It looked like some electronic things in these boxes. The crates were wooden, and then there was some waterproof covering inside that. I saw inside one just as Doug was closing the box.

"'What's these things?' I asked him.

"'Radios, Vasili. Just radios. If the Communists take over Tihwa, we might need to have some radios so I am burying these out here in the desert so we could pick them up later.'"

When they buried the "radios" Mackiernan carefully fed antenna wires out of them, up through the earth that covered them, and laid the wires out on the surface of the desert, with just a thin covering of dust over them here and there.

"'What are the wires coming out of the boxes Mr. Mackiernan?'

"'Oh, that's just some string so we can find them again easily, Vasili.'"

Fifty years later Zvansov laughs when he tells this story. He now believes that perhaps these "strings" were antennae, coming out of the atomic detection equipment, in order to transmit data back to Mackiernan in Tihwa.

"At that time, I believed him. He was very good. How was I supposed to know we were burying things that could find out if the Russians blew up an atomic bomb? I was just looking how to protect my life."

THE RUSSIAN ATOMIC TEST SITE

SEMIPALATINSK, KAZAK SOVIET SOCIALIST REPUBLIC

AUGUST 29, 1949

"The length of time the Soviet Union needed to develop the atomic bomb was determined more by the availability of uranium than by any other factor."

Stalin and the Bomb, David Holloway

When Douglas Mackiernan went to bed the night before Stalin blew up his first bomb, he was the only American in Tihwa. The State Department, watching the course of the Chinese civil war, ordered the Tihwa consulate closed on August 15. Consul Paxton led an exodus, famous in State Department history, that included all Americans except Mackiernan. Paxton's wife, Vincoe, Vice Consul Robert Dreesen, and more than a dozen local employees went out with Paxton. He took out the local hires—including the driver Erwin Kontescheny (and Erwin's five-year-old son, Leonid)—because he feared their known loyalty would endanger their lives when the Communists took Tihwa. Theirs was an amazing journey south around the western edge of the Taklamakan Desert, in western Tibet, and then through the Himalayas into India.

Mackiernan was ordered by the CIA to remain in Tihwa to continue his work despite the Communist conquest of China. Kontescheny remembers that when they left Mackiernan at Tihwa he seemed unhappy. Mackiernan was the sole American anywhere within one thousand miles of Stalin's top-secret atomic test site at Semipalatinsk.

The night of August 28–29 was cold and windy in the center of Asia. Clouds covered the sky. A light rain fell. The feather grass on the treeless, sandy steppe rippled in the wind. Anywhere else on the Eurasian steppe the grass rippled in unbroken waves in all directions.

Four hundred and fifty air miles northwest of the American consulate in Tihwa the steppe was not empty. A dirt road cut through the grass to a ninety-foot-high steel tower surrounded by a workshop bathed in bright worklights. Inside the workshop, a small group of men gathered around an odd collection of machinery. They were focused on a small half-sphere of uranium being lowered by a giant crane.

At two o'clock in the morning, the notorious chief of Stalin's secret police, L. P. Beria—a man responsible for the death of millions—was one of the eight men watching the final assembly of the U.S.S.R.'s first atomic bomb. The father of the Russian bomb, Igor Kurchatov, directed the well-rehearsed movements of the team he had assembled during the past four and a half years, ever since he received the "pay any price" command from Stalin. Each piece of metal before them had to be precisely assembled, or the atomic bomb would not explode.

Two half-spheres of plutonium, each only nine centimeters in diameter, were clamped together forming a sphere around the sensitive electronic device that would initiate the explosion after the plutonium had been compressed. A sphere of uranium surrounded the plutonium sphere, and a sphere of high explosives surrounded the uranium. The design is somewhat like nested Russian dolls—except the design was an exact copy of the American bomb first tested in New Mexico in 1945.

To start the atomic explosion the sphere of high explosives was specially designed to implode rather than explode outward. This implosion would create a sphere of high pressure, moving inward at an extremely high speed. That pressure wave would compress the uranium, which would then surge inward and compress the hollow plutonium sphere. This brought enough plutonium atoms into a small enough space that they became critical: an atomic reaction began, causing the atomic explosion.

This precise series of events took place within millionths of a second. If any one of these events was mistimed, the bomb would fizzle, and there would not be an atomic explosion. If it succeeded, America's atomic monopoly would be over, and Stalin would have exploded his first atomic bomb.

All seven Russian scientists in the room knew that more than just the success or failure of their years of hard work was at stake as they placed each of these pieces within one another. Beria had made it clear long before that some, or all, of these men would be shot if the bomb failed to explode. Each had an understudy, who was supposed to know everything he knew—so the men assembling the bomb could more readily be shot. Even so, fear of Beria was not their primary motivation; rather it was the fear of the American monopoly on the atomic bomb.

These men at the top of the Russian atomic pyramid were supported by an army of men and women who supplied the precious few kilograms of uranium and plutonium that are at the heart of an atomic bomb. Just as in the United States, the Russians had to build an atomic industry in order to build their bomb. The uranium had to be found, mined, and purified. Then reactors had to be built, so that the refined uranium could be turned into plutonium. It had taken the Russians almost exactly the same amount of time to create their atomic industry as it had taken the Americans before them. When they built their bomb between 1945 and 1949, the Russians had two advantages that the Americans did not have when they built theirs between 1942 and 1945.

The Russians had stolen a complete design of the atomic bomb from the United States by using British, Canadian, German, and American spies. In addition, the Russians made widespread use of prison labor to mine, refine, and shape the uranium and plutonium required.

Little is known about the lives of the estimated two hundred thousand people who lived and died in this nuclear gulag. Few of the prisoners condemned to these camps ever left them alive. Those who did not die because of their exposure to radioactivity were not allowed to leave the gulag, even after their sentence was served. Since they knew too much, they continued to work in the gulag until they died.

Much is now known about the lives of Klaus Fuchs, Ted Hall, the Rosenbergs, and the other atomic spies who gave away the American atomic secrets to Stalin. In every case, these spies have said they did not trust the United States to have an atomic monopoly. They believed that they were making the world a safer place by sharing the schematics of an atomic bomb with the Soviet Union. The Russian scientists who built the bomb for Stalin, based on the stolen American designs, shared the conviction of the spies. The Russian scientists, unlike the men and women whose lives were sacrificed in the nuclear gulag, knew the dangers of uranium. Yet they accepted higher radiation exposure levels because they understood the vital importance of acquiring an atomic bomb for Russia. The Russian physicists believed that the Americans were attempting to use their atomic monopoly to blackmail Stalin. To the Russians, America's political might was based on uranium.

The scientists knew the incredible cost of the nested spheres of plutonium and uranium. The few kilograms of purified uranium and plutonium was priced at thousands of lives per gram. The mass graves of the uranium miners from the gulag have never been opened. Uranium, not stolen American science, was the key to the Russian bomb. Murray Hill had been a very smart idea.

The Russian scientists had actually devised their own technique for building an atomic bomb—one, when later tested, that worked. In 1949 Stalin insisted that they use the American design. It was not the science that slowed the Russian bomb, nor had it been the stolen American designs that primarily speeded it up. At most, the stolen American science is estimated to have sped up production of the Russian bomb by one year.

A lack of uranium, more than any other factor, slowed the development of the Russian bomb. The Russians assembled their first bomb within weeks of having enough purified uranium and plutonium to build one. Even Stalin was aware of how difficult it had been to acquire the uranium. When the scientists gave Stalin their final briefing before testing the bomb, he had only one question. He asked if it were not possible to divide the existing plutonium in half, creating two less powerful bombs, so that one could be tested and one could be held in reserve. The answer was no; after four years and unknown thousands of lives, Stalin had produced enough uranium for only one bomb.

General Groves had been right with Murray Hill. Keeping uranium out of the hands of the Russians was one thing that could slow them down. Groves had been wrong when he'd thought that the Russians could not find enough high-grade uranium inside the Soviet Union and from the mine in the ETR with which to build a bomb. How much Groves and his successors at the Atomic Energy Commission knew about the supply of uranium to the Russian project remains a mystery. U.S. records about American atomic intelligence inside of the Soviet Union remain sealed, and they may never be declassified.

Douglas Mackiernan may have known a great deal about Stalin's bomb. Perhaps he tried to blow up the uranium mine at Koktogai that summer or earlier. Perhaps he had White Russians at Semipalatinsk that night as the bomb was assembled. It's possible that his agents installed sonic detectors within a few miles of Semipalatinsk. The most mysterious possibility is that through these efforts Mackiernan alerted the United States to an impending test explosion six months earlier.

In August 1949—eleven days before the Soviet atomic test—the State Department was asked, by other agencies, what it would feel if the United States *could* know whether the Russians had tested an atomic bomb. State Department foreign policy officials were excited by the prospects. The simple fact that they, and others in Washington, were asking questions about the possibility of an impending Russian atomic test indicates that there may have been some intelligence alert about the impending test. History as now written states that Harry Truman had no advance alert to the Soviet explosion.

General Lewis Mundell—who was running things for General Yates at an AFOAT-1 base in Alaska in 1949—made an interesting comment in 1999: "General Yates knew from some intelligence source that he did not reveal to me that the U.S.S.R. was about to explode an atomic bomb and so he urged us to get the long-range detection system, or our part of it with the air filters in specially modified aircraft, done as soon as possible. And in fact we got that system up and working just in time to detect the first Russian bomb."

The intriguing possibilities that this statement and other evidence raise cannot be proven until the CIA declassifies the history of Mackiernan that it wrote in 1998. Despite American silence, the Russian records, which reveal the history of their first atomic explosion, have been declassified. They tell the story of Russia's first bomb, and David Holloway's fine book, *Stalin and the Bomb,* drawing on those sources, narrates the first test in great detail.

The assembled bomb was raised up into the steel tower. When dawn came to the steppe, the area around the tower with the bomb in it was strangely silent. After weeks of incessant human activity, no one was there. Everyone within a fifteen-kilometer circle around the tower had been evacuated.

In the early morning, it was already intensely hot on the sandy steppe. The wind blew. Even birds were rare, with only the occasional hawk high above, or a small flock of black starlings. Silence reigned.

The assembled scientists, Communist Party members, secret police, and Red Army troops were all focused on the toy tower in the far distance.

When all was clear, Igor Kurchatov ordered the detonation sequence to begin. Once it was set in action, it ran automatically. Radios crackled with the seconds until explosion. Three. Two. One.

Unbearable light on the tip of the tower. A fireball rising from it. A blast wave sweeping out from the center of light. The bomb assembly buildings, machinery, houses, walls of brick and steel—all of this was instantly swept up in a blast wave, billowing out from the atomic explosion. All of that steel and brick and cement instantly reduced to a wall of smoke. The fireball at the center rising, growing, revolving, turning red and orange. A fine purple radioactive haze flickered for brief seconds around the fireball as it rose.

All of this had been seen before at the first atomic explosion in New Mexico, and later at Hiroshima. The Russians added a new touch to the modern myth. They had prepared a special lead-covered tank. Just ten minutes after the explosion, the tank rumbled out to ground zero with scientists inside; no one had ever seen ground zero that soon after an explosion and lived to tell the tale. The metal tower had vaporized. The yellow sandy soil had coagulated, turned to glass, and crackled eerily beneath the tracks of the tank as it lurched through the blast zone. The tank tracks threw up molten lumps of sand, still glowing with heat and their invisible load of alpha, beta, and gamma rays. An oil tank burned, and thick black smoke drifted across the scene of devastation. The test had been a great success.

Within hours, Kurchatov was back at his hotel handwriting a report for Stalin that was then dispatched by airplane to Moscow. Within six weeks, Beria had prepared the list of state honors for the scientists who gave Stalin the bomb. In deciding who would get what level of state recognition, Beria is said to have used a simple principle.

"Those who were to be shot in case of failure were now to become Heroes of Socialist Labor; those who would have received maximum prison terms were to be given the Order of Lenin, and so on down the list."

Douglas Mackiernan is the only known agent who worked on atomic intelligence concerning the Russian acquisition of uranium. His messages to the State Department in August 1949 remain almost all classified or have simply vanished. The State Department, mysteriously, cannot locate any trace of more than one hundred messages between Mackiernan and the State Department, which its own records prove once existed. These messages cover the period leading up to the Russian atomic test. Though the messages have vanished, entries in a file card system, which refer to the vanished documents, have survived. Only one document itself escaped this curious disappearance in an odd corner of the National Archives. It directly links Mackiernan to Hegenberger's atomic explosion detection project.

TOP SECRET

DATE: August 10, 1949
FROM: Tihwa
TO: Secretary of State
FOR BUTTERWORTH EYES ALONE FROM MACKIERNAN

Advise Hegenberger Tihwa Consulate being closed. I am staying behind wind up disposal property (for about three months) and will continue operate TR during that time. Advise disposition equipment on my departure.

On the afternoon of August 29, Douglas Mackiernan checked the sonic detectors—called the TR device. He also may have received data from other monitor equipment nearer to Semi. Either way, once he had the data he converted it to numbers, encoded them, and then sent the encrypted message to his brothers back in Massachusetts. Once this data arrived in Washington—for reasons still not declassified—it was not analyzed for at least one month. The first alert to Stalin's explosion did not come from Mackiernan in Tihwa. It came instead from an Air Force Air Weather station in Alaska.

By August 1949 Hegenberger's long-range detection project was operating, but just barely. Because of the unexplained speed-up, the

U.S. Air Force's squadron of WB-29s based in Alaska had at least one Air Weather plane making a daily flight between Alaska and Japan along the Russian Pacific border. Each of these planes carried air filters that collected any radioactive fallout in the prevailing westerly winds from the interior of Russia.

On September 3, 1949, a plane flown by Air Weather Service First Lieutenant Robert C. Johnson picked up the first fallout from the bomb Americans would soon be calling Joe-1. Sergeant Eugene Tews at the Alaska base examined the filter when it arrived and detected the radioactive dust particles in it. None of these men in Alaska knew what their filters were for or what startling news they had discovered.

The raw intelligence was passed routinely up the chain—through Andrews Air Force Base, which is where Stuart Mackiernan was also sending his data, to Hegenberger's data analysis center in Washington, D.C. Once the significance of the data was understood, additional data collection flights over the Pacific were ordered. By September 6 several labs were confirming the presence of high levels of barium, cerium, and molybdenum, all by-products of an atomic explosion.

Carried by the jet stream, the radioactive debris cloud continued its course over the Pacific Ocean. It was tracked across the forty-eight states. Finally, even British planes alerted by the United States were able to pick up traces of Joe-1 over the British Isles. Once the filter data had been collated and examined, the scientists were certain that an atomic bomb had been exploded sometime between August 24 and 29. The filter detection system also revealed that the plutonium core of the atomic bomb had been surrounded by a uranium "tamper"— just as had America's first bomb—and that it had probably exploded atop a tower. It would be six more months before the United States completed its analysis of the data and understood that the design was an exact copy of the stolen American plans.

Using only filter data, the scientists determined that the explosion had taken place somewhere north of the Caspian Sea—a point fifteen hundred miles farther west than the actual test site at Semipalatinsk. It was only a month later after all the sonic data—including Mackiernan's—was examined that Hegenberger's team of scientists could determine the exact location and the exact size of the explosion.

The airborne filters provided the first alert of the explosion, while Mackiernan's data revealed the exact size, time, and location of Joe-1.

On September 21, 1949, President Truman was told that in the opinion of his top scientific advisers the filter data proved beyond any doubt that Stalin had tested an atomic bomb. On September 23, the president's press secretary distributed a presidential announcement: halfway through the announcement newsmen rushed the doors to get the news out to the world. By 11:05, the news was on the wires: ". . . Within recent weeks an atomic explosion occurred within the U.S.S.R."

Every query about the president's source of intelligence for this startling announcement was met with stony-faced silence. The public assumed that the intelligence came from radioactive fallout, detected from a great distance. They also assumed that the United States had been able to track such fallout since 1945. No one in government disabused the public, or the Russians, of this partially correct assumption. In fact, the technology that allowed the United States to detect the Russian explosion had been installed just in time.

Hegenberger was awarded the Oak Leaf Cluster to the Legion of Merit for heading AFOAT-1, but his work remained top secret until the 1980s. Mackiernan's role as a CIA agent was never mentioned, outside Chinese and Russian circles, in any printed source until 1996. To this day, the CIA officially refuses to "confirm or deny the existence or nonexistence" of Douglas Mackiernan. Their denials can no longer obscure the facts.

Douglas Mackiernan worked to identify one of the uranium sources for Stalin's first atomic bomb. He may have covertly worked to close that mine, but certainly he provided the information about the quality and quantity of uranium coming out of it. He utilized Osman Bator and White Russian agents to do so. Mackiernan provided intelligence used to determine the precise location and strength of Stalin's first atomic bomb test. He designed, and his brothers operated, America's first long-range radio system to pick up vital coded data from the global net of scientific monitors used to detect the explosion. He installed and operated one of the monitor stations himself, and he may have managed a team of White Russians who installed such monitors deep inside the Soviet Union. He also may have alerted the United States to the impending Soviet test months before it occurred, though this remains speculation. Some believe that it is because of Mackiernan atomic successes that all of his work remains classified top secret. These matters, according to one CIA employee, are still "considered national security secrets."

Mackiernan's CIA cover as a vice consul has been zealously guarded for fifty years. Charles Ziegler, an expert on the creation of America's atomic explosion detection system, had never heard of Douglas Mackiernan when he was asked about him in 1999. Even so, Ziegler's comments about the detection system reveal the essence of Mackiernan's work.

"In the period 1945–49 . . . the U.S. established a state-of-the-art technological monitoring system, global in scope, whose sole purpose was to assess the status of the U.S.S.R.'s atomic program by detecting and analyzing the first (and subsequent) Soviet atomic bomb tests.

"The U.S. system for monitoring the first Soviet atomic bomb test relied primarily on radiological methods of detection that were incapable of pinpointing the time and location of the explosion. However, this vital information was provided by sonic detectors which, because their development was then in its infancy, were limited in range and thus had to be placed on the very borders of the U.S.S.R. . . . That this difficult and hazardous placement was accomplished is a tribute to the skill and courage of those responsible."

Everything about Mackiernan's work has been kept so secret that only now, fifty years later, are we able to obtain even a first glimpse of America's first atomic intelligence agent. This secrecy has created confusion and disagreement, even within the CIA, regarding why everything about Mackiernan remains classified. Some CIA employees say that if it were only his atomic work at stake, there would no longer be any real national security reason to keep everything classified. When pressed some say that the answer to the continued secrecy about Mackiernan lies in Tibet.

Curiously, Douglas Mackiernan, this uniquely effective atomic intelligence agent, is also the man that the United States government chose to lead its only covert mission into Tibet.

PART TWO

THE JOURNEY TO TIBET

"Those who have long enjoyed such privileges as we enjoy forget in time that men have died to win them."

—PRESIDENT FRANKLIN D. ROOSEVELT

TIBET
SUMMER OF 1949

Tibet was a country of fiction, and everyone wrote a different story: reality was intentionally obscured.

China said Tibet was an ordinary Chinese province, the size of western Europe—25 percent of the surface area of China—a province where no one spoke Chinese, where no Chinese taxes were collected, where no Chinese lived, and where no Chinese soldiers were stationed. Through its embassies around the world, China expertly promoted its fictional view of Tibet in the Western press. No state was allowed to establish diplomatic relations with China unless it accepted the Chinese fiction that Tibet was part of China.

The Tibetans made it easy for the Chinese—they refused to establish diplomatic relations with anyone. The Tibetan nobility said that Tibet was a special land, protected by the Buddha, and said essentially that the entire notion of statehood, and diplomatic relations, meant nothing to them. Tibet did not need an army. Nor did Tibetans require roads, newspapers, factories, radios, airfields, or any wheeled or motorized vehicles. All were banned. Such worldly creations might have tempted the monks out of the vast monasteries, or offended the gods. Such were the fictions that allowed the Tibetan nobility to ignore the rest of the world—and preserve its rule over Tibet unchallenged from within.

When Britain invaded Tibet in 1904, it stumbled into this strange pair of opposing fictions and turned them both to its own advantage. The British invaded Tibet after hearing rumors that Russian troops were to be posted along the northern border of India, Britain's largest colony. Once installed in Tibet—and when no Russian troops were found there—Britain convinced the Chinese that it would defend their fictional claim over Tibet and convinced the Tibetans that it would defend their isolated independence. For half a century, Britain was the only major foreign power allowed to have an embassy in Lhasa—a trade representative's office to the Chinese. By playing Tibet and China off each other, and promoting the antimodernization faction within Tibet, Britain maintained Tibet as a demilitarized buffer state, thus defending India's northern border. In the British fiction, Great Britain was Tibet's true friend.

The hooded eyes of Gyalo Thondup, elder brother of the Dalai Lama, glitter with restrained rage, and cynical humor, as he tells how Britain aborted the emergence of a modern state in Tibet, and then summarizes Tibet's own responsibility in the affair.

"Tibetan government officials were ignorant of the world and of power politics. . . . People don't realize how badly the Tibetan government was behaving, no one was thinking about Tibet."

In one meeting with Tibet's foreign minister, during Thondup's youth, the minister was smoking opium. Lounging in his brocade robe, the minister laughed at the idea that China would invade. "Mr. Thondup, our high mountains, our vast deserts . . ." The minister paused, took another puff from his pipe, and waved his stoned hands in the air, as he struggled to sketch the vastness of Tibet's defenses for the silly boy before him, ". . . Mr. Thondup, these will protect us!"

Thondup's lips curl with laughter as he describes how Great Britain compounded this Tibetan malfeasance.

"What is truly amazing is how all of these powers used Tibet and Tibetan ignorance! The great powers helped to maintain our ignorance, and then they used it for their games of power politics."

In the summer of 1949, Tibet's usefulness to Britain ended— India had freed itself from centuries of British colonialism. As Britain departed, it insisted that the vague responsibilities it had toward Tibet—whatever those were—were now India's. India derided this notion and accepted the old fiction that Tibet was part of China.

At this time, the conflicting visions of Tibet were mutating. The British fiction about Tibet appeared now as plain betrayal. In a macabre twist, the People's Republic of China insisted it was nothing but the truth. Tibet was part of China, even Britain said so. Useful new definitions were being born. Mao Tse-tung occasionally spoke about the true rationale behind China's fiction.

We say China is a country vast in territory, rich in resources and large in population; as a matter of fact it is the Han (*Chinese*) nationality whose population is large and the minority nationalities whose territory is vast and whose resources are rich. . . . The population of the minority nationalities in our country is small, but the area they inhabit is large. The Han people comprise 94 percent of the population, an overwhelming majority. . . . And who has more land? The minority nationalities, who occupy 50 to 60 percent of the territory.

The underlying truth is that Tibet as a nation was betrayed: by its rulers, false allies, and a ruthless neighbor intent upon colonizing a technically backward nation, which was unable to defend itself—a nation that possessed the resources its larger neighbor sought.

America, when it first appeared on the Tibetan horizon, accepted Chinese and British explanations of the Alice-in-Wonderland nature of Tibetan politics. There was no American self-interest that prompted it to do otherwise, not as long as China was its major Asian ally during World War II. Only when postwar China began to fall to the Communists was that blind acceptance questioned—only when Mao repeated what Chiang had always said about Tibet. In July 1949 the American ambassador to India, Loy Henderson, summarized the policy transition.

> Recognition of Chinese suzerainty over Tibet had been principally to strengthen the Government of China because of our friendly attitude toward the Chiang Kai-shek regime. With the Communist victories in China, however, our attitude toward Tibet is unrealistic and not to our interests.

As American interests in Inner Asia began to change, in 1949 and 1950, the State Department undertook a Tibet policy review, which listed the pros and cons of recognizing Tibetan independence. The strongest argument for recognition of Tibet was American self-interest.

> If Tibet possesses the stamina to withstand Communist infiltration . . . it would be to our interest to treat Tibet as independent rather than to continue to regard it as a part of a China which has gone Communist.

As this debate in Washington continued, officials realized that everything the United States knew about Tibet was based on third parties. Britain could not be trusted as an objective reporter, yet the United States had no other source of information. By 1949 officials in the State Department were insisting that the United States must send a covert mission to Tibet. The purpose of the mission was simple, at first:

> To secure first-hand information and as an indication of our friendly interest, it would be desirable to send a suitable official . . . to Tibet if this can be done inconspicuously and without giving rise to speculation that we may have designs upon Tibet.

The State Department discussed the issue for months. Any U.S. mission had to be a covert one, unless the United States wanted to speed up the Chinese invasion of Tibet. By the summer of 1949 America's Tibetan policy had one rule: Do absolutely nothing to hasten the apparently inevitable Chinese Communist invasion.

Planning for the covert mission to Tibet was slowly infected by developments in Inner Asia and China. In the summer of 1949, just north of Tibet, the United States became involved in a secret war aimed at preventing a Communist takeover of Inner Asia. The people of Inner Asia were making a last stand against the Chinese, as they broke out from behind the Great Wall. America sought ways to turn this anticolonial war into an anti-Communist crusade. Both America's covert mission to Tibet and its Tibetan policy became slowly enmeshed in these larger affairs. In the summer of 1949, Frank Bessac and Douglas Mackiernan were also caught up in the Inner Asian war, in different ways, before they headed to Tibet.

DINGYUANYING, INNER MONGOLIA
MONGOLIAN PEOPLE'S DELEGATE CONFERENCE
AUGUST 1949

It was a school auditorium filled with the elders of Inner Mongolia. A cement box filled with exotically dressed old men. Owl feathers floated atop silk hats. Fermented mare's milk was the drink of choice. Prince De—Frank Bessac's Mongol friend from his Peking days—had called the Banner chiefs to this city on the edge of the Ordos Gobi Desert, north of the Great Wall. They were making a last stand. They had traveled by airplane, truck, horseback, and camel caravan from all along the treeless steppe lands of China's northern border with Mongolia. The elders listened to Prince De carefully, but then each man rose to present the views of his Banner. Electric fans whirled above. Fine yellow dust from the Gobi Desert blew in through the open windows and coated every surface. The conference went on week after week. Each day the Chinese Communist armies marched one day closer to Dingyuanying (modern Bayanhot).

Perhaps now that Chiang Kai-shek had lost the Chinese civil war the Mongols of Inner Mongolia would declare independence and create their own state—or try to join the Mongolian People's Republic. Maybe they would send a representative to the Chinese Communists to ask for an autonomous status within the emerging Chinese Communist state. Nearly every option was openly debated. Even Frank Bessac was asked to speak.

He was dressed in a Mongol robe and spoke in Mongolian. He told the Inner Mongolians that in his opinion they had to seek independence. He felt somewhat like the French revolutionary Marquis de Lafayette rising to speak for American independence during the American Revolution. The British would have gladly executed

Lafayette in the 1770s if they could have caught him. The Chinese—Communist or Nationalist—might well have done the same to Bessac if they had caught him.

What had brought a student, recently retired from the CIA, from Peking in 1947 to Dingyuanying by the summer of 1949? Most of all, it was Bessac's heart. The more he studied the Mongols the more passionately he believed that these people were not Chinese and had as much right to their own country as the Chinese had to theirs.

After Bessac quit the CIA in the fall of 1947, he continued his language studies and applied for a Fulbright scholarship. In the summer of 1948 he took a summer job with a relief operation run by UNRRA (United Nations Relief and Rehabilitation Administration). He went to Inner Mongolia where he distributed grain to starving Mongolians that summer. By fall of 1948 his Fulbright came through. He had no sooner accepted that grant and begun further Mongol studies than the Chinese civil war threatened Peking. Forced out of the capital he went south to Shanghai, where he discussed a possible job with UNRRA. He did a small job for them while they considered hiring him. He even considered giving up his Fulbright for the position as UNRRA chief at Dingyuanying. Bessac says that because of his glaucoma, diagnosed two years earlier, UNRRA decided not to hire him.

In Shanghai Bessac asked an old friend in the CIA to help him exchange his Fulbright scholarship money for gold bars. Then he flew inland away from the advancing Communist armies to Chengdu in southwest China. He underwent an operation for his glaucoma at a missionary hospital in Chengdu, alone in a town where he knew no one, as civil war spread through China. Peking fell in January 1949, Nanking in March. Nevertheless Bessac sat playing chess by touch, his eyes bandaged, without knowing if the operation had given him several more years of sight or blinded him. Only when the bandages were removed did he know that he could still see, a saga that did not go unnoticed by the American community in China, despite the civil war. One American in China in 1948 revealed what a small community it was when she asked, fifty years later, even though she had never met Bessac in China, "What happened to Bessac? Did he go blind?"

By the time his bandages came off in the spring of 1949, the entire American community in China was headed east toward the Chinese coast and a steamship home. Bessac went in the other direction. Bessac took his tiny hoard of gold bars and boarded a China Civil Air Transport (CAT) plane to Lanchow, the last Chinese city before the deserts of Inner Asia. From there he drove to Dingyuanying, a walled oasis city. He arrived at the crumbling old caravan town on the edge of the Ordos Gobi Desert at about the same time that the delegates for the Inner Mongolian conference did, in July 1949.

Bessac says he was totally unaware of the intelligence plots that were swirling around Prince De that summer. He insists today that he went to Dingyuanying to continue his study of Mongolian on his Fulbright scholarship and that he had no connection to the CIA at that time.

But Sechin Jagchid does not agree. He insists that Frank Bessac *was* a U.S. intelligence agent that summer. Jagchid grew up in a family that had always been a traditional supporter of Prince De. He was one of Prince De's closest associates until 1949, when he fled China for the United States. He tells an interesting story about U.S. intelligence, Prince De, and Frank Bessac in his remarkable book, *The Last Mongol Prince*.

Jagchid was present in May 1949 at a meeting Prince De had in Canton with a U.S. intelligence agent he calls Raymond Meitz. Meitz had already trained several young Mongols as radio operators. He planned that these Mongols would go underground after the Communists took over Inner Mongolia and would provide radio contact between Prince De and the Americans, as well as intelligence from occupied Inner Mongolia. Furthermore, Meitz told Prince De that he was negotiating with UNRRA, Bessac's recent employer, so that when UNRRA shut down, its entire remaining stock of food, communication equipment, and trucks would be handed over to Prince De. But Jagchid is not the only witness who says that the United States wanted to aid Prince De in the summer of 1949. Commander of the U.S. Seventh Fleet, Admiral O. C. Badger, urged the same thing.

U.S. military strategists, and U.S. intelligence agents, had begun to wonder if the non-Chinese people of Inner Asia, like the Inner Mongolians, the Tibetans, and the Kazak, could be used as anti-

Communist guerrillas. Admiral Badger wrote directly to the Joint Chiefs of Staff about his concerns. He wanted the United States to stop the spread of Communism and was certain that if all of China fell then Communism would spread to Southeast Asia and India. After Chiang collapsed, he saw only a few fighters worth supporting.

> In all probability the fight against Communism in Western China will continue actively under such regional leaders as . . . Ma Pu Fang, and the Mongol Prince De . . . however these leaders need a fair share of arms and funds. These potentialities . . . are too promising to be discarded.

Badger wrote the Joint Chiefs about Prince De because he knew that in the summer of 1949 a Military Assistance Program (MAP) was working its way through Congress. Soon there would be money to stop the Communists in China, money not for Chiang but for the Inner Asians. MAP was designed to reverse a Communist victory in China or, if that failed, contain the Communists within China. Badger wanted to see the MAP funds given to non-Chinese, non-Communist guerrillas in Inner Asia because like many military leaders he had given up on the Nationalists. In August 1949 the military supported President Truman when he cut off all aid to the Nationalists. At that same moment, the State Department released its China White Paper, which attempted to show the U.S. public that it was Chinese corruption, not lack of U.S. aid, that caused the collapse of the Nationalist armies. Instead, the White Paper reignited the "Who Lost China?" debate. The State Department had hard intelligence that Republican senators and lobbyists were working closely with the Nationalist Chinese, as they venomously slandered the U.S. government during that debate. Even so, the political climate had become so charged that few Americans would ever see this foreign hand in U.S. affairs. To the average American everything was already clear. The reason for this certitude was the success that Nevada's Senator Pat McCarran, and others like him, had in selling Chiang's propaganda. "Our own State Department peddles the Communistic propaganda line . . . it is time something was done about it."

As the red scare flared anew, the Military Assistance Program of 1949 began its final journey through the House and Senate. In that climate, following immediately the announcement of Russia's atomic bomb and China's fall, no representative could be seen opposing a fund that would fight Communism in the "general area of China."

After the bill passed, the Joint Chiefs of Staff recommended that the United States use some of the MAP money to covertly aid the Inner Asians and assigned the CIA that job. The funding for such covert actions was in a part of the MAP legislation called Section 303. MAP-303 allowed the CIA to start arming "anti-Communist" people—the Kazak, the Inner Mongols, and the Tibetans. The Cold War game of dominoes and proxy wars with the Russians and the Chinese was being born in Inner Asia—a game that would soon shift to Vietnam.

In 1949 the Mongols, the Kazak, and the Tibetans did not see themselves as U.S. tools. They wanted weapons to fight off all Chinese, Communist or Nationalist. Today, Inner Mongolians say that perhaps a million Mongols have been killed by the Chinese since 1949, and millions of Chinese have settled on Mongol lands.

Prince De and the men around him saw this coming. In the summer of 1949 in Dingyuanying, the Knights of Genghis Khan debated how to stop this invasion. Sechin Jagchid felt it was impossible. He convinced Prince De not only to leave Inner Mongolia once the Communists took over but also to flee to Tibet. Prince De felt it was politically important for the Mongols to declare independence while in Inner Mongolia. The prince planned to use the trucks and other equipment CIA agent Meitz had promised that UNRRA would deliver to transport his strongest supporters away from the advancing Communists. Once up in the mountains, they would walk into Tibet. Prince De expected to set up a government in exile in Lhasa, and then to lead the fight for Inner Mongolian freedom from there.

According to Jagchid, this is where Frank Bessac again enters the story. Some of Prince De's supporters at the conference were growing afraid. Others, actually secret Communist supporters, tried to sway the convention toward China. Prince De needed to keep his support lined up. When one of the prince's supporters began to show doubt about declaring independence, Jagchid secretly told the man about the UNRRA trucks, and the plan to escape to Tibet. The promise of U.S. support—based on an assurance by Meitz—boosted Prince De's influence at the conference.

Jagchid says that Frank Bessac was the representative of UNRRA and an American intelligence officer with Raymond Meitz's group when he arrived at Dingyuanying in July 1949. Jagchid notes that Bessac told the Mongols he would try to get the UNRRA materials delivered to Dingyuanying and that he was authorized to receive the materials, as well as to transfer them to the Mongols. Bessac denies all of this. He says that he was turned down for the UNRRA job and had quit American intelligence in 1947. He denies any U.S. government connection that summer, except as a Fulbright scholar. Nevertheless, Jagchid reports that it was Frank Bessac who brought the bad news to Dingyuanying—the UNRRA material was handed over to the local Nationalist leaders in Lanchow, who would soon hand it over intact to the invading Communist armies.

The loss of the UNRRA material was a fatal blow to Prince De. When the aid did not show up, Prince De began to lose support at the conference. Without U.S. support, Prince De decided to flee to the MPR when the Chinese Communists took over Dingyuanying. He dropped his plans to flee to Tibet. Jagchid himself flew to the United States—flights were still running in and out of Dingyuanying even days before the Communists arrived there. Bessac could have left as well. In fact, Bessac says that he sent a report about the conference to the U.S. consulate in Shanghai on the same plane that took Jagchid out—but insists this was a friendly gesture, not the act of a paid agent. Instead of flying out himself, Bessac again elected to go deeper into the interior of Inner Asia. A Mongol Banner chief helped him rent a string of camels, and he set off across a stretch of the Ordos Gobi Desert toward Sinkiang.

Bessac says that he left Dingyuanying, ahead of the Communists, because he did not want to be involved in any fighting that might erupt. As the town changed hands, he wanted to find a band of nomadic Mongols in Sinkiang and continue his Fulbright-financed study of Mongolian language and culture.

Frederick Latrash, a retired CIA agent, chuckles and vehemently shakes his head when he hears this. He says that the CIA told him in

1950 that Frank Bessac was a contract CIA agent using Fulbright cover. He claims that this is the very reason why Bessac is so insistent that he was not a CIA agent—it was, and is, illegal for the CIA to use a Fulbright scholarship as cover for any agent.

Frank Bessac grows agitated when these conflicting viewpoints are presented to him. "I was not a spy, damn it!"

Bessac has a different explanation of his motivations that summer. He quit the CIA in 1947 and was using his Fulbright to study the Mongols because he identified with them, not because the CIA sent him there under Fulbright cover. He urged the leaders of Inner Mongolia to seek independence for the same reason he went to China in 1945—to help a colonized people throw off their oppressors. He did not go there as part of any U.S. plot to covertly arm Prince De. At the same time he says it is possible for Jagchid to have misunderstood these facts, just as he is certain the Chinese Communists may well have seen him as a spy. When he hears that Chinese claim, Bessac's eyes flash with rage.

To Chinese eyes, anyone who wanted to help the Inner Mongolians was a spy. Anyone who wanted to help the Inner Mongolians keep their country was seen as an enemy. It has been that way since the Great Wall was first built. Bessac says that he encouraged Prince De that summer because he opposed colonialism. It was his heart, not any government order, that motivated him. He understands that this may be hard for a younger generation raised on Vietnam to believe but insists that it is the truth.

HAMI TO TIHWA, SINKIANG
SEPTEMBER 9, 1949

The eternal wind of Inner Asia threw up a cloud of dust around the adobe shack that served as the air terminal at Hami. An old tin sign rattled in the gale. The peeling signage on the dilapidated Russian plane proudly announced in Russian and Chinese that it was a passenger aircraft of the Sino-Soviet Friendship Airline. The twin-engine propeller plane taxied to a stop, but the propellers kept on turning.

The door in the rear of the plane banged open from inside. The copilot peered out from the darkness of the plane into the dust and sunlight and then beckoned to Frank Bessac. On board, Bessac discovered why it had been so easy to book a seat: he was the only passenger. Russia had an agreement with Chiang Kai-shek to keep this airline running, from Russia through the ETR to China. It was the same spooky airline that Pegge Lyons had flown on from Tihwa to the ETR when she made her trip for Mackiernan in 1947.

Bessac sat down across from the open door at the rear, which was slammed shut by ground staff as he buckled in. The plane taxied out from the terminal and took off for Tihwa. They had been airborne only a few minutes when the door beside him blew open with a loud clang. He glanced out to the earth far below.

Bessac got out of his seat and went forward to the cockpit. He shouted to the Russian pilots about the door, but when they found it a matter of no concern he returned to his seat. He carefully buckled himself and settled in to enjoy an excellent view of the Turfan Depression. They flew over sand dunes, salt pans, and then a plain of black gravel.

Leaving the desert, the plane circled north around the glacier-carved summit of twenty-four-thousand-foot Bogdo Shan. The white peak was wreathed in clouds. From that frozen summit, the southern face of the mountain swept down and out into the wastes of the Turfan, where temperatures soared above 130°F in summer.

Looking at the peak reminded Bessac of flying over the Himalayas during World War II when he had first flown into China from India, a raw OSS-SI agent. Same open door. Same white peaks. He had flown into China then around the southeastern edges of Tibet, and now here he was, after five years in China, flying past the Tien Shan far north of Tibet. Between India and China there had been deep gorges cloaked in tropical forests. Here they flew over empty steppe, and then along the Tien Shan. At least this time there weren't Japanese fighters shooting at the plane.

When Tihwa appeared, it amazed him to see signs of civilization in such a remote wilderness. They circled low over the walled city as they approached the airfield. Children dashed up onto roofs from the courtyards below to wave at the plane as it flew over.

Frank Bessac knew no one in Tihwa, had never been there, and had not told anyone he was going there besides his Mongol friends in Dingyuanying when he set out after the conference.

The air terminal at Tihwa was another adobe shack. Beside the shack stood a 1948 Willys Jeep, with an American flag whipping in the dusty afternoon wind. As Bessac clambered down from the plane, a neatly uniformed Chinese chauffeur trotted out from the car toward him.

The chauffeur walked up to him and spoke in Chinese, shouting over the turning propellers. "Mr. Frank Bessac?"

Frank grabbed at his Mongol hat, which threatened to blow off in the wind and peered at the driver in surprise.

"Yes, I am Frank Bessac."

"Vice Consul Mackiernan has asked me to bring you to the American consulate. Please come this way. Do you have any bags?"

"But I don't know a Mr. Mackiernan."

"Never mind sir, you are expected."

The driver bundled Bessac's bags into the back and then held the door for Bessac to get in. It took a second for him to realize the door was being held open for him.

The driver tooted his horn loudly as the Jeep inched its way into the afternoon traffic. Camels, donkeys, sheep, goats, and cows had returned after a full day grazing outside the city and were now causing a traffic jam at the city gate. The Nationalist solider smoking a cigarette in his niche within the adobe gate did nothing to change the situation. Finally, they passed through the narrow tunnel that pierced the city walls and drove through the cramped dusty lanes of the walled city. Uighur men in their long robes clambered up out of the lane and into shops to allow the consulate car to pass. The driver ground the Jeep back into first and drove deeper into the maze within the walls.

The car drove past the Chinese Nationalist garrison. Peering through the gate in the walls that surrounded it, Bessac could see three hundred men lazily sitting around in tatty uniforms. The nearly shredded red, white, and blue flag of the Chinese Republic fluttered from a lone flagpole in the center of the parade ground.

Fifteen minutes after he stepped off the plane, Bessac was driven through the gate of the American consulate compound in Tihwa. An American flag billowed atop a pole in front of the solid bungalow with large deep-set windows that sat on one side of the inner courtyard.

A tall dark-haired athletic man strode quickly down the steps to greet him as the driver hopped out and held the door open for Bessac.

"Hi. I'm Doug Mackiernan and you must be Frank Bessac. Welcome to Tihwa. I'm really glad you turned up."

"It's very nice of you to welcome me like this, but I am so surprised, no one knew I was coming . . ."

"Ah, don't worry about that. We have our ways around here. Come on into the living quarters of the consulate back here and let's have some lunch. You must be starved."

Mackiernan led Bessac through the courtyard past a truck parked in one corner loaded with wooden crates.

Lunch was served on American china with knives, forks, soup spoons, teaspoons, and napkins, all properly laid out, on a table set for two. Leonid Shutov, a blond-headed Russian kid, age twenty, tall and skinny, entered with a towel draped over one forearm and proceeded to serve soup. Bessac glanced around slightly wide-eyed as Mackiernan and he sipped their soup. When it was finished, Mackiernan shouted something in Russian, and Leonid came back out to remove the soup bowls.

"This is Frank Bessac," Mackiernan said slowly in English. "Say hello to Leonid, Frank."

With introductions over, Leonid scurried out with the soup bowls. Bessac turned back to Mackiernan.

"You have to excuse my amazement. I just spent nineteen days on camels crossing the Gobi Desert, and I haven't sat down to eat properly in a long time." Bessac gestured to the Foreign Service accommodations that attempted to simulate in Tihwa, as much as was possible, a normal American world.

Leonid returned with the next course, which turned out to be a very tough chicken, but it was the first chicken Bessac had eaten in months.

Over tobacco and coffee after lunch, Mackiernan got down to business.

"You saw that truck out there?"

Bessac nodded, as Mackiernan continued to explain.

Well, it's filled with documents that the Department of State would like driven down to the Pakistani border around the west end of the Taklamakan Desert. And then, well . . . and then you'd need to find porters and see if you couldn't get the boxes walked through the Himalayas to Pakistan. We would pay all your expenses, of course. You might not have heard yet, but actually, the consulate was officially closed on August 15, and I have stayed on to wrap up outstanding business. The consul and most of the staff left last month. I got a message from them a few days back, and they are still heading south to the Himalayas and are still planning to walk through to Ladakh. Seemed like a more interesting way home than flying back into Red China. What do you say? Sound like a good trip to you?

"That sounds fine. I'm always ready to help out Uncle Sam."

Is that so. I'm glad to hear that. Well anyway, that would be a big help if you could do that. However, it will be a few more days until that truck is ready to go. So meanwhile, Stephan here will show you to the guest room. The Nationalists are still in control here, and it's plenty safe to walk the streets, so you might enjoy seeing Tihwa. I have to get back to the office to finish some reports and such. See you for dinner. Say about six?

"That sounds fine, Mr. Mackiernan. I'm just amazed."

"I bet you are. You can call me Mac."

TIHWA-URUMCHI, THE PEOPLE'S REPUBLIC OF CHINA
SEPTEMBER 26, 1949

Frank Bessac spent his days walking the streets of Tihwa when he wasn't helping Mackiernan.

That morning he walked along the lane past the mosque and listened to the prayer leader call the faithful to prayer. He stood beneath the squat adobe minaret in the early morning and listened to a language he could not understand as the prayer leader chanted. The Muslim faithful of Tihwa, men in their ikat dyed silk robes, were already gathering in the courtyard of the mosque.

He bought peaches and grapes in the market. He wandered the Inner Asian oasis town until he found the post office. Then he sat down under a poplar beside the chuckling irrigation channel that ran throughout Tihwa and wrote a quick note to his folks. (They received the letter—for Christmas—and it was their last word from him till June 1950.)

Walking back to the consulate past the Chinese garrison, he peeked through the gates again. Fluttering on the flagpole was a shocking scarlet banner with four yellow stars. Chiang Kai-shek's red, white, and blue flag had vanished overnight.

Nearing the consulate, a crowd of urchins surrounded him and began to chant in their poor Chinese a phrase that they had just learned.

"Long Live Mao Tse-tung! Long Live Mao Tse-tung!"

They laughed and chanted and pointed their thumbs at him and then at the earth.

The guard at the gate of the consulate, who had been asleep when he went out for his morning walk, stared down the lane as he opened the gate to let Bessac inside and then quickly shut it behind him. Bessac wandered through the half-empty offices of the consulate until he found Mackiernan and a Russian, who looked to be about thirty years old, in front of the fireplace in the public room.

"There you are, Bessac. Have you met Stephan?"

Stephan Yanuishkin, a solidly built Russian, looked up at Bessac from the fireplace where he was burning papers. Mackiernan rushed on in his clipped, terse way.

"The garrison turned belly-up last night, without a shot—the Chinese troops here have gone over to the Communists. So they say. Can you help me get all those documents out of the office in there and burn them?"

It took hours. They traipsed back and forth from the offices to the fireplace, and even had to uncrate things from the truck that Mackiernan had originally asked Bessac to drive, and burned everything. The two Americans stopped frequently to smoke, and then turned back to uncrate more papers. The onion skin burned easily, but there was so much of it that Mackiernan and Bessac carried on burning papers even after Stephan, and his assistant, Leonid, left to make lunch.

Finally, the two Americans sat down in Mackiernan's office for a final smoke before lunch—Bessac lit a cigarette, while Mackiernan lit his pipe. Heaps of unclassified U.S. government publications stood around them. Mackiernan's half-open file drawers were empty. The adobe floor was covered with bits and pieces of torn paper, abandoned paper clips, Bessac's cigarette butts, and piles of gray ash where Mackiernan had tapped out his pipe.

The blue smoke rose to the wooden rafters high above them. Yellow sunlight poured into the room from the south-facing windows. Mackiernan sat behind his desk while Bessac stood near the open windows staring out into the courtyard. When Bessac turned his eyes back toward Mackiernan, he found Mackiernan scrutinizing him. Without any prelude, Mackiernan said one word to Bessac.

"Oregon."

Bessac heard the word and suppressed his natural inclination to say, What did you say?

He knew that word. It was the recognition code given to him by the CIA in 1947. He thought for a second about his reply. Damn, that's why Mac knew his name. The Outfit must have sent Mac an encrypted radio message with his name and his recognition code. And of course he worked for the CIA, or he would never have had the code in the first place. Mac had to be a CIA officer using State cover.

Bessac knew he could say nothing or blow his reply to the recognition code. If he chose to reply correctly, though, he knew he would be under Mackiernan's command, or at the very least available if he was needed. A contract agent.

During the few moments that Bessac considered his reply, Mackiernan kept his eyes locked on Bessac's. Finally, Bessac sighed, flicked his butt on the floor of the office, and ground it out beneath his heel. He looked back up from the floor into the eyes of Mackiernan, which remained fixed on him, waiting.

"D. The letter *D*."

Mackiernan let out a breath and relaxed. Then he got up out of his chair and came around to shake Bessac's hands. As he drew near, he spoke again.

"Well, I am glad you replied, buddy. You had me worried for a minute."

Bessac's few leading questions over lunch were all parried by Mackiernan with monosyllables, just as they had been before Mackiernan coded him. The Outfit had warned Mackiernan that Bessac was coming to Tihwa, but how had they known? When had Mackiernan joined the Outfit? Mackiernan wouldn't even openly admit he worked for the Outfit, though his use of the code guaranteed that. Only CIA agents had access to the recognition codes. Being coded was a two-way street—it identified the *user* and the *replier* as members of the Outfit. Within minutes, Bessac remembered the way it worked. Need-to-know. What did he have a need to know?

"Where are you going now that the Reds have taken over?"

Mackiernan grunted and looked at Bessac for the first time since he had coded him. Mackiernan probably viewed Bessac as a contract agent so long out of the reins that he was having trouble slipping back into them. He rewarded Bessac's awareness of his need-to-know status with an answer.

"You can't get south with a truck anymore, so you can't drive out all that stuff in the truck. I hear the Chinese troops in all of Sinkiang have gone over to the Communists without a shot. So I thought I might go meet this Kazak chieftain named Osman Bator."

Mackiernan's eyes were concentrated now on his plate as he methodically continued speaking and chewing.

"Osman's not going to go over to the Communists. I bet he's gonna need some time to think about this—we expected he would have at least a few more months before this happened, but things have speeded up. I know he would like to be independent, he'd like his own country. He is a Kazak first, and they have been trying to get independence, or maintain it when they had had it for centuries. From both the Russians and the Chinese. I'm going to join Osman, at least for a while.

"Anyway, the Reds aren't here yet; it's just the Nationalists turning belly-up without a fight—as they have done everywhere—so

Osman has some time to think about it. These Nationalist troops won't bother him, and it might take months for the Reds to get their own men in here. I think we could just travel with Osman for a while as he thinks about this. He is going to need some time to figure out what he is going to do.

"I've had Vasili, a White Russian who works for me, pick out two men, and we have them here on standby. One is Stephan here, the other is Leonid. The three White Russians will go over the wall when it gets dark. You and I could drive out the front gate tomorrow morning with our passports. I don't think the guards are going to stop me in my command car. They have known me for four years."

With a small sigh, Mackiernan finished the longest speech he had made since Bessac met him. Then he looked up from the table and asked Bessac a question, "Want to go out and join the nomadic Kazak with me?"

Bessac replied instantly, without any thought.

"Sure, that sounds great. When are we leaving?"

"We'll finish packing today and leave tomorrow, early."

Loading Mackiernan's command car, Bessac noticed a government-issue field radio, machine guns, rifles, ammunition, and even a box of grenades. He did not see the hundreds of tiny gold bars, shaped like double sugar cubes, that Mackiernan had crated and put in the car earlier, nor the $10,000 that Mackiernan had strapped to his body. Nor did Bessac know that the Air Force, the CIA, the AEC—or all three—had ordered Mackiernan to stay behind in Sinkiang, as long as he could, to operate the atomic detection devices.

Vasili Zvansov found Mackiernan sometime on his last afternoon in Tihwa and received his orders to go over the wall after dark. Mackiernan told Vasili where to meet them outside the city the next day. Zvansov still remembers the conversation clearly.

"Doug had received orders to exit Sinkiang via Tibet while we were in Urumchi, before Mao took over Sinkiang. I am quite sure about this. When the Chinese turned over to the Communists, I told him, 'I have to go, this is very dangerous for me, the Communists will kill me.'

"And Doug said to me, 'Don't worry. We are going together through the Taklamakan Desert and through Tibet to India.'"

Zvansov's first impression of Bessac, upon his arrival in Tihwa, was: "He comes in from Inner Mongolia, I thought, well, he is probably working for the CIA too." Zvansov, a man running for his life from all Communists, could not imagine any other reason why a sane man would willingly walk into the trap that he was trying to escape.

LEAVING TIHWA
SEPTEMBER 27, 1949

The final packing took longer than they had planned. It was afternoon when Mackiernan, alone in the radio room of the consulate, sent the last coded message from Tihwa to Washington.

"Consulate Tihwa, officially closed."

With that final message sent, he then burned the last consulate code material that he wasn't taking with him. As Bessac climbed into the command car beside Mackiernan, he had no idea he was headed for Tibet. He had no need to know, and so wasn't told anything except that they were going out to join up with Osman Bator.

The guard at the gates of Tihwa glanced in the back of the car to be sure no one was there. Then he had a cursory look at Mackiernan's and Bessac's U.S. passports and waved them out of the city.

Mysteriously, one "Mr. Simmons," a British subject working for International Supply Corporation, was still in Tihwa when Mackiernan and Bessac left town. Bessac wrote in 1950 that Simmons had several vehicles in a large compound in Tihwa. What relation Mackiernan had to Simmons is unknown. ISC is not unknown—it was owned by Civil Air Transport, based in Lanchow, and CAT was in the process of being taken over by the CIA. CAT became famous later under its new name: Air America. In early 1949 ISC purchased, with U.S. funds, thousand of weapons and flew them to the Muslim warlord, General Ma Pu-fang in Lanchow. Since ISC also had an agent in Tihwa it would have been quite possible for them to have also supplied weapons to the Kazaks through Mackiernan. All of this remains speculation—except that the ISC agent was still in Tihwa when Mackiernan left and ISC was supplying arms through CAT to northwest China in the winter of 1949. If Mackiernan was deeply involved in arming the Kazaks the mysterious Mr. Simmons was somehow involved. That stage of Mackiernan's operations apparently ended when he left Tihwa.

Two miles outside the city, they unloaded the car and then waited for the arrival of Vasili, Stephan, and Leonid. Mackiernan told Bessac that they were also expecting a group of mounted White Russians from Osman's party to meet them there. Bessac climbed a tree and kept lookout.

Sitting in a lone poplar, Bessac watched the afternoon inch toward sunset. Bessac did not see any people. Instead, it was the vast steppes, deserts, and mountains of Inner Asia that greeted him. He looked out at the peaks of the Tien Shan to the east and west. To the south lay the vast emptiness of the Taklamakan Desert. Setting in the west over Kazakhstan and Russia, the sun cast its last red rays on Bogdo Shan east of Bessac and upon the steppe around him. The fading sun turned the glaciers and snow red, and then pink, as the treeless steppe gradually changed from gold to pale yellow.

His appreciation of the landscape was interrupted by loud bangs from below. Mackiernan had the hood of the car open and was hacking around inside with a hammer, destroying parts of the engine. Finally, Doug pulled out a machine gun and shot up the tires, doors, and gas tank. The vehicle did not explode; the gasoline seeped away into the sand.

The sound of machine-gun fire sharply brought home to Bessac exactly what they were doing. By joining Osman, they became enemies of the state. Sitting in the tree looking out over the steppes and mountains, Frank Bessac realized the seriousness of their actions. The Chinese would want them dead or alive.

At last, Vasili, Leonid, and Stephan trudged in after their long walk from Tihwa. Then Bessac spotted a party of mounted men galloping over the steppe skyline, trailing a dozen riderless horses behind them. Bessac shouted the news to Mackiernan, who pulled out his binoculars.

"Yep, that's the White Russians from near Osman's camp, with our horses. Come on down, I have something for you."

Bessac climbed down from his perch in the tree and leaped the last few feet to the ground as the horses arrived. Stefan and Leonid were already loading crates onto the cargo horses. Vasili chattered away in Russian to his compatriots.

Mackiernan reached into a crate and pulled something out.

"Here, take this, Bessac. You might need it."

It was a small, handheld machine gun. The gun rarely left Frank's hands until he finally handed it over to Tibet's Foreign Office in Lhasa.

As they set off on the horses, Vasili Zvansov recalls that Mackiernan was quite clear about where they were going.

"We go to Tibet, but we have to go first to visit the White Russians' camp near Osman, and then we go to the camp of Osman Bator at Lake Barkol."

When they stopped at the camp of the White Russians, Zvansov recalls that Mackiernan "gave the Russians some help, gold . . . I think if I am not mistaken, one bar they got, because Vasili Burigin he divided the gold, because he had an instrument to cut it . . . [the gold bar was] eight inches long, thicker than one inch."

These were not the small gold bars that Stuart Mackiernan saw his brother with the year before. Nor was it the gold that Duncan Mackiernan believed was secreted in a radio battery. Unless the gold had been melted, this was still more gold that Mackiernan was carrying.

Stuart Mackiernan thought his brother was taking the gold to China for the White Russians—to buy friendship or intelligence. Among these men at the White Russian camp was Ivan X, the sole survivor from the five men Mackiernan had sent to raid the uranium mine. What else this group of about two hundred White Russians had done to earn Mackiernan's gold—the CIA's gold—remains unknown. If the mysterious Mr. Simmons of the International Supply Corporation in Tihwa was working with Mackiernan to land weapons in Sinkiang, these Russians would have been among those who received them. While this is a reasonable assumption there is no evidence to prove it—the few survivors of this group refused to be interviewed. Zvansov describes this group of escapees from Soviet Russia as, simply, "anti-Communists, that was the point."

Mackiernan made a promise to the refugees in the White Russian camp when he gave them the gold. Zvansov says that Mackiernan was only restating a promise he had already made to them on other occasions.

"Mackiernan . . . promised that all these Russians, approximately one hundred and fifty or two hundred people, who fought against the Communists, that they all are going to be safe. . . ."

Zvansov hesitates to say it outright, but he feels that Mackiernan promised them that they would all eventually be taken to the United States as a reward for their work for the U.S. government. This promise included a guarantee of Zvansov's own safety and a U.S. visa.

After an overnight stop with the Russians, the Mackiernan party moved on to meet up with Osman Bator. Zvansov describes the Mackiernan party as they left.

"There were twenty-one horses only for us five people. . . . We got the radio put on the saddle, then the gold and some other things on the horses. Some weapons, we had a lot of weapons, we had American rifles. I had Belgian rifle, two machine guns, hand grenades, one box I think." In addition to the Geiger counters and the gold, of course.

Zvansov's estimate of the gold Mackiernan carried is more precise than that of anyone else, since he picked it up and loaded it on the horses every day of the journey to Tibet. "Maybe ten kilos of gold, at most."

LAKE BARKOL, NORTH OF HAMI, WITH THE KAZAK HORDE OF OSMAN BATOR
SINKIANG, THE PEOPLE'S REPUBLIC OF CHINA
OCTOBER 29, 1949

Douglas Mackiernan stood in front of the yurt within Osman's camp looking out at the falling snow. The temperature had dropped, and the first thick flakes were blanketing the plains around the lake. The snow muffled the whistles and yells of the nomads herding their flocks out of the corrals of stacked stones and up to the mountains that girdled the lake.

The smell of burning dung drifted out of the smoke hole of the yurt. Bessac brushed aside the felted yurt flap and walked out to stand beside him.

"So, the snow has come," Bessac said to Mackiernan.

Mackiernan replied with a tight smile. "You afraid of a little snow?"

"No, Mac, but I don't see what good we are doing these Kazak by staying here."

"Yeah, there isn't much I can do now. Osman is talking about going to the Mongolian People's Republic if he can't make it work here with the Communists. What they really want is independence, though. They keep asking for guns. That's all they really want from us, and we haven't figured out how to get them up here."

"What about some airdrops up here, give Osman what he is asking for?"

Mackiernan looked sidelong at Bessac and smiled. Mackiernan knew, if Bessac did not, that he did not have to be present for the airdrops. Several sources indicate that CAT and ISC were busy all over northwest China with weapon deliveries. What ever they were doing, Mackiernan was not talking about it. Bessac spoke into the silence.

"I know you want to help these people, Mac. But whatever is going to happen you can't do them any good staying here in the camp with them. The Communists have got to know we are here by now."

Bessac had been trying to convince Mackiernan to leave Barkol for days, but Mackiernan was lingering—for reasons that Mackiernan did not share with Bessac. They stood in silence for a while before Mackiernan spoke again.

"Red troops marched into Tihwa last week. It's not just Nationalists there now, and they are sure to know we are up here with Osman."

"So are we just going to stay and draw the Red troops up here?"

"No, Frank, we are going to leave. Tomorrow."

"Do I need to know where we are going?"

"Tibet."

In the yurt that night before heading south toward Tibet, Zvansov was with Osman and Mackiernan the last time they saw each other. He watched as Mackiernan handed over some of the gold.

Zvansov remembers little about the conversation except that "Most of the talking was about how to fight the Communists. Osman was very happy because he felt at least an American comes to help him." A CIA employee, writing an unpublished letter about Osman Bator said this much about Osman that winter:

> He provided vital intelligence, and if war had broken out, his forces could have been very useful. . . . These . . . matters are still considered national security secrets . . . and are still, in a very practical way, sensitive.

It's a safe assumption that the "vital intelligence" Osman provided was his help with one of Mackiernan's atomic intelligence projects. Though Mackiernan may have completed those projects, the CIA wanted to have armed groups like Osman's—and the White Russians—ready for U.S. intelligence missions if the Cold War ended and World War Three erupted. Failing that, Osman was also useful as a guerrilla who could harass the Chinese Communists after they took over. Six months earlier the United States had dreamt of much more.

Back in February, Mackiernan wrote a tantalizing letter to his wife Pegge, which indicates what Mackiernan planned with Osman, and perhaps others. Dated February 12, 1949, it was one of the few letters to make it back to Pegge in Fairfax. Though he speaks of Muslims—and Vasili Zvansov was brought to Mackiernan by a Muslim Chinese general—these same ideas probably applied to the Kazak, the Mongols, and the Tibetans.

> There is the rumor that the Moslems of Sinkiang, Kansu, Chinghai and Ninghsia are joining force to prevent the spread of Communism into the NW. . . . My personal opinion is that the Sovs will continue strong in Sinkiang, and that the Moslems will form a sort of anti-Communist island in Kansu, Chinghai, and Ninghsia.

During a brief period—from Stalin's first atomic test in August 1949 until the Korean War began in June 1950—the United States believed that the people of Inner Asia could be useful to the United States. America hoped the Kazak, the Mongols, and the Tibetans might make good anti-Communist warriors. Earlier, Owen Lattimore had tried to explain that these people were not Chinese, but no one listened. Now that they might be used, within a larger plan, America's attitude toward them—and their claims that they were not Chinese—was changing.

Mackiernan must have radioed Osman's requests for arms back to the United States. In June 1950 *The New York Times* would go so far as to say that Mackiernan "played a leading role in assembling the forces under Osman." If Mackiernan received instructions from the CIA to arm Osman—as the facts indicate—the CIA refuses even now to de-classify the documents that would allow modern historians to study the issue. Nevertheless, Mackiernan probably told Osman that if he assem-bled the Kazak people and they publicly declared their independence from China, Osman's request for arms would have a greater impact in Washington. Mackiernan probably assumed that surviving units of the Nationalist army in Sinkiang were heading into the mountains on the fringe of Tibet, and they too wanted arms. If these groups united, they might be able to block the Communist drive into Inner Asia. By October, the situation was not looking as good as it had in February when Mackiernan had talked optimistically about a Muslim-held anti-Communist island. Even so it is possible that Mackiernan still hoped that the Kazak and the Nationalist armies from Sinkiang might all retreat into Tibet, to help the Tibetans make a last stand, and that he, Mackiernan, would help arm the Tibetans, just as he helped the Kazak.

Mackiernan's ideas and the events in Inner Asia unfolded in lockstep with decisions by the Joint Chiefs of Staff back in Washing-ton—which was probably not a coincidence. Osman Bator wanted weapons. Prince De wanted weapons. MAP was the first presiden-tial, unvouchered, discretionary fund in the peacetime history of the United States, especially designed to pay for such weapons. In Octo-ber 1949 the JCS had a committee review what to do with the money. It reported back to the chiefs with precise ideas.

If we recall Prince De's and Osman Bator's request for arms, the most important detail in the JCS documents is the talk about funding "those special operations which will most effectively interfere with Communist control of China."

Who would run the special operations?

The JCS stated that the program of special operations in China "should be initiated by the Central Intelligence Agency."

The CIA was charged with giving "assistance to underground resistance, aid to guerrilla and refugee groups, and support of indigenous anti-Communist elements." The fact that many of these elements were more anti-Chinese that anti-Communist was ignored.

The JCS granted covert operations in China, Taiwan, and Tibet an initial budgeted line item of $30 million. The money was budgeted in October 1949, as Mackiernan sat at Lake Barkol listening to Osman ask for weapons, about the time Mackiernan handed gold bars to the White Russians and Osman Bator.

Mackiernan and Bessac were each affiliated with indigenous anti-Chinese—Osman and De—who both wanted assistance. Now the two Americans—one an employee of the CIA and one an alleged contract agent—were headed to Tibet. The Tibetans were already asking for U.S. military aid, as were the Inner Mongolians and the Kazak.

A new balance of power was emerging that winter, an atomic stalemate that prevented the United States and the U.S.S.R. from directly attacking each other. That stalemate was the beginning of the Special Operations and Proxy Wars that defined the Cold War. The Military Assistance Program of 1949 provided the military, the State Department, and the CIA with a slush fund that allowed them to fight a new kind of war.

Mackiernan and Bessac were both deeply committed to the nationalist feelings of the people they worked with and may have never fully understood how cynically the bureaucrats in the United States manipulated those passions for America's anti-Communist crusade. Regardless of intentions it is a simple fact that the MAP funds, after failing to contain China within the Great Wall (or to contain Communism within the boundaries of ethnic-China), were diverted to Vietnam. Ironically the secret roots of Vietnam can be traced to the funds that supported Mackiernan and others in Inner Asia.

A winter gale swept out of the northwest that night as Mackiernan and Bessac climbed into their Air Force–issue sleeping bags. On the morning of October 30, as Mackiernan, the three White Russians, and Bessac headed south for Tibet with four Kazak guides, a gale wind blew at their backs. No one came out of the yurts to wave good-bye.

THE WHITE HOUSE
OCTOBER 31, 1949

Since Secretary of State Dean Acheson was out of town, President Truman showed the map to Acting Secretary of State Webb. The map of Inner Asia had different colors on it to indicate which groups of tribal people along the Russian border were Muslim and which were Buddhist. Osman was Muslim; Prince De was Buddhist, as were the Tibetans.

President Truman assured the secretary that "these people" were "fundamentally antagonistic" to the U.S.S.R. Someone had been talking to the president about covert action in Inner Asia. Perhaps it was the CIA or the secretary of defense. The president's request to the secretary was phrased succinctly.

> He wanted us to try to develop some plan by which part of the $75,000,000 [from MAP] might be used to penetrate these peoples if such was feasible through covert activity.

The president of the United States wanted to use the MAP funds for covert actions in Inner Mongolia, Sinkiang, and Tibet.

At the State Department, Webb turned Truman's idea about the MAP money over to the CIA and circulated a memo within State only to a few people. Within a few months, the president, the State Department, and the Joint Chiefs of Staff all separately asked the CIA to prepare plans for covertly arming the Inner Asians.

On October 1, 1949, Mao Tse-tung proclaimed the establishment of the People's Republic of China in front of a million people gathered in Tiananmen Square in Peking. The celebration parades of American trucks and jeeps, filled with millions of dollars of captured

U.S. weapons, went by street corners for close to eight hours. It is estimated that on that day up to half the military might of the People's Republic had been made in America.

China within the Great Wall was secure. There was nothing to stop Mao from occupying all of Inner Mongolia and Sinkiang as he prepared to invade Tibet. Nothing except a few ragged bands like Osman's, or Prince De's.

The presidential memo from the October 31 meeting was classified TOP SECRET. One of the four men in the State Department who received a copy was Under Secretary of State Dean Rusk. His basic rationale about the use of the MAP-303 money as a covert tool of American policy was much the same in 1949, in China, as it would be in Vietnam twenty years later. He felt the United States should use covert aid to anti-Communist forces as a means to foment dissatisfaction with Communism. The United States "might provide arms for some guerrillas as form of payment and . . . should employ whatever means were indicated in the . . . furtherance of our interests— arms here, opium there, bribery and propaganda in the third place." This was Rusk's general attitude toward MAP-303 as he received President Truman's instructions about Inner Asia. Within eleven months, Dean Rusk would complete the president's instructions. Rusk found one of his first dominoes in Tibet.

FAIRFAX, CALIFORNIA
NOVEMBER 1949

Pegge Mackiernan enjoyed the back porch of her tiny home, especially the view of the dry, brown hills above Fairfax. Her husband had managed to find the money to buy her their first house. She sat in the morning sun, in a rare moment of peace, writing in her diary as she tried to add up the sums of her life. She missed her life in Asia as much as she loved her twins and delighted in watching them grow up. She admitted to her diary that it was difficult arithmetic.

It was a long leap from the life of a correspondent, dashing around Asia, to being a mother stuck in a suburb with two kids. No time to write, no cocktail parties to attend, no savvy friends with whom to debate the headlines, and no husband in sight to make it all worthwhile. Women paid for moments of passion with their lives and bodies, while men went on to more passion and more adventure without seeming to pay the price that women did.

From the time she met Douglas in July 1947 until the fall of 1949, she had spent eight of those twenty-eight months with her husband. She swung between bitterness and desperate longing, between gall and hope, between wedded love for Douglas and hoping she would never see his face again. It was bad enough when he was still in Tihwa, and they could manage the occasional exchange of letters or telegrams. During the first eight months of separation they had made plans for her to travel out to India by boat and then trek through the Himalayas with their infant twins to Tihwa. When the State Department caught wind of this fantasy, Assistant Secretary of State W. W. Butterworth wrote her a letter specifically forbidding it. But such letters were rare. Weeks went by without any word at all.

She dreamed of simply packing up the babies and flying off to South America. She was sure her $109 a month would go further there. In South America, she would have the time to write and something to write about. If a month went by and Pegge heard nothing from Douglas, she began to dream of the Andes. Then a letter would arrive, and she pored over every word.

His letters no longer restored her faith in him. Her sense of disconnection became so strong that she began to write him about her true feelings. In his replies, he simply ignored those parts of her letters—if he ever got them—and continued to write to her as though they were an old married couple with no serious problems between them. Perhaps her estrangement from her husband would have evaporated if she could have seen him or talked to him.

In July 1949, a month before the consulate was closed at Tihwa, Mackiernan, apparently thinking he would leave with Paxton, cabled and asked Pegge to meet him in Kashmir in the fall of 1949. Pegge cabled back saying the State Department wanted her to stay put.

Around August 20—five days after Paxton had left Tihwa and nine days before the Russian atomic test—a Boston paper carried a story saying that all Americans at Tihwa were en route through the Himalayas. Pegge went into a tizzy of preparation, only to have her hopes dashed a week later.

On August 26, the State Department sent the impoverished mother a collect telegram.

AM CONSULATE OFFICIALLY CLOSED BUT YOUR HUSBAND REMAINING TEMPORARILY HANDLING DIS-POSAL U.S. INTERESTS stop DATE HIS DEPARTURE NOT YET DETERMINED.

Pegge sensed now that there was more to all of this than anyone was telling her.

Despite the total collapse of the Nationalists in China by September 1949, Mackiernan managed to get a cable to her on their first wedding anniversary. Then Chris Rand, the *New York Tribune*'s correspondent in Hong Kong and an old friend, got word to her that "they" had radio contact with him, and everyone expected him to fly out soon on a CAT charter flight. CAT flew in and out of Tihwa even in September; Mackiernan could have flown out but he did not.

His last letter to Pegge from Tihwa made it to the United States by October 3. He wrote that he had no idea when he would get home. He also reminded her just how much he loved her, but the words rang hollow to a woman who had been raising twins alone for a year.

At last on November 28, 1949, Pegge got a letter from the State Department, again written by Butterworth, telling her where her husband was and when she might expect to see him. Butterworth was now one of Secretary of State Acheson's top men, though Pegge had known him in China as Mackiernan's buddy.

Doug is in Tibet. I just had a letter this morning saying our State Department was notified Doug left Tihwa the first of October, for India, via Tibet. He is expected to be in India the first of December and home for Christmas!!!

AROUND THE TAKLAMAKAN DESERT FROM LAKE BARKOL TO TIMURLIK

OCTOBER 30—NOVEMBER 29, 1949

The Mackiernan party traveled at night and slept during the day to avoid being seen. Since Communist troops were busy on the road into Tihwa, the Americans left camp at 2 A.M. and rode across the highway. The only highway connecting Sinkiang with China, it was the last automobile road they would see until they reached India. They rode on through the nights into a landscape that grew ever more lifeless. They camped on a stony plain without any trees or grass to hide them. Only the vast scale of the land itself hid them from observation when the sun rose. They were ten kilometers from the road by then. They had already disappeared into the northeast fringe of the Taklamakan Desert. When night fell, they rode on.

They woke one evening in the ruins of an old watchtower that stood on the lip of a five-hundred-foot-deep canyon rim. At sunset they watched the last of the light linger on the deeper desert beyond. Five nights of hard riding had taken them from the snow and meadows around Lake Barkol to the eastern fringe of the Taklamakan Desert. As night fell, the four Kazak guides, assigned to them by Osman, led the line of ponies down the steep narrow gorge and out onto the wastes beyond.

Though Frank Bessac had trained in the U.S. Cavalry, he was not prepared for the wiles of a fat-bellied central Asian pony. At sunset when he saddled the beast, he failed to kick it in the belly before cinching it up. It swallowed a belly full of air before it was saddled and, once under way, it exhaled and Bessac's saddle came loose. An hour after dark his saddle started sliding around. Bessac fought the pony just to keep it in line with the others, and then in the dark his saddle slipped around. He went down with a thump, onto the machine gun on his back. He was knocked out and cracked a vertebra. It was some time before the rest of the party noticed Bessac was missing. They found him with the pony standing quietly over him. He was unconscious but had held on to the reins. Mackiernan was not impressed.

After a week of night travel, they rode through the day and pressed on to a low-lying stand of tamarisk along the north bank of the shallow Kuruk Gol river. They had dropped from nine thousand feet at the Barkol camp to eight hundred feet.

The Kazak led them day by day across dry wastes, from river to spring to dried-out waterholes. They had to keep the ponies watered, but some days they rode for fifteen hours to reach water. For several days they crossed a black-sand desert called the Kara Gobi (black desert). Bessac stopped his horse in the middle of that waste to look for something alive or that had once been alive. In all directions he saw nothing but his own party and black sand.

By November 5 the horses were exhausted. At one point, the party went three days without water, which took a terrible toll on everyone. After a night's rest, with or without water, they went on. On November 7, when they finally reached good grazing—at 4,400 feet on a ridge above the eastern edge of the desert—they had to spend a day letting the animals feed before they could go on. On the next day, November 8, no water and no grazing greeted the party following a fifteen-hour ride.

Their lives settled into a routine, dominated by the quest for often brackish water and the search for grazing for their horses, which was often thin at best. The men also ate off the land, and it was Vasili Zvansov who fed them.

Zvansov remembers stalking a desert antelope early one morning after a twelve-hour ride the day before. He got a good shot and a clean kill. The animal fell hard against the ground. After a twenty-minute walk back to camp to pick up a horse, he rode out to gut the kill and butcher the antelope, expecting to be back at camp with the butchered meat in an hour. He was back in camp in half that time. In the forty-five minutes it had taken him to walk in and ride back out, vultures had descended and picked his kill clean. The Kazak laughed at him. Then they showed him how to cover his kill with the reeds that grew near the watering holes where the antelope gathered.

At night, Mackiernan had a routine. He pulled out his barometer and conducted a series of calculations to determine the altitude. He enjoyed plotting their course on the several maps he carried, one of which was from a nineteenth-century travel book. It seemed to Bessac that Mackiernan saw himself as a nineteenth-century explorer, but there was another side to the explorer.

Two or three times a week, Mackiernan had to match their travel schedule to that of his CIA radio contact schedule. As Zvansov slowly turned the hand-cranked generator, Mackiernan tapped his encoded messages to the CIA's listening posts in Turkey and Iran. His messages made their way from there to Mackiernan's handler at the CIA—someone we know only by the pseudonym "John." From there, parts of his messages were sent to Mackiernan's liaison at the State Department, W. W. Butterworth.

Every night, Mackiernan pulled out his travel log and entered the day's data as he sat by the flickering fire. His entries were quite terse— it was the expedition's log, not a diary.

November 13—Camp #20
Left #19 at 8 a.m.—rode up river valley for 8 hours (SW) to Khul-yastay—a campground with excellent water and food for horses. Alt. 7750'. No one living there.

On the day that they finally climbed up out of the Taklamakan for good, Mackiernan was inspired to his version of eloquence.

November 18—Camp #24
Left #23 at 11 a.m.—Rode until 3 p.m. to *awl* (camp) of HxxxxB Bastik. Everything fixed up for us. Yurt and best Bursak (fried bread) so far. Also big horn sheep meat—fried—very good. Alt. 9600'. Will probably stay here 4 or 5 days getting ready for trip to Gas Kol. Need mittens, more camels and make up bursak and cooked meat. Yurt at this instant is full of young Kazak—most of whom have never seen foreigners before. They are interested in my writing.

The party traveled across the northeastern fringe of the Taklama-kan and then, by November 18, their Kazak guides led them out of the desert to begin the ascent of the Kunlun Mountains. The Kunlun rise out of the southern edge of the Taklamakan and form the northern rampart of the Tibetan Plateau. In eighteen days they had traveled nearly three hundred miles.

As Mackiernan predicted, they had spent four days at Camp 24. It took that much time to find the fresh camels and horses the party needed to make the final push on to a camp the Kazak called Timurlik Bulak at Gas Kol. After a final five-day march—past the skeletons of men, horses, and camels—through absolutely barren, treeless valleys, and over a twelve-thousand-foot pass, the party made its way to the southernmost Kazak *awl,* in Sinkiang.

Hussein Taiji, the well-known leader of this band of Kazak, had a yurt prepared for the arriving Americans. Somehow he had known they were coming. The *awl* of Hussein Taiji was the richest camp Mackiernan had ever seen. After a short talk with Hussein, Mackiernan realized that he could not press on over the nineteen-thousand-foot pass and up onto the sixteen-thousand-foot Tibetan Plateau that loomed above them just north of Timurlik. Winter had come. Crossing the northern half of the plateau—called the Changthang—during winter was impossible. There was no other way to Lhasa except the three-month trek across the Changthang. They would hole up at Timurlik for the winter. Mackiernan could have been home for Christmas if only he had not stayed on collecting atomic intelligence in Tihwa. If only he had not lingered with Osman Bator. Now it was too late.

WASHINGTON, D.C.
NOVEMBER AND DECEMBER 1949

Mackiernan's radio message announcing his stay at Timurlik most likely went to the CIA and then to Butterworth. Six months earlier it had been Butterworth who had ordered Mackiernan to collect intelligence on the Russian uranium mine. During August, Mackiernan's atomic intelligence messages for General Hegenberger were routed through Butterworth as well.

Before Butterworth was promoted back to D.C., he initiated work on a treaty with the Nationalist Chinese that would have given America exclusive access to all the uranium in China, and denied it to the U.S.S.R. Butterworth was one of the most able members of the U.S. Foreign Service. Secretary of State Acheson promoted him to the post of assistant secretary of state for Far Eastern affairs, and considered Butterworth one of his most trusted advisers.

In the fall of 1949, Butterworth had helped edit the China White Paper, which essentially placed the blame for the collapse of Nationalist China on Chiang Kai-shek's corruption. The China lobby was pointing its finger at Butterworth as one of the Commies who had lost China.

President Truman knew from first-hand experience that the White Paper was telling the truth, but the constraints of office tempered his speech for twenty years. Decades later he told Merle Miller that the crooks around Chiang "stole seven hundred and fifty million dollars out of the thirty-five billion that we sent to Chiang. . . . And that's the money that was used and is still being used for the so-called China Lobby."

Even now few realize that it was the China lobby that made it politically impossible for Butterworth, the State Department, and President Truman to change America's policy toward Tibet. The United States had recognized Chiang's claim over Tibet, as a gesture of goodwill. To withdraw that gesture when Chiang was fighting for his life would have given the China lobby more "proof" of Communists in the State Department.

By the fall of 1949 Tibetans were asking the United States for military support. The American radio personality Lowell Thomas and his son, Lowell Thomas, Jr., were invited to Tibet during the summer of 1949. Upon his return, Lowell Thomas, Jr., took the Tibetan appeal straight to President Truman. The Tibetans wanted "to see Tibet accorded diplomatic recognition by the West, admit-d to the United Nations, and given assistance to develop an army ng enough to defend its borders."

hat message was repeated in official letters the Tibetans sent to the

U.S. and British governments. Tibet also sent a message directly to Mao Tse-tung, pointing out that Tibet was an independent country and asking Mao to reassure them that China would not invade. The Tibetans sent the U.S. and the British copies of that communication and asked for aid. The British told the Tibetans not to provoke China by insisting upon its independence—they had washed their hands of Tibet.

Butterworth not only oversaw communication with Mackiernan, but he also managed the American response to the Tibetans' aid request in the fall of 1949. He told them that consideration was being given to their request, but that no decision had yet been reached. The U.S. Tibet policy review—under way since the beginning of the year—was yet ongoing. Some men in the State Department felt that a small number of arms might allow the Tibetans to hold off the Chinese, and that the United States could then recognize Tibet as independent. That fall the United States was still waiting for the dust to settle after the civil war. Tibet could not be resolved until China was. If Chiang totally collapsed and Mao invaded Taiwan, then that would be the easy moment for the United States to recognize Tibet. Until then, Chiang could cause the U.S. administration so much damage that it was politically impossible to recognize Tibet.

The Chinese were not waiting for the United States to decide. On November 24, Radio Peking announced that the twelve-year-old reincarnation of Tibet's second-highest lama, the Panchen Lama, was now in the hands of the Communists. This prescient boy had written to Mao Tse-tung, asking him to "liberate" Tibet. The Tibetans sent representatives to the United States, Great Britain, and the UN. On December 3, 1949, as these missions set off, the Tibetan government wrote to the United States and the British.

> There is now imminent danger of Communist aggression towards Tibet. To preserve our future independence and freedom, we consider it most essential for Tibet to secure admission of her membership in the United Nations General Assembly.
>
> We are sending a special mission to the United States in this connection but, in the meantime, we shall be most grateful to you and your Government if you would kindly help us and place our humble appeal to the United Nations immediately through your good office

so that Tibet could take her place in the United Nations as a member state.

Secretary of State Acheson's reply was blunt:

> Any Tibetan effort to obtain United Nations membership at this time would be unsuccessful in view of the certain opposition of the USSR and of the [Nationalist] Chinese delegations. . . . The Tibetan plan to dispatch a special mission to obtain United Nations membership may at this time serve to precipitate Chinese Communist action to gain control of Tibet.

The Tibetans were diplomatically forbidden to apply for UN membership, and were told that this was in their own best interests. On January 10, 1950, the U.S.S.R. walked out of the Security Council when that body renewed recognition of the Nationalist Chinese government. The walkout left only one nation on the Security Council that would have refused to grant Tibet UN membership: Nationalist China. From January to June 1950 only Nationalist China could have kept Tibet out of the UN.

Britain and the United States held that since Tibet was not officially recognized as a state, neither country would issue Tibetans visas for their missions. The Tibetans were not allowed to send representatives to plead their case and were forced to recall their missions.

Tibetan desperation grew. In early January, 1950, nations around the world began to grant recognition of the Chinese Communist government of China. Britain and India were among the first to establish diplomatic relations with China, renouncing relations with the Nationalist regime in Taiwan and with Tibet. Nations that wanted to establish normal diplomatic relations with China had to accept a precondition. They had to accept that "Tibet had always been part of China."

THE FOURTEENTH DALAI LAMA
DHARAMSALA, INDIA
DECEMBER 1, 1994

The Dalai Lama does not want to talk about what happened in 1949 and 1950. "Past is past," he says, "the future we can still change."

There is no bitterness in his voice or on his face when he speaks about the events that led up to the destruction of his country. Yet he does not try to hide the bitter truth. He has written, "In the winter of 1949 and 1950, when something could have been done, we approached everyone, India, USA, Britain, the United Nations, but no one helped us."

And recently he has said, "At the same time, the Americans had no courage to formally recognize Tibet as an independent nation. . . .

"At that time, I do not think there was genuine sympathy toward Tibet. Simply, it was according to their master plan: what is best for Britain, what is best for America. So after the People's Republic was established in China, then America . . . did not come forward to recognize Tibet as independent. The courage was not there.

"But also there was some desire to stop the Chinese forces from invading Tibet. So with this policy, there was going to be covert actions. . . . On the Tibetan side, we were at that time very much eager to receive some weapons, some help, from foreign countries—whether India, England, or America. So if someone comes to talk . . ."

It did not occur to the Tibetans that the person sent to talk with them could have carried a kiss of death before he even arrived.

SECRETARY OF STATE DEAN ACHESON
WASHINGTON, D.C.
JANUARY 12, 1950

The Tibetans wanted to send a mission to the United States to ask for military aid. Tibetans in Washington would present the State Department with complicated questions about their status and irritate the Nationalist Chinese. The United States' reply on January 12 was the same response the Tibetans had heard again and again. Any overt moves to assert Tibetan independence could precipitate a Chinese Communist invasion—we forbid you to send a mission to the United States.

Some of this might have crossed Secretary of State Dean Acheson's mind as he glanced at the latest message to the Tibetans. Perhaps Acheson was planning to use Mackiernan for covert talks with the Tibetans; he certainly knew that Mackiernan was waiting to enter Tibet in the spring. Acheson did not personally write the cable that was sent to the Tibetans that day—at most he glanced at it. His thoughts were on China.

Acheson felt that the best plan for China was to wait for the dust to settle. The CIA was telling him that Chiang Kai-shek might not survive the winter. An invasion of Taiwan could happen at any moment. The CIA believed the Nationalist army in Taiwan could not resist such an invasion. U.S. policy stated that America would do nothing to stop it. Acheson was more worried about relations between Communist China and the U.S.S.R. He wanted to cause a schism between the two. He chose Sinkiang to show that Mao was kowtowing to Stalin—hoping to rouse Chinese nationalism. He made his pitch in a major foreign policy speech, at the Foreign Press Club in Washington on January 12.

The Soviet Union is detaching the northern provinces (areas) of China from China and is attaching them to the Soviet Union. This process is complete in Outer Mongolia. It is nearly complete in Manchuria, and I am sure that in Inner Mongolia and in Sinkiang, there are very happy reports coming from Soviet agents to Moscow. That is what is going on. It is the detachment of these whole areas, vast areas—populated by Chinese—the detachment of these areas from China, and their attachment to the Soviet Union.

But there was a flaw in Acheson's argument. Chinese did not populate these areas. Sinkiang was less than 4 percent Chinese that year. To argue that Outer Mongolia or the MPR was really part of China was a distortion of history. The Mongols had voted for independence in 1946 and Chiang Kai-shek had accepted the verdict of the Mongol voters. Acheson was distorting history in an attempt to divide the Chinese and the Russians.

Acheson was sending several messages through the headlines to Russia and China. He may have been talking about the Russians detaching the Eastern Turkestan Republic for the uranium there.

Acheson's speech was relayed to Mao, who was in Moscow with Stalin on the only foreign trip he ever made in his life. The new Chinese Communist leadership of Sinkiang was there as well—Governor Burhan—the only provincial leader so honored. Mao let the Sinkiang leadership reply to Acheson for him.

On January 30, a Shanghai newspaper blared back the Chinese response to Acheson's speech. China's decision was to call Douglas Mackiernan, who was now headed for Tibet, a spy.

SHANGHAI, THE PEOPLES REPUBLIC OF CHINA
JANUARY 30, 1950

NOTORIOUS LIAR OF AMERICAN IMPERIALISM ACHESON MANUFACTURES STRING OF SHAMELESS FABRICATIONS IN AMERICAN NATIONAL PRESS CLUB SPEECH ON JANUARY 12TH

NEW CHINA NEWS AGENCY JAN 30— TIHWA Mr. Mackiernan, former American Vice Consul, Tihwa, found to be spy, as American imperialists schemes of sabotage in Sinkiang comes to light. . . . Sinkiang Governor Burhan issues statement on American imperialists designs against interests of Sinkiang people. In this speech, Acheson maliciously said: "In Sinkiang there are very happy reports coming from Soviet agents to Moscow." . . . Sinkiang people, who have joined hands with more than 400 million people throughout country, are now striving to build up new democratic China. Probably Acheson thinks that in this way Sinkiang is to be regarded as falling into hands of Soviet Union. . . .

On behalf of the 5,300,000 Sinkiang people, I wish to make fol-lowing statement. Chinese people have now smashed imperialist shackles of Republic of China. As result of the utter defeat of KMT reactionaries, American imperialists have lost interest and capital in terms of arms and ammunition invested in Chiang Kai-shek. Suffering from such heavy blows, Acheson has invented preposterous lies that Soviet Union was invader Sinkiang. Mere little children do not believe such ridiculous statements. Before peaceful liberation of Sinkiang, even to use Acheson's words, there must have been very unhappy reports to Washington coming from American imperialist agents in Sinkiang. . . .

After Mackiernan went to mountains near Fuyuan he abandoned jeep and arrived at lair of bandit Wusman [*sic,* Osman], running dog of KMT. . . . On Sept 29, he went to Janimkhan, former head of Finance Department, who absconded and turned traitor because of his agitation's. This time He instigated them to flee to Chensi. Mackiernan took two radio sets with him and maintained communications with KMT secret agents whole time.

He told bandit chief Osman and Janimkhan and few Kazak and White Russians, Bodyguards of Osman, that they oppose it. He said that 3rd World War would soon break out and they must keep themselves armed and be ready for action. Such are iron facts of . . . intervention in Chinas domestic affairs . . . Mackiernan stayed with Osman and . . . other bandits for more than 20 days. Upon leaving he gave bandits Osman and 94 White Russians, 25 taels of gold as fund for insurrection. He took 14 horses from Osman and was escorted to Tibet. . . . Thus intrigues of American imperialism in Sinkiang met with bitter-failure."

FAIRFAX, CALIFORNIA
JANUARY 30 AND 31, 1950

January 30 I was suddenly informed a radio newscast had carried a story from Peking, China, that Doug S. Mackiernan was a spy. That he had "fled" into the Himalayas bound for India after organizing resistance group in the now communist province, Sinkiang.

Pegge Mackiernan's telephone began to ring—if the twins and her husband prevented her from being a journalist now she could at least be a news story. The *San Francisco Chronicle* and the *San Rafel Independent* both wanted to send reporters to interview her. The local Mutual radio station—KFRC—did a quick interview over the telephone and played it on air that afternoon. Several radio stations carried the story throughout the day. Pegge sat crouched before her radio, with the twins in their playpen nearby, as she rolled the glowing Bakelite dial across the spectrum, searching for news about her husband. At one point, she could pick up three simultaneous broadcasts about the brave U.S. consular officer trying to escape from the Reds.

It may have been news she was expecting. She had known since November that he had left Sinkiang for Tibet. She also knew Doug wasn't escaping. She put quotations around the word "fled" in her diary. He wasn't escaping anywhere, he was working. Pegge had long suspected he was some sort of agent.

The Dalai Lama commented on this in 1994. "On the Chinese side they called these Americans spies, this was something bad for them. For those who sent them, they called it intelligence. There is no contradiction here."

The day after the announcement, on the morning of January 31, the State Department in Washington called. Tony Freeman from the division of Chinese Affairs was on the line. They had received a radio message from Mackiernan.

"Am safe and well. Expect to return in the Spring."

Pegge was relieved to have news. Freeman sounded as if he cared about her—a pleasant change from the treatment she had been receiving.

When Freeman put down the telephone, Pegge immediately rang right through to the Associated Press. Old loyalty from her China days. They had paid her something for the few Tihwa reports she had been allowed to file before the army had cut her off. She got the local AP guy on the line and gave him the news.

She dressed the twins. Reporters came, and also a photographer. Flashbulbs popped. Headlines and captions told the story: MRS. PEGGE MACKIERNAN AND HER TWINS, MARY AND MIKE, WONDER WHERE DAD IS. CONSUL REPORTED HOLED UP IN THE HIMALAYAS. RADIO MESSAGES FROM HIM REPORT ALL WELL. REDS ACCUSE U.S. CONSUL AS SPY.

The story was headline news in American newspapers the next morning and made it to the front page of *The New York Times*. Friends from all over the country, some from whom she had not heard in years, tracked Pegge down on the telephone and sent her clippings. Her parents were thrilled to open their local Pennsylvania paper and find their daughter and their grandchildren beaming out at them from page two. Mackiernan's folks opened their local Boston paper and saw the same photo. They were not happy about the publicity. They thought that Pegge was courting the press. Family members say that the State Department complained to them about all the press reports. Perhaps the publicity might be dangerous for Mackiernan.

The newspapers also said that Mackiernan had a radio. Someone had slipped up, either Pegge or the State Department. State later issued statements to the press saying that Mackiernan did not have a radio. The escape cover had to be protected.

U.S. CONSUL IS SAFE IN HIMALAYA TREK

WASHINGTON, JAN. 31 (UP)— American Vice-Consul Douglas Mackiernan has got word to the State Department that he is "safe and well" on his hazardous trek across the Himalayas from Communist China to India, it was announced today.

The Department said Mr. Mackiernan, who fled his post at Tihwa in Sinkiang Province Sept. 27 when the Chinese Reds took over sent the word over a small portable transmitter somewhere in Asia. It was relayed to the State Department last night.

He is making his way to Kashmir, nearly 1,000 miles away over an ancient caravan route. The message said he is "safe and well" and expects to return "in the spring."

The Department relayed the news to Mrs. Mackiernan in Fairfax, Calif.

The Department refused to say where the message was received, explaining it did not want to further endanger Mr. Mackiernan, who already has been branded a spy by the Chinese Communists.

While insisting that there is no truth to reports that Mr. Mackiernan is stirring up "guerrilla revolts" against the communists, the department did not explain why it is taking him so long to reach India. New Delhi dispatches said several caravans of Chinese refugees who left Tihwa in early November— about two weeks after Mr. Mackiernan—reached Kashmir the end of December.

CHINA REDS CALL U.S. ENVOY A SPY

SAN FRANCISCO, JAN. 30 (AP)—The American Vice Consul in China's

wild west was accused by the Communists today of being a "spy" who sought to organize the bandits of the Sinkiang wilderness.

This latest in a long series of Red propaganda attacks on U.S. diplomats charged that Douglas S. Mac-kiernan "has been exposed as an espionage agent."

(In Washington, State Department officials called the Red report the "usual fantastic yarn.")

Page one of *The New York Times:*

U.S. AIDE ACCUSED AS SPY BY PEIPING
Vice Consul Said to Have Paid Three Sinkiang Tribal Chiefs To Resist Communists
by TILLMAN DURDIN
Special to *The New York Times*

HONG KONG, JAN. 29—The Chinese Communists produced a new American spy case today with a radio broadcast charge that Douglas S. Mackiernan, former United States vice-consul at Urumchi, Sinkiang capital, gave gold and instructions last year to anti-Communist Kazakh tribal chieftains in Sinkiang.

Mr. Mackiernan left Sinkiang last autumn for India. The Communists charged that before he departed he had visited three "bandit" leaders in Northeast Sinkiang, urged them to continue to resist the Communists and gave them twenty-five taels of gold (about $1,200).

[The Associated Press reported that State Department officials in Washington had called the Communist charge the "usual fantastic yarn." These officials said Mr. Mackiernan had been ordered by Washington to leave his post. The last report the department had was that Mr. Mackiernan was trying to get out of China by the route to India.]

The Communists described as the source for their story confessions of three White Russians who had gone with Mr. Mackiernan on his visit and who had since surrendered to the Communists. The Russians were quoted as having said that "the former United States Consul (J. Hall Paxton) who left Urumchi before Mackiernan" had also visited the tribesmen earlier in 1949.

(When Mr. Paxton, of Danville, Va., was ordered to leave his post last August, news agencies reported, he left Mr. Mackiernan behind to liquidate consular property. Mr. Paxton, Mrs. Paxton and Vice Consul Robert Dreessen, of St. Louis, Mo., reached India last October after an arduous trip, afoot and by horseback over the Himalayas.)

The Russians' story is that Mr. Mackiernan left Sinkiang Sept. 28 with an American student, whose name was given as Frank B. Besson, and the three Russians, bringing along two radio sets. Their jeep was said to have been abandoned in the mountains near Fuyuan and thereafter the party proceeded by horseback to call at camps of Osman Bator, Janmin Khan and Sultan.

At the last rendezvous, in Chenhsi, Mr. Mackiernan is stated to have instructed the three chieftains "on how to undermine the democratic work of the Chinese peoples." He was said to have told the chiefs to continue opposing the Communists and guaranteed that the United States would give them assistance. They were asked to "accumulate their forces for the present to await the outbreak of a 'third world war.'"

Offered to Take Sons

Mr. Mackiernan was said to have proposed to take the sons of the three men to the United States with him for "training" but the chieftains did not agree to this; instead three other young men went with Mr. Mackiernan. One of the White Russians, Vasili Zvantsoff, was said to have been especially trained as a radio operator by Mr. Mackiernan. The chieftains whom the Communists linked with Mr. Mackiernan were Kazakh who in recent years have consistently opposed the pro-Communist activities of some other Kazakh leaders in Sinkiang, particularly the Iii group of Ahmed Djan who in 1947 formed a virtually autonomous pro-Soviet regime in the three northern districts of Sinkiang. Osman Bator gained world publicity by aiding the Nationalist garrison at Peitashan Sinkiang, against an incursion from Soviet-dominated Outer Mongolia in 1947. Thereafter he and allied Kazakh Moslem chieftains were visited by a number of Americans, including newspapermen.

IN CONSULAR SERVICE SINCE 1946
Special to *The New York Times*

CANTON, MASS., JAN. 29—Douglas S. Mackiernan Jr., 36, has been in the consular service since 1946.

He was born in Mexico City and was educated in Mexico and at the Stoughton (Mass.) high school.

Later he attended the Massachusetts Institute of Technology.

During the war Mr. Mackiernan was in the Air Corps, attaining the rank of lieutenant colonel. He was engaged in communica-tions work in the Asian theatre. His wife, Mrs. Margaret Parker Mackiernan, and their twin children, Michael and Mary, less than a year old, are living in California.

PEKING AND WASHINGTON, D.C.
JANUARY 20, 1950

Radio Peking had a few words to say to the world about Tibet on January 20. China not only intended to invade Tibet, but it knew America had never denied Nationalist China's legal right to do so. The Communist Chinese planned to inherit that right. America's support for Chiang Kai-shek's claim over Tibet was backfiring—onto the Tibetans.

Unless America changed the precedent it had helped establish and recognized Tibet as independent, America would be in the position of defending the legal right of Communist China to invade Tibet. The United States was in an untenable position and the Communists knew it. Radio Peking gleefully put a vicious spin on the fiction that America had helped to create. "Tibet is the territory of the Chinese People's Republic. This is known to everyone in the world *and is a fact, which has never previously been denied.*" China went on to say that any U.S. contact with the Tibetans was "nothing but a puppet show played by American Imperialism and its conspirators in the invasion of Tibet."

That same day Butterworth's staff in Far Eastern Affairs at the State Department gave Secretary of State Acheson his briefing notes for a press conference. It contained an executive summary of Tibet policy.

If asked about Tibet and Chinese communist threats to that area it is recommended that you reply that Tibet for a long time has enjoyed autonomy under Chinese government suzerainty. *This government has never questioned this arrangement.* We believe the best interests of the Tibetans would not be served by attempting at this time to change this status perhaps thereby jeopardizing the autonomy they now enjoy.

In March, Dean Rusk was about to replace Butterworth. Rusk changed the secretary's briefing card on Tibet.

If asked to comment on the policy of this government concerning Tibet it is suggested that you reply along the following lines:
"I do not believe there is anything I can usefully say on that subject at this time."
Background for the Secretary (SECRET)
We can no longer afford to state that we have never questioned Chinese suzerainty over Tibet. [Or that] Tibet is primarily a responsibility for the British and Indian Governments. *We certainly do not want to hand it to the Communists.*

Tibet was part of Rusk's anti-Communist crusade, and that crusade now had a budget, the Military Assistance Program of 1949. Yet Tibet was only a footnote as the MAP pie was cut up. Tibet was at the very bottom of the list given to the secretary of defense—the smallest anti-Communist pawn. Even so the Joint Chiefs of Staff did recommend that the United States provide covert military aid to the Tibetans as part of the $30 million anti-Communist program for mainland China, Taiwan, and Tibet.

These plans for Tibet as a pawn in a larger anti-Communist game hardly amounted to the American invasion of Tibet that the Chinese Communists were predicting. Nevertheless, America was preparing to help the Tibetans. This military policy had to be coordinated with the State Department, and that coordination was slow to develop.

In March the State Department continued telling the Tibetans that they should not expect any military aid. The United States still refused to recognize Tibet as an independent country despite the Tibetans' begging them to do so.

The U.S. and British governments effectively forbade the Tibetan government the right to put forward their case in public forums. And Senator Joseph McCarthy's support for Chiang Kai-shek would soon make it even more difficult. Tibet was being swept up into the emerging Cold War.

In six months China had been lost, the Russians got the bomb, and Russian atomic spies were discovered in the United States. This wave of bad news created a sense of public hysteria. Against this backdrop Senator McCarthy helped set the United States on its way to Vietnam, and destroyed Tibet's last hopes for help from the United States.

SENATOR McCARTHY'S SPEECH
WHEELING, WEST VIRGINIA
FEBRUARY 9, 1950

There are different reports about what Senator Joseph McCarthy said at the meeting of the Ohio County Women's Republican Club. David M. Oshinsky culled through the conflicting reports in his book *A Conspiracy So Immense*.

> The theme of the speech was rather simple: America, the strongest nation on earth, the center of "the Democratic Christian world," was losing the Cold War, and losing badly, to the forces of "Communist atheism." Why? Because the Department of State, led by Dean Acheson—"this pompous diplomat in striped pants"—was filled with dupes and traitors, men and women who wanted the other side to win.
>
> ... Then, according to several witnesses, [McCarthy] said: "While I cannot take the time to name all of the men in the State

Department who have been named as members of the Communist Party and members of a spy ring, I have here in my hand a list of 205 . . . a list of names that were known to the Secretary of State and who nevertheless are still working and shaping the policy of the State Department."

Fifty years later, we know that the handful of people in the State Department who actually did have Communist inclinations during the 1940s had been far from policy-shaping circles. They had all been ferreted out shortly after the war and had resigned in order to avoid security investigation. Every case ever brought to trial after McCarthy's new technique of trial by public slander either died in court or was eventually overturned by the U.S. Supreme Court.

That is not to say that Russia did not have spies working in the United States. Those spies did deliver U.S. atomic secrets to the Russians, and Klaus Fuchs had confessed a few weeks before McCarthy's speech. The widely publicized Fuchs arrest, coming on top of the loss of China and the Russian A-bomb test, helped spawn the fear that gripped America in February 1950.

"The air was so charged with fear," recalled the American cartoonist Herb Block, "that it took only a small spark to ignite it." McCarthy was the spark. The resulting explosion left a crater in U.S. foreign policy for decades to come.

McCarthyism had a direct impact as the State Department considered changing its established policy toward Tibet. In the weeks after Wheeling, the entire government was hamstrung by fear.

Few Americans were listening when President Truman said that Senator McCarthy was the Kremlin's greatest asset in the United States. The public was listening more closely to McCarthy. Secretary of State Acheson received daily death threats. He worked in this toxic environment as he considered which American he would send to Tibet. Though Mackiernan had been in Timurlik for six weeks, Acheson had yet to ask the Tibetans for permission for this U.S. vice consul to pass through Lhasa.

SECRETARY OF STATE ACHESON MEETS LOWELL THOMAS, SR.

FEBRUARY 17, 1950

Lowell Thomas's trip to Tibet was the crowning journey even for a man who had skied glaciers in Alaska and shot game in Africa. He was only the eighth American to visit Tibet. Soon after his return to America, Thomas demonstrated the influence that had gotten him invited to Tibet and repaid the Tibetans for their hospitality. He called on the president for a chat. Then he went over to see the secretary of state. Acheson recorded the conversation.

> Mr. Thomas . . . referred to his earlier conversation with the President and said that he had come out of Tibet with two ideas, which he had expressed to the President, and which the latter had seemed to think worthwhile and of interest to me.
>
> Thomas thought that the United States should send a mission to Tibet, ". . . to see what could be done and what the situation was. The terrain was admirably suited for guerrilla operations and Tibetan forces could put up strong resistance through such operations to any military force that could be sent into Tibet.

Acheson was not about to get into a deep discussion of what was afoot, but Lowell's position allowed Acheson to hint at developments. Acheson said that:

> Suggestion of a mission seemed to have merit and we had for some time been considering such a possibility but a major difficulty was that of avoiding publicity which would draw Chinese Communist attention and probably serve to hasten their move against Tibet. I said that we would give further study to this question.

Despite the threat of a Communist invasion of Tibet and despite outrage from Taiwan, the United States was still considering some contact with the Tibetans. As the U.S. government consulted Britain, India, and others on the idea, Indian Prime Minister Jawaharlal Nehru said an American mission to Tibet—when the Chinese were already talking about a British-U.S.-Indian plot to invade Tibet—would "do more harm than good." He believed it might hasten a "Communist invasion of Tibet." Everyone consulted gave the same warning, and Acheson himself was well aware of the danger to Tibet if the U.S. mission became public. As recently as January 24, he had told the U.S. embassy in New Delhi that he concurred with their suggestion that circumstances—which had supported a U.S. mission to Tibet a year earlier—had changed. It was now inadvisable to send any U.S. government official to Tibet.

Douglas Mackiernan still sat in Timurlik, awaiting permission for him to pass through Tibet.

WINTER AT TIMURLIK
NOVEMBER 29, 1949, TO MARCH 20, 1950

The guides Osman Bator had sent with them rode ahead to warn the local chief, Hussein Taiji, of their arrival in Timurlik. The baying mastiffs were chained up as the Americans rode their long line of camels and horses sedately toward camp. Hussein walked nearly a hundred yards from his yurt, near the center of the *awl,* or encampment, to welcome the Americans with a two-handed handshake. His senior wife had hot tea with mare's milk ready for them inside. As they drank, Hussein suggested they pitch their tent near the guest yurt that awaited them. Every traditional honor was extended to the Americans.

There were about one hundred yurts in the Timurlik *awl,* scattered for miles around in the surrounding meadows, out of sight, allowing the flocks sufficient grazing. The white beards, as the Kazak called their elders, visited Hussein's yurt nearly every day. They walked into the yurt, seated themselves by the fire, and joined in the daily discussions about community decisions—without waiting for any invitation. They were family. Hussein's wife only looked up from her cooking, noted the arrival, and added more mutton to the pot boiling on the fire.

That winter the white beards decided to ban the traditional raids on the camps of other nomads. Young Kazak men traditionally raided Mongols or Tibetan nomads—going on raids as distant as several months' round-trip—in order to steal sheep, horses, camel, yaks, or children. Animals stolen on a raid were the most highly respected form of bride-price. It paid for the bride with panache by demonstrating the manly powers of the groom. During the winter of 1949–50 in the face of the invading Chinese, the white beards took a diplomatic step to try to unite all the different nomadic tribal groups of Inner Asia. The young men were not impressed by the idea that they had to work together with those they had previously always raided.

Young men galloped wildly in from the horizon, laughing and whooping as they came to Hussein's yurt in the center of the *awl*. Frank Bessac, watching the performance for the first time, thought someone was going to get hurt. Instead, to everyone's amazement, these daredevils slung themselves down under the bellies of their galloping mounts. When the horses came to an abrupt halt in front of the yurt, the watching crowd—drawn out by the ruckus—appreciated the grace with which the young men seemed to fall off their horses.

That winter some young men ignored the edict of the white beards. A week's ride away, a group of Mongols, whom the Kazak had pushed out of Timurlik only a decade earlier, were preparing to move their herds north across the Kunlun Mountains into Tibet. The Mongols were already afraid the Communist Chinese would destroy their nomadic lifestyle as the Chinese took control of Sinkiang. The Kazak raiders from Timurlik swept into the Mongol camp, killed two people, and galloped out again with hundreds of head of livestock. There was no triumphant return from the raid—the young men had, after all, undermined any unity among the nomads in the face of the Chinese invasion.

Instead, upon their return the young men crept up in the night and tied a few head of sheep or goats to the yurts of many people at Timurlik. That was the only public announcement of their successful raid. Even the Americans found a sheep tied to their tent when they woke up the next morning.

Bessac and Vasili Zvansov noticed another result of such raids. There were several Tibetans at Timurlik who acted and dressed like Kazak. They had been kidnapped on raids into Tibet over the past decade. Tibetans to the north would be primed to shoot anyone who looked Kazak.

Bessac spent much of his time at Timurlik noting such anthropological details. He did not go out with Mackiernan and Stephan when they discussed politics with Hussein Taiji and the white beards. At night, sometimes, he heard the gist of these discussions from Mackiernan.

"They want us to supply them with weapons. Arms, ammunition. That's all they keep asking for—exactly like Osman."

Zvansov also does not recall much political detail about their stay in Timurlik; he says that Stephan did all the translating for Mackiernan with Hussein Taiji.

He does remember that "we were in a dangerous position when we got to Timurlik. The Red Chinese already knew we were there. The passes around us were covered with snow. I asked if to save our life they could get us airplanes and Mackiernan said, 'No, our State Department would not allow this.'

"I asked why and he said it was a complicated thing with airspace between India and Tibet and so on."

Mackiernan must have had talks with the CIA and the State Department about such issues. His work with the Kazak—and his planned work with the Tibetans—must have been linked to MAP-303 and U.S. intelligence planning. The State Department and the CIA are unable to locate, unwilling to declassify, or have shredded the dozens of messages that were transmitted between Timurlik and Washington that winter.

Dr. Linda Benson, author of the most comprehensive biograp' of Osman Bator, is one of the leading U.S. historians on Sin] today. She agrees that we are not allowed a full picture of Mack' work because of government secrecy: "I am absolutely sure that the American government sought to organize non-Chinese ethnic groups to resist Communism, during 1949, as the Communists came to power. I am also certain that Douglas Mackiernan was a player in that effort."

Relations between the Americans and Hussein Taiji went smoothly for much of the winter. Bessac was invited to a wedding and to a shaman healing. He observed how the Kazak made the felt that covered their yurts, and the carving over the wooden doors. The Kazak had a penchant for eating condensed mutton fat as though it were taffy. Bessac was applauded the first time he gagged a piece down with a smile on his face. The Kazak also admitted their love for *kumiss,* fermented mare's milk. Though the Koran prohibits wine—and the Kazak are faithful Muslims—the nomads at Timurlik said the Koran spoke only of wine, and so it was all right to enjoy *kumiss.*

The nomads at Timurlik lived according to their own laws, and interpreted those of others as they saw fit. Bessac was told that marriages were arranged. He then asked what happened if the young woman did not like the choice made for her. A young woman listening to the older women describe things as they should be intervened with a laugh and patted her belly as she spoke: "One can always be made pregnant by the fellow one loves."

It was the same with the new Chinese Communist leaders. Hussein was willing to help the Americans on their way to Tibet—but still he was pragmatic. When a group of Chinese Communist officials came for a visit, the outriders gave the nomads several days' advance notice of their impending arrival. The Americans, their tent, and all sign of them disappeared. When the Communist officials asked specifically about the Mackiernan party, Hussein denied that any Americans had come that way.

The nomads had led their own lives, making their own rules for as long as they could remember, a way of life that would soon be destroyed by enforced collectivization and other regulation by the Chinese state. During the Manchu Dynasty, these nomads—though recognizing the power of the distant emperor—had been left to their own devices as long as they did not raid settled Chinese farming communities. Peking's relationship with the nomads was focused on preventing such raids. In the 1970s and 1980s the mineral wealth underneath the nomadic lands of Sinkiang eventually caused such a great rush of Chinese into Sinkiang that the nomads would become a minority in their own land. Today 90 percent of the total oil reserves of China lie underneath the deserts and mountains of Sinkiang. The nomads have disappeared from much of their old range, and the remaining nomadic people are slowly being turned into a population of settled farmers—as Lattimore predicted, they are made to be Chinese.

It was a trying winter for Mackiernan, who was clearly more at ease on the move. There was only so much time he could talk with the Kazak about their hopes for weapons. He went out shooting sometimes with Zvansov—but the Russian was the better hunter. On one occasion after Zvansov had made a shot, Mackiernan rode off with both horses. Zvansov had to walk back to camp. That entailed an overnight stay at a yurt he stumbled upon. Mackiernan did not explain his actions. Zvansov knew something was bothering Mackiernan.

Bessac also thought something was eating Mackiernan. On one occasion, Mackiernan tried to unburden himself. He approached Bessac and started to talk about what Bessac calls "Doug's women problems." Bessac had heard vaguely that he had an American wife in the United States. Mackiernan cynically told him several times, "Never get married." And Bessac heard that Mackiernan was upset about leaving his Russian wife in Tihwa. He was vague. Mackiernan tried to bring up the subject just that once. After Bessac brushed him off and went back to reading *War and Peace,* it never came up again.

Mackiernan prided himself on his expert relations with the locals. In the last few weeks before they left, he made a mess of his attempts to buy the meat-eating horses and camels the expedition needed to make it across the Changthang into central Tibet. There would not be enough grazing for the animals until summer, and the Americans were planning to set off on March 15. They would have to take meat-eating animals. The Kazak pointed out that meat-eating camels and horses were rare and asked twice the normal price for them. Mackiernan was willing to pay in gold, but the animals that were tied up in front of the American's tent the next day were a swaybacked lot. They would never make it to Lhasa with those mounts. Mackiernan flew into a rage.

This was simply a bargaining position by the Kazak, but Mackiernan's public fit of anger made it impossible for further negotiation. Hussein Taiji called Mackiernan to his yurt, but Mackiernan refused the invitation. At last, Bessac, watching this unfolding drama, went in Mackiernan's stead. After a tongue lashing for the unseemly behavior of the Americans—after all, the Kazak had lied to the Chinese about the Americans' presence and helped them through the winter in many other ways—Bessac was sent on his way. The next day a fine train of fifteen meat-eating camels and two meat-eating horses were tied up in front of the Americans' tent. Mackiernan weighed 45 ounces of gold, sent it over to Hussein Taiji, and after that the incident was never spoken of again.

There was one final arrival at the yurt of Hussein Taiji in March shortly before the party set off for Tibet. A rider came in advance to notify Hussein that Qali Beg was arriving. Qali Beg, a Kazak leader from around Lake Barkol, was an ally of Osman Bator. He had decided not to stay for the independence conference Osman had called. Instead, he had made his way across the Tarim Basin during the cool of the winter to Timurlik. He planned to band together with the Kazak at Timurlik, or if that failed, to retreat through Tibet to India.

What promises Mackiernan made to Qali Beg cannot now be proven. We know that Hussein Taiji did not walk out from camp to meet his newly arrived ally. There was unknown conflict between the men. Perhaps Hussein hoped to live with the Chinese Communists, and feared Qali Beg, who was too openly aligned with Osman.

Douglas Mackiernan saddled up and rode out to meet Qali Beg even if Hussein Taiji did not. Bessac rode out with him. Bessac says it was the only instance at Timurlik that winter at which he was present for political discussions between Mackiernan and the Kazak.

Qali Beg rode a fine white stallion and was dressed in an astounding full-length coat of snow-leopard fur. Several big cats died to clothe this Kazak warrior chief. His high cheekbones and slanted eyes showed the Mongol blood in his ancestral past. One of the camels in his caravan had a large wooden bedstead lashed to its back. Qali refused to part with it no matter how much the people laughed at his bed. Several other camels carried the massive yurt a leader of his stature required. Behind Qali Beg and his senior wife plodded the long train of Kazak who had chosen this man as their leader. The arrival of so many new people with their herds was bound to spark some rivalry with the Timurlik Kazak.

Mackiernan and Bessac were not focused on intratribal rivalry. Their concern was Kazak independence in the face of the invading Chinese.

Riding into camp with Qali, the Americans talked about the problems looming before the Kazak. Bessac said that he hoped for Kazak independence.

Qali Beg caught the remark and turned in his saddle. "That's the best thing anyone has ever said to me about the Kazak."

Later, during further discussions, Mackiernan and Qali Beg decided that the American would carry a letter from Qali Beg to the Dalai Lama's government. It requested that the Tibetans allow intelligence couriers from the Kazak to pass through Tibet. Mackiernan was probably working with Qali Beg to allow intelligence from his own network—the White Russians or others—to be passed to Qali Beg, who would then pass it on to American agents in India through Tibet. It's also possible that Mackiernan planned only for Qali Beg to collect intelligence on Chinese troop movements in Sinkiang and then pass that to the Tibetans.

If the Chinese Communists learned of Mackiernan's plan, they would have said that an American spy was organizing Kazak and Tibetans to spy on the People's Liberation Army. Or that Mackiernan was organizing a revolt. They had already accused Mackiernan of these types of actions at Lake Barkol. It is impossible to know if Mackiernan was, or was not, under orders to set up this intelligence link. If true, his actions may have been linked to a planned Nationalist Chinese withdrawal into Tibet. There are hints that Mackiernan headed to Tibet to prepare the way for a withdrawal of Kazak and Nationalist troops from Sinkiang into Tibet.

Bessac does not recall details about Qali Beg's letter, which Mackiernan carried to Tibet when they left Timurlik on March 20. He had a general idea of what was planned.

"What Doug wanted to do was to allow the people of East Turkestan and Tibet as much independence as possible. If that meant Qali Beg should send messages through Tibet, then of course he would try to help that happen."

Historian Linda Benson is able to expand on the situation: "It's clear that in 1949 the United States wanted to arm people, like the Tibetans and the Kazak. The details of Doug's involvement in that are not clear. The details may never be completely revealed to us because of government secrecy.

"It is clear that the whole thing, however, was disorganized from the start. They thought they would have more time. No one thought Chiang Kai-shek would collapse so completely, so fast. When he fled to Taiwan they at least thought that non-Communist forces would hold western China for some time. Of course, they were wrong and that's why the effort in Tibet was so hopeless to begin with. It was doomed from the start. But of course the agents in the field would have thought, at the time, 'Look, all we need are some weapons out here and these people are ready to die fighting the Communists.'

"Generals in Washington, who had never seen the Gobi Desert, never seen the Himalayas, they could not conceive of how impossible it was going to be to effectively arm these ethnic groups—who really did want to fight off the Chinese.

"So this effort was doomed from the start. Our ignorance and the sheer numbers of the Chinese proved insurmountable. God knows how many Kazak and Tibetans were killed as a result. Of course the American agents involved could just go home and retire.

"After the total humiliation of losing China, America had to do something to save face. Like getting your agents into Sinkiang to try to arm the anti-Chinese ethnic groups. But of course there were terrible miscalculations in all of this. China exterminated all anti-Communist and anti-Chinese resistance much quicker than America thought they could. This is what happened to the Kazak and the Inner Mongolians and the Tibetans. They got caught up in this and paid for it with their lives."

Today, the meadows at Timurlik are empty of nomads. The followers of Hussein Taiji and Qali Beg were among the fifteen thousand Kazak who fled Sinkiang for India after running battles with the Chinese broke out in the spring of 1950. In a 1954 *National Geographic* article, Milton Clark reported that only three hundred and fifty of these refugees survived the trek through Tibet. The survivors reached Kashmir in 1951 and were eventually resettled in Turkey after U.S. intervention.

A LETTER TO TIBET, STATE-CIA RELATIONS
MARCH 30, 1950

The Mackiernan party was en route to Tibet for six months. The State Department did not request permission from the Tibetans allowing the party to pass through the country until after the Americans had entered Tibet. Mackiernan left Tihwa in September 1949, knowing he was going to Tibet. His wife Pegge knew it in November, and the Chinese published the news in January 1950. Even during the months when Mackiernan was in radio contact with the State Department from Timurlik, the U.S. government never contacted the Tibetan government. The Americans sent their request to the Tibetans only on March 30. That was ten days after the Mackiernan party had left Timurlik and a week after they were inside Tibet. Why was the American letter sent so late?

The U.S. embassy in New Delhi offered one explanation: "The Communists would go to great lengths to make sure that no member of this party reaches the outside world alive." The State Department may have thought it was protecting the Americans by not announcing U.S. plans to the Tibetans until after Mackiernan left Timurlik. That explanation makes little sense, as China knew Mackiernan was headed into Tibet by at least January 30, when it trumpeted that news in the newspaper.

There is another possible explanation. The State Department and the CIA were at war that spring. It was the State Department's responsibility to ask the Tibetans for permission for Mackiernan to enter Tibet. Since Mackiernan was a CIA agent, they were required to liaison with the CIA beforehand. In 1950, that legally mandated liaison process was dysfunctional because of Senator McCarthy's crusade and its effects on American politics.

George Kennan, a trusted adviser of Secretary of State Acheson, headed the Policy Planning Staff. He was also the State Department's representative on the State-CIA liaison committee, which ensured that all covert CIA operations were in line with State Department policy.

That spring, Kennan wrote an impassioned letter of complaint. A State Department official had issued guidance to the CIA about a covert project. Instead of taking that policy guidance at face value, the CIA—without notifying anyone in the State Department— reported the policy guidance to the FBI as "possible evidence of political unreliability on the part of the State Department official concerned." Kennan was stunned.

> It was never to be expected that covert operations could be . . . conducted . . . unless those charged with their conduct could command the cooperation and the confidence of all agencies of the United States Government.
>
> Experience has indicated that the issuance of political guidance to the Director of the CIA in these matters is, in present circumstances, liable to distortion and exploitation in ways dangerous to . . . the persons concerned in this Department.
>
> In these circumstances I would consider it unjust to permit any official of this Department to have anything to do with this work. . . . It is obviously not a tolerable state of affairs that men should be asked to work in this atmosphere and in this jeopardy . . .

George Kennan wrote this plea on March 30, the same day that the State Department finally sent a letter to the Tibetan government asking it for permission for Douglas Mackiernan to pass through Tibet. When the State Department and the CIA should have consulted about Mackiernan's trip to Tibet, Kennan says that the two bureaucracies were not talking to each other. One retired agency employee says, "Washington was on Mars" in the spring of 1950.

Agents in the field were not receiving the policy guidance they needed. He laughs at the idea that the State Department could have effectively guided covert operations at the time. By March 1950 Secretary of State Acheson was spending as much time fighting off the attacks of McCarthy and other Republicans as he was working on policy. Acheson could not take any action without first considering how it might expose him to the charges that McCarthy and the China lobby were continually hurling at him. It was in this witch's brew that Butterworth—Mackiernan's old friend and supervisor in State— became a scapegoat for Acheson.

Acheson wrote that he removed Butterworth from his post as chief of Far Eastern Affairs, on March 28, because of attacks against the man by opponents of Acheson's China policy. Looking back, some believe that Acheson removed Butterworth to defend himself from those attacks. If he reshuffled the staff, which had been making China policy, perhaps the attacks would cease.

Acheson knew that Dean Rusk had good relations with the Republicans in the House and Senate. Rusk's suggestion that he take over the hot seat at Far Eastern Affairs helped Acheson deflect Republican attacks against himself. It also thrust aside a man whose policies were 180 degrees opposite those of Dean Rusk. Butterworth—like Lattimore, Mackiernan, and Bessac—recognized the nationalism of the Asians and knew it was the key to gaining their support. Dean Rusk saw a global Communist conspiracy guided from Moscow. Butterworth felt that Chinese nationalism would never allow Mao to let China become a Russian colony. Butterworth wanted U.S. military aid to Vietnam to be given to the Vietnamese directly. Rusk had that aid handed to the French colonialists, who used it to suppress Vietnamese nationalism, as much or more so than they used it to suppress Communism.

The appointment of Rusk to replace Butterworth is one example of the countless ways in which American foreign policy was shifted to the right by McCarthyism. A generation of China experts was purged. Though no evidence was ever produced in a court of law sufficient to indict any of McCarthy's smear victims, the fear of McCarthy and others like him was sufficient to change the course of American foreign policy.

As America and Dean Rusk set off on their long journey together, one of Rusk's first actions was to allow Douglas Mackiernan to be sent to Tibet. He did it even though Mackiernan was already a known spy, and U.S. policy toward Tibet was to do nothing that might hasten the invasion. He sent Mackiernan to Tibet though he could have walked around Tibet to India, or been flown out by an American plane. This apparent lack of coordination between State Department policy and the covert actions of the CIA remains the central mystery of Mackiernan's trip to Tibet. Perhaps, as suggested, State and the CIA were simply not talking that spring. Perhaps State and the CIA believed they understood the risks but still felt the risk was worth taking.

The message from Washington, requesting the Tibetan government to allow Mackiernan to pass through Tibet, reached Lhasa a few days before April 15. The courier with the message to allow the Mackiernan party into Tibet left Lhasa on April 15. It took two weeks for a horseback courier to ride from Lhasa to Tibet's northern border with Sinkiang. It was likely the delay in Washington that caused the shooting on the border on April 29,1950, because the Tibetan guards had standing orders to shoot on sight.

McCARTHY AND LATTIMORE
WASHINGTON, D.C.
APRIL 1950

If Butterworth was a secret victim of McCarthyism, Owen Lattimore was the most public one. First, Senator McCarthy let the media know that he was about to name "the top espionage agent in the United States, the boss of Alger Hiss." Hiss was living proof to the public that indeed there were Communists in the State Department; he had been convicted of perjury just two months earlier. McCarthy's sensationalism received a lot of attention, and he let it build for several days.

On March 21, 1950, McCarthy called Lattimore the "top Russian spy . . . the key man in a Russian espionage ring . . . I am willing to stand or fall on this one."

Overnight a man unknown to the average American was infamous. Lattimore was in Afghanistan—on an aid project, back when the United States was first interested in "nation building" there—when the story broke. Upon his return, the professor was besieged at the airport by the press. Lattimore denied McCarthy's charges. By April 6 he was in front of Senator Tydings's committee, which was investigating the loyalty of State Department employees. The professor was calm, for he knew he was innocent of the charge. He said, "The Senator has stated that he will stand or fall on my case. I hope this will turn out to be true, because I shall show that his charges against me are so empty and baseless that the Senator will fall, and fall flat on his face. . . ."

During a long day of testimony, Lattimore rebutted every one of McCarthy's charges. Senator Tydings was impressed.

Tydings announced that J. Edgar Hoover and five members of the committee had reviewed Lattimore's FBI file, and that the senators were all of one mind. "There was nothing in the file to show that you were Communist or had ever been a Communist. . . . The FBI file puts you . . . in the clear."

Despite this poor start, Senator McCarthy came up with more charges. When one charge was disproved, he brought up another. Lattimore tried to redirect attention to the China lobby, and how McCarthy was acting as their "stooge." No one listened to him, or to President Truman, when they hinted that Chiang Kai-shek was funding McCarthy.

Few American's ever understood that the Red Scare was in part a Chinese pogrom, which aimed to shift U.S. policy toward Chiang. Instead, Lattimore went through five years of questioning about the books he had written and every action of his career in China. The FBI tapped his telephone. Dozens of agents investigated his life. In the fall of 1951 he was denied a passport. His speaking engagements dried up, and *National Geographic* no longer published his cover stories. Lattimore was tainted, though every charge against him was disproved. On the other hand, Chiang Kai-shek was about to become an ally of the United States. He was never held accountable for his corruption, theft, or the disastrous shift in U.S.-Asian policy that he helped achieve.

Owen Lattimore was one of the few men who could have helped guide the United States as it faced the Chinese Communist victory in China. One of the facts cited to prove that Lattimore was a Communist was his support for the Tibetans and others who wanted freedom from the Chinese. Since Lattimore supported an independent Mongol state, which was also championed by the U.S.S.R., he was branded a Communist. The ideas that Lattimore espoused were discredited, not after a free discussion but because of cowardice. People feared following his advice, worrying that if they sounded like Lattimore they, too, might be branded Communists.

ACROSS THE CHANGTHANG
MARCH AND APRIL 1950

The fifteen camels knelt in a circle around the canvas tent close enough for Frank Bessac to hear them grinding their teeth in the bitter cold, windless night. Awake at night listening to the camels, he rarely smelled the unwashed feet and smoky fire inside the tent. Whenever he first entered the tent, the smell of humans and fire was coppery and startling after the pure thin air of the Tibetan Plateau. The cold was always there, though. Nothing but sleep ever made it disappear. At night the temperature fell to thirty degrees below zero. All he could do was huddle against the bone-chilling night in the sleeping bag and wait for sleep to wash over him.

Often unable to sleep, Bessac would listen to the wind, the camels, and the snoring inside the tent—and the occasional distant wolf on the edge of hearing. Once a big cat yowled in the night. Mackiernan said it had to have been a snow leopard. The cold crept up from the frozen earth through the felted sleeping mats the Kazak had sold them. Night became something Bessac hoped only to sleep through.

Toward dawn, Leonid yawned and began to blow on the coals of the last night's fire. The fire woke slowly. First it was a diffuse red glow in the darkness, lighting Leonid's face brighter each time he blew. When the heat began to snap at the air, Leonid laid a small handful of grass and twigs on the fire, followed quickly by a large sprinkling of dry camel dung. In Bessac's mind, the interminable night ended and another day began as the fire took the dung and leapt into flame.

The canned jam lasted almost to the border. They were still munching the Kazak fried bread the women had made for them in Timurlik; it got harder every day, but they learned to let it dissolve slowly. The tobacco was finished, but there were the butts they had saved. Zvansov, sitting by the fire, broke open the butts and rolled them into new cigarettes for them. Leonid flaked the rough tea off the bricks of black Chinese tea they had bought in Timurlik and boiled it for hours, thick with rough sugar. The water boiled only minutes after setting it on the fire, but Leonid let it boil on and on. If they had enough, he'd replenish the water, letting it moisten the air. Mackiernan demonstrated their altitude by sticking his hand in the boiling water. It didn't even burn.

They did not descend below sixteen thousand feet for forty days. The lack of moisture left their cuticles and lips bleeding. Dried hunks of blood came up when they blew their noses. They could not get enough water to drink, so they kept the tea on to boil whenever they were in the tent. Unable to bathe, they all developed boils that had to be lanced throughout the trek. Their diet, composed mostly of wild game shot by Zvansov, left them with scurvy, bleeding gums, and dreams of fresh vegetables. Bessac's teeth grew loose in their sockets, and the Russians lost a few.

Another worry was simply finding their way. Following the instructions of the Kazak—Mackiernan's maps were blank for parts of the trip—they had already crossed three passes. They were told to look for grave mounds. The first pass was called Kalibek and was named for the man who lay at the top of the pass, beneath a mound of stones. On the treeless, shrubless plateau that mound was visible from miles away, marking the pass they trekked toward. The graves, always on high passes, were the trail markers. A week later, they found the mound of Kasbek, and finally they went east from there to find the mound of Abul Kasim, in another notch between the mountains. At Timurlik, the Kazak told them that the mounds were the graves of Kazak who had died on the return journey from raids on the Tibetans. Some died from wounds, some from altitude or cold or lack of food. Following the dead Kazak, they made their way into Tibet.

In the hour before dawn, the men sat snuffling around the fire, breathing in the water in the fire-warmed air, loudly sipping their first cup of tea of the day. They rubbed butter into their cracked and bleeding hands, into their lips and noses. They rubbed boot oil into their precious boots. If there was anything to be said, it was said now, since the wind made conversation during most of the day impossible.

One morning, sitting in the dark, Mackiernan told a joke.

"There was this group of twelve guys, and they had gone out to cut lumber in Alaska, and no one wanted to cook. A bit like us here, where Leonid has done the cooking, because no one else will have the job."

Bessac laughed, and then listened in silence as Mackiernan told the first line of the joke in Russian. He went back and forth in English and Russian so everyone could understand, and Zvansov still remembers Mackiernan's joke. "As long as they were in the woods cutting timber, these twelve guys, they cooked every day for themselves. One day a guy said, why don't we make one guy the cook and the rest will work. When we come back hungry, he will have food prepared, and we will be happier. So they thought this was a good idea and agreed on it. They said, how are we going to decide who is going to be cook, because nobody knows how to cook. Ended up, they decided to draw straws, long and short. One guy says, 'Wait a minute, what happens if people say you're not a good cook.' And they say, 'Well if somebody says you're not good at cooking then that man is going to cook as his punishment.'

"So one guy pulled the short straw and he was cooking one day, two days. Nobody said he was a bad cook or anything like that. But that guy got real tired of cooking. The horses were close so he put in a couple of scoops of horseshit into the kettle. He cooked it very well. And there you are. They start to eat the horseshit. In the soup. One man came and said, 'Hey, this one smells and tastes like horseshit. But it's still tasty!'"

Mackiernan watched as Stephan, Leonid, Zvansov, and Bessac laughed and sipped their tea. There was something to be said for just making it here alive. Mackiernan had gotten them this far.

The three White Russians rose up out of their sleeping bags first. There was nothing to put on except their outer coats and boots since they slept in all the rest that they had. As Mackiernan and Bessac sat sipping their tea, still snug in their bags by the fire, there came through the tent the loud sound of frozen meat being chopped with an ax. The camels would carry this fodder for a few hours in blood-soaked bags, until by midday the meat had defrosted enough so that they could eat it. The camels grazed when there was something for them to nibble at around a camp, but that was not enough to sustain them. Both Bessac and Zvansov say that unless the camels had eaten meat, daily, the party would never have made it across the Changthang.

It was still night when they struck the tent and loaded the camels. Zvansov grunted and heaved Mackiernan's heavy bag, the one with the gold, onto the camel and lashed it down; then they loaded the other fourteen. Setting off into the dark, still night Mackiernan led the way as he followed a bright star he had set his eye upon. Bessac walked the first stretch in the dark, striding along beside his camel, which he had named Sam. By then, he knew that if he rode he would get cold sitting atop the swaying camel in the night. Mackiernan rode at the head of the caravan, and Sam followed behind him with Bessac trudging beside. Sam made a gargling noise, and then spit at Bessac, who had just stepped away when he heard the sound; one of Sam's predictable habits. The White Russians straggled along behind, keeping the long train of camels from straying in the night.

In the east, the sky turned a lighter shade of black, then deep indigo. The higher peaks in the east stood out, a jagged black silhouette against the brightening sky. The earth around them remained black without detail for the longest time. A line of light then landed on the highest peaks in the west and slowly moved east toward them. Once the sun rose above the mountains in the east, leaving them at last in light, Bessac clambered up on top of Sam and looked at the bright earth that had emerged from night.

The sun was warm after the long cold night, and those moments before the wind came were the best of the day. The temperature had not risen above freezing in four months. Riding in the first light of day atop his camel, after a long walk through the night, it was almost possible to remember sitting in a warm armchair, in a warm house, longing for the adventure of crossing a vast, empty land by camel caravan. Gazing out at the land, such thoughts often caused an ironic chuckle.

They rode across a yellow plain, yellow with the short fuzz of dead grass. They rode toward a line of twenty-thousand-foot mountains in front of them. No tree, no shrub, nothing interrupted the flat yellow plain of dead grass except the mountains. They rode through a vast tawny valley, across the plain between ranges of mountains until they came to the next line of mountains. Then they rode up through a canyon to a snowbound pass. Once again, they rode down another canyon and out onto another yellow plain, across which they could see the next mountain range, which they would soon have to cross. The adventure of this journey was only anticipated beforehand or recalled afterward—the journey itself was cold, windy, interminable, and mundane.

No human beings had ever settled the Changthang. Few people—from the beginning of time—had ever walked across it. Only a handful of Western explorers had ever come this way. The last was the great Swedish explorer Sven Hedin in 1901. The Mackiernan party rode across this vast world, unpopulated by humans, day after day. They rode their camels and sucked slowly on the hardtack biscuits the Kazak had fried for them. When sleep finally came to Bessac, he dreamed about dead yellow grass, and the bright glittering earth. He kept waiting for the distant white mountains, for the white drifting clouds, for the glaciers, and for the lakes. But every night it was specifically remembered bits of earth and tufts of grass. The Changthang had been burned into a brain blank with cold and exhaustion.

The most outstanding feature of the sixteen-thousand-foot plateau was the wind. It rose every morning just after daylight, building from a barely audible whisper to a deafening roar. They couldn't smoke; they couldn't open their eyes; and they couldn't hear one another because of the wind—ruffling, roaring, and rattling in their ears all day long. They chewed the grit of dust that hovered in the air. They could shriek at one another until noon, brief barked commands, but after that they could hardly hear their own shouting. By then each man was lost in his own world of endurance. They rode on peering out from behind their high collars only occasionally to see if they were behind the lead camel. They forged ahead into the deafening howl, hoping only for the day and the wind to end and night to come again.

Even the interruptions of this monotony became predictable. A herd of animals would appear on the horizon. They waited for the herd to get close enough to decide whether they were antelope, wild ass, or wild yak. If they needed meat, Zvansov climbed on their one horse and rode out to make the kill. The line of camels never ceased its southward march.

The wildlife was unafraid of them since most had never seen men. If it were a herd of wild ass, the animals sometimes ran rings around the caravan, inspecting them. One curious male darted in close to the line of camels, its nose raised in the air, sniffing. The curiosity died quickly if Zvansov shot one of the herd to feed the camels. At the sudden crack of gunfire, the startled herd would race off into the vast distance, throwing up a cloud of dust.

Several times the line of camels approached a solitary male yak standing still on the plain, apparently unaware of them. These fifteen-hundred-pound bulls were so unaccustomed to men and so unafraid that they simply stood their ground, forcing the caravan to go around them.

One afternoon coming upon such a solitary yak, Zvansov rode up and shot it in the chest, a clean heart shot, and the black beast dropped and thrashed about briefly. It was far too big to take much of the meat with them. Zvansov had shot the yak for its skin, hoping to make new soles for his boots, but the hide proved too tough to cut. After taking a few of the best cuts of meat, he left the yak in the trail of the caravan. The scarlet steaks, hung from the pommel of his saddle, were flopping about as Zvansov galloped in with a brilliant smile on his face. The black dot of the yak was still visible the next day when they climbed up a mountain valley and headed up over the next pass. They could see the tower of vultures circling above, preparing for a second day's feeding.

Many days the wind blew so sharply that by late afternoon they couldn't carry on. They looked for a camp with some grass and rarely found it. They looked for a camp with snow to melt, having at one point forgotten that water ran in streams. They looked day after day for someplace to camp that possessed some of what they needed to survive, but never found grass, fuel, and water together at a single site.

When they found a suitable place, they dumped the loads off the camels and struggled to erect the tent in the gale. Inside, with the tent flapping loudly around them, they had a cigarette and tea. That was a moment they relished.

If it was a radio night—and Bessac recalls that Mackiernan made contact at least a few times a week—Mackiernan encoded a brief message and tapped it out in Morse code, while Zvansov rhythmically turned the crank on the radio's generator. There were a number of alternative possible radio contact times, during which the CIA, whether he broadcast or not, always listened for Mackiernan. While Zvansov cranked and Mackiernan tapped out the message or scribbled down an incoming one, Frank read *War and Peace* under the glow of the lantern. Leonid boiled the meat for dinner, and outside Stephan hacked up meat to feed the starving camels. The sound of the turning crank, the boiling meat, and the hacking outside became part of a nightly ritual. Once or twice Mackiernan shared news from the radio with Bessac.

"Washington says we should take care on the way into Tibet. No law except God and bandits until we drop down below the 34th parallel."

After the radio transmission, they would eat boiled wild ass and rice, or boiled antelope and rice. Then they waited for sleep and listened to the camels chewing outside the tent in the abrupt silence that came with sunset. Little broke the pattern of their journey. Things that did were memorable. Around April 20, Mackiernan stopped his camel moments after the morning sun finally hit them. He scrambled down and waited for Bessac and the rest of the party to reach him. He indicated that all of the camels should kneel down. He called Bessac over to him, and with one of the camels sheltering them he shouted to Bessac.

"You can head off this way toward the west, with Stephan and Leonid. No need for you to go through Lhasa with me. You can go through western Tibet to Kashmir. I'll take Vasili with me through Lhasa."

Bessac says that he did not get into an argument with Mackiernan about this outrageous request.

"Where is the radio going, Mac?"

"With me."

"I'm not going to argue about this Mac, it's a waste of time. I could tell you that I don't think we should split the party if we are going to all make it out alive. But let's keep it simple. Where the radio goes, I go."

Bessac never knew what prompted Mackiernan to attempt to send him off on his own through western Tibet. He doubted that he and the two White Russians could have found their way without Mackiernan and his maps to guide them. When Bessac flatly refused the idea, Mackiernan just frowned and rolled his eyes. They all got back on their camels, and the caravan moved on across the Changthang. This strange episode was only one of numerous such incidents, noticed by everyone in the expedition during the last week before they reached the first Tibetan nomad camp. In that last week, Mackiernan changed. Zvansov noticed it. He remembers, "A few days before the Tibetan border, he acted strange. You know, I thought it was high altitude. You cannot talk much. Just walking. Everybody gets strange with altitude."

Bessac wondered about Mackiernan's mental stability. Ever since Mackiernan had tried to open up to Bessac at Timurlik, he hadn't spoken about his problems again.

One afternoon the wind died down early. As the last light of day passed over the vast plain, the surrounding ring of peaks on the horizon turned deep yellow, a golden fence encircling them, almost as if they had arrived at the center of the world. After they unpacked the camels, Mackiernan pulled out his pistol, stuck it under his belt, and stalked out to a boulder twenty yards away from camp. He sat there with his gun in his hand for nearly an hour watching everything carefully, not looking at anyone, not moving. The rest of the party knew to leave him alone and went about the business of making camp. As the sky turned to indigo and the peaks to scarlet, the last golden light left the vast plain. Only after the Milky Way stood above them did Mackiernan wrap his great coat around himself, stand up, put his revolver away, and return to the tiny scurrying circle of life around the tent.

There are hints, and circumstantial evidence, of what may have been bothering Mackiernan. He had a radio and was in regular communication with the State Department in Washington. He may have left a radio with Osman Bator, or Nationalist troops near the Kazak may have communicated his news to the United States. If Mackiernan learned about the massacre at Lake Barkol, which happened sometime around the middle of April, he would have been terribly upset. His covert aid to the Kazak, so publicly blown in Chinese and U.S. newspapers on January 30, could well have provoked the massacre.

The best-known account of the massacre was published in the November 1954 issue of *National Geographic,* in a story entitled "How the Kazak Fled to Freedom." Here is the tale of the massacre by a Kazak leader Sultan Sherif, who eventually escaped across Tibet to Kashmir, as told to Milton J. Clark.

During the fall and winter of 1949–50 the Kazak had dealt with the Communists, asking guarantees of religious freedom, preservation of tribal customs, and liberty to travel at will within Sinkiang. But the new regime let it be known that *it* would set the terms of Kazak "cooperation."

Many of the Kazak made long journeys to reach the Barkol council. Then a winter storm killed much livestock; the sheep, which were lambing, could not be moved to shelter. It was the kind of time of which the Kazak say, "Ice is our bed and snow our blanket."

By March of 1950 the panorama at the rallying place must have been cause for pride and even reassurance. Kazak by the thousands populated the broad valley, still white with snow. Tents were strewn for miles across the landscape, the sons' placed around those of the fathers.

Within sight of Sultan Sherif's tent door were assembled at least 15,000 people, 60,000 fat-tailed sheep, 12,000 horses, 7,000 head of cattle, and more than 1,000 camels.

On March 28 in that Year of the Tiger a congress of 1,000 Kazak leaders and family heads cast their vote to leave the golden cradle of their birth and make for the southern passes that led toward India.

A week later the council set up an autonomous Kazak government, naming Janim Khan governor and Osman Bator commander
in chief of the fighting men. Neither leader survived long to exercise
his new authority. At Barkol the threat of tribal destruction hung,
like the Damoclean sword, over every tent, every horseman, every
mother, every infant heir. Yet the Kazak clung stubbornly to the
customs and ritual of daily life. The herders' work, the elders' prayers,
the children's play—all went on as usual.

In mid-April the Communists swept down in a surprise attack on
the Barkol encampment. Brief warning by outpost sentries scarcely
gave women and children time to strike tents and head for the hills,
driving flocks and herds before them.

Puppet troops in quilted drab poured into the valley in trucks,
armored vehicles, and on horseback, heavily armed and plentifully
supplied with ammunition.

For the spirited Kazak, used to unequal odds, even such formi-
dable armament held no new terrors. Shouting battle cries and riding
at full gallop, the warriors struck hard in righteous anger. "One shot,
one dead enemy," states the Kazak standard of marksmanship. But
against an enemy equipped with modern arms, there could be no hope
of victory. Kazak fighting men died by the hundreds.

"Janibeg!" called out the chiefs at last, using one of the war cries
that are old-time heroes' names. "Break off battle and flee!" Southward streamed the shocked, enraged, depleted company of tribesmen.

Sultan Sherif told me that 12,600 of the more than 15,000 of his
people assembled at Barkol were killed, captured, or dispersed.

Osman managed to escape the attack and fled south along the route
he had sent his old friend Mackiernan on six months earlier. Zvansov
says that about one hundred of the two hundred White Russians—
from his old group the Eskadrone—survived the massacre, and they
too set off for Tibet. It is possible that news of this attack reached
Mackiernan in the last week of his journey to Tibet. He may have
wondered if the CIA had used these people and then left them to die.
He may have wondered what role he played in all this.

It was probably his own certitude that came crashing down upon
him there at the heart of the Tibetan Plateau, when a feeble radio

message finally conveyed to him the price of using people as pawns. Sometimes they are slaughtered.

The Kazak massacre could well have caused even Mackiernan's hubris to crumble. A man alone in a wilderness so vast it belittles all human motivations, facing the fact that he was wrong. Worse than being wrong; other people were paying with their lives for his failure. This is the most likely explanation of why Mackiernan sat there, gun in hand.

Bessac had been through this crisis much earlier. As early as 1947 he wanted to learn what Asia looked like when not viewed through U.S. government motivations—though to what degree he achieved that freedom remains unknown.

From what we are allowed to know of Mackiernan he apparently only began to question his use of his family as well as whole tribes and peoples for the benefit of the United States in the last days before he arrived in Tibet. There in the heart of the Tibetan wilderness some part of Mackiernan may have had a bloody glimpse into the future, toward the ultimate result of the policies that guided his actions. Perhaps as he sat there the Himalayan panorama before him faded—replaced by the roofline of Saigon. Perhaps his frozen skin suddenly warmed and a tropical sweat rolled down his back. Perhaps for a moment Mackiernan stood on the roof of the U.S. Embassy as America evacuated Vietnam.

Did he feel the heavy gun in the hands of his successor? A CIA agent, gun in hand, beating back Vietnamese who were loyal to America. In their eyes the terror of defeated pawns now certain that the victorious Vietnamese Communist will murder them. Pawns clawing their way up the ladder on the roof, fighting for a place on the last U.S. helicopter out of Vietnam.

MORNING

APRIL 29, 1950

There were signs that they had descended from the highest part of their trip. Each day the temperature grew warmer. The frozen stream they camped alongside the previous night had running water at its center when they left camp. Since they had left Timurlik two months earlier Bessac hadn't heard the sound of running water. They even stumbled upon remnants of an old camp—an abandoned fire pit and mounds of goat dung.

As they headed south that morning, Bessac saw the first patches of green fuzz on one tawny mountainside. They were fast approaching the edge of the frozen world. It was sunny all morning long as they walked downhill. The wind no longer seemed as strong, and the air they breathed seemed a little thicker. The worst of the Changthang was now finally behind them.

That morning, Mackiernan mentioned it was his thirty-seventh birthday, and there had been some joking as they walked on into Tibet, everyone's spirits lifted. Mackiernan dropped his guard a fraction and made one of his few remarks about his work to Bessac: "Well, we've communicated with the Tibetans and they know we're coming." Mackiernan went even a little further than that. According to Bessac, "He implied that he had a mission in Lhasa . . . he knew that I had made the assumption that it was somehow to covertly assist Tibetan independence. That's what he had just been trying to do with the Kazak. I think he was . . . sent to Tibet to do the same thing. I had the impression that he was sent to Tibet to somehow covertly arrange military assistance for the Tibetans."

At about 11 A.M., Zvansov first pointed out to Bessac the black spot on the horizon. Bessac watched it as they drew closer. It did not appear to be a herd of yak, or a herd of gazelle, or a herd of antelope. It was large, dark, and unmoving, unlike anything they had yet seen.

Bessac rode up alongside Mackiernan on his camel. The wind had not reached full roar, so they were still able to hear one another.

"It's a tent," Mackiernan shouted. "I think it's our first Tibetans!"

As they drew closer, Bessac could make out a black yak-wool tent, sprawled low over the earth like a spider's web, big enough for twenty people inside.

Zvansov came up to speak to Mackiernan.

"Douglas knew I was five years in that turmoil with Kazak, fighting against Communists and so on. I well knew the situation between Kazak and all Asians and how they are. Whatever I did, normally Douglas would follow me. Like brothers. If I said, 'Douglas we go this way and we do this and this,' he listened to me.

"That brotherhood ended when we put up the binoculars and see the Tibetan teepee the first time. Those Tibetan tents, whatever you call them.

"I said to Douglas, 'Let's go up there, on that high plateau above without them seeing us. We go around that way. We get the camels to lay down and make camp up there and we watch these Tibetans. Then we send someone to contact them with a white flag, one man, and then later we can walk slowly up to their tents.'

"'No,' Mackiernan replied, 'I don't want to do that. Let's do what I tell you to do.'"

Zvansov shakes his head as he remembers the dispute with Mackiernan. "I always been okay with him, always together. But this time he is strangely separated." Mackiernan was adamant.

"No, you got to listen to me. Let's go right to the tent and park our camels there and lay them down next to the Tibetans and put up our tents."

Bessac had learned long ago to simply not ask questions. If Mackiernan thought there was something in that Russian conversation that Bessac needed to know, he would have told him. Mackiernan didn't think Bessac needed to know that he was ignoring the advice he had always before relied on, so he did not tell him about this conversation with Zvansov, and the whole group marched toward the Tibetans.

As they drew closer to the Tibetan tent, Bessac and Mackiernan walked together alone, half a mile in front of the caravan. Striding downhill with Mackiernan toward the Tibetan tent, it felt as if they had reached a land where spring could come. Bessac and Mackiernan looked at each other and smiled with deeply mixed feelings. They both knew that the next few moments were critical. They felt the camaraderie of men not just in an adventure but at war.

"We didn't know, but one or both of us could be shot," Bessac remembers.

The Tibetans noticed their arrival and sent a beautiful young girl out to parlay with them. The two men approached her slowly, showing their empty hands, though Mackiernan's rifle was in a holster on the side of the horse that trailed on its lead behind them. It was such a wonderful shock to see another human.

The girl stood in the sun with them, her flock of sheep behind her, and Bessac listened to Mackiernan try to talk with her. He watched her smile coyly at Mackiernan, and took a deep breath and relaxed. They had at last made it across the desert, the Kunlun Mountains, and the Changthang plateau into Tibet. It was hard to believe but they had actually made it here alive.

STRANGE AND
TERRIBLE THINGS
SHEGAR-HUNGLUNG, THE TIBETAN BORDER
33.40 NORTH, 87.20 WEST
2PM, APRIL 29, 1950

The three White Russians—Vasili Zvansov, Leonid, and Stephan—thought Mackiernan had selected a great campsite. For once, everything they needed was in one place. The small stream was not even frozen. Plenty of dried yak dung for their fire lay scattered about. The camels smelled the plentiful grazing and grunted as the men coaxed them to kneel. The tent was unloaded first. Bessac and Mackiernan struggled to erect it in the wind. As soon as the tent was up, Zvansov unloaded a crate of guns and brought it inside.

The Tibetan girl watched the proceedings and then strolled back to her tent as they carried on. Bessac volunteered to follow her to the camp of their new neighbors and try to establish relations. Mackiernan stood in the open tent flap watching Bessac walk toward the nomads' tent. Zvansov crouched beside him in the tent, unlimbered a gun, loaded it, and stacked it with several others.

Zvansov glanced up from the guns when Mackiernan said, "Bessac won't make it."

It seemed a strange thing to say. Zvansov asked, "What you mean?"

Mackiernan replied, as he continued watching Bessac walk away, "Mr. Bessac is going to die today. I just have this feeling."

They were still unloading the camels and setting up camp when the first bullets began to rip through the camp. Mackiernan and the Russians looked around in terrified bewilderment, until one of the camels was hit and began to writhe and squeal in pain. Then the men dropped to the earth. In a flurry of diving and crawling, they struggled for cover as they craned about trying to spot the shooters.

The shooting did not come from the tent to which Bessac had gone, but from the direction of another group of tents, tents they had not even seen. A party of horsemen had ridden up quite close to them from that camp, while they were distracted unloading the camels.

Two camels lay dead by the time the men crawled into the scant safety offered by crates and bags within the tent. Outside, two still-loaded camels squealed in terror as they rose to their feet. Another camel was suddenly hit and thrashed against the tent, dying before it fell hard. Though their only horse ran at the first shot, some of the camels did not move; they stood in a bewildered circle around the tent as bursts of gunfire continued.

Through holes in the tent the men glimpsed the Tibetans slowly encircling them. Most of the shooters gathered thirty yards from the front of the tent. Some crouched on the ground, while others fired from horseback.

Despite protests, the Russians obeyed Mackiernan's order not to shoot back. Finally, Zvansov had another idea. He shouted at Mackiernan.

"Let's cut some white cloth and wave it out the door!"

Mackiernan, stooping beside him, peered out the tent flap and nodded his agreement.

Almost as quickly as Zvansov could say the words, he cut a swatch

The Mackiernan brothers with skis: (*left to right*) Malcolm, Stuart, Angus, Douglas, Duncan. Massachusetts, circa 1940. (Courtesy of Duncan Mackiernan family)

Kazak Yurts and horsemen, Tekes Valley, Sinkiang, circa 1926. Appeared in *National Geographic,* October 1927, p. 412, William J. Morden/ Morden-Clark Asiatic Expedition.

Owen and Eleanor Lattimore at their wedding, Peking, March 4, 1926. (Courtesy of David Lattimore)

Margaret Lyons (Pegge Parker) on a parachute jump with the U.S. Army, Paratroop School, Fort Benning, Georgia, circa 1943–1944. (Courtesy of U.S. Army Signal Corps, *Sunday Times-Herald,* April 4, 1948)

(*opposite*) Qali Beg, the Kazak chief Douglas Mackiernan asked to pass intelligence from Sinkiang, through Tibet, to India. Photograph circa 1952, in Kashmir, by Milton J. Clark. Appeared in *National Geographic,* November 1954.

Osman Bator, near Peitaishan, Sinkiang, July 1947—on a white horse in the center. (Courtesy of Pegge Parker—Margaret Lyons Mackiernan Hlavacek, *Sunday News,* October 19, 1947)

Vasili Zvansov, circa 1950. (Courtesy of Vasili and Alex Zvansov)

Prince De and his shortwave radio, Inner Mongolia. (Photograph by Walter Bosshard © 2002 Artists Rights Society (ARS), New York/ ProLitteris, Zurich)

(*opposite*) Douglas S. Mackiernan and Pegge Parker. U.S. consulate, Tihwa, Sinkiang, July 1947. (Courtesy of Pegge Parker—Margaret Lyons Mackiernan Hlavacek)

The brothers Mackiernan in World Weather's Radio House at the Green Lantern, Stoughton, Massachusetts, circa 1950: (*front*) Stuart, (*middle*) Malcolm, (*back*) Duncan. (Courtesy of Duncan Mackiernan family)

The gate in the walled city of Tihwa, through which Mackiernan and Bessac passed as they left in September 1949: as it was circa 1926. Appeared in *National Geographic*, October 1927, p. 419, William J. Morden/Morden-Clark Asiatic Expedition.

U.S. Air Force General Albert F. Hegenberger, head of AFOAT-1 in 1949. (Courtesy of National Archives and Records Administration)

Camel caravan and tents, Altai Mountains, Sinkiang, circa 1926. Appeared in *National Geographic,* October 1927, p. 428, William J. Morden/Morden-Clark Asiatic Expedition.

(*next page*) His Holiness the 14th Dalai Lama of Tibet, circa 1950. A photograph sent to the Mackiernan family by the Tibetan Regency. (Courtesy of Duncan Mackiernan family)

of white cloth from the double-layered canvas tent, jabbed it on a stick, and waved it out the tent flap. The Tibetans stopped firing as soon as they saw the white flag. With only the wind now attacking the tent, Zvansov spoke again.

"Doug, we got to go out there. One of us got to go out there, while the rest cover him from here with the machine gun."

Mackiernan replied tersely. "No. I do not want to do that. Do what I tell you to do."

"And what's that?"

"We're all going out together. Leave all the weapons inside the tent, and put your hands up and let's walk out."

"That's crazy!"

"We're gonna do it my way this time. No guns."

An instant cold sweat broke out all over Zvansov when he heard the conviction in Mackiernan's voice. In absolute disbelief he listened to Mackiernan repeat the order to Stephan and Leonid. If the American government hoped to negotiate a covert arms deal with the Tibetans, Mackiernan might have been under orders not to shoot these potential new allies, no matter what. Alternatively it is possible that Mackiernan was so distraught about the massacre at Lake Barkol that he simply refused to use a gun. In the heat of the moment Mackiernan offered no explanation of his order to the Russians.

He stood up inside the wavering tent and looked down at them. His hard, penetrating stare said everything. The Russians looked at him, then at one another, and slowly rose to their feet behind him.

They raised their hands above their heads exactly as Mackiernan had ordered. Leonid and Stephan spread out in a line right beside Mackiernan and walked behind their leader, directly toward the Tibetans gathered approximately thirty yards in front of the tent.

As they walked toward them the Tibetans watched them closely, and a few of their guns sagged downward. Mackiernan continued to walk straight toward the Tibetans with his hands above his head. Zvansov began to sidle slowly toward a few larger rocks off to the left. He slowed his pace and held back, though he kept his arms up and walked with all the rest.

Zvansov looked over Mackiernan's shoulders, right down the barrels of the guns pointed at them. Mackiernan had the white flag in his hand and held it high as he walked steadily, but slowly, toward the Tibetans. The scrap of cloth whipped in the wind. The Tibetan in front stepped back a pace.

Waves of panic and fear swept over Zvansov. They were now just ten yards from the line of Tibetan gunmen. He thought to himself, "Douglas has gone crazy. He is going to get us all killed."

The sound of the guns startled Zvansov into instant action, though he no more heard the guns than he took the time to think about what he was doing. Everything suddenly accelerated, yet somehow seemed to slow down at the same time. There was no more fear. No more doubts.

He ducked low to the earth and turned sideways to the gunmen. As if his life depended upon it, he ran two steps one way, and then whirled and zigzagged off just as fast two steps in another direction. The world spun around him.

He heard Leonid scream one word in Russian.

"Momma!"

Dodging the bullets with all his strength, Zvansov's ears heard and his eyes saw—but he felt nothing. He saw shards of twisting sky, clods of turning earth, and the jerking bodies of Mackiernan and the others as they fell against the ground.

All his mind and body focused on being the smallest target imaginable. With his chest squeezed down and his body crouched low darting one way and then another in the thin air, it was impossible to breathe enough to run for more than a few seconds. After he had given it everything, his body involuntarily straightened and gasped for a lungful of air. His friends were down, and all the gunmen were now shooting at him alone.

He sucked in one breath on the run and then ducked down again as he threw himself toward the guns in the tent. When he tried to go back down his leg wouldn't bend and he stumbled. The next step seemed all right. Yet on the third step, his leg buckled, and he fell directly in front of the tent. The Tibetans suddenly stopped firing. Zvansov looked at his leg and was amazed to see blood on his knee. Stunned, he reached to touch the wound. He had felt absolutely nothing and still felt nothing; there was simply no pain.

After a few seconds he crawled inside the tent and grabbed the loaded machine gun.

Did he speak aloud or only think to himself? "Jesus Christ, this is it." As soon as the words formed themselves he was thinking again. Kill enough to frighten off the others. Then he would grab a horse and ride on into Tibet. He couldn't go back now, the Communists would get him. He saw himself in his mind's eye doing these things as he stared out through the sights of the machine gun at the men who had killed his friends. Then he saw Bessac walking slowly and shouting at the Tibetans. And that was when he recognized that the Tibetans were not looking at him but were instead riveted on Bessac.

As he watched the incredible drama unfold he wavered between opening fire and simply watching. His leg now started to hurt, and he knew he could not survive alone. He knew he had to kill as many of the Tibetans as he could if they were to get away, but he also knew he needed Bessac to escape alive. If he opened fire, the Tibetans might shoot Bessac.

When Bessac knelt in front of the Tibetans, and they didn't shoot him, Zvansov began to think there was another way. He watched closely as they tied Bessac's hands and headed for the tent. He realized that if he surrendered now, they probably wouldn't kill him. So he threw the machine gun away before they reached him. The Tibetans walked over and grabbed the gun. They gathered around him, shoving and staring down at him. One poked at Zvansov's pistol, tucked under his belt. Zvansov handed it over. They wanted to know how to shoot it, so he showed them.

After he gave lessons on how to use his Soviet T.T. pistol, he picked up a few rocks. He put one down and said, "Lhasa." He placed another down some distance away and pointed at himself. Like Bessac, he began to chant the mantra, "Dalai Lama. Lhasa."

The dirty-faced men had their long hair up in braids, wrapped around their heads. As they watched this pantomime their wide leathery foreheads wrinkled in curiosity. One of the beardless faces shouted at the others. Sharp words were hurled back and forth. The man who had taken the pistol stood up and left to join the rest of the Tibetans searching through the camel loads. The remaining Tibetans with Zvansov glanced briefly at him and then turned to join the others.

Zvansov had a burst of hope. Maybe they had understood. Maybe they would not kill them. As hope flared in Zvansov, the Tibetans moved on to break open the boxes and cases. One of the Geiger counters turned on and clicked a few times before they smashed it against the ground. The gold bars provoked some shoving, before the bars and biscuits disappeared into the folds in the robes of many different people.

Twenty yards away, Bessac was trying to see who it was that had been killed, but his captors had taken his glasses. He suddenly recognized that the foot in front of him was Mackiernan's. With his hands tied behind him he hobbled on his knees to get a closer look. He had to be certain. When he saw the look on Mackiernan's face, he wanted to turn away, but he could not.

Mackiernan's open eyes and mouth revealed nothing but disbelief—to travel this far, only to be shot by the first Tibetans he met. And yet within his eyes there was peace. Bessac's own eyes stung at how honestly he envied Mackiernan that peace. Tears came as he thought, "I should have died. Not Mac. He had so much to do. I should have died."

One of the Tibetans shoved Bessac aside and began to search Mackiernan's pockets. The Tibetan found a piece of fried bread that Mackiernan liked to tuck away in his pockets to suck on during the long days of travel. The Tibetan pulled it out and jammed it between Mackiernan's bloody teeth. Then he pulled it out and offered it to Bessac. Bessac shrank back and the Tibetan laughed.

The Tibetan again jammed the biscuit between the teeth of Mackiernan, and then gleefully popped it in his own mouth, watching Bessac as he ate. When the Tibetan got up to walk away Bessac was still staring at Mackiernan's face. He watched in horror as the jaw sagged slowly open to the Tibetan sky above.

Bessac had no more time for the dead. He moved to help the living. He put a tourniquet on Zvansov's knee, and then he had to help the Tibetans capture and load the camels because they were afraid of them.

When the Tibetans picked up Zvansov and helped him toward a horse, he used a tent pole as a crutch and made sure to walk past his friends, lying as they had fallen beside the stream. Now that the sun was moving toward sunset rime ice had formed on the edges of the brook. Blood dripping from the dead men's gaping mouths had already frozen. In the golden light of the afternoon Zvansov prodded the bodies with his crutch. Though his knee hurt he bent over and touched Stephan's body. It was already stiff.

When the Tibetans hoisted him onto a horse he wrapped the green down sleeping bag Mackiernan had given him around his leg; it was soon soaked with blood. As Zvansov rode out of camp, Bessac joined him. Some Tibetans stayed back in camp looting and loading goods on the remaining camels.

Neither Bessac nor Zvansov ever looked back. They did not see the Tibetans pull out their swords and behead Douglas Mackiernan and Stephan and Leonid. They did not see them load the heads onto the last remaining camel. Within half an hour, a tower of vultures circled above the site of the abandoned camp.

Then Bessac suddenly remembered that it was Mackiernan's birthday. He thought about Mongolian sky burial. Neither cremation nor burial was common in Tibet or Mongolia. There was no wood on the steppe for cremation. For eight or nine months of the year, the earth was too frozen to allow burial. Tibetan Buddhists and Mongols consider it auspicious to feed the remains of the dead to scavenging birds. They call it a sky burial.

As they left the three corpses at Shegar-Hunglung, Bessac consoled himself that sky burial was not such a bad thing. Without his glasses now, he followed blindly behind the wounded Zvansov as the captives were taken into Tibet.

WHEN THEY HEARD MACKIERNAN WAS DEAD

Mother Mackiernan woke up early on April 29, 1950, at about the time the family believes that Douglas Mackiernan was killed. Stuart Mackiernan shakes his head in amazement as he tells the story:

"I was living across the back meadow, in my own house with my wife, Kathleen. And it was so early in the morning, when she came running across the meadow. She was crying and going on, and at first I couldn't make out what she was going on about.

"Then I started to make sense of her words.

"'Dougie's dead. Dougie's dead.' I could just make that out between her sobbing and tears.

"'Whad'ya mean, Mom? Dougie's dead? Who told you that?'

"'I just know, he's dead. Dougie's dead.'

"It must have been on Dougie's birthday, you know, that same day he got shot. And I don't know how she knew, but she did. No radio message or nothing. The State Department wouldn't know anything for a month, and they wouldn't tell us anything till July. But there was Mom, coming across the field in tears on Dougie's birthday. Crying her eyes out. Strangest thing I ever saw." Stuart's own recollection about his brother's death complicates things. He says that the story told by Zvansov and Bessac is not what the family was told by government officials in 1950.

"There are two different stories. The official story is that they came out unarmed and then the Tibetans shot them down. And he was buried. But we were told that he was shot because he came out with a gun—they shot him because he had a gun. Then there is the other story—the one where they were shooting in the distance. That is not the story that we were told."

The White Russians who survived the massacre at Lake Barkol eventually escaped along the same path to Tibet that Mackiernan had taken. In Lhasa, eight months after the shoot-out, they met a doctor.

> They . . . learned about Mackiernan's death from a doctor in Lhasa who had buried the body and who treated Zvansov for his wounds. The doctor heard that Mackiernan had been shot because he was carrying about thirty bars of gold eight inches long [about one inch thick] with him.

The news of Mackiernan's death reached Erwin Kontescheny—the driver in Tihwa who had escaped with Consul Paxton—three months after the shoot-out, at his new job in Tehran. He recalled the sharpshooter he knew on the drive to Peitaishan and could not believe that Mackiernan was dead.

"I was convinced that this was one more miracle by Mr. Mackiernan. It was what they call a cover story. They tell you he is dead, so he can go and do something even more amazing. I was sure he could not be dead. Not that man. He is too clever."

When the news of Mackiernan's death was given to her in June 1950 Mackiernan's wife was not told the truth. The State Department and the CIA decided that she had no need to know that he had been beheaded. A State Department employee, whom Pegge believes was Tony Freeman, was sent out to break the edited news of Mackiernan's death to the widow. Even at eighty years of age, she recalls the moment perfectly. He had told the State Department story, but he did it with such kindness.

"Of course, all he said was that there was a shooting, and he was buried on the scene. I was in a state of such terrible shock, because nothing prepared me for this. . . . Douglas, no matter how dangerous the situation, was a survivor. And I had the shock of the news plus the reality—I still had to change diapers and warm bottles."

It was only in 1999, as an eighty-year-old woman, that Mackiernan's widow heard the full truth about her husband's beheading. As the truth settles in after fifty years of living with a well-intentioned lie, Pegge turns to Douglas's clear-eyed daughter, the radiologist Dr. Mary Mackiernan.

There is more Mackiernan in Mary than just the name. This is a women who loves science and says she is a radiologist because radiology uses a tool that never lies. X rays show the truth—a truth that sometimes brings her patients pain and sometimes bring them joy. But the tool is honest. The Mackiernan in her, and her love and respect for the truth, is present when she comforts her mother.

"Listen, compared to what people are doing to people every day today, we should all be so lucky as to be quickly shot and beheaded and left to the open sky."

PART THREE

THROUGH TIBET AND HOME AGAIN

"After the People's Republic was established in China, America . . . did not come forward to recognize Tibet as independent. The courage was not there."

—The Dalai Lama

NOMADS AND GRENADES
ON THE CHANGTHANG PLATEAU
APRIL 30 AND MAY 1, 1950

The Tibetan soldiers who shot Mackiernan dead at point-blank range led the two survivors of the Mackiernan party south toward Lhasa, Tibet. Frank Bessac stumbled on behind the wounded Vasili Zvansov. After a few hours trudging across the plain, Zvansov squinted through the wind and saw black dots on the horizon, just as he had seen through Douglas Mackiernan's binoculars earlier that morning. An hour later, their captors marched them into another nomad encampment.

Three Tibetan mastiffs, one chained at the door of each black tent in the camp, began to bay when the arriving party of camels and horses was still a mile away. The tents were pitched on bald spots in the turf—denuded by thousands of animals—and around them the ground was covered inches deep in goat and sheep dung. The mastiffs, black and gigantic, pawed in the dung and howled.

The captives were not led to the tents. Instead, they were taken to a nearby ditch about twenty feet long and eight feet deep. It looked like an open grave to Bessac and he was terrified when the soldiers ordered them into it—they were herded unwillingly, perhaps to their deaths, despite their pleas. But the prisoners were not shot. A single guard was posted over them and the Tibetans turned their attention to looting.

All the bags were ripped off the surviving camels and gleefully torn open. Bessac convinced the Tibetans with sign language to give them their sleeping kit. After that a free-for-all broke out around the loads. The sugar and raisins were fought over, as were the gold and the guns. The radio, Mackiernan's handmade altimeter, the barometer, the books, and the maps were all churned into the dung, battered and knocked about as the nomads and the soldiers broke open bags grabbing at their haul. Nomad children begged for sweets on the edge of the surging knot of looters. Items were traded back and forth, and haggling soon broke out. Bessac glanced at the scene as he tried to tend Zvansov's wound, wondering what the locals planned to do to them in the ditch once the looting was over.

In the last light of day, herds of goats and sheep were driven into camp. The nomad women tied up the females in long lines. Once the herds were in the milk line, the women shuffled down it from teat to teat, sitting on their low milking stools. As they milked, they craned their heads and cast excited eyes toward the camels and the looting soldiers.

After dark, Bessac lay back and waited for the hours to pass. He waited for death. For the longest time he thought about little except dying. A long time after that the dark shadow of a girl appeared and handed them two bowls of unidentifiable gruel.

When he handed the bowls back to her, he could smell his tobacco on the wind. From the sounds of laughter, too, it seemed the soldiers had discovered more than the cigarettes and had found the last of the Scotch.

He didn't want to sleep, fearing the Tibetans might be waiting for exactly that, and that they would be shot in their sleep. Indeed, a couple of the soldiers did wander over, one with Zvansov's Soviet T.T. pistol in his hand, to look down at them. Despite his fear, he eventually fell asleep. He awakened with a start and a loud ringing in his ears, so shocked he immediately thought, "So this is what it feels like to be dead. Not so bad. And I got here without any pain."

Gradually he realized he was still alive, which meant he had been asleep and was now awake. Tibetans surrounded the ditch. They were yelling and pointing. Bessac crawled out of his sleeping bag and climbed up to the top. A small crater pocked the earth. Several of the yelling Tibetans, who were pointing at the crater in the ground, had grenades in their hands.

From the smell of their breath and the general laughter, it was obvious they were drunk on the Scotch. They had opened the crate of grenades. A lethal combination. When Bessac gestured that they should not play with the grenades, they seemed to get the message. Apparently, they had not been trying to kill them. One of the soldiers even handed him a cigarette in the dark as the others went off in search of more excitement.

In the morning, Bessac found shrapnel from the grenade buried in the ground a few feet from where he had been sleeping. Soldiers invited them into a nomad tent. They were fed more gruel and endless cups of the Tibetan version of tea. The black tea was boiled, and then salt, soda, and butter were added and the whole concoction was churned together. Zvansov hated it. Bessac thought it was surprisingly good, considering. Both made appreciative noises.

As they sipped tea by the fire in the early morning, one of their captors brought out Bessac's bag of tobacco and began to roll a cigarette in a slip of paper that Bessac realized had been torn out of his copy of *War and Peace.* Another solider practiced his English vocabulary.

"Helloo!" he shouted at Bessac. The group of Tibetans in the tent laughed when Bessac replied with the same word.

When he finished rolling the cigarette the soldier handed it to Bessac. It was the same guy who had told him to "kowtow."

Bessac offered a smile in return and was repaid in kind. Maybe the Tibetans didn't intend to kill them. If he could only get himself and Zvansov out of this alive. As he tried to get to know his captors, Bessac learned a name. The man in charge of the soldiers was Tsering Dorjee, the man who had first opened fire on them. Tsering Dorjee.

THE ARROW LETTER, "A MISTAKE"
THE CHANGTHANG, TIBET
MAY 1, 1950

The dot on the horizon was white, not black. As they drew nearer, Zvansov could see that in fact it was a startling white tent covered with swirling blue patterns. A string of rainbow-colored flags fluttered from the top. The tent was not made of the hand-loomed black yak wool as were all they had seen thus far. Nor was it designed like the nomads' tents: those had hovered low to the ground. This tent stood up like a house; it looked almost like an army mess tent, except for the exuberant blue pattern scrolling wildly all over it.

As they rode up, Zvansov heard shouting. Tsering Dorjee, the man Zvansov was certain had started the shooting spree that killed three men and wounded himself, was bent low at the waist in front of a tall, well-dressed man, who was the source of the shouting.

The shouting man grabbed Zvansov's T.T. pistol from the belt of Tsering Dorjee and strode up to Zvansov. He clucked his tongue as he saw the wounded knee.

Zvansov heard again the Tibetan word he had heard so often when people saw his wound.

"Nyingje! Nyingje!"

Abruptly, he thrust the T.T. pistol into Zvansov's hands. When he turned away, leaving Zvansov somewhat bewildered, the shouting continued. Once Bessac arrived, the shouting man rushed up and gave Bessac his own pistol, a fine American-made Colt .45. Then he called over Tsering Dorjee, whom he had been berating, and the man who had shot Mackiernan kneeled in front of Bessac. The shouting man made it clear that Bessac was free to shoot Tsering Dorjee.

Bessac stood there with the gun in his hand in absolute shocked amazement. The shouting man pulled out from his robe a scroll of red cloth wrapped around an arrow. He bowed as he presented it. Bessac accepted it and gingerly unrolled the scroll. It was covered with a fine Tibetan cursive script in black ink.

Though the scroll was unreadable to Bessac, all around him the soldiers silently scrambled forward to bow their heads to the scroll. They pushed forward, bent low, and touched their heads to it. They unfurled their pigtails, normally wrapped around their heads, as they rushed forward with their tongues out—a Tibetan sign of honor. Some dropped to their knees. Bessac watched the reaction sweep through the Tibetans around him. The man shouted at everyone who had been traveling with Bessac and Zvansov. No one replied. All eyes were cast to the ground.

Bessac drew a circle around each of his eyes. His glasses were produced. For the first time in two days, the Tibetan horizon snapped into view: the bright red scroll, fluttering in the wind; the bowed heads; the fine tent stretched taut in the sunlight.

Bessac began to understand.

He could not understand the words, but nevertheless he began to comprehend the situation. The scroll was an order from the Dalai Lama's government, alerting the Tibetan border guards to expect the arrival of distinguished American guests, an order to escort them to Lhasa as quickly as possible. All Tibetans were ordered to provide horses, food, and porters, as the party required. The letter said they were important state guests.

The letter was two days late. The *da-yig,* or arrow letter, with the urgent government instructions to let them pass, had simply been late. Yet standing there, with the red scroll fluttering in his hands, Bessac already understood. Three men were dead because of a mistake.

THE U.S. EMBASSY
NEW DELHI, INDIA
MAY 2, 1950

The Indian clerk clipped the item from the paper without much notice. The American supervisor added only one note before he sent it off to the State Department in Washington: "Press item said to be from Peiping Radio Broadcast."

PEKING CLAIMS 5,000 CASUALTIES IN SINKIANG

HONG KONG, MAY 2—Peking Communist radio reported last night that 5,000 "bandits" under American direction had been killed, wounded or captured by Communist units in Sinkiang province. The "bandit" leaders were described as "chiefs of Kuomintang remnants" directed by "American imperialist agent Douglas S. Mackiernan." The radio said they led 7,000 men to Chensi County, north of Sinkiang, to undertake robbery and sabotage following the Communist occupation of Sinkiang. Mr. Mackiernan was formerly U.S. vice-consul at Sinkiang.

Few people in Washington could look at this story and make the simple summary. Mackiernan was dead, and Osman Bator was on the run. Fifty years later, the U.S. government still has not released much information about this massacre. Was it five thousand Kazak killed when America abandoned them, as reported by the Chinese, or twelve thousand as reported by *National Geographic*? Kazak living in exile today do not talk about numbers. They talk instead about a hill of bones.

Aynur Caksýlýk, a young Kazak woman, writes that after the massacre at Barkol it was a time of fighting. Osman fled south toward Tibet and was eventually captured in January 1951. Other Kazak tried to flee north into the MPR. Aynur, a daughter of a survivor of these dark days, assumes that everyone knows the nightmare that haunts the scattered refugees, like her, who live in Turkey, Germany, and Kazakhstan.

> There is a valley called Bulgun, in the Altai Mountains, and the border runs through it. Mongols call it *Hasag Yias,* which means Kazak's Bones. In those terrible days as the Kazak fled Lake Barkol the Russians and the Mongols trapped them at the border, and then bombed and strafed them. Even now it is impossible to walk in Bulgun because of all the skeletons. One mound there, a small hill, by the river, is called Kazak's Bones, because that is what it is made of.
>
> But this is unknown in your country?

SHENTSA DZONG, TIBET
MAY 6, 1950

Since Bessac had Mackiernan's binoculars back as well as his glasses, he could identify the small white dots on the horizon as houses. Two days after meeting the Tibetan government representative they arrived at their first Tibetan village.

The steep two-thousand-foot drop to the village had Zvansov moaning in pain. His knee had swollen to twice its normal size. As they descended, Bessac saw high snow-covered mountain ranges on the horizon to the north, south, and east. The General—that is what Bessac had decided to call their shouting savior—led the two survivors past the crowd of curious Tibetans, who had gathered to watch the caravan come down off the windy plain.

The houses were built of dried mud and cut rocks. They were whitewashed, and some were decorated with slashes of red mud. The color was splashed down the sides of the houses from the roofs after the whitewashing. The few tiny windows had only paper glued in wooden lattices—there was no glass in this village. The roofs were lined with precious bundles of thorn, and even a few pieces of wood, the first wood they had seen since Timurlik. People gawked from upstairs windows and doorways as the camels and horses and foreigners passed by. Men and women alike were clad in red or black woolen robes, wearing brightly embroidered wool boots.

The General drew his horse to a stop in front of the biggest house in the tiny village. A woman with her tongue stuck out bowed low in the door, motioning them to enter the inner courtyard of her house. The men nearby bowed and pulled their pigtails from the tops of their heads, the same gestures Bessac had seen when the government's letter had been handed to him. Bessac now recognized these signs of submission and respect.

The General dismounted and lowered his head slightly to the bowed woman, who never raised her eyes, as she gestured for the party to enter her house. Men rushed forward at shouted commands from the General. Two of them grabbed Zvansov under the shoulder, plucked him off the horse, and hustled him into the house. Others held the rein of Bessac's horse as he dismounted.

In the house, Bessac was seated on a raised platform covered with bright carpets along one wall beside the fire. The household bustled around him as he sat down near Zvansov. Water was placed on to boil. Plates and bowls were taken out. A girl kneeled to blow on the fire before adding a handful of dung. The General issued orders, nonstop, as he stood in the doorway, surrounded by Tibetans who rushed off in different directions.

The herbal doctor arrived by the time water had been boiled for tea. He went directly to Zvansov and ordered him moved into a private room. Zvansov watched with horror as the doctor cut the pants off his grotesquely swollen leg. He kneeled beside Zvansov and took his pulse. He prodded the wound, quickly finding the entry and exit hole of the bullet on the front and back of his knee. He bathed the knee in boiled water. Finally, he pulled out a tiger-skin bag and began to measure out handfuls of numerous dried herbs.

Fifteen minutes after the doctor arrived he was daubing Zvansov's entire leg, from crotch to ankle, with thick handfuls of the herbal concoction he had mixed in the boiled water. It formed a solid layer over his leg, like wet mud or plaster, and Zvansov found it instantly soothing. He took a deep breath and relaxed. The doctor seemed to know what he was doing.

Bessac was given his own room in the house on the second floor, facing onto a sunny courtyard. Below him their horses and camels were unloaded and fed. He sat on his bed and drank more salt and butter tea, as girls rushed into the room, filling a giant cauldron with buckets of hot water. Sparrows chittered in the piled brush above.

He was inside and out of the wind under a solid roof for the first time since he had left Tihwa seven months earlier. He could hear distant laughter through the thick walls. He felt as if he just walked off a ship after a long sea voyage—but instead of swaying for days as though still at sea, his ears rang for lack of the wind. He stripped down and took his first bath since Tihwa. The serene room with a roof overhead and the steaming bath has stayed with Bessac for the rest of his life.

Zvansov remembers that rambling adobe house because it was where he recovered his life. The herbal wrap stopped the pain, and he was able to sleep for the first time since he had been shot.

The next day, Bessac was forced to understand that they would wait in the village for Zvansov's leg to heal, as well as for a messenger to return from Lhasa. He discovered that the messenger sent to Lhasa was Tsering Dorjee, the man who had led the firing on April 29.

After a meal, the General managed to let Bessac know that his name was something like Bambo Rubin. After an hour of generally frustrating conversation, Rubin led Bessac to a house where a rather pretty young girl greeted them. They went in for tea by the fire. After a few minutes, Rubin stood up and roughly pushed the girl down next to Bessac. The girl giggled and glanced up at Bessac, then she grabbed his beard in her fingers and stared in amazement.

Rubin slammed the rough wooden door behind him as he left the house. The girl served Bessac more tea and then made it clear that they could have sex if Bessac wanted.

The herbalist greeted Zvansov the next morning by peeling off a piece of the dried herbal paste to see how the patient was doing. He had a look at the skin, and then proceeded to rip off the dried herbs, pulling Zvansov's leg hairs away with the herbs. When Zvansov complained about the pain from his hairs, the doctor examined the patient's hairy legs with amazement. He showed the leg hair to a knot of householders who had gathered to view the undressing. The Tibetans all leaned closer to see. The doctor then ripped off the rest of the paste with a firm hand and a smile on his face. Zvansov grimaced and tried to laugh along with everyone else.

Within a few minutes the doctor had applied another thick paste of herbs to the entire leg, and Zvansov drifted back to sleep.

SHENTSA DZONG, TIBET
MAY 11, 1950

That afternoon Bambo Rubin had a treat for Bessac. The unlucky soldiers who had shot Mackiernan and looted the expedition were called into a village street, along with Bessac. As the American watched, the Tibetans were stripped and whipped. Bessac recorded the event in Mackiernan's travel log. Although Mackiernan's entries have almost no local details and are composed entirely of trail descriptions, Bessac's entries are more personally revealing.

> Army officer who had gone to Shegar-Hunglung returned with most of our articles including the gold. For his cut, most of the clothing of deceased and many things no longer of use were given him. The soldier under Tsering Dorjee's command who had accompanied

us was given the second series of 40 across the bare buttock today. Tibetan officials greatly incensed at looting after incident and I was asked to witness. Man is laid flat on ground with BTM skyward in this ceremony officers whip from both sides. I must admit that I derived some satisfaction from proceedings. Mac's, [Leonid's] and Stephan's faces and bodies as they lay by the streambed kept coming to mind—especially Mac's after the bursak had been put to his teeth. Also that of the twenty-year-old boy [Leonid]. He looked as though he died crying. It will be a long time before this smarty pants of a soldier sits down. This is all the punishment he will receive. Opinion here is that Tsering Dorjee will be beheaded in Lhasa. I will stop this if possible, but will not object if he also gets a taste of the lash. Also am going to try to arrange it so that he gives me three good kowtows on a stone floor. I have been brought to my knees but once and the person who caused it must reply in kind with interest.

During the next few days, more of the looted goods appeared in Bessac's room. Gold bars showed up (though we may never know the total), along with the radio, their clothes, Mackiernan's U.S. driver's license, Treasury bonds, and nearly everything else. Mackiernan's trip log was among the recovered items. Bessac picked up that journal where Mackiernan had left it off. He wrote notes about Mackiernan's death, their travels since the shooting, and concluded with the whipping.

The following week, Zvansov was able to hobble into Bessac's room. He set up the radio on the mud floor, though his leg remained swollen and he felt pain whenever he moved. When Mackiernan's radio contact came on the air at the appointed hour they tried to send, but they did not know Mackiernan's ID signal and the codebook was missing. Excited Tibetans watched from the doorway as Zvansov and Bessac tried to work the radio. Their efforts were useless. They could not establish contact with the CIA listening post in Turkey, no matter what they tried. Mackiernan had not taught Zvansov enough for him to run the radio. Though they broke in on other Morse conversations on the same channel, they were ignored—since procedure was not being followed. The Tibetans did not know that the Americans had not established radio contact with America. What the householders saw, and what they told the villagers, was that the Americans had a radio that could broadcast to America.

Before Bessac and Zvansov could leave Shentsa Dzong, wild rumors were spreading across the plains of Tibet. American government officials had come—with gold and a radio and grenades—and the Tibetan government was hoping to secure U.S. military assistance through them. Tibetans, who could not understand them, had shot the Americans in the back, at Shentsa Dzong, in the middle of the village. Those who had come to help were shot. What sad karma Tibet has.

TRIP TO LHASA
MAY AND JUNE 1950

When the Tibetans told Zvansov that it was still a twelve-day ride south to Lhasa, he thought, "Jesus, I never can make it." Despite rest and some healing, the bullet wound festered. On the first day's journey out of Shentsa Dzong, Zvansov almost passed out on the horse from the pain.

Bambo Rubin issued orders for villagers to carry Zvansov on the second day. Six Tibetans struggled to carry his one-hundred-ninety-five pounds on a stretcher. Every bump sent a wave of agony through Zvansov. On the third day, Rubin had twelve men, in two groups of six, who took turns carrying the giant wounded Russian. Some days out of Shentsa Dzong, a horse galloped up from the south to meet the party. The government had sent a Tibetan, who spoke Chinese and English and had studied a smattering of Western medicine in India, from Lhasa. He was carrying the newly available wonder drug, penicillin. He is forever immortalized in Zvansov's memory as simply, "the doctor."

The doctor looked briefly at Zvansov's leg and took out a hypodermic needle. He injected him with two doses of penicillin, one in each arm, and gave him a third shot—of morphine—for the pain.

When the doctor injected him as he lay on the grassy plain—the porters in a wide-eyed ring around him—Zvansov felt that "my life was given back to me." From the next day, his knee began a rapid recovery. The doctor arrived with orders to bring the survivors to Lhasa as quickly as possible in good health.

Even with the doctor, Zvansov still had the problem of transport. His leg could not hang down from a horse or it would swell up. He felt terrible watching six Tibetans struggle to carry him. Because of the doctor's language skills, for the first time Zvansov and Bessac could have detailed conversations with their hosts.

Zvansov pleaded with the doctor, "I just can't watch this. I can make a much better way to transport me."

"What are you saying? The Tibetan government gave me an order to carry you in a stretcher. I cannot do anything but what they say."

The doctor finally relented and Zvansov set to work building a saddle that allowed him to lean back on a camel and keep his wounded leg propped up so that it wouldn't swell.

Building that, he destroyed several Tibetan saddles and was digging through all their bags looking for rope and other things. When he opened one bag his mind at first simply could not name what his eyes saw. With each passing second his mind began to grasp what his eyes could only stare at.

"There was three heads, Mackiernan's, Leonid's, and Stephan's. . . . It's gruesome, but there was no smell and no flies. It is very cold and dry there in Tibet. So the heads were preserved."

Zvansov remembers the doctor's explanation of why the Tibetans were taking the human heads—and even those of several camels that had been killed—to Lhasa.

"They brought those heads to show to the government. That's exactly why—to prove what they have done, like American Indians would scalp. . . . They had to show them to the government, so they brought them all the way to Lhasa."

Upon arrival in India, Bessac and Zvansov were warned never to talk about the beheading of Douglas Mackiernan. It was only in 1991 after the State Department declassified reports written by Bessac in 1950, which recorded the truth, that either of the two men spoke about the beheading of their companions by the Tibetans.

As they traveled south, they descended slowly off the Changthang Plateau that marks Tibet's northern border. They made their way past blue lakes and over green plains into the lower valleys—at twelve thousand to fourteen thousand feet—in the center of the country, where the majority of the Tibetan population lives. There were still nomads up on the mountain pastures, but now in the valley there were fields green with the first shoots of barley. By the end of May, the lowest meadows were thick with new grass. The villages they passed through seemed more prosperous than what they had seen in China. There were fewer people, and they all seemed to have plenty to eat. The herders on the high plateaus and mountainsides were allied with the farmers. They were all one people. All the Tibetans spoke Tibetan, wore the Tibetan robe, and in appearance were distinct from that of both the Chinese and the Mongolians. Not a single word of Bessac's hard-won Chinese or Mongolian was understood by these people. There were no Chinese in Tibet, and few had ever lived there.

They had penetrated the rings of desert, mountain, and wilderness that encircled the hidden land, and now at last they descended into the fertile valleys at the center. Men and women working together in the fields were singing. No one was begging. In the villages, people thronged the temples. A caravan of red-robed, shaven-headed monks passed by on their horses. Villages grew larger the farther south they traveled.

Day by day, the temperature grew warmer. The lower they went the gentler the afternoon winds became. A few days outside of Lhasa, on the outskirts of a village, they ran into a regiment of the Tibetan army camped in a meadow with an army band. The army band played in the golden afternoon light to the delight of the villagers. They performed old British Indian army ditties like "God Save the King," since the only training the Tibetan army had ever received was from the British. On the same memorable day the travelers spotted their first trees. They were now below fourteen thousand feet for the first time in months. A line of willows swayed alongside the river.

The doctor asked Zvansov and Bessac if they would stand on the platform beside the parade ground. The two foreigners agreed. Zvansov remembers the awed eyes of the Tibetans as they watched the two foreigners strutting back and forth for their inspection, while the band played "Marching Through Georgia."

On the last day before Lhasa, the doctor went out of his way to make sure the two arriving visitors understood what had happened. He spoke to Zvansov and Bessac and gave them both a similar message.

The area where the shooting had occurred, Shegar-Hunglung, was patrolled by the Home Guards of the Dalai Lama to defend against Kazak raids. The Kazak had stolen children and animals in the past on these raids—as the Kazak at Timurlik had boasted to the Americans. In the troubled days of 1950, the Home Guard had received orders to shoot raiders on sight. The message from the American government, asking permission for the Mackiernan party to enter Tibet, had been received only on April 5. Government orders were rushed out to soldiers all along the vast northern border. The orders to welcome the Americans had not reached the party of soldiers Mackiernan had run into, so following their orders they opened fire. Nothing but a tragic mistake. The government was in fact eager to receive them. The looting, Bessac was told, was of course another issue, and the offenders would be punished in Lhasa to Bessac's satisfaction.

Looting was a time-honored pastime among the Tibetan nomads, just as it was among the nomadic Kazak. Heinrich Harrer—who so famously lived seven years in Tibet—wrote that looting was still standard practice in the Tibetan army of 1950. The nomadic roots of Tibetan culture ran deep.

"Instead of mentions and distinctions, the Tibetan solider receives more tangible rewards. After a victory he has a right to the booty, and so looting is the general rule."

The history of looting was not explained to the survivors, though Bessac knew the reality of nomadic warfare. The fault was placed on the local soldiers. The Tibetans did not even try to point out that the U.S. request had arrived in Lhasa only on April 5 and that the Tibetan government had moved quickly when it was received. Never once did the Tibetans complain to Bessac that the delayed U.S. message underlay the tragedy. The State Department had had six months during which they could have contacted the Tibetans, and the Americans' delay was the most likely cause of the death of Mackiernan and the two White Russians.

By the time the survivors approached Lhasa, Zvansov was feeling well enough to be offered the services that Bessac had been offered earlier on. The party was traveling with a *lamyig*—a road pass—issued by the government. When presenting the road pass in each village, the villagers were compelled to supply horses and porters for the next day's journey. The letter was often stretched to include sexual services for the passing visitor as well. Without a *lamyig,* you could not travel anywhere in Tibet. With one, everything was available.

On the road to Lhasa, Bessac was twice offered the privilege of personally executing the soldiers who had shot his companions. The soldiers were alive only because Bessac refused the offer. The feudal lords wanted to give their visitors anything they wanted, even though the soldiers were obeying orders when they had opened fire.

TIBET, TAIWAN, AND CHINA
SPRING 1950

That spring Gyalo Thondup, the Dalai Lama's brother, was in India trying to get the Tibetan Regency to wake up to the impending Chinese invasion.

Thondup's father-in-law had gone to the same military academy as Marshal Chu-deh, now commander in chief of the People's Liberation Army. In the winter of 1949–50, he sent back-channel messages from Marshal Chu-deh to Thondup, who passed them on to Tibet's rulers. The Communists said that Tibet's rulers could keep all their estates and all their serfs and that Tibet's traditional status would not be altered. They could have all this if they would just send a delegation to China. The Regency sent no reply to these messages. In January 1950 the Communists gave up on this back-channel discussion and announced the impending "Peaceful Liberation of

Tibet." Today, Thondup accuses the Tibetan government of throwing away this chance. Others say that it was a simply a Chinese trick and that the PLA would have invaded in any event.

In March, the PLA occupied Kangding (Dartsendo) on the traditional ethnic dividing line between China and Tibet. In April, thirty thousand troops of the People's Liberation Army pushed farther westward into the Tibetan province of Kham, where the population had always been more than 90 percent Tibetan. Since the leaders of Kham had only occasionally accepted direct rule from Lhasa, the Tibetan army was not stationed in Kham.

Some of the invading Chinese troops had been specially trained in minority nationalities policy, which Bessac had seen evolving in Inner Mongolia in 1947. When the PLA entered Kham, they treated the Khampas with great respect and paid above-market prices for anything they needed. Some Chinese said they would help the Khampas create their own independent state of Kham. Local Khampa lords received high-sounding titles and large salaries. This velvet invasion exploited Khampa hatred of the central Tibetans. These first Chinese invaders insisted that they had entered Tibet to help the Tibetans. When Tibet was improved and was capable of self-rule, their Chinese brothers would leave.

In this first phase local collaboration was essential. China had not yet built the roads it would require to supply its armies: some supplies were being air-dropped. True Chinese intentions were not exposed until the roads linking Kham with China were completed.

By April 1950 Thondup was frustrated with the lack of response from the Tibetan government. He packed his bags and took his wife and young daughter to Hong Kong. Nationalist intelligence agents had penetrated his father-in-law's house there. When the Nationalists discovered that Thondup was in contact with the Chinese Communists, they invited him to visit Taiwan.

Upon arrival, Chiang Kai-shek's agents retained his passport. Thondup learned that his hotel was in effect a prison. He had been kidnapped and would not leave Taiwan for nearly eighteen months. From April 1950 until September 1951—during the period of the Chinese invasion of Tibet—Thondup was cut off from all sources of information. Chiang offered Thondup patient teachers, who explained that the Communists were like a seductive prostitute: beautiful on the outside but diseased inside. On May 21, 1950, once Thondup was in his hands, Chiang Kai-shek's office in Taiwan distributed a press release. It said that the Dalai Lama's brother had arrived to seek military aid from the Americans. Chiang looked forward to receiving more U.S. dollars to use for the liberation of this Chinese province.

That May, the U.S. government resumed aid to the Nationalist government on Taiwan that had been discontinued in August 1948. One of the first beneficiaries of this aid was Taiwan's covert action project.

Despite support to Taiwan, there was still no final decision to arm the Tibetans. Gyalo Thondup escaped from Taiwan only after he sent a letter covertly to Secretary of State Dean Acheson in 1951. Acheson replied to Chiang, and Thondup was released. By then Communist Chinese troops were in Lhasa.

LHASA, TIBET
JUNE 11, 1950

A steady rain fell as twenty eight-year-old Frank Bessac rode alone into the fringe of the Tibetan capital, ahead of the rest of his party. Low clouds at first obscured the distant roofs of the Potala. When they parted and a shaft of sunlight hit the golden roofs Bessac caught his first sight of the most famous building in Tibet, floating like a vision above the emerald-green barley fields.

His pony picked its way down a muddy lane lined with tall poplars. He gazed at Tibet in awe.

A group of women threaded their way down to the river, singing, with heaps of flowers in their arms. Perhaps they were headed to offer flowers to some protector deity in the fields. Maybe they were just weeding wildflowers from a field. Bessac never knew. In his mind it all created a general impression of wealth, greenery, and happiness. And the women were pretty, too.

A few miles outside the city, he found an embroidered tent erected in a meadow alongside the road to welcome him. Several officials from the Tibetan Foreign Bureau were waiting for him. They held his reins as he dismounted, drew him into the tent, made him a gift of new Tibetan robes, and plied him with food and tea. He was introduced to his government-appointed translator, Tse Gung, and aide-de-camp, Driesur Nu, who was deputed from his official position as Telegraph Master of Tibet. The Tibetans were dressed in gorgeous silk robes. The wore long dangling earrings from their pierced ears and other adornments, indicating their rank within the highly stratified social structure of Tibet. As government officers, they all wore round yellow government officer hats, fat felted wool saucers perched atop their heads. Bessac found the reception committee endearing. They all kept repeating that the death of Mackiernan was a terrible accident and hoped Bessac could convince the U.S. government that such was the fact behind the tragedy.

As Bessac enjoyed the traditional welcome, he noticed in the corner of the tent a man ten years his senior who was certainly not Tibetan. He stood out in the crowd if only because he was the only person in a European-style suit. He was one of the eight Westerners allowed to reside in Tibet. Heinrich Harrer says he went out to the edge of Lhasa "thinking that it might be some comfort to the young American to have a white man to talk to."

Harrer began a friendship with Bessac as the two men rode into town, their mounts ambling together down the muddy lane in the rain. Harrer later described his first encounter with Bessac in his book.

> We met the young man in a pouring rain. He was as tall as a hop-pole and completely dwarfed his little Tibetan pony. I could well imagine how he felt. The little caravan had been months on the road . . . and . . . their first meeting with the people of the country in which they sought asylum brought three of their party to their deaths. . . . I . . . hoped to convince him that the Government could not be blamed for the incident, which it deeply regretted.

Harrer's dapper suit made Bessac aware of what a bearded mountain man he had become during the trek from Tihwa. As they rode on into Lhasa, Bessac's eyes kept wandering off over the barley, amazed that it was already knee high at this low elevation of twelve thousand four hundred feet. The fields stretched down to the edge of the Kyichu River, which meanders through the vast Lhasa valley. Sixteen-thousand-foot mountains rim the valley, but those peaks were hidden in black monsoon clouds. Riding through the endless barley fields on the outskirts of Lhasa, Bessac's eyes were continually drawn back to the Potala. The hilltop fortress on a solitary crag stood like a tower in the middle of the flat valley bottom.

Lhasa remained obscured by willows until they drew closer. There was no city wall around it, as in Peking or Tihwa. At first sight, Lhasa was a line of low-lying whitewashed buildings peeking above willows that dotted the grazing lands around it. The city had a population of thirty thousand people in a one-square-kilometer area, yet it was the largest city in Tibet. Tse Gung and Harrer explained to Bessac that *Lha-sa* means, literally, God-place, or place of the gods. As they rode through the willows toward the flat-roofed buildings, Bessac noticed a flock of golden pagoda roofs in the center of the city that hovered above the roofline. No building in the city was higher.

The golden roofs were those of the Jokhang temple, the first Buddhist temple built in the country, established about 640 A.D. The Dalai Lama calls it the "holiest shrine in all Tibet." Tibet's greatest ruler, King Songtsen Gampo, built it with the aid of visiting Nepalese craftsmen. Though periodically sacked by invaders over the centuries the temple remains the finest relic from Tibet's imperial age. During the seventh century, King Songtsen Gampo unified the many feuding Tibetan fiefdoms into a single nation. He and his sons led the Tibetans on a century of conquest. The Tibetan empire eventually reached to Nepal and India and even occupied Sinkiang. They even pushed to the walls of the Tang Chinese emperor's capital at Changan. A wing of the Great Wall is said to have been built to hold back the waves of Tibetan nomads who made an annual sport of seeking tribute from the lowland farmers of China—just as had their nomadic brothers the Manchu and the Mongol.

The Nepalese and Chinese kings, threatened by invasion, each concluded a marriage alliance with Tibet. Both kings sent one of their own daughters to wed King Songtsen Gampo. The princesses—both uddhist countries—brought images of the Buddha with them of their trousseau, thinking to tame the barbarians who threatened their homelands with the philosophy of peace. The Jokhang was built under the instruction of the Nepalese princess to house the Buddha statue she had brought, which is why it resembles ancient Indian and Nepalese Buddhist temples, from which the Chinese also took architectural inspiration. Buddhism in Tibet dates from its introduction to Tibetan royalty by the two princesses.

As the survivors of the Mackiernan party entered the city through winding alleys, the trail beneath them became muddy with urban traffic. Donkeys laden with clay pots and other trade items shared the trail with them. Tse Gung explained that all the different areas of Tibet had slightly different dialects, types of robes, and jewelry. He pointed out the mingling of the various Tibetans in the streets of Lhasa. Khampas were obvious because of the hulking size of the men and the red silk tresses with which they braided their hair; Monpas stood out because of their spiky hats of felted wool. The noble ladies of Lhasa had their hair up on three-foot arched frames that supported their extravagant hairdos; nomad women wore their hair in one hundred and eight braids. The hair of nobles and nomad women was studded with coral, seed pearls, amber, and turquoise. The country was as big as western Europe, and the diversity of Tibet was evident on every street in Lhasa. Roadside vendors sold homemade pea noodles, tea, and dumplings from bamboo and reed baskets. Snow leopard and tiger skins hung alongside Indian and Chinese silk. Mounds of spices and tea were arrayed beside piles of nails and stacks of matchboxes. Tall towers of aluminum pots from India seemed to be the most popular import. Silver nomad jewelry, carpets from Kashmir and Kashgar, Nepalese handmade paper, and black-and-white photographs of the young Fourteenth Dalai Lama all vied for buyers' attentions in the crowded bazaar.

For more than a thousand years, Lhasa had been the city of the temple for a nation of nomads. In winter, the nomads descended from the high pastures to Lhasa and combined a pilgrimage with trading. Over the centuries, farming increased in the river valleys and the farmers brought their wares to the bazaars of Lhasa. In time, the bazaar around the Jokhang became the largest in the country. Slowly an urban elite, which gained its wealth by taxing the isolated nomads and farmers, developed the area around the Jokhang with town houses for visiting lamas, government offices, shops, and residences for the ruling aristocrats. A distinctive urban architectural style developed in a country that was traditionally without cities.

The bulk of the Potala grew out of a solitary rocky spur just beyond town, soaring four hundred feet above the plain of Lhasa. For centuries, it was the largest single building in Asia. Bessac had not seen anything so grand since he had left Peking. It was entirely different from any Chinese building. The Potala represents the coherence, originality, and strength of Tibetan culture, comparable in that way to the Egyptian pyramids, or to the Taj Mahal. Thousands of workers constructed the building between 1645 and 1705, during the reign of the Great Fifth Dalai Lama. The first four Dalai Lamas were religious leaders and had little political power. During the reign of the Great Fifth, his sect, the Gelukpa school of Buddhism, seized political rule over Tibet with the backing of Mongol devotees. The Mongols helped place their teacher on the throne of Tibet in 1642, two years before the Manchu ousted the Ming from the Chinese throne. From that time, the Dalai Lamas became kings of Tibet, as well as heads of the Gelukpa sect of Buddhism. The Potala was commissioned by the Great Fifth at this high point of Tibetan civilization.

Bessac was stunned when he arrived in Lhasa. The crush of the bazaar and the glory of the Potala and the Jokhang were overwhelming. There was nothing Chinese about Lhasa, nor could the Chinese call these people barbarians. The Potala alone ensured the Tibetans' claim to cultural equality with China. The Tibetans were descended from the ancient Tibetan nomad culture Bessac had seen on the Changthang. That culture had more similarities to the nomadic culture of the Mongols and the Kazak than to that of the Chinese, leaving few traces and few grand palaces. In ancient times, the Tibetans had drawn on Indian and Chinese civilization, and with their own native genius they fused elements from both, creating a unique culture indelibly their own.

Tibet, one-third the size of the United States, had then a population of only three or four million. In 1950 there were no airplanes, automobiles, railroads, telephones, wagons, bicycles, factories, hospitals, newspapers, magazines, indoor plumbing, running water, heating, or sewage systems. The Buddhist monks of the nineteenth and twentieth centuries interpreted their religion in a way that allowed them to forbid all of these things. They appealed to the xenophobia and superstitions of the common man. Mining would hurt the gods of the earth. Spectacles were un-Tibetan, and so was football. Heinrich Harrer reports that a hailstorm occurred, destroying crops near Lhasa, immediately after a football game: football, which had just been introduced, was banned overnight. This same thinking banned English schools and Western hospitals. When Harrer was helping to make a map of Lhasa, parts of the city had to be mapped by pacing. Even measuring tapes were banned at the Dalai Lama's Summer Palace. The most conservative monks insisted religion was more important than these Western toys. Such outside influence might loosen the grip of religion on the people—threatening the rule of the nobles and monks. The British had encouraged this isolation of Tibet since 1904, for it left them as the sole Western nation with access to Tibet. "Don't you want any of the conveniences of the modern age?" Lowell Thomas, Jr., asked when he visited Tibet in 1949.

"Well, perhaps," replied one official. "We are willing to accept them as we accept alms."

This describes well how the Tibetan elite viewed its relations with the world. Tibetan Buddhist teachers were preceptors to the Mongol emperors when they ruled the largest empire the world has ever known, of which China was but a sliver. Tibet was the only country within that empire that had been granted self-rule—even when the Chinese had been crushed by Mongol heels. Was it not a Tibetan teacher who convinced Kublai Khan to quit sacrificing hundreds of Chinese in a lake for a Mongol ritual and converted him to Buddhism? The first Manchu emperor received the Fifth Dalai Lama as an equal head of state, and successive Dalai Lamas were Preceptors to the Emperor throughout the Manchu Empire. If the Chinese insisted that any Mongol conquest was China's—thus proving Tibet had always been part of China—Tibetans said, "But we were even higher than the Emperors—we were their religious teachers," showing that Tibet's religious relations with the Mongol emperors was no modern basis to prove anything about the Tibetan nation.

As Bessac rode through Lhasa he was told that all this ancient history was now a matter of urgent concern. Harrer and the Tibetans said that the Chinese Communists' radio broadcasts now repeated daily their threat to "liberate Tibet." After expressing their concerns about the Chinese his hosts broached a few polite questions about Bessac's status. Bessac tried to summarize who he was and how he wound up in Lhasa.

"I'm a lost Fulbright student." He explained that he had a Fulbright scholarship to study Mongolian and then was pushed west by the civil war. Then he met up with Mackiernan who invited him to travel with him through Tibet to India. After riding through Lhasa, the men from Tibet's Foreign Bureau took them to the house that had been prepared for Bessac and Zvansov. Harrer calls it a "garden-house with a cook and servant to look after them." A mansion called Tride Lingka, it was nestled within a walled compound by the Kyichu River, a half mile out of Lhasa. Lowell Thomas and his son stayed in the same state guest house when they visited Tibet in the fall of 1949. The walled house was set amidst grazing meadows, studded with knots of willows that lay between the town and the Potala. The windows and roof of the villa afforded a sweeping, panoramic view of the river flowing past Lhasa as well as the Potala on its crag.

The eleven surviving camels, the boxes of ammunition, the machine gun Bessac carried, the U.S. ARMY–stenciled radio, and the gold were unloaded when they reached the house. Bessac says he never made any effort to hide any of this cargo from Harrer or anyone else. Impressions were being made, and many eyes were watching.

MR. LATRASH'S
LHASA "ASSETS"
CALCUTTA AND LHASA
WINTER AND SPRING 1949–1950

The first encoded cable about the Mackiernan party, from CIA head-quarters in Washington, lay on Vice Consul Frederick Latrash's desk for him one morning in May 1949. Latrash had caught the consul, who knew Latrash was the CIA agent in Calcutta, India, snooping around his desk often enough that he finally shoved his desk into the farthest corner of the room. It gave him a great view of the reeking streets below and a clearer earful of the cacophony echoing up from the rickshaw pullers and shouting hawkers.

The cable announced that either Mackiernan or Bessac had been shot dead on the border, and that the survivor was headed to Lhasa. That information was given to the U.S. embassy in Delhi as soon as the Tibetan government heard the news and was quickly passed to the CIA.

In messages that followed, Latrash was given "the address" for Mackiernan and Bessac, since he had a need to know. The Outfit told him that Mackiernan was a career CIA agent, working under State Department cover. He was also told that Bessac was a contract intel-ligence agent, working under deep Fulbright cover. Bessac has no idea why Latrash says this; he asserts, as discussed previously, that he quit the CIA in 1947.

In the weeks that followed the shoot-out, as Bessac made his way to Lhasa, Latrash was ordered to get ready to go to Lhasa. He was to lead a rescue mission.

"My function would be to go up there and get Bessac and Vasili and debrief Bessac." He was told that Bessac "was . . . undercover and that I should bring him down, debrief him, and send him on his way back to the States." Latrash hoped that an overt rescue mission would provide the cover he needed to go to Tibet and pull together the intelligence assets he had been creating during the past year.

All that winter and spring the State Department's message to Tibet followed U.S. policy: Tibetans were told that they could not send a Tibetan mission to the United States; they were refused visas to allow them to join the UN; any overt U.S. mission to Tibet was impossible. The United States said that any of these moves might precipitate a Chinese invasion. Simultaneously, Latrash covertly prepared to arm the Tibetans, when Washington finally—as he tells us—"got their thumb out of their ass."

During the winter and spring of 1949–50, the Dalai Lama was studying very hard and was allowed only a few hours a day to play on the roof of the Potala. His favorite pastime was to watch the world beyond the Potala through his telescope. One day, he saw people clearing rocks away from a long strip of land in the Lhasa valley. He would not know for fifty years that this was the hand of the Outfit at work.

Frederick Latrash had an airfield cleared that winter, just in case it was needed. An airfield would make it easier to send weapons into Tibet if the United States decided to arm Tibet. Latrash had accomplished much in Lhasa by spring of 1950.

"I knew every day who was being tortured down below in the dungeons at the Potala . . . we had excellent coverage and capabilities and were reporting all this back to the Agency. We had at least fifteen disseminated intelligence reports a month out of Lhasa . . ."

By 1950 such clandestine information collection was part of the standing mission for a CIA agent.

"I don't need any special authorization from anybody back home to do that. I have funds that allow me to do that because this is a standard mission. That was clear. They never said, 'Stop it.' They knew we were paying people. Paying agents for information is different from the covert action."

Some of the sources for this clandestine information network were in the Tibetan military and government. These same people were appealing for U.S. aid, but the only connection to the United States that they were allowed was a deniable one with Latrash. "There was no task force, there was no interagency coordination on what do we do about Tibet that the Agency or its representatives were invited to.

There are those coordinating offices today. They didn't exist back then, and I think Tibet just fell between the cracks."

Since there was no policy decision forthcoming, Latrash decided, on his own, that the United States needed to be ready to supply the Tibetans and went ahead and set up the means to do that by building the airfield. At this point, he may have stepped over the line from information collection to covert action. Since this was technically forbidden, Latrash had to build the airfield without agency money.

"I'm not going to get into sources and methods, but there's a lot of things that get done because Agency people ask that they be done. . . . There are a lot of people who will do a lot of things that might be helpful, because they are patriotic.

"Sometimes you have to do things with mirrors, and since we were getting no positive reaction out of Washington, we did it with mirrors. It was not paid for by the Tibetan government."

A preferred "mirror" for field agents like Latrash was to get the money from the enemy—Latrash indicates that there were times in his career where the source of money for such mirrors was the local Communist Party.

Tibetans were desperate for U.S. aid and so would have gladly built a strip that might be used to ship U.S. weapons to Tibet. Latrash says that Washington did not object to the field either. "There's some times when you have to do things. We just did it . . . and then we said, it's done."

Latrash also created a link that would have allowed encrypted radio communication between the United States and the Tibetan governments. Latrash was doing his job as he understood it, and the feedback he got from CIA-D.C. was that he should carry on. In fact, he was commended. The CIA said that he was producing intelligence of a quality "no one else was producing on Tibet . . . And . . . they were not getting anything comparable to that from anywhere else." Though they did not condemn him for his work, they also did nothing with the resources that Latrash created. While U.S. policy regarding the provision of aid to Tibet was still under debate, a CIA field agent was "doing what was right." His actions may have led people in the military and the government in Lhasa to believe that ultimately the United States would help them. The CIA had come a long way from its OSS days. Now it was creating foreign policy, by default, while the McCarthy-led terror held Washington in its grip.

Because of all his work in Tibet, Vice Consul Latrash was pleased when a plausible pretext for him to go to Lhasa fell into his lap. The tragedy at the border gave him a believable cover story. State and the CIA wanted Latrash to go in and rescue Bessac, whether he needed it or not. In Lhasa, he could meet his sources face to face. He thought that he might be able to ". . . for the first time put policy and the clandestine engine together. Why do you think I was selected [to lead the rescue mission]? Because I had the strings on the clandestine side, and I was a foreign service officer under consulate cover. I was perfect to do these things. I had the contacts and would have had the directions as to what they wanted me to say [to the Tibetan government]."

THE FOURTEENTH DALAI LAMA, "A U.S. AGENT PASSING THROUGH LHASA"
DHARAMSALA, INDIA
DECEMBER 1, 1994

For fifty years no one asked Tenzin Gyatso what he and his government thought of the Americans who were sent to, or who passed through, Lhasa in the summer of 1950. When he is first asked about them, the Dalai Lama speaks in Tibetan for a while and then his political secretary answers. "His Holiness's view is that if you will ask whether there was an American agent specially stationed, or sent to Lhasa, then there was no such agent. But, if the question is whether an American agent passed through Lhasa . . ."

The Dalai Lama is not primarily a politician. He is, as he says, a simple monk. As the secretary carefully dances around the question for him, the Dalai Lama is unable to restrain his basic nature. He interjects and cuts to the truth.

"Yes, it happened. And during his stay in Lhasa he had some consultation with Tibetan officials . . . You see we considered him as . . . something official. Because he had a radio and money. He reached Lhasa, not under instruction, he simply escaped. He cannot discuss with the Tibetan government officially. But at the same time, he was somehow, we thought, an American government official—he had a radio. So you see he offered . . . [the] Tibetan side was very much willing at that time to discuss things."

The Tibetans thought of Bessac as a deniable U.S. secret agent passing through, and they availed themselves of his services. It is possible that, like Prince De, the Tibetans may have misconstrued Bessac's position, and that Bessac, as he says, was not a CIA agent while in Tibet—and truly gave the Tibetans no reason to think he was. Neither Bessac nor the Tibetans had any way to know that Mackiernan's cover was blown before he arrived in Tibet, which destroyed the "deniability" not only of Mackiernan but of anyone traveling with him. The appearance, for the Chinese, was that Bessac was a U.S. intelligence agent, and even Bessac admits this. That appearance alone may have damned Tibet.

The debate about whether Bessac was, or was not, a U.S. agent did not concern him when he arrived in Lhasa. He was still thinking about the tragedy on the border, not politics or dates of service with the CIA. He kept asking himself what those who have watched their friends die always ask, "Why me? Why them?" Feelings of guilt, remorse, sadness, and inadequacy were Bessac's constant companions. These feelings may have also motivated him to take on Mackiernan's mission. "I was the second American . . . not the person in charge. . . . Doug should have been left. Doug shouldn't have died."

Yet it was Bessac who survived the trip to Lhasa, not the supersleuth Mackiernan.

FAIRFAX, CALIFORNIA
JUNE 11, 1950

As Bessac fell asleep in Lhasa after his second hot bath in eight months, Pegge Mackiernan sat in the morning light on her back porch, sipping her coffee. Tony Freeman, who had been so pleasant to her on the phone back in November, had flown out from the Chinese Affairs Division of the State Department in Washington to bring the news to her personally.

"The Tibetans, being very antiforeigner anyway, and not realizing Doug was a friendly U.S. official, fired on them." Of course, Tony had not come there to tell her that the State Department, having sent its message to Lhasa too late, might have caused Mackiernan's death. No, what he told her was that they were not 100 percent certain Mackiernan was dead, but it was looking bad. Someone had been killed on the border, and it might well have been Mackiernan. Only when the survivor reached Lhasa would they get final confirmation. Then they would notify her once more.

Every time the telephone rang her "heart bellowed." At the same time, she was under strict orders to talk with no one about the news she had been given. Freeman offered her a job in Washington in the same breath that they told her she had to keep quiet.

It would be one year before Pegge realized that one of Tony Freeman's jobs was to find out how much Pegge knew about her husband's real work. Fifty years later, the director of the CIA would call her up on a stage in the foyer of a gleaming multimillion-dollar building in Langley, Virginia, to point out Mackiernan's nameless star carved into a marble wall. The first star on the CIA's Honor Wall. That's what they call Mackiernan's star at the CIA today, first star on the wall. But even then no one would be telling Mackiernan's widow how he had died, or why.

On June 14, 1949, Tony Freeman called her back to confirm that Mackiernan was dead. Her first thought was how she and her twin children would survive. As the news of his death sank in, Pegge realized she had to go to Washington herself to deal with the federal bureaucracy. She didn't know if Mackiernan had a will, who would pay her pension, or what salary was still outstanding.

She could not deal with the details from Fairfax. As a single mother she would have to leave the children at the Green Lantern in Massachusetts. Only then could she go to Washington.

MEETING THE DALAI LAMA
LHASA, TIBET
JUNE 1950

Although Bessac and Zvansov had walked two-thirds of the way across Tibet, they could not leave their house until they met the Dalai Lama. Their hosts from the Foreign Bureau explained that "the Dalai Lama has to bless you if you are going to stay on his territory." Tibetans believe that the Dalai Lama is the fourteenth human body to serve as a vehicle for the spirit of the Bodhisattva *Chenrezig*. That Bodhisattva was the father-creator of the Tibetan race, and he continues to reincarnate as the Dalai Lama to guide his children.

While waiting for their audience, the commander in chief of the Tibetan army and the secretary of Tibet's Foreign Bureau came to speak with Bessac. Bessac gave them briefings about the current situation in China, Inner Mongolia, and Sinkiang. His message was " the Chinese Communists could not be trusted."

One morning, the translator and officials from the Foreign Bureau came to escort them to the *Norbu Lingka,* the Jewel Park. It was the third week of June, and the Dalai Lama had already made his annual procession from the Potala to his summer home. The Dalai Lama hated living in the cold and gloomy Potala. He says that he looked forward to his annual move to Jewel Park—to its open parks, its ponds and trees—more than any other event of the year.

Bessac and the much-recovered Zvansov rode their ponies to the soaring southern face of the Potala, about a half mile out of Lhasa. Then they turned west and rode a mile farther away from the city to a fifty-acre parkland, enclosed within a twenty-foot-high wall. There were no houses between the Potala and Jewel Park. They galloped their mounts past willows, ponds, and meadows, a beautiful ride.

At the gate of Jewel Park, the bodyguards of the Dalai Lama asked them to dismount. They walked through a brightly painted thirty-five-foot-high gate, through the whitewashed wall, and then strolled through the outer parkland. Some Tibetans had pitched tents for picnics. Voices, accompanied by the Tibetan guitar, the *dranyen,* echoed under the trees. It seemed as if they had at last found the garden of peace, the place of refuge in a troubled world. Shangri-la at last.

One hundred yards into the park they reached the yellow Inner Wall, which surrounded the Inner Garden. Stepping through a small gate they walked mesmerized past the Dalai Lama's private menagerie, wandering unafraid in the Inner Garden. Peacocks strutted about and a herd of deer grazed peacefully. Finally, they entered the courtyard of a small Buddhist temple built by the Seventh Dalai Lama back when the Norbu Lingka was founded in the seventeenth century.

The windowless interior was lit only by light from the doorway and butter lamps glowing in front of the Buddhist images. On the raised platform at the front of the temple stood a pair of fine cloisonné Chinese elephants that had been given to a previous Dalai Lama by a previous Chinese emperor. The temple was overcrowded with such donations, made by patrons over the centuries—some Mongol and some Chinese. Statues, silk hangings, and fine porcelain filled the room. The Dalai Lamas of Tibet have been revered as Asia's greatest spiritual teachers since 1578 when the Gelukpa teacher Sonam Gyatso was given the title Dalai Lama (Oceanic Teacher) by the Mongol lord Altan Khan. Patrons sent their teachers these offerings, hoping to gain merit for their own spiritual development.

Bessac and Zvansov passed through the temple and then upstairs and across a rooftop courtyard choked with potted flowers. A door hanging was swept aside for them, and they entered a south-facing room. The south wall was composed entirely of small glass panes set in wooden frames. The young Dalai Lama, dressed in wine-red robes, was seated on a raised platform in the morning sun, smiling at them as they entered. Monk attendants ushered them directly to him. Bessac and Zvansov took turns bowing and approaching the Dalai Lama for his blessing as they had been coached to do.

Zvansov bent at the waist as he approached the boy, who put one hand on his head and said a few words of prayer. When Bessac bowed, the Dalai Lama reached out both hands and rested them on Bessac's head. Tibetans believe the double-handed blessing is one of the highest forms of blessing by the Dalai Lama.

Tea was served. The Dalai Lama smiled at Bessac and Zvansov, and they smiled back. They had been warned neither to speak to the young boy nor to expect him to address them. The regent of Tibet forbade it. During an audience with the Dalai Lama, he blessed you and smiled at you and then you left.

Before his exile in 1959, the Dalai Lama received only ten Americans in Tibet. Lowell Thomas and his son were numbers seven and eight in 1949. Bessac and Zvansov were the ninth and tenth Americans to meet him. They also became the last Americans to meet the Dalai Lama in Lhasa.

In 1999, looking back on these ritual audiences during which he was not allowed to speak, the Dalai Lama laughs and utters just one word when asked to describe them: "Useless."

He is obliquely criticizing the nobles who ruled Tibet in his name. The silent audience reflected the feudal grip on power. By the summer of 1950 that structure was unable to respond effectively to a Chinese invasion that had already begun.

The regent was more concerned about the power of his own monastery than in the fate of a nation. He could not take tax revenue from his monastery to fund an expansion of the army. He was unable to make that choice, though the Chinese invasion had been a threat for at least two years.

Riding from the Norbu Lingka to old Lhasa today, a visitor sees the result of this overweening focus on religion—and the nobles' focus on their own wealth rather than the security of the nation. The road is lined with Chinese shops, Chinese restaurants, a Chinese piggery and butchery, Chinese houses of prostitution, and rows of barracks to house the estimated eighty thousand Chinese troops in the Lhasa valley. Nearly all of the meadows and willow forests are gone. The People's Liberation Army filled in all the uninhabited marshes between the Potala and the Norbu Lingka. The PLA has turned a profit building the modern Chinese city to house the estimated one hundred thousand Chinese civilians living in Lhasa. Meanwhile, the Tibetan population of thirty thousand in 1950 has grown to only about one hundred thousand at present.

Old Lhasa remains, a square kilometer where the population is still 90 percent Tibetan, but the character of the area has been decimated by the destruction of more than half of the original Tibetan buildings between 1985 and 2000. Thirty square kilometers of modern Lhasa surround that ancient core by the Jokhang and 90 percent of the population in New Lhasa is Chinese. By all objective estimates, the city is now well over 50 percent Chinese. The Dalai Lama today warns that this colonization, if allowed to continue unchecked, will soon make the Tibetans a minority in all of Tibet.

DINNER AT TRIDE LINGKA
LHASA, TIBET
JUNE 15, 1950

Thick white Tibetan barley beer, called *chang,* flowed from a silver urn into delicate silver bowls. The cook had made a great Chinese dinner, served with chopsticks. An American radio tuned to the BBC played Western classical music. A kerosene lantern hung from the ceiling, hissing. The gaily painted Tibetan furniture and fine Tibetan carpets glowed like bright jewels. Dressed in a Tibetan silk robe, Bessac sat at a table full of men and women similarly dressed.

The commander in chief of the Tibetan army and a senior official from the Tibetan Foreign Bureau updated Bessac on the situation with China. Chinese radio broadcasts had frightened the Tibetans. The message since January was that China had a "sacred duty to liberate Tibet." If the Tibetans negotiated, they could arrange a peaceful liberation. In May, the broadcasts had switched to Tibetan and were received in Lhasa three nights a week. The broadcasts had become filled with the ominous alternative to peaceful liberation. Neither the broadcasts, nor the Communist troops moving in on the eastern border of Tibet, had evoked serious help from India, Great Britain, or the United States. Everyone at dinner was deeply frustrated by the apathy of the world's great nations and terrified of the looming invasion.

Bessac shook his head as his frightened hosts told the sad tale. The Tibetans had begun to understand that the big powers might not help Tibet develop its army. If the West would not help, the Tibetans had no choice but to try to negotiate—if only to gain time in which to build up their defenses. In early 1950 the Tibetan government decided to arm and to negotiate. Neither effort went well.

An order was given to increase the size of the army from thirteen thousand to one hundred thousand. Though the Indians did increase the shipment of light arms and ammunition to Tibet in March 1950, the Tibetans had not mustered the resources to increase the army. In the previous six months, military expansion had faltered, since Tibet had to pay cash for the weapons. Any serious military effort would have required foreign aid, new taxes, or a slice out of the taxes that now went to the monasteries and nobles. Since the serfs of Tibet were already heavily taxed, the ruling elite was faced with a difficult choice. Since foreign military aid had not appeared, the nobles would have to hand over taxes that were going into their own pockets to the military. Their reluctance caused the effort to expand the army to falter.

In February, the Tibetans dispatched a diplomatic mission to talk with the new Chinese Communist government, in Hong Kong, a neutral third country. The trails from Tibet to China were terrible. Far quicker to ride a horse to India, and then fly to Hong Kong from there, than to travel overland to China, which was how the mission, led by Minister Tsipon Wangchuk Deden Shakabpa, tried to travel but it never got any farther than India.

The British and the Indian governments "were both convinced that no good would be achieved by any attempt on the part of the Tibetans to contact the Beijing Government." Again, Britain forced its decision about Tibet onto the Tibetans. Just as Britain and the United States had refused visas for the Tibetans when they wanted to apply for UN membership, Britain kept the Tibetan mission trapped in India.

Various British maneuvers prevented the Shakabpa mission from leaving India. The Tibetans were first refused visas while the matter was studied. Then they were advised it was better to negotiate with the Chinese in India, not Hong Kong. Britain went so far as to prevent the Tibetans from boarding a plane in Calcutta for Hong Kong, though visas had been accidentally issued by ill-informed consular staff. A member of the British Foreign Office described the British position accurately: "We can hardly wash our hands of Tibet, as we seem to have done, and then prevent her from taking her own line."

By June 1950 the Communists believed that foreign imperialists had purposely thwarted their attempts at peaceful negotiation. The gist of China's first Tibetan-language radio broadcasts in May were repeated to Bessac over dinner by the excited Tibetans. The broadcasts reveal that the Chinese had closely followed the discussion in the ruling circles in Tibet.

> We have heard that the Tibetan government is mustering forces to fight us: Chiang Kai-shek did that and failed. What chances have the poor Tibetan troops against us?
>
> We have two objectives before us: the liberation of Tibet and of Formosa and we are determined to achieve both at any cost.
>
> We have heard that you have deputed your representatives to negotiate with us, but they have not arrived yet. *Do not listen to what the capitalists have to tell you.* There is still time before you—it is not too late to mend matters by sending your representatives quickly.

In June the tone of the broadcasts changed yet again. It was as if the Tibetan government had ceased to exist.

> "Our people of the province of Tibet need not be apprehensive because we are coming. We are not coming to put you into further

trouble but to liberate you from the shackles of the Capitalists. You have nothing to lose but your chains and may therefore rest assured that the end of your privation is within sight.

Everyone at the table had an idea. Chinese talks of negotiation were simply a ploy to get the Tibetans to surrender without fighting. The Chinese would invade anyway, no matter what. Wasn't it time to fight for Tibet, win or lose?

No one mentioned that some nobles were already shipping gold bullion out of Tibet. One recent case, the subject of much gossip, showed the fearlessness and strength of the Chinese.

Some traders had come from Kham and went about freely in Lhasa making propaganda in favor of the Communists, apparently unnoticed. They carried letters from the Communists addressed to the Dalai Lama, the regent, and the Kashag, asking the Tibetans to send negotiators. When the traders were finally arrested and their rooms searched, a radio transceiver was discovered. The Chinese had spies in Lhasa with radios. Bessac was fascinated to hear the inside story of how the Tibetans were reacting to the Chinese threat. It reminded him of dinners in Dingyuanying with the PLA pounding on the city gates one year before and dinners with Mackiernan in Tihwa in the fall of 1949, when the tide had swept that far. In his mind, Bessac could look back over the last year and see a wave of Chinese, moving ever farther beyond the Great Wall. Now they were pounding on the gates of Lhasa. If only the Tibetans could gain the time that the Mongols and the Kazak had not had to build up their defenses. It was the only hope. Every day the Tibetans gained, every day they held off the Chinese, was one more day to train more troops.

The wife of one of the officials, a beautiful woman, sat quietly during the discussions, unable to speak English. A gold charm box, studded with coral and turquoise, rested heavily on her breasts. Her long black hair lay against her fair skin as she served food to the group with unconscious grace.

Two men who were brothers sat beside Bessac at dinner. First one and then the other talked to him about "my son Mingma." Each, separately, asked Bessac if he could help him get "my" son into an American school. After a few glasses of *chang,* Bessac realized that both men were referring to the same son. They were co-husbands in a polyandrous marriage. They were both married to the same wife, as was the custom among many Tibetan families: in order to keep the family wealth intact. Two brothers had several sons, who married one wife, and so the family wealth could be passed down, unbroken, from generation to generation. Everyone had a polite laugh when Bessac figured this out and obliquely broached the subject. Then the conversation moved on. Would Mr. Bessac please come round to the Tibetan Foreign Bureau for further talks on the next day?

As the party ended, one of the men had a few words with him. "I could not help noticing you admiring my wife tonight."

Bessac blushed.

"Aren't you lonely?"

"Well, sure I am."

"I think I can help you there."

And that was how "Pema" and "Lhamo" came into the lives of Bessac and Zvansov. The next evening, two young women showed up to have dinner with them. Heinrich Harrer speaks of this form of Tibetan hospitality. "Sometimes it happened that a pretty young servant girl was offered to one, but the girls don't give themselves without being courted."

Bessac recalls that the courtship lasted one or two nights. After that, the lady was his nightly companion as long as he was in Lhasa.

THE TIBETAN FOREIGN BUREAU
LHASA, TIBET
JUNE 16, 1950

Bessac took what he still calls "the holy walk" around the Potala and Lhasa each morning during the six weeks he was in Tibet. Tibetans call this practice *kora*. Every morning thousands of devotees walked around the sacred palaces and temples of Lhasa; such ritual circumambulation is an ancient form of popular Buddhism. Every morning Bessac put on his Tibetan robe, shoved an old felt fedora down low on his head, and walked with the pilgrims.

Kora was Bessac's only opportunity to slip away from his Tibetan minders. They preferred to be with Bessac whenever he talked with anyone, and he usually needed a translator. They let him know that he should not talk with Hugh Richardson unless they were present. The Tibetans were increasingly convinced that the British had let them down.

Gyalo Thondup today thinks of the late Hugh Richardson as the British colonial "hand behind the curtain." Westerners regard him as a scholar because of his vast knowledge of Tibet and his several published books. He spent his last years living just near the golf links at Saint Andrews, Scotland, before his death in December 2000 at the age of ninety-three. Though British, he was the Indian representative in Lhasa in 1950—he had served as the British representative in Lhasa before the Indian colony achieved independence. After 1947 Richardson was retained for some years by the Indian government and remained in the same compound in Lhasa, a practical decision since no Indian had the mastery of the Tibetan language or politics as had Richardson.

Bessac wanted to make radio contact with his government, but he could not get Mackiernan's radio to work. He peered into the gate of the Indian mission on one of his morning walks. Servants in red livery escorted him to Richardson, who had already seen many messages about Bessac since the U.S. radio messages to the Tibetan government had been sent through him. Their meeting was brief. Bessac wrote out a message, for the U.S. embassy in New Delhi, and Richardson agreed to radio it out in code for him.

Richardson asked the same question everyone was thinking.

"Are you an official representative of the U.S. government?"

Bessac replied that he was a lost Fulbright scholar, and then returned to his walk around the city.

After completing the five-mile walk around Lhasa, Bessac had a cup of milk tea at his house and then walked into the city. He made his second daily stop at the center of all the *kora* paths—in fact, it is the center of Tibet—the Jokhang temple. He discovered that the monks in the central cathedral chanted every morning at 11 A.M. shortly before they were fed. He liked to stop in and listen to them. On the way into the Jokhang, he paused to look at the stone pillar in front of it. Carved in stone in 822, it records a solemn treaty between the Tibetan and the Chinese emperors.

"Tibet and China shall abide by the frontiers of which they are now in occupation. All to the east is the country of Great China; and all to the west is, without question, the country of Great Tibet."

Inside the Jokhang, hundreds of shaven-headed monks in red robes sat in parallel lines in the main chapel. Skylights and flickering butterlamps dimly illuminated them. The monks rocked back and forth as they solemnly chanted Buddhist texts; Bessac was mesmerized. In that vast echoing chamber, lined with thousand-year-old paintings and carvings, he could hear the heart of Tibet throbbing, as though nothing had ever changed, and nothing would ever change.

Long lines of pilgrims, each with a small pail of butter, stood in line to enter the chapels around the central hall. Bessac joined the line to light a butterlamp before one of the ancient bronze statues. The pilgrims added dabs of butter to the ever-burning butterlamps before the statues in each chapel. The more chapels visited, the more merit for a better rebirth the pilgrim acquired. Women prostrated themselves to the statues, their children held between their knees bowing with their mothers. The central focus of this devotion was the ancient Buddha statue, known as the *Jowo,* brought from China to Tibet a millennium ago. Though the Nepalese wife's statue had at first been installed in the Jokhang, the statue was eventually replaced by the Chinese bride's statue of the Buddha.

The Chinese image of the Buddha was almost invisible behind the offerings of silk brocade, golden canopies, and an encrustation of turquoise and coral that smothered it. During the 1960s, the People's Liberation Army desecrated the Jokhang by slaughtering pigs in the most sacred temple in Tibet. Its walls were blood-spattered for at least a year. Many of the statues, including the ancient Buddha from China, were damaged or destroyed. After 1979 the temple was restored and worship was again allowed there, but no Tibetan can ever forget the low point of the Cultural Revolution in Tibet. Bessac was the last American to see the Jokhang before the Chinese invasion.

After lighting a butterlamp in the crush of pilgrims, Bessac sat down against a wall and looked upward to the one hundred and eight carved tigers atop the soaring pillars. The ancient art, bearing a patina of the ages, the prostrating masses, and the chanting monks stilled his heart. A child laughed and that high-pitched note echoed in the chamber above the deep bass of the chanting monks. Bessac breathed deeply. Then he saw the nomad men, cloaked in their sheepskin robes, such tough characters turned suddenly so devout. They unfurled the pigtails wrapped around their heads and bowed low before the ancient Chinese statue of the Buddha.

That gesture brought back the first time Bessac had seen nomads take their pigtails down. The soldiers had done so when they saw the arrow letter on the Changthang. Then came the cascade of uncalled, involuntary images—pictures that suddenly were more real than the temple before his eyes.

Mackiernan's face in its death grimace. Smoke rising up from the firing guns. An awful flash of the heads in the bag bouncing along on the way to Lhasa. The biscuit in Mackiernan's mouth, and then the nomad laughing as he ate it. Bessac could not stop the flood of memories. With each picture an involuntary shudder ran through his body, and he was soon covered in a cold sweat. When at last the temple filled his eyes once more he sighed deeply, got up off the floor where he had been sitting, and left.

Bessac pushed through the thronging pilgrims, down a dark passage, past tiny chapels each with dozens of statues lit by butterlamps twinkling at their feet. Then he walked out into a sunny courtyard filled with pilgrims and monks, where the all-pervasive smell of Tibetan incense, composed primarily of juniper and tiny petals from a miniature rhododendron that grows only above sixteen thousand feet, filled the air. Tibetans say the incense contains one hundred and eight precious herbs. A solid white tower of smoke rose into the sky from one corner of the central courtyard, where a six-foot-high censer was constantly fed by newly arriving pilgrims. Bessac worked his way through the crowds, out of the brilliant light and into another long dark passageway. The halls, chapels, and courtyards were permeated with the smell of butter and juniper—a scent that brought all of Tibet to him.

Bessac climbed out of the next courtyard on a set of mud, timber, and stone stairs to the second floor housing the Foreign Bureau. The offices overlooked the Barkor, the main bazaar that circles the Jokhang temple. He entered a series of small interconnected rooms. Each room had four pillars to support the flat mud roof. On every pillar hung ancient Tibetan letters—some were red scrolls from arrow letters, like the one sent to him, others were folded handmade paper. Hundreds hung from the pillars, all covered with dust. The Joint Foreign Secretaries of the Foreign Bureau appeared at the office around 11 A.M. As in every Tibetan office, one was a monk and one was a noble— dual administration, representing the two dominant forces in Tibet.

What percentage of Tibetans were serfs; what percentage of the land was owned by nobles and monks; what were the conditions of life for the serfs: all of this has been a matter of furious debate since China invaded Tibet. China gleefully excuses its invasion by saying it was only, "liberating the oppressed masses." Some supporters of Tibet have tried to downplay the difficult conditions that many Tibetans lived under. The "truth about feudal Tibet" remains elusive. Despite this modern debate two things are clear. No problem inside of Tibet justified China's invasion, and Monks and nobles held nearly all political power in Tibet.

In this feudal society, many of the farmers of central Tibet were bound to the soil, owned by monks or nobles, similar to the plight of European peasants in the Middle Ages. These serfs were not supposed to leave the estate to which they were bonded without permission of their lord. When the land was sold, the peasants usually went with it. The nomads escaped servitude, but even they paid an annual tax in butter to one of the great monasteries. The Khampas in eastern Tibet were not subject to this system. The monks, too, were immune to the nobles' demands for "corvée labor." The Fourteenth Dalai Lama, according to Heinrich Harrer, was eager to reform this system as soon as he came into his majority. The Chinese hoped to exploit the system as Tibet's Achilles' heel. If enough Tibetans resented feudalism, perhaps they would view the Chinese invasion as a political liberation.

The lay secretary, Surkhang Lhawang Topgyal, was sumptuously dressed in silk robes with his long pigtails tied around a turquoise topknot. He was an elderly gentleman, descended from one of the two hundred noble families that ruled Tibet. *Surkhang* means "corner house" in Tibetan, and his clan had held on to the finest corner house on the Barkor since the seventeenth century. The family had taken the name of their house. The Surkhangs were one of Lhasa's most distinguished and powerful aristocratic families. One of Surkhang's sons was the chief minister of Tibet; another was a general. Surkhang's brother was commander in chief of the Tibetan army. Surkhang and the commander in chief had both met Bessac at dinner the previous night.

The much younger, religious, secretary of the Foreign Bureau, Liushar Thupten Tharpa, showed up after they had been talking awhile. He was dressed in red woolen robes with his head freshly shaved, like all monks. Surkhang and Liushar administered the section together. These two men had written President Truman and Secretary of State Acheson in January. These men had proposed to send a Tibetan mission to the United States to seek U.S. aid and to apply for UN membership. They were rebuffed for their own good, as they were told.

The Foreign Bureau secretaries saw Bessac as "officially unofficial" and even the Dalai Lama says they wanted to talk about the supply of arms in 1950. Bessac sat down with the secretaries in Lhasa, behind closed doors, and talked for several days. In 1994, forty-four years after the talks took place, the U.S. government declassified Bessac's report about his meetings with the Tibetan Foreign Bureau, which he wrote in India after he had left Tibet.

> They asked me for advice concerning the possibility of relationships between the Government of Tibet and the Government of the United States of America. In reply, I first made certain that they understood that I was not an American official, and anything that I said would be of necessity in an unofficial capacity. They replied that they understood this, but that I might be of value both to the American and Tibetan Governments in the role of an unofficial adviser, and they again requested that I help them. I replied that I would do all that I could to further the relationship between the Government of the United States of America and the Government of Tibet.

The first issue the Tibetans wanted to discuss was whether Bessac agreed with them about their decision not to allow the planned American rescue mission to come to Lhasa. The Tibetans explained that earlier the United States had refused to allow them to send a mission to America, because it might precipitate a Chinese invasion. The Tibetans replied in the same way about the proposed U.S. rescue mission. Sending Frederick Latrash, known to some of the highest Lhasa officials as an undercover CIA agent, to Lhasa might also precipitate a Chinese invasion. Bessac agreed, as he wrote in 1950.

> I agreed with the Tibetans in their action. Elaborating I said that any *overt* action done now which might aggravate the Chinese Communists would endanger the safety of Tibet.

This was in accord with stated U.S. policy toward Tibet, though Bessac had no contact with the State Department. The CIA or the State Department, or both, wanted to change that policy by sending Frederick Latrash to rescue Bessac. Latrash did not know Bessac had a hand in nixing his trip until 1998. When the two men met in September 1950 on the Tibetan-Indian border, which was as far as Latrash was allowed to go, Bessac never mentioned to Latrash his discussions with the Tibetans.

Latrash was issued orders to travel to Lhasa sometime in May or June, just before Bessac arrived in Lhasa. Latrash says they were the only State Department orders ever issued with Lhasa as their destination. Latrash believes that he could have activated the assets he had established by face-to-face meetings in Lhasa. But that was not to be. After their discussion with Bessac the Tibetans confirmed their decision not to allow a rescue mission. Latrash was ultimately allowed only up to the Tibetan border—leaving him always wondering what he could have achieved if only he had been able to make the journey.

The issue of military aid formed the centerpiece of Bessac's talks in Lhasa. The Tibetans and both Bessac and Latrash knew what was required—even if Washington had not made up its mind. Bessac did what he thought Mackiernan would have done, and what he thought was best for Tibetans. It is doubtful if any U.S. official could have sounded more official than Bessac did when he wrote his report.

> I deemed it necessary that first the Governments of Tibet and the United States of America should establish secret radio communications. This could easily be done by use of the already existing Tibetan

radio in Lhasa. This radio has sufficient strength to make and maintain contact with American Stations in Japan or Iraq. I stated that if this proposal were acceptable to the American Government, cypher pads would be sent to the Government in Tibet. To my knowledge there is no danger connected with this operation.

"I then asked what sort of military aid the Tibetans would need." The Tibetans replied that they would have to send that question up the chain of command to the regent and to the Kashag. Bessac plunged on.

I also stated that the American Government could hardly be expected to give military assistance to any nation or area in which there is no American representative; and suggested that an American military and economic adviser be covertly assigned to Lhasa in order to report to the American Government upon the situation in Tibet; that this American adviser's actual position be unknown to anyone but the Foreign Bureau; that he reside in Tibet under a different capacity, such as a student, missionary, doctor or newspaper reporter.

There was one last item on Bessac's agenda. He "urged" the Tibetans to cooperate with the Kazak from Timurlik—he wanted couriers from there to be able to pass safely through Tibet. Mackiernan had arranged for intelligence reports coming out of Sinkiang to be passed on to Timurlik. By urging the Tibetans to let the Kazak couriers come through Tibet, Bessac was forging a final link for intelligence to flow from Mackiernan's intelligence network in Sinkiang through Tibet to U.S. agents in India.

After asking if they had any questions, and receiving the reply they had none, I asked if they approved of this plan. They stated that they did, but that they would have to refer the matter to the Regent, Cabinet, and National Assembly. I said that was fine as far as I was concerned, and that I wished an early reply.

The United States wanted to see Tibet covertly armed, but without the Chinese hearing of it. It appears that two CIA agents, Mackiernan and Latrash, worked toward that goal before the Chinese invasion. Latrash suspects that the State Department and the CIA in Washington may have been arguing about this policy. Perhaps the Outfit was encouraging activity not authorized by the State Department. Or perhaps liaison between different agencies of the federal government was mismanaged because of confusion and paranoia resulting from McCarthyism. What is certain is that actions that should have been covert—according to U.S. policy—were not.

CARVING CROSSES
LHASA, TIBET
JULY 30, 1950

Vasili Zvansov carved the crosses slowly. The Tibetan Buddhist carpenters had made the Christian crosses, three of them, from a sketch Zvansov had provided. After they were made, he took about a week to carve them, according to the old school of Christianity in which he had been raised in Kazakhstan. He sat carving on the flat mud roof in the sun, as his leg continued to heal.

He had separate rooms in the government villa, and the doctor stayed right with him. The penicillin shots continued. The doctor changed his bandages and cleaned his wound. The cook made his meals. The woman the government sent came at night. The Tibetans were taking good care of him. Life in Lhasa had become a ritual, and the doctor was always there.

At first he had been happy just to rest, but after meeting the Dalai Lama he slowly began to have more interest in life. Some days when he sat in the sun carving, the only other White Russian in Lhasa came by to chat. Heinrich Harrer calls this man by the name Nedbailoff. He was a refugee from Stalin's dictatorship in Russia, like Zvansov, but twenty years older. He had been wandering about Asia since the Marxist revolution in 1917. He finally landed in the same internment camp from which Harrer had escaped. In 1947 the British had threatened to deport him back to the U.S.S.R.—and certain death. In desperation, he escaped and fled to Tibet. When the British seized him near the Tibetan border, he was allowed to remain in Sikkim—an independent Buddhist kingdom—since he was a mechanic. By the summer of 1949, Nedbailoff was assisting an English engineer hired to install the new General Electric generators for the Lhasa hydroelectric project.

Zvansov listened to Nedbailoff as he carved. From his accent, he could tell the man came from a noble family, not serfs. They talked about the revolution and the pogroms of Stalin from which Zvansov had fled. Every day for a week they talked. Lenin one day. The camps the next.

One day as Vasili carved, he had stopped to drink from a glass of water.

"I was holding a glass in my hand when he suddenly said, 'You know, I think that the Soviets are going to get us.'

"I dropped the glass, I was so shocked, and then I said, 'They are going to kill us, what the hell are you talking about!'

"I think he was testing me. He was doing a professional job, to see whether I was red or white. I thought he was a professional CIA worker."

"Wait a minute," Zvansov thought to himself, "this guy knows how to find out who is who. That Russian was a real artist, he really surprised me, looks like he had good schooling."

After that, Nedbailoff never came to talk with Zvansov again. Zvansov continued his carving. Yet the incident made him look closely at the few foreigners in Lhasa. He knew better than to talk about it, but he formed his own opinions.

"I also felt that Harrer was working for someone, the CIA or somebody—but we did not talk about it. For me then if they were against the Communists they were okay with me. Who was going to stay there in Tibet without working for someone?"

Only during the past ten years, State Department documents have been declassified that show Harrer may have been involved with several covert operations for the Americans after he left Tibet.

Some nights Bessac and Zvansov had dinner together with their Tibetan girls. They did not have much else in common. Bessac wore Tibetan robes the Foreign Bureau had given to him. Zvansov donned a Western suit sewn for him in the bazaar by a Barkor tailor and he managed to buy a pair of boots that fit him.

The two men were headed in different directions. Zvansov was thinking of Mackiernan's promise that he would be given a U.S. visa when they made it out to India. He was a refugee looking toward America as a safe haven in a world at war. Bessac was an American who had gone as far into Asia as you could go, but he was headed still deeper into Asia every day he spent in Lhasa.

Each day Bessac went off with the Tibetans, and Zvansov worked on the crosses.

THE FLOGGING
LHASA, TIBET
JULY 1950

Shortly before Bessac left Tibet, the soldiers who shot Mackiernan were punished, as Bessac described for *Life* magazine once he got home. In an article titled "This Was the Perilous Trek to Tragedy," Bessac and James Burke wrote,

> Just before we left Lhasa, I was told that the six border guards had been tried and sentenced in Lhasa's military court. The leader was to have his nose and both ears cut off. The man who fired the fatal shot was to lose both ears. A third man was to lose one ear, and the others were to get 50 lashes each. The men receiving the lesser sentences ... had argued with the leader against shooting. Since the Tibetan Buddhists do not believe in capital punishment, mutilation is the stiffest sentence given in Tibet. But I felt this punishment was too severe, so I asked if it could be lightened. My request was granted. The new sentences were: 200 lashes for the leader and the man who fired the first shot, 50 lashes to the third man and 25 each for the others. I was asked if I would like to witness the punishments. I watched and enjoyed the whole proceeding and took ... pictures.

THE POTALA
LHASA, TIBET
JULY 1950

The whitewashed room where the Kashag met was about the size of a basketball court deep within the Potala, A lightwell, coming down through the courtyards within the Potala, lit the vast room from above. Bessac says that Heinrich Harrer guided him up the massive front steps of the Potala, through the battle-gated courtyard, and up the steep steps to the assembly hall. Before they went in, Bessac took a photograph of Harrer on the roof of the Potala, wearing his black European suit and porkpie hat. Bessac says he then went to the meeting, alone, and sat quietly in a corner, watching.

There was a long debate, back and forth in Tibetan, which Bessac could not understand. Members of the Kashag sat among the monks and others who composed the audience until it was their turn to speak, and then they rose to stand on the raised platform as they addressed the power elite of Tibet. Tibetan sources believe that Bessac may have been confused. They say he probably attended a meeting of the National Assembly, not the Kashag.

Bessac's understanding of this meeting is that the Kashag was debating whether to request covert military aid officially from the United States. Bessac had discussed their situation several times with the Foreign Bureau secretaries and the commander in chief. He felt they knew that such a request, if revealed to China, could cause a Chinese invasion, but that the Tibetans were willing to take that risk. Furthermore, during his discussions in Lhasa, Bessac had developed the firm opinion that the Chinese would not invade Tibet that winter. It was already July, and they had not invaded, so it seemed impossible to think they would invade the Tibetan Plateau in winter. Bessac had crossed the Changthang in the spring and could not imagine a winter invasion. He and the Tibetans assumed China would invade in the spring of 1951, which meant Tibet had to get the weapons it needed from America that winter.

Tibetan records of the meeting have been lost, and most Tibetans in attendance have since died, which leaves Bessac as the sole witness. The Dalai Lama remembers only that Bessac held some talks with government officials, but does not recall further details. Bessac says that at one point he actually got up in front of the Kashag and presented the reasons why the Tibetans needed to make an official request for covert military aid.

If that is true, it recalls his address to the Mongol delegates conference almost exactly one year earlier. It is a remarkable image: twenty-eight-year-old Frank Bessac in his Tibetan robes, addressing the ancient nobility of Tibet, deep within the Potala, a six-foot tall, silk-robed American standing less than fifty yards from the massive gold tombs of the previous Dalai Lamas of Tibet. Bessac's address to the Kashag is no small matter—it is a matter of historic import that before now has remained hidden. No one has ever before suggested that an American citizen addressed such a government body in Lhasa, not to speak of an American of his era urging the Tibetans to request U.S. weapons. His address could justify Chinese claims, made after their invasion, that they invaded Tibet to abort "imperialist plots."

"I was just trying to do something for Tibetans as I'd tried to do with the Mongols and with the Kazak. For their . . . independence. I got them to accept an American there, an official covert military adviser. I presented it to them, and then they officially sent out a document asking for that. I had to justify their signing this.

"'If you want help from the Americans, you have to officially ask for it and receive it. You can do it covertly, but you have to ask for it. There has to be a document. I will covertly, safely, take the document without the Chinese seeing it.'" Bessac knew there were risks, but felt it was a grim time which justified them.

It was impossible to keep the purpose of the meeting secret. Frederick Latrash "assumed" there were Chinese spies in the Kashag. Latrash says that he would *not* have sought the public approval Bessac did.

"I would've said screw that because all you are going to do is get enough people knowledgeable about it that you're going to provoke the invasion. . . . You want a document from the Dalai Lama, one guy? Fine, if that's what you want. But they [Washington] never asked."

Latrash is convinced that Bessac, without knowledge of what was already in the works, had "screwed up the United States government . . . because I could have completed certain loops that remain never connected again. . . . My capabilities and resources up there, I could have discussed things on the spot with them. . . . They were doing so much up there, in terms of building a machine to get something done, I wouldn't have had to do it remotely. I would have been able to do it directly."

Bessac was not the only American talking with the Tibetans about U.S. aid to Tibet. During the summer of 1950, the United States was in regular contact with the Shakabpa mission that had been stuck in India for the previous six months, trying to reach Hong Kong or Singapore for talks with the Chinese. Shakabpa had a number of discussions with U.S. embassy and consulate officials about possible aid for Tibet. On June 16—probably a few weeks before the Kashag debated the Bessac proposals—he bluntly asked the U.S. ambassador in India if the United States was going to supply military aid in case of a Chinese invasion. Ambassador Loy Henderson reported to the State Department that

> In response to Shakabpa's direct question . . . [the ambassador] stated we could not in fairness encourage Tibetans to believe that the U.S. Government would consider it feasible to offer such aid.

At the same time, Henderson told Shakabpa that their conversation was unofficial. Henderson explained he would have to pose the question to policy makers in Washington to obtain a final answer on the matter.

Shakabpa was reporting his conversations in Delhi to the Kashag, thus we can assume that they had his report by the time they considered Bessac's proposals. This means that Latrash's presumed Chinese spy in the Kashag would have heard about *two* Tibetan-American contacts regarding the covert supply of weapons.

Despite the urgent nature of Shakabpa's request, it would take the

Americans until August 7, 1950, to reply to his request for military aid. Nine weeks. In that time America's Postwar thinking about A had changed: it had changed in twenty-four hours.

On June 25, 1950, two weeks after Bessac arrived in Lhasa, North Korea invaded South Korea. First America had lost China; now it looked as if it would lose Korea. Asian nations were falling to Communism, one after the other, like dominoes. Unfortunately for the Tibetans, the ideals behind the Truman Doctrine—established during the period of America's atomic monopoly—came due at a time when America was finding it demanding to live up to those ideals. In seventeen days, outnumbered American troops retreated seventy miles in front of North Korean troops, one of the longest retreats in U.S. military history. Atomic bombs could not prevent it. It began to look as though the United States would be thrown off the Asian mainland, making it quite difficult for the Americans to establish further overt commitments in Asia, particularly to a country as remote as Tibet.

The Korean War added urgency to Bessac's talks in Lhasa. There was a feeling that a third world war might break out any day.

LAST DAYS IN LHASA
LATE JULY 1950

At night, Bessac could hear the sound of the Happy River flowing by the villa on the outskirts of Lhasa. He stood on the flat roof smoking. Under a full moon, the Potala loomed above silvered meadows and enshadowed willows. A tower of white incense rose above the temple. The deep bass sound of the twelve-foot-long copper horns at a ritual in the Jokhang drifted out from the city.

In the distance someone laughed, and then a song began. Heinrich Harrer had come and gone. He had brought the maps of Lhasa, and the maps of routes through the Himalayas on which he and his friend Peter Aufschneiter had spent years working. No one else had ever actually mapped Lhasa with modern techniques. Now the U.S. government would have them. Harrer knew that the Chinese should never hear of this gift, or they would think he and Aufschneiter were spying for the Americans.

Harrer said that he and Aufschneiter wanted to "secure credit with" U.S. government sources for supplying the maps. They were just as eager to be sure that no one outside the U.S. government ever knew who had supplied them. Bessac folded up the 5 x 9-foot map of Lhasa and slipped it into his bags, eventually handing it over to the State Department in New Delhi. Today, it is in the National Archives at College Park, Maryland, a historic document in need of better conservation than it has thus far received.

The Tibetan girls, Pema and Lhamo, had also been by that night for dinner and farewells. There were no tears, only laughter and jokes. As Bessac looked out at Lhasa in the night, he knew that he would miss her.

There was a campfire on an island in the stream only fifty yards away, and someone was rhythmically thumbing the strings of a Tibetan guitar. It was foot-tapping music, and he could just make out the line of dancers around the fire. A high wailing song drifted in above the sound of the water. The moonlight glittered on the rippling water. The music sounded like the songs the Mongols sang at night in the desert. Wild wails under a star-studded sky.

Then there was the letter from the Tibetan government, which the Foreign Bureau had handed over to him. Bessac had gone to the Foreign Office to collect the official response. As he bid farewell to the Tibetan secretaries, he pulled out his machine gun.

"Here, you might need this if World War Three breaks out."

The Tibetans' response to receiving the one gun is not recorded. The official letter of request was already packed in Bessac's bag along with Harrer's maps. Sitting on the roof in Lhasa, perhaps he wondered about Qali Beg and Doug Mackiernan. In his mind's eye, could he see Mackiernan receiving the letter in the yurt before they left Timurlik? Mackiernan dead, and the letter fluttering away across the Changthang. Bessac had done his best to complete Mackiernan's work.

GOVERNMENT OF TIBET
FOREIGN BUREAU
UNDATED
CONFIDENTIAL NOTE

What you have told us during our last meeting here was reported
to His Highness the Regent of Tibet through the Kashag, and the
following statement is the reply from our Government:

"We have fully understood the contents of the letter sent by [Qali
Beg] the Chief of [Timurlik] to His Holiness the Dalai Lama, which
though lost at [Shegar-Hunglung], was roughly explained by you
verbally. Therefore, if they send any messengers towards Tibet with
secret information about communist movements, then we shall send
orders to our frontier posts not to stop them."

Whatever stay-behind agents Mackiernan had left in Sinkiang now
had a clear channel through Tibet with which to get their intelligence
out to India. Looking back on it now, Bessac is still glad he involved
the Tibetans in this operation. "What Doug had wanted to do was to
allow the People of East Turkestan and Tibet as much independence
as possible. If that meant Qali Beg should send messages through
Tibet, then of course he would try to help that happen."

Then there was Bessac's discussion with the government about the
covert supply of U.S. weapons to Tibet. The Tibetans had the idea
that the United States would provide them weapons in exchange for
certain intelligence about their own army. If they told Bessac exactly
how many soldiers they had, it was believed the Americans would
arm them in exchange. The Tibetan reply was a direct appeal for U.S.
military aid.

We would like you also to ask the American Government to help
to defend the cause of Tibet. . . .

In this connection, you suggested that in order to supply Tibet with
big guns, machine guns and other effective weapons of the latest type,
we should furnish American Government with full information regarding the total number of troops in Tibet, and also out of the total
number of men, how many men could properly handle big guns,

machine guns, etc. The total strength of our army is one hundred thousand men [*the true figure was twenty thousand*] and if there is any emergency we can recruit more men as required in addition to the above number. Out of the permanent troops, there are one thousand soldiers who know how to use howitzers and about two thousand men who can use machine guns and Tuis guns, two thousand men who can use Bren guns and Sten Guns, three hundred men, out of which some are trained and others being trained to handle 2" and 3" mortars. The remaining troops are well trained in firing rifles. Therefore please ask the US Government confidentially to supply our Government adequate number of latest type of howitzer guns, 50mm light machine guns, 75mm horse pulled rifles [cannon] and the new weapon called bazooka etc. Which are useful for Tibet. We also need some portable field service radio sets for our army and also sufficient number of American dollars for the purpose of our military expenditure.

If the US Government agrees to sanction the above aid to Tibet, then we may have direct radio communication between Washington and Lhasa; and we would like to ask the US Government to make a new code book for this purpose and send one copy to our Government enabling us to send wireless telegrams for the purpose of consulting the US Government regarding importing the above arms through India secretly and also about sending of secret representatives to Tibet etc.

Please discuss the matter fully and approach President Truman and other US authorities as to obtain their agreement with regards to the above aid for Tibet when you arrive in America and let us have an early reply.

The Foreign Bureau secretaries said that all the talk of negotiation with the Chinese was simply a stalling action: they were delaying until they had received enough weapons to hold them off when they did invade.

Before Bessac left Lhasa, there was one more thing the Tibetans wanted him to do. Tibetans, including the Dalai Lama, believe that in every generation there is a human being who can go into trance ¹ ⸰llow Tibet's special protector deity, Dorje Drakden, to seize his   ice. Tibetans called this monk—who lived at Nechung   —the state oracle of Tibet.

The Nechung oracle is asked only about the most serious questions facing the Tibetan nation. In late July, before Bessac left Tibet, the oracle was asked to make predictions about the fate of Tibet as it faced the Chinese threat.

Bessac says that he was invited to attend the trance session, because the Tibetans somehow believed that his arrival in Tibet at that moment was not entirely accidental. "They thought it would be important that I come . . . because I was concerned about the invasion, and he was going to make predictions about the invasion."

Bessac rode a horse out to Nechung Monastery, a few miles north of Lhasa. The oracle was a diminutive man, dressed in a mass of silk robes. When his ninety-pound headdress was put on his head, he needed two men to help him stand. Within a few moments, after he had slowly fallen into a trance, the power of the protector deity surged through the man. Suddenly, the body of the frail man was electrified. He jerked about the stage as though his heavy headdress was feather light. He foamed at the mouth. He made the strangest noises, which only a very few specially trained monks could translate. Bessac reports: "You know the report of the oracle on that occasion? Oh, he said that the Chinese were not those who were going to overthrow Tibet . . . that it was not that period and Tibet would be powerful and prosperous and would defeat its enemy."

By July the Chinese had grown tired of hearing that Tibetan negotiators were on their way to Tibet; they based their actions on intelligence from spies, not oracles. They had begun to believe that the Tibetans were stalling and using the time gained to try to obtain arms. China was already training an army at high altitude, near the Tibetan border, that would invade when the order was given.

There were more picnics on the islands in the Happy River that flows in front of Lhasa than there were in most summers. The nobles took out their coracles, bedecked with parasols, and set up their tents on the willow-shrouded islands in the stream. Servants prepared ten-course luncheons. The *chang* flowed freely. Vast embroidered tents were erected. Tibetan guitars were brought out, and people sang and danced. Bessac was invited to one such picnic and remembers it well. The golden roofs of the Potala in the distance, reflecting in the stream, overhung with willows. Tibetan peasants—men, women, and children—bathed unabashedly nude along the banks of the river, while the children of the nobles cavorted in the latest imported bathing costumes.

That was in July. In October, when the Chinese troops began their invasion of Central Tibet, the Tibetan Kashag was having another picnic on the Happy River. The first news about the invasion was radioed in from eastern Tibet, but there was no response. The Tibetan official radioed Lhasa again. Despite his persistence he could not get any instructions from the Kashag. Eventually, an aide-de-camp to the Kashag told the desperate official—who would soon flee the Chinese army without any instructions from Lhasa—that the Kashag could not be disturbed because they were at a picnic.

As China invaded Tibet, the last words from eastern Tibet were those of a Tibetan frustrated at the nobles in Lhasa who were unable even to respond to an invasion of their country.

He said, "Shit on the picnic!"

Then the radio went dead.

MACKIERNAN'S DEATH ANNOUNCED
JULY 29, 1950

The State Department in Washington, D.C., and the U.S. embassy in New Delhi were arguing about when and how to announce the death of Douglas Mackiernan and the presence of Frank Bessac in Lhasa. Thus far they had kept the news out of the press.

The embassy advanced many arguments for postponing as long as possible the announcement of Mackiernan's death. The State Department assumed the Reds would exploit Bessac's presence in Lhasa for propaganda purposes, but that would be done no matter when it was announced. The State Department argued for an announcement, and the embassy argued against it. Finally, the State Department grew exasperated and advanced another reason for making an announcement.

"Should be noted that with present Korean crisis occupying prominent press space story RE Mackiernan would probably not draw undue public attention [at] this time."

Two days after Bessac and Zvansov left Lhasa, all these arguments were overturned. A garbled account appeared in a New Delhi paper on July 28. The State Department contacted Reuters in America and attempted to suppress the story. When that proved impossible, the United States preempted any reporting by issuing a cover story. Despite the Korean War, Mackiernan's death made page one of *The New York Times* on July 30. Not a shred of investigation into the State Department's press release was attempted.

U.S. CONSUL FLEEING CHINA, SLAIN
BY TIBETANS ON WATCH FOR BANDITS

WASHINGTON, JULY 29—Douglas S. Mackiernan, forced to flee his post as United States vice consul at Urumchi in Northwest China last September, was accidentally shot and killed by Tibetan border guards at the Tibetan border on his way out of Communist China.

Ten months after Mr. Mackiernan's hasty departure from the capital of Sinkiang Province, now held by the Chinese Communists, the State Department announced today that the vice consul, who was 37 years of age, had been shot last April 13. The guards, according to the department, had apparently mistaken the party, at that point traveling by camel, for bandits or Communist raiders.

A native runner took twenty-seven days to carry the news of the incident to Lhasa, the capital of Tibet. The messenger's sketchy report was then relayed to United States authorities in New Delhi, India, Mr. Mackiernan's destination.

Mr. Mackiernan was accompanied on his caravan by Frank Bessac, a scholar from Lodi, Calif., who had been studying in Northwest China. Mr. Bessac was not hurt and is now making his way to New Delhi. Two native servants, however, were killed in the shooting and another was injured.

The report in the *Lodi News-Sentinel,* Bessac's hometown paper, was not a two-column piece on the bottom of page one. In Lodi, it was a banner headline all across the top of the paper: FRANK BESSAC, LODIAN, ESCAPES COMMUNIST CHINA THROUGH TIBET.

Bessac and Zvansov were in a yak-skin coracle floating south down a branch of the Tsangpo River. Lhasa was behind them, and the golden roofs of the Potala were the last traces of it to disappear. They were lost on the broad, braided river floating rudderless, back and forth across a treeless valley surrounded by rocky crags.

Zvansov remembers the stench of human corpses thrown into the river—after a Sky Burial—as they left town. Bessac recalls the birds feeding by the river.

Traveling the last leg toward India, Bessac lost himself in reverie. He thought of the Japanese excuses he had heard for the Japanese invasion and colonization of China when he had first came to China. The Chinese needed their elder brothers to help them develop. Asians had a different standard and had to band together to oppose Western colonialism. Today, he trembles with rage when he hears old Japanese nationalists saying that there was no "Rape of Nanking"—three hundred thousand Chinese were not killed by the Japanese Imperial Army, they say, which is similar to the Chinese who say that Tibet has always been part of China and that the long history of independent Tibet is a fiction created by enemies of Chinese nationalism.

None of it had anything to do with Communism or anti-Communism. It was about colonialism. America somehow gave up that fight after World War II—a fight that had its origins in America's revolt against Britain in 1776—and went off on another course during the birth of the Cold War.

That course would lead America deep into Southeast Asia in the defense of French colonialism there. As Bessac left Tibet the first MAP-303 aid—originally intended for China and Inner Asia—was landing on the docks of Saigon in South Vietnam.

MINISTER SHAKABPA VISITS THE U.S. CONSULATE
CALCUTTA, INDIA
AUGUST 4, 1950

At last, the State Department had a response to Minister Shakabpa's blunt request for U.S. military aid. Shakabpa was called into the Calcutta consulate because the Americans thought that might be more private than the U.S. embassy in New Delhi. U.S. Consul Steere had good news for Shakabpa. Despite Ambassador Henderson's June remarks to the Tibetans that they should not expect aid, the U.S. State Department had come to a different conclusion, stating that ". . . if Tibet intended to resist Communist aggression and needed help U.S. Government was prepared to assist in procuring material and would finance such aid."

Yet the United States insisted that the Tibetans should first obtain permission from India for that aid to transit through India. Shakabpa knew that India was collaborating with Great Britain in keeping him penned up in India. In addition, he may have known about Frederick Latrash's airfield in Lhasa. He tried another tack. He wondered about the possibility of an airlift to Tibet.

The American consul discouraged Shakabpa about "these ideas." The Americans wanted a detailed list of what the Tibetans needed. It was agreed that the Tibetans would send a special military aid mission to India from Lhasa to discuss Tibetan requirements and the means that would be used to supply them.

There is no record of what the Tibetans thought about this second request for a military aid list when the Kashag had just sent exactly that list out with Bessac, but surely it caused confusion for the Tibetans. It gives the appearance that there was little coordination between State and the CIA.

Frederick Latrash says that he was under orders *not* to talk with State Department staff about his covert work in Tibet. He reported all of his intelligence and his covert assets (like the airfield) to the CIA in Washington. Then the CIA decided what the State Department needed to be told. Only then would the State Department in Washington send back to New Delhi what it had decided the U.S. embassy in India needed to know. This ineffective intelligence distribution system rivals the one that allowed the United States to collect intelligence warnings about the possible bombing of Pearl Harbor without having gotten it to the right people in time to prevent it. The new peacetime intelligence outfit wasn't proving any better than the older, military one.

THE EARTHQUAKE
AUGUST 15, 1950

The fifth-largest earthquake in recorded history, was felt all across Tibet and much of northern India. Thirty or forty massive explosions ripped through the air. People reported what the Dalai Lama calls a strange red glow in the sky. A massive landslide cut off the entire flow of the Tsangpo/Brahmaputra River. A lake formed. When it burst, a wall of water sluiced down through the Himalayas and flooded hundreds of villages and took thousands of lives.

For the people of Tibet it was a sign from the gods—the ancient gods, protector deities of China and Tibet, were at war. An omen. The Chinese invasion was at hand. The Dalai Lama, even now, feels that it was something unusual.

> Perhaps there is a scientific explanation, but my own feeling is that what happened is presently beyond science, something truly mysterious. . . . At any rate, warning from on high or mere rumblings from below, the situation in Tibet deteriorated rapidly thereafter.

The earthquake hurt neither Bessac nor Zvansov. They arrived in Yatung, the last town in Tibet, on the tenth of August. They sat waiting for the party from the U.S. embassy to reach the first Indian town on the other side of Jelap Pass. Several embassy officials had come to the border, including Frederick Latrash. Telegrams were sent back and forth.

Finally, on August 19, Bessac and Zvansov rode their short-legged Tibetan ponies up to the pass, which kept vanishing and reappearing among thick monsoon clouds. A week's trek down through Sikkim to India remained, and throughout the journey the transition from Inner Asia to South Asia overwhelmed Bessac.

Trees. The loud call of cicadas and crickets. The sound of wind among green leaves. Bessac had not heard such sounds in more than a year. There were also annoyances he had forgotten about. Mosquitoes and leeches. His skin stayed wet and sticky because of the 100 percent humidity. Leather began to grow moldy patches. After a few meals he had diarrhea.

Though they had left dry and treeless Inner Asia behind, they could not see the Himalayas because of thick clouds. Day by day, they descended from the Tibetan Plateau through green clefts in the Himalayas and down to the plains of India. The mule track grew wider. The mule teams carrying rice to Tibet and bringing wool down were decked out with bells that rang loudly as they passed. Indians and Nepalese shared the trail with Sikkimese. On the outskirts of Kalimpong—a town that thrived on Indo-Tibetan trade—the party was hailed in English. Prince Peter of Greece had worked for the OSS during World War II. He and his wife, Princess Irene, a White Russian, had settled in Kalimpong. Bessac's arrival was the scuttlebutt of the trail from Lhasa. Prince Peter had caught wind of it. They chatted about the latest news from Lhasa, and then the Americans moved on.

When the track at last became wide enough to carry a car, just beyond Kalimpong, they came around a bend and found one waiting for them. The luggage was transferred from the mules and everyone piled in. After a rough two-day drive, they reached an airport, and on that night, August 28, they flew to Calcutta.

LATRASH AND BESSAC
CALCUTTA, INDIA
AUGUST 29, 1950

Frederick Latrash reviewed the latest reports from his Lhasa assets in the morning before he had his meeting with Bessac. Strange messages started to filter in from Lhasa. Latrash's Lhasa sources wanted to know who Bessac was, what he was doing in Lhasa, and if he was legitimate.

Bessac looked better after he had a shower and a shave, but still Latrash thought the guy had been out in the boonies too long. They were sitting in Latrash's Calcutta office, and all of Calcutta was out the window—shouting, beeping, the smell of coriander and chiles, rickshaw bells ringing, typical Calcutta madness, monsoon heat. Bessac came to pick up his tickets to Delhi, as he was supposed to fly the next day. Bessac also brought in a leather box and a duffel that contained all of Mackiernan's personal effects, and Latrash agreed to ship them on to Mackiernan's widow, Pegge.

They had been talking for a few minutes when Latrash tried to insert the code word into a sentence, casually.

He might have said something like, "I guess you haven't read the Oregon *Post* in a while?"

Bessac looked up at him sharply when he heard the word "Oregon." He had last heard it from Mackiernan.

Did he hesitate again, as he had with Mackiernan? Latrash does not recall, though he does remember that Bessac responded correctly.

"Yeah, I particularly liked the article in section D."

The letter *D*.

As far as Latrash was concerned, that was it. The code had been given and the correct reply was given back. So they now had a secure environment. He had been ordered to debrief Bessac, and now that they had established that they both worked with the CIA, the debriefing should have begun. Latrash says that's not the way it went, though.

Bessac said, "Well, I need more code."

"There isn't anymore. That's it. . . . If you think there is more, your memory is faulty. That is the end of the code. There is no more. . . . So you either accept that or go."

Latrash was stunned when Bessac cut him off.

"But tell me more."

"What do you mean tell you more?"

Bessac was very firm. "I need more recognition."

"There isn't anymore. That's it."

After a pause Bessac replied, "Okay, fine. . . . I'll talk with people back in D.C."

Still Latrash tried to begin his debriefing of Bessac. He had been ordered to begin with finances. Latrash recalls that Bessac should have accounted for one bar of gold that the CIA had given him before he left China for Inner Mongolia. Latrash was never told about the gold bars Mackiernan was carrying when he set off for Tibet, so he did not ask Bessac what had become of them. Bessac at first seemed willing to talk about his one gold bar. Bessac's explanations made little sense to Latrash. He said he had cut off a piece to buy some horses, but then the horses died, and they ate them. The size of the pieces was not clear. No one had a scale, so he didn't know. Latrash tried another tack.

"Do you have any information, do you have any records, do you have anything you can give me, any studies, any documents?"

"No, I don't have any."

Bessac failed to mention Mackiernan's travel log, which he was carrying. Nor did Bessac say a word about his talks in Tibet, or the written request for military aid that he was carrying. To Latrash it appeared that Bessac had simply been out of touch for too long.

THE U.S. EMBASSY
NEW DELHI, INDIA
AUGUST 30–SEPTEMBER 22, 1950

Bessac and Zvansov stayed at the U.S. embassy in New Delhi. Bessac and the embassy, after consultation with the State Department, prepared a press release because of great public interest in his story. On August 30 the press came to the embassy and Bessac read his prepared statement and answered questions.

Bessac had arrived at Tihwa and discovered that Mr. Mackiernan was the last American there. When Sinkiang went over to the Communists, Mackiernan "decided to leave Sinkiang and advised me to accompany him. . . . Neither I nor any of the three refugees held any official positions in the American government." Newspapers all over the world printed the story on September 1.

Bessac stayed three weeks in Delhi while he wrote reports and was interrogated by embassy officials. He gave Mackiernan's journals and the maps from Heinrich Harrer to the State Department in New Delhi. Most important of all, he gave the embassy the official request for military aid from the Tibetan government—which he had not shown Latrash.

On September 1, 1950, the day after Bessac had arrived in Delhi, the Tibetan government's request for military aid was transcribed and sent by encrypted telegram to Washington. The other documents from Bessac followed slowly, but the official aid request went out first.

On September 12, 1950, the Kashag's request reached the office of Dean Rusk, undersecretary of state for Far Eastern Affairs. The retired CIA agent Kenneth Knaus says that by this time Dean Rusk was "calling the shots on U.S. policy in Tibet." Rusk also told Knaus that he kept President Truman and Secretary of State Acheson fully briefed on his actions.

By September 19, 1950, Rusk had decided to covertly supply military aid to Tibet, and had begun discussions with the CIA about how to implement that policy. The document that proves this was declassified only in September 1999. Whether a decision had also been made to send that aid to Tibet without the cooperation and permission of the government of India remains uncertain. There is evidence that points in that direction. If President Truman signed an executive order authorizing Rusk's actions it has not been declassified.

The importance of the official request for military aid, which Bessac had carried out of Tibet, and the cascade of events that the meeting and the letter set off have not previously been recognized. The U.S. government has always insisted that it did not send any aid to Tibet before the Chinese invasion, and that there were no U.S. agents there.

The chain of events that brought the Kashag's letter to Undersecretary Rusk is probably what China is pointing to when it states that it invaded Tibet in 1950 to forestall U.S. plots to "invade" Tibet.

CALCUTTA, INDIA
SEPTEMBER 15, 1950

Frederick Latrash has an odd recollection about the few last weeks before China invaded Tibet. He had been sending a simple message to Washington repeatedly throughout the previous year: You can help the Tibetans if you decide to. He recalls saying, "If you are going to do anything, you've got the airfield now, you can do it. There are people who will receive it. It's not going to be stolen off planes and sold."

The frustrating reality for Latrash during the past twelve months was that those in Washington did not utilize the assets he had created. Shortly after Bessac left Calcutta, and less than a month before the invasion, Washington changed its mind.

In 1950 Latrash did not know that Bessac brought out the letter, nor that Dean Rusk was having conversations with the CIA. Perhaps it is a coincidence that at the very moment Rusk began to act on Bessac's letter, Latrash received a flurry of interest from Washington. If it is not a coincidence, it suggests that, just after receiving the letter from the Kashag and The Regent, the U.S. government began to initiate covert action.

Latrash suddenly received messages from Washington, which asked about positioning a U.S. aircraft carrier in the Bay of Bengal. He assumed that the aircraft carrier would let planes take off, air-drop weapons into Tibet, and return without involving the Indians.

From Latrash's viewpoint, it was absurd. He expressed his feelings to Washington. "It's too late. That's what we asked you to do a year ago, eight months ago, every month in between. Do something, do something." He had been saying that for a year, and nobody wanted to. Now they were too late.

It is Frederick Latrash's impression that the United States began to drop military supplies into Tibet only weeks before China invaded. The U.S. government denies that this ever happened. In July 2000, the Dalai Lama said for the first time that U.S. weapons may have reached the Tibetans before China invaded.

MRS. DOUGLAS MACKIERNAN GOES TO WASHINGTON
STOUGHTON, MASSACHUSETTS
OCTOBER 4, 1950

Pegge Mackiernan waited in California as long as she could, but finally she flew east to see Mackiernan's parents. It had already been decided that when the State Department assigned her the widow's posting she would leave her twins with her husband's parents. She would have to go overseas alone to work for a year or so until she got on her feet. The State Department, despite its assurance that she would get a job, had still not lived up to its word four months later. Meanwhile, her financial situation was critical.

She heard that Frank Bessac was due in the United States soon, and she was determined to talk with him. He would know the inside story.

Finally she had a letter from the State Department, but it wasn't word on her job. Instead, they had written to invite her to a memorial service for Mackiernan on October 18. Maybe she could see Bessac then, too.

BESSAC IN WASHINGTON, D.C.
OCTOBER 1950

Washington was a shock in many ways. The big American houses, the big American cars, and the big American people all amazed Frank Bessac after three years in Asia. He couldn't help but compare the size of the vast buildings in Washington to the yurts and adobe houses to which he had grown accustomed. Only the Tibetan Potala had been built on this imperial scale. And the American cars. So many of them, so large and new, speeding down well-paved roads lined with trees. The guards at the CIA headquarters were such big men, but then so was everyone in this well-fed country. What would the skinny Indians think to see these fat people? What would the butter-spattered monks of Tibet think to see so many well-scrubbed faces?

So much had changed. OSS's little old schoolhouse down by the Watergate on the Potomac was now a distant World War II memory, and so was Q Building. The Outfit had moved into new digs in Virginia. There were all these new boys running around with their crew cuts. Old friends from OSS, including Marge Kennedy, who had given him his Oregon code back in 1947, were still with the CIA. But they were all in Research and Analysis, and out of the field now. The moment Bessac got back and started debriefings at the State Department, they called up and said, "You must come over. So much to talk about."

He darted around Washington, from State to Outfit and back again. State gave him a desk where he prepared his reports. Everyone was thrilled to get the intelligence firsthand from him. So many bright American faces, and they were all so optimistic about saving Tibet.

"When I arrived, I just talked about everything I had done and what we were trying to do. . . . I got the feeling when I was at CIA headquarters that they were certainly going to try to arm the Tibetans that winter." It was also Bessac's understanding that the CIA "was working with all sorts of Tibetans to do that."

"The problem that they ran into was that the Indian government wasn't cooperating. I don't think I ever asked them, or if I did I've forgotten, how they were going to get around the Indian thing. I think it was beginning to worry them how they were going to get enough weapons by airlift in there before the Chinese came. I was there the week before the Chinese invaded, and I was still optimistic. We all were. The CIA was going to do their best to arm the Tibetans, and then the State Department would recognize Tibet.

"I think the CIA was very sincere in hoping for Tibetan independence. . . . When they were talking of secret aid to the Tibetans, they were doing it for Tibetan independence."

Bessac did not know it but as these plans proceeded in Washington, the Tibetan military mission, which Shakabpa had promised would arrive in India to discuss how U.S. military aid would reach Tibet that winter, arrived in New Delhi on October 4. Shakabpa himself had finally met with a Chinese Communist negotiator in India in September. The Chinese had three points that were not open to negotiation: either Tibet accepted them or China would invade. The first of these tells the whole story: "Tibet must accept that it is part of China." When informed about this condition the Kashag ordered Shakabpa to stall, apparently hoping that the new military mission could get some guarantee from the Americans before China invaded.

The day after the Tibetan military mission arrived in New Delhi to begin talks with America about the supply of weapons China began the invasion of Tibet. It was October 7, 1950. Forty thousand Chinese troops had been waiting on the border for the order to invade. Bessac knew none of this. Bessac and the CIA assumed the Chinese would invade Tibet in the spring of 1951 and the plans to arm the Tibetans were based on that assumption.

Bessac found similar plans at the State Department. At last, policy and covert action seemed to be coordinated. Secretary of State Acheson assigned an old China hand, Edmund Clubb, who was in charge of the China desk, to show Bessac around as the department debriefed him. Clubb, born in China to missionaries, spoke even better Chinese than did Bessac. He had been the U.S. consul at Tihwa during World War II when Mackiernan was there. In fact, Clubb had made the very first report about the existence of uranium in Sinkiang in 1943. Bessac, who was considering an offer of employment after a week in the State Department, remembers the general tone of his conversations with Clubb.

"Clubb told me he wanted Tibetan independence and that the Mackiernan trip was to supposed to help that. People just took for granted that I knew that the Mackiernan trip was for Tibetan independence at the State Department and at the CIA.

"As far as I understood it, the State Department and Acheson wanted to help the Tibetans as much as possible, following the same line which the Tibetans had told me and which I accepted . . . which was to give them as much covert aid as possible and when they became powerful enough [to resist Chinese invasion] to recognize them.

"I think I'm agreeing with Acheson that it was worth taking a risk of sending somebody like Doug Mackiernan to Tibet even though this might aggravate the Chinese, in order to prepare the ground so that Tibet could be in a position to receive American aid and then repulse the Chinese invasion, and be recognized as a sovereign independent nation."

It seemed to Bessac that an immense change had taken place inside the State Department during the past three years.

"The State Department had finally gotten off the China lobby . . . not fully but in part. They could think about the Tibetans as a people who were not necessarily Chinese and that to help the Tibetans was not just being an imperialistic power."

Until that time, the China lobby had made sure that the State Department toed the Chinese line—if you supported Tibet "you were a colonialist" dismembering China. Now some people in State "wanted to help the Tibetans defend themselves against the Chinese.

"Acheson didn't buy it anymore . . . this holiness of the Chinese empire . . . and they could look upon the Tibetans as a people . . . regardless of whether Tibet was Chinese yellow on Chinese maps or not."

This policy change allowed the CIA to start planning the covert supply of arms to the Tibetans.

After decades of Chinese control over America's understanding of Inner Asia, the State Department finally began to see that the Mongols, the Kazak, and the Tibetans were simply not Chinese. The next step was to say openly that the Inner Asians had as much right to independence as did the Chinese. That step was never taken. All military aid to Tibet remained forever covert, and the United States has never officially recognized Tibetan independence.

The men most responsible for the change in policy about Tibet were under intense attacks as alleged Communists. Edmund Clubb would eventually retire from the State Department after a bitter attack by Senator McCarthy. Because of McCarthy's smear campaign—and 38 percent of American citizens felt McCarthy was on to something—it was difficult to recognize Tibetan independence. Out of touch with American news during his epic trek across Tibet, Bessac had no idea of the power that Joe McCarthy now wielded. That power was amply demonstrated to him at the memorial ceremony for Douglas Mackiernan.

THE STATE DEPARTMENT
WASHINGTON, D.C.
OCTOBER 18, 1950

About one hundred people gathered in the Interdepartmental Auditorium on Constitution Avenue for the State Department Honor Awards ceremony. Dozens of people were awarded medals that day. Mackiernan was to receive the department's Superior Service Award, its second-highest medal, posthumously. The audience was composed primarily of State Department officials receiving medals and their families. There were also a few members of the Washington press corps to report the ceremony. Among the press in the last row, Bessac vanished into the crowd. Pegge Mackiernan was a widow in black, but still dressed fashionably. Bessac and Pegge did not meet that day. They have completely different memories of the event.

Pegge, angry at an insensitive bureaucracy that couldn't be bothered to bestir itself to help her support her children, brushed off the service in her diary.

> Oh yes, the medal. Doug was awarded a State Department Foreign Service Distinguished Service Medal. I was invited, expenses paid, to Washington. The Mackiernans came with me. The ceremony was composed of Marine Band music—bla, bla speeches—but the presence of DEAN ACHESON who opened his mouth and said something when he made a brief talk. I was first to receive the medals and on the platform stood beside Acheson as the Asst. Sec. read the Citation. Then I said to him: "Thank you on behalf of my twins."
>
> He smiled automatically. Then the word Twins registered.
>
> "Er, oh! Well, well," he blurted.
>
> The medal is dull silver on a red ribbon.

The State Department was pleased with Bessac's work in Tibet. They were set to hire him as a young vice consul and send him off to Iran. Bessac was pleased by the offer, though his glaucoma eventually disqualified him. Still, he went to the Honor Award ceremony with his heart set on trying to join the State Department. At some point during his prepared remarks, Secretary Acheson gave an off-the-cuff defense of Owen Lattimore, which was not reported in the press records of the event. That moment, for Bessac, was the end of his hoped-for Foreign Service career.

Lattimore was in the middle of a trial by torture. Acheson was so outraged by the unfounded attacks on the good professor that he spoke about it during the memorial service. Bessac was stunned. "When Acheson defended Lattimore, I went into shock, because Lattimore wrote the Bible on the Inner Asian Chinese frontier. . . . He invented the term Inner Asia. I knew Lattimore as . . . a grand old man from my area and I was shocked that he was under attack. McCarthy from Appleton, Wisconsin? Well he didn't know a damn thing about anything."

Acheson was not alone in his defense of Lattimore. A few brave people stood up, people who felt strong enough to withstand any attack on their livelihood or good name. Even President Truman entered the Lattimore debate. In public, the president said that the charges were absurd, though that did not put an end to Lattimore's nightmare. Privately, Truman wrote Lattimore's sister.

> I think our friend McCarthy will eventually get all that is coming to him. He has no sense of decency or honor. You can understand, I imagine, what the President has to stand—every day in the week he's under a constant barrage of people who have no respect for the truth and whose objective is to belittle and discredit him. While they are not successful in these attacks, they are never pleasant so I know just how you feel about the attack on your brother. The best thing to do is to face it and the truth will come out.

It would be four more years before McCarthy would be censured by the Senate; the damage he did to the State Department would not be repaired for a generation. The full story of McCarthy's involvement with Chiang Kai-shek has never come out. Unfortunately for Tibet, Lattimore was one of the few people in the United States who could have argued coherently that Tibet was an obviously independent country.

For Bessac, the end of Acheson's defense of Lattimore was a decisive event in the course of his life. "I remember the conclusion. That being a State Department official was risky business and you better get a doctorate before you got into it. Apparently, many thought the same thing. I wasn't the only person after McCarthy who came to this conclusion."

Bessac was not the only young Chinese-speaking American watching the public humiliation and career detonation of the Chinese-speaking Americans in the State Department. A whole generation of qualified people shied away from the State Department. Many within State were purged for being the messengers of Asian nationalism. This is one of the reasons former Secretary of Defense Robert McNamara cites when he talks about how the United States got mired in Vietnam.

> When it came to Vietnam, we found ourselves setting policy for a region that was terra incognita. Worse, our government lacked experts for us to compensate for our ignorance. . . . The irony of the gap was that it existed largely because the top East Asian and China experts in the State Department . . . had been purged during the McCarthy hysteria of the 1950s.

W. W. Butterworth, one of Mackiernan's old allies in China, was fighting to get the United States to recognize the reality of Vietnamese nationalism, shortly before he was replaced by Rusk, a man who would later see Vietnam only through his anti-Communist lens. We might be living in a different world if someone like Butterworth, who knew Asian nationalism, had been secretary of state in 1960, rather than Dean Rusk. McCarthy, and fear of him and others like him, helped to make sure that never happened.

The cost of Chiang Kai-shek's persecution of his enemies—through the offices of the likes of Senator McCarthy, the U.S. China lobby, and the Cold War hawks who inherited the mantle—is long, and it runs from Tibet through Vietnam.

BETHESDA, MARYLAND, AND DRUKHA MONASTERY
OCTOBER 19, 1950

Did Bessac know on October 19 that Tibet had been invaded on October 7? Certainly, he did not hear it on October 7, as the news was slow to reach the press. On the seventh, the world was focused on American troops crossing the 38th parallel into North Korea.

Maybe China suspected that the United States, while occupied in Korea, would not want to open a second front in Tibet, and thus moved on Tibet as the United States went into North Korea. Maybe the Chinese invasion was linked to the arrival of the Tibetan military mission in India. It may well have been a combination of all these factors.

No one in press or government circles outside Tibet would suspect for another week that forty thousand Chinese troops crossed the Yangtze/Drichu River into Tibet about the same time the United States went into North Korea. The Chinese moved with lightning precision and cut off the retreat route of the Tibetan troops back into central Tibet. A good portion of all of Tibet's forces were encircled without any chance of resupply, and radio contact with Lhasa— where the Kashag was busy with a picnic—was quickly cut off.

The plan for the invasion of Tibet was drawn up by the PLA's Southwest Military Region, which included Deng Xiaoping among its top three commanders. By October 19 it was over, and the Tibetan army in eastern Tibet surrendered to the Chinese at the monastery of Drukha. It was obvious to the Tibetan generals that without modern weapons—which had not arrived in eastern Tibet despite a too-little-too-late CIA operation to supply them—it was fruitless to resist Chinese troops armed with the latest U.S. weapons. The Chinese were still hundreds of miles from Lhasa, and would not enter central Tibet until 1951, but the fighting was over.

The news of the Chinese attack reached Lhasa only on the fifteenth, and was withheld from the public for fear of chaos. Distorted reports of the attack on Tibet were reported in Indian papers on October 12, but they were denounced as false rumors for days. *The New York Times* reported the Chinese invasion only on October 14.

Pegge Mackiernan had sent a letter to Bessac at the Raleigh Hotel on October 15. They agreed to meet up in Bethesda, where Pegge was staying with Ann Wheeler from State, who had provided Pegge a home when she was last in D.C. with Mackiernan in 1948.

Pegge's letter set the stage for the encounter.

Dear Frank Bessac,
    Will you please reserve some time Thursday Oct. 19, for a visit

with me in Washington? This is a very special favor I am asking—
but I do want very much to see you alone. . . . I must speak to you
privately . . .

Before we meet Frank let me *assure you* I am not concerned with
the facts you must conceal. My appeal is solely as a human being concerned with human qualities. I have a great feeling of understanding for you—and too, I am of your world. . . . You need not explain
or elaborate on anything for me. We have already shared an experience which must remold both of our lives—so except for a momen-
tary qualm, why should we dread the inevitable meeting? . . .

Sincerely,

Pegge Mackiernan

On October 19 Tibetan generals in eastern Tibet delivered an
order no Tibetan had ever given before. They ordered the Tibetan
troops to surrender their arms to the Chinese who had surrounded
them at Drukha Monastery. The troops did as they were told. They
were so outnumbered and outgunned that the only other choice was
death. Inside the dark monastery, not far from the silent Buddhas
on the altar, Chinese cameramen set up perfect positions for film-
ing. The brilliant movie lights came on and filled the dark temple
with sharp shadows. The Tibetan commander of eastern Tibet,
Nagpo, signed the surrender document on cue as the cameras
began to whir. Nothing lay between the PLA and Lhasa except a
few hundred miles of treeless steppes and unbridged canyons. Later
the Chinese announced that only one hundred and eighty were
killed or wounded, and 5,738 Tibetan troops were liquidated in the
brief war. Reports say that most of the "liquidated" troops were
simply allowed to return home after being disarmed. Nagpo was
kept for reeducation by the Chinese, and within a few years he
would emerge as the pliant front man for the new Chinese administration in Tibet.

On the morning of October 19, Pegge was dressed as fashionably as
ever when Bessac arrived. He would have seemed more solid and
dashing in his Mongol or Tibetan robe, but now, shorn of Asia, there
was something merely slender about him.

Pegge sat them down and insisted that Bessac relate the "the final chapter of Douglas Mackiernan with brutal candor." According to Pegge's diary, that is what Bessac proceeded to do. She quotes him at length in her October 19 entry.

"Doug sought death—" Bessac explained, "and meeting you probably prolonged his life or effort for life . . .

"I know something was bothering him—made him irrational at times—made him want to remain behind in villages—even at the point of risk . . ."

In the Black Gobi, Doug did a foolhardy thing, said they'd manage without water, at the cost of three days without any. He removed his ring when his fingers began to swell from frostbite. He referred to me as "my wife" not frequently and not often by name. He said often to Frank: "Don't ever get married."

Once he almost committed suicide. He walked off from camp with a revolver through his belt. Vasili (a Russian in the party) followed him. Doug sat on a rock with the revolver beside him for a long time. Then came back to camp. The mood passed. Bessac said that it may have been thoughts of "my wife" that helped him over this.

Bessac suspected a strain of hero-illusion in Doug. He wanted to appear tough and rugged before the Russians and others.

Had Doug survived (pure conjecture) and Bessac been killed, the experience would have snapped Doug out of his somewhat erratic mental state, or it would have been the other extreme.

Bessac nobly said of the two of them, Doug's survival would have been of the greater value, had Doug come back to normal.

Bessac repeated several times, "I wish I knew what the hell was eating Mac."

This is most painful, but Bessac said he had mistresses—Tartar women. It was his weakness that foreign women, and just plain foreignness, appealed to him. The most I did for Doug was offer some stabilizing influence and probably held him—as best he could—to the long road out.

Perhaps by the end of the encounter Bessac realized that he was causing Pegge immense pain, and that his honesty might not have been what a widowed American mother of twins had in mind when she asked for candor. As they headed out the door, Bessac tried to make amends.

"Mac died in the Cold War, he did some good in a sense of security to his country. Don't forget him to spare a hurt to your pride at his unfaithfulness. You were the only woman who meant anything to him."

By then Pegge was reeling. On the curb as they waited for Bessac's cab, she dazedly asked him what time it was. Bessac looked down at his wrist, and so did Pegge. Realization dawned over them both at about the same time. Bessac was wearing Mackiernan's watch, and Pegge wondered how it had gotten on Bessac's wrist. She did not ask, though in her mind she saw pictures of the watch being removed from her husband's lifeless arm. She wondered why Bessac had not offered it to her right away. What if she had not accidentally asked the time?

As the taxi came up, Bessac looked away and unstrapped the watch.

"One of your children will want this," he said as he handed the watch to Pegge. Then he was gone.

Bessac did not record his meeting with Pegge Mackiernan at the time. When Pegge's diary extracts were read to him, in 1999, he was stunned. Bessac denies saying most of what is attributed to him in the foregoing passages. "I tried to cover up for Doug about whatever she'd heard about Russian women and so forth. She said all sorts of things, putting Doug down and I was trying to be gentle towards Doug."

Bessac denies that he told her Mackiernan had lovers on their trip, or that he tried to commit suicide, though what other source the widow could have for the suicide story recorded in her diary is difficult to imagine. He says that he told the widow only things that would not hurt her. He did not tell her that Mackiernan, at Timurlik, had said he was divorced from Pegge. He did not tell her the truth about Mackiernan's death. No one did until 1999; the State Department and the CIA had ordered Bessac and Zvansov not to speak about it with her or anyone else.

After the meeting, Pegge was heartsick. She called Tony Freeman—who was still handling her over at State—and told him what she had heard. Freeman was at her house in Bethesda the next morning.

Of course, he assured her, Bessac's stories were all false. And, yes, the State Department would work out her finances right away. What did Bessac tell you? Freeman's calming assurances helped her try to forget the past and move on. She felt better after talking with him, but she would remember that betrayal, bitterly, when she later learned Freeman's true role that morning. Freeman was sent there only to find out what she knew.

WASHINGTON, D.C.
OCTOBER 27 AND 28, 1950

The gold light of a fall evening in North America shot through the windows and fell on the lanky shape of Frank Bessac folded in a corner. Pegge had burst into Thebolt Taylor's office at the State Department, eager to talk with Taylor about her financial situation and the promised job. Taylor asked her to wait. That was when she saw Bessac looking at her.

Pegge turned sharply, walked out of the office back into the hall, and took a chair to wait, as she had been instructed. Bessac followed her out into the hall and squatted down beside her.

"May I see you before I go home?"

"You will not distress and upset me further?"

Frank blushed, looked at the floor, and shook his head from side to side.

"No," he said in a very quiet voice.

To Pegge, it seemed as though Bessac had something important to tell her, and that he wanted privacy in which to do it. She agreed to meet the next day. On Saturday, they met and walked for hours. Bessac seemed more comfortable walking than sitting in a room. He talked to her about his years with the Mongols, and about the walk across Asia with Mackiernan, but he focused now on the amazing and funny things about the trip. He told her about meeting the Dalai Lama. He told her about going to Genghis Khan's tomb in Inner Mongolia in 1948 when he was first learning Mongolian. He told her about drinking mare's milk, about the wailing songs of the nomads, about the winds that blow every day over the treeless land, about the hard life of the nomads, about their yurts—about the people of Inner Asia that he and Mackiernan had so admired.

And then he told her that most of the things in the box he had shipped back from Calcutta were his own, and talked about getting them back from her after she removed Mackiernan's things. Finally he gave her the name of a man in Washington. Mackiernan had asked Bessac to give the name to Pegge if something ever happened to him. As they parted that afternoon, Bessac strongly urged her to call the man. Pegge calls him "John" to protect his identity, even in her diary. Mackiernan had named John as Pegge's SOS contact at the Central Intelligence Agency. He was Doug Mackiernan's handler.

PEGGE AND JOHN, FIRST MEETING
WASHINGTON, D.C.
NOVEMBER 8, 1950

Pegge's security clearance was not complete. It was one bureaucratic snafu after another for five months. Eventually they offered her a temporary job in Washington as a secretary in the Middle Eastern section while they tried to get her clearance approved. It was a temporary job so she could make ends meet.

She phoned Mackiernan's handler at the CIA, who agreed to meet her the same day at her office. He arrived exactly at the appointed time. He seemed handsome, calculating, watchful, and composed. He looked to her as if he might be an actor, or a radio commentator, between jobs.

"John" identified himself and admitted that he had tremendous admiration for Mackiernan and had highly regarded his abilities. He told Pegge that Mackiernan had carried out a dangerous mission, and that if he had been caught he would have been executed. John said that because of this Mackiernan was under a lot of stress on the trip to Tibet. He said that this explained Bessac's comment that something was eating Mackiernan. John also said that the CIA was going to miss Mackiernan.

"We needed his technical skill—he would have been kept right here."

By that fall, the Mackiernans' World Weather was grossing more than $100,000 a year. They were setting up a new West Coast operation.

LIFE MAGAZINE
NOVEMBER 13, 1950

Frank Bessac took advantage of the GI Bill and applied for graduate school at the University of California–Berkeley. The *Life* money helped. So did his payment from the CIA. Bessac reports that the CIA paid him the same amount as if he had stayed on the payroll in 1947— effectively giving him two years' back salary as though he had never resigned. As though he had been using his Fulbright for deep cover under CIA direction, which Bessac insists was not the case. The Outfit said they would have paid much more than that for the intelligence Bessac brought out. He was able to buy a used 1947 Chevy and to rent a cottage in the Berkeley hills. Bessac denies that this payment effectively turned him into a CIA contract agent, after the fact, even if he had not been acting as one during his time in Tibet. His most memorable comment on this confusion is: "I was a spy but I didn't know it."

When the *Life* story came out Bessac was livid. Bessac felt that Henry Luce turned his trip to Tibet into an anti-Communist homily.

He wished the article had stressed the Inner Asians' fight for freedom from Chinese colonialism. Instead, he was made into a Cold Warrior.

The *Life* map showed them going west around the Taklamakan, because it was necessary to hide the time they had spent with Osman Bator. Cold War propaganda created many false statements. The most obvious regards the kowtow. Bessac did kneel to the Tibetan border guards, and probably saved his life by doing so. But that was not the world of Luce. *Life* wrote the facts as they should have been.

> When I was within talking distance, one of them waggled his rifle at me and shouted "Ke t' ou!" This was the Chinese phrase meaning "Kneel and touch your head to the ground." Unthinking, I was infuriated. I shouted back, "I will not. I am an American."

Pegge was enraged to see Bessac making money off the story. To her it seemed he was making money off of Mackiernan's death. After the *Life* article came out, Frank Bessac and Pegge Mackiernan never spoke to each other again.

She wrote to her acquaintance, Clare Boothe Luce (wife of the publisher, Henry) who wrote the editor. *Life* agreed it was terrible that the widow of Mackiernan had not been paid for the article. The editor sent her a check.

PEGGE AND JOHN
WASHINGTON, D.C.
NOVEMBER 24, 1950

John picked Pegge up at night, during a rainstorm. He refused to come into the lighted lobby of her building to do so. Pegge laughed at the game. She loved how John played his espionage role, just as much as she had when Mackiernan did so in Tihwa.

We drove to a side street and parked for four hours. It stopped raining and a misty midnight moon glowed dully on the still wet shiny streets. And John asked and asked and asked, even with a threat.

What did I know? How much did I know? He would MAKE me tell him. I MUST tell him. Doug would want me to; he was Doug's boss. But not a word, <u>nothing, nothing</u>, did I say.

John changed the subject and said that the CIA could offer her a clerk job in Washington if she wanted. He wanted to offer her some option if she was not satisfied with the widow's pension that the CIA was thinking to give her. He told her that he thought she would make a good agent with careful training. Yet he said that it would be difficult because of her children.

You always go back to your children. Your attachment for them is very deep and close. Concern for them might limit your activity.

In discussing Mackiernan, the past came up. John seemed to know everything. He said a strange thing as they sat in the dark car, with midnight Washington looming around them—apparently about Mackiernan's illegal marriage to the Russian girl in Tihwa.

"We are not concerned with morals—only security."
It was a hell of a lonely place, Tihwa.

TIBET
WINTER 1950–1951

The Chinese pushed only a few hundred miles into Tibet. Then they stopped and again urged the Tibetans to send a negotiating team to China. Frederick Latrash says that this was not unusual. "That's the way most of these invasions are in these crazy places. All you have to do is show the intention that you're mounting it. You don't have to actually invade and bang, bang, bang, shoot a bunch of people and take over the city: the city falls."

When Latrash was transferred to New Delhi that winter, he had the chance to speak with Ambassador Henderson, who had fought so hard in 1949 and 1950 to get the United States to reconsider its policy toward China and Tibet.

One afternoon, they were talking about what Latrash had done in Tibet in 1949 and 1950, specifically about his sources. Latrash didn't tell him details—CIA agents are never supposed to talk about sources and methods—but he made it clear that he had created assets in Tibet. The ambassador was furious that he had not been informed.

Latrash expressed his regret: "And here I had the engines and he had all these dreams. I had the reality and he had the dream. Why didn't somebody put us together?"

The invasion of Tibet had many consequences. The Dalai Lama was propelled to power less than a month afterward. The regent resigned, which put a fifteen-year-old boy in power at Tibet's most dangerous hour; there was simply no other alternative. By the time he came to power many around him felt they had been given reason to expect that military aid would be forthcoming from the West.

When that aid did not materialize in useful quantities even after China invaded it began to dawn on Tenzin Gyatso exactly what had happened.

"We did curse them. I remember that. Regretfully we would say, 'Now we have destroyed ourselves.' Or, 'Now we have [been] completely betrayed by these people.'"

That winter the Dalai Lama fled to the Indian border, and Tibet made an appeal to the UN in 1951. But nothing came of it; the United States and the U.S.S.R. together voted to prevent the Tibetan issue from being debated in the UN. Tibet was forced to begin negotiations with China. It was a bleak winter for the young Dalai Lama.

"Then eventually, we returned to Lhasa. [When no foreign aid] came, then several months passed and this old monk said, 'For a long time we have heard that the Americans are coming. But even if they were sliding all the way to Lhasa along the ground on their butts, still they should have reached here by now.'"

The Dalai Lama laughs when he finishes telling this story.

The invasion revealed the lack of support from India, Great Britain, and the United States. China had warned the Tibetans during 1950 not to listen to the "imperialists." Here was the proof—China had neutralized them all. China offered India a grand postcolonial alliance if India did not help the Tibetans. Britain worried that by helping Tibet China would challenge its colonial claims to Hong Kong. And Chiang Kai-shek neutralized America, giving the Chinese a free hand with which to invade Tibet without paying any price. Now that China had proven to Tibet that no help was forthcoming, she could focus her energy on forcing the Tibetans to cede Tibetan independence—under threat of an armed invasion if they did not agree to Chinese terms.

Frederick Latrash says that there were a few small airdrops in Tibet that winter, but it was too little too late, and he could not understand why the CIA even bothered. Up to now, the CIA has denied the existence even of these airdrops, so it is impossible to gauge just how large they were until the CIA releases its Tibet files, which the CIA refuses to do. One CIA source complained, "Hey, this is history. We released everything about the Bay of Pigs and that failed covert operation was in 1960. Why should something that happened ten years before *that* be kept secret now? It's history."

People with such beliefs are not in control at the CIA. The faction within the CIA that opposes releasing the history of America's covert involvement in Tibet between 1949 and 1972 believes that a stable Sino-American relationship is worth any price. They do not want to threaten the status quo. Trade and corporate profit make that taboo, whether it is a Republican or a Democratic administration.

Then there is the issue of atomic intelligence; the CIA avoids revealing U.S. atomic intelligence. Americans hear about foreign atomic spies in the United States, but never a word about American atomic spies in other countries.

The Chinese invasion of 1950 revealed that the United States might support Tibet covertly, but it would not do so overtly. That winter the State Department made noises to the contrary. State told the British Foreign Office that "should developments warrant consideration could be given to recognition of Tibet as an independent country." In the fifty years since that statement, conditions have never warranted the recognition of Tibet. This policy has continued up to the present. When the United States wants a stick with which to beat China, it reaches for Tibet. Yet it never changes policy—Tibet is part of China—though that policy has little popular support and is based upon neither history nor facts.

Tibetans learned what was in store for them when they took their appeal to the UN after the invasion. It was a major fight to get any nation to bring the invasion of Tibet to the General Assembly. How could Tibet be invaded if it was already part of China? Britain specifically did not want to challenge colonial rights. It was the same with France: if China could not invade and occupy Tibet, what about the French in Vietnam? The United States had more pressing concerns: getting China off its back in Korea where the U.S. Army was being mauled and Americans were dying by the thousands.

Each nation had its own interests, and Tibet was not one of them. Tibet had been prevented from joining the UN a year earlier and now, brutally, that was used against it. When tiny El Salvador finally brought the question of Tibet to the UN in 1951, the United States joined the U.S.S.R. in voting to postpone any debate about Tibet. It was one of the very few times that the United States joined the U.S.S.R. on a vote. Senator McCarthy did not call anyone Communist for doing it and did not speak of a global Communist conspiracy guiding the State Department.

Nations of the world hoped that Tibet and China could negotiate a peaceful and honorable settlement. India assured all that this would happen. By 1952, 90 percent of the food that the Chinese occupying army needed to remain in Tibet was shipped through India. India actually fed the Chinese army in Tibet. China returned the favor in 1962. Once established in Tibet, the Chinese invaded India. India was surprised.

This was the level of self-serving disinterest the Dalai Lama faced when he came to power, and this is why he had no other choice than to send a team to negotiate with the Chinese. The Chinese promptly told the Tibetans that they must accept all Chinese terms or the invasion would resume. Under duress, the Tibetans allowed the Chinese to forge the government seals that the Dalai Lama had specifically *not* sent to China so that no agreement could be made in the name of the Tibetan government, especially under duress.

The 17-Point Agreement was signed. For the first time in its history, Tibet "legally" became part of China. Tibetan independence was signed away and the nine-year period of coexistence between the Dalai Lama and the Chinese began. Deng Xiaoping probably wrote the terms under which Tibet joined China. The promises were certainly worthy ones.

> Now that the PLA has entered Tibet, they will protect the lives and property of all religious bodies and people, protect the freedom of religious belief for all the people of Tibet, protect all lamaseries and temples, and help the Tibetan people to develop their education, agriculture, animal husbandry, industry, and commerce, so as to improve the livelihood of the people. The existing political system and military system in Tibet will not be changed.

China would violate every one of these promises in the coming decades. Instead of protecting Tibetan temples, 90 percent to 95 percent of them were razed during the Cultural Revolution. How was Tibetan agriculture improved? Somewhere between three hundred thousand and one million Tibetans starved to death when Chinese experts forced Tibetans to replant their barley fields with new strains of Chinese wheat, which then failed. Tibet is 25 percent of the surface area of the modern Chinese empire. Tibet has the largest uranium reserves in the world, not to speak of gold, oil, and other riches. Most of all, there was always the hope of land for China's growing billion. Today, none of this is an international affair; it is an internal affair, and China brooks no criticism of its rule in Tibet.

"Tibet has been part of China since ancient times. None of the previous governments in the United States have recognized Tibet as an independent country. The United States maintains that Tibet is part of China also."

—Chen Kuiyuan,
Secretary of the Tibet Autonomous Regional Party Committee
March 22, 2000

Few Westerners know enough Inner Asian history to contradict Chen's lie about ancient Tibetan history. Few know how close the United States came to recognizing Tibet—and why that effort to oppose Chinese colonialism failed. Few can understand the vicious barb Chen hurls at the colonized Tibetans when he twists the blade of history in their wounds. America, too, says Tibet is part of China.

Chinese colonial rule in Tibet has been even more disastrous for the Tibetans than French rule was for the Vietnamese, or British rule for the Indians. In Tibet, estimates of Mao's death toll range between one and two million. Today, after abandoning Communism, the new rulers of China find that there is money to be made in Tibet. What the Communist dictatorship did not destroy, the capitalist boom in present Tibet—where hundreds of thousands of Chinese colonists have arrived to make it rich—may finish off. At the current rate of migration into Tibet, Chinese will become an absolute majority of the population (as they have already become in Sinkiang and Inner Mongolia) within twenty years, at most.

Communist Party General Secretary Jiang Zemin told President Bill Clinton in 1998 that the very few Chinese who were in Tibet were there only to help the Tibetans and would of course all eventually return to China. Why was it so important to Jiang to insist that the hundreds of thousands of Chinese in Tibet were there only as aid workers? Because even now, when the Chinese colonization of Tibet has advanced so far it may be irreversible, even now Chinese cannot admit to themselves that they are colonizing Tibet. Chinese have a vehement sense of victimization stemming from their own colonization by Manche, Mongols, Europeans, and Japanese. To admit that they are now repeating the same sin on another people would be to condemn the Chinese nation in its own eyes. And so China lies to itself, and the world, distorting history because the facts are unacceptable: Tibetans are Chinese; Tibet has always been a part of China; Chinese colonialists in Tibet are aid workers who will all leave when the Tibetans have been civilized by the superior Chinese. Chinese colonization cannot exist—so it does not exist.

In 1950 there were no Chinese in Tibet. Today, Chinese are a majority even in Tibetan towns as small as thirty thousand. On the treeless steppes where the nomads roam, Tibetans are still a majority. No Chinese want to live there for now, but there are signs that irrigation, a new railway, and new petroleum finds may change this.

Throughout all of this the United States has always recognized China's legal right to occupy Tibet. It was a promise made to Chiang Kai-shek that the United States kept for Mao. It was not because of history, or law, or because it was right that Tibetan independence was not recognized. As Frank Bessac says, "America would have helped, if it had been easier."

Or as the Dalai Lama says, "The courage was not there."

WINTER OF THE COLD WAR
WASHINGTON, D.C.
1950–1951

The twins had to be left with their grandparents outside of Boston. It hurt Pegge Mackiernan to do that, but she had no choice—there wasn't enough money to do anything else. Every time she left them their fat little fingers clung to her neck, and they cried.

In Washington she spent her free time trying to get her pension from the State Department. That meant correspondence and meetings with a faceless bureaucracy that did not understand she was a widow of a solider killed in a secret war—and she could not tell them. At the same time, she pursued contacts with John.

She discovered that the CIA had paid Mackiernan an annual salary of $8,344, including his $2,200 cover salary from State Department. She also found out that Tony Freeman had been assigned to "watch for any 'hunch'" she might have of Mackiernan's true job; Tony's solicitude to her in the prior months was now frightening to Pegge. His friendship had been an act. She wondered who else was lying to her.

The Civil Service Commission got back to her with its decision about her widow's pension. It was based on Mackiernan's $2,200 cover salary at State. She received only 25 percent of what she would have gotten if they had applied Mackiernan's CIA salary. The State Department pension was $11 a month per child. Pegge had been scraping by on $109 when Mackiernan was alive. These facts fell on her like blows, day after day. Friends were not friends, and she was a pensionless widow.

On February 2, 1951, Pegge had another meeting with John. Her FBI clearance had finally arrived, and State was talking about sending her to India. She was also eager to talk with John about any insurance money or pension from the CIA. He assured her that everyone in the Outfit agreed she was entitled to Mackiernan's pension from the CIA. The bad news was that he could not find any record of any insurance for her. She pushed on.

> I brought up the point of wanting to know who ordered Doug to stay behind. John looked at me sharply. Denied it had been the Company. "State's orders," he said.
> "I wonder," I continued, "had it been Butterworth?"
> John wisely, "wasn't sure."

John was lying when he told Pegge it was State, not CIA, who had ordered Mackiernan to remain in Tihwa in August 1949, as Pegge herself eventually discovered. The other vice consul who left Tihwa earlier with Consul Paxton finally told her the CIA had ordered Mackiernan to stay. Her heart nearly broke when he told her how sad Mackiernan was to be left behind when the American caravan left Tihwa in August 1949. No one would tell her for years that Mackiernan's sacrifice, at the order of the CIA, provided the most precious atomic intelligence the United States has ever received.

On February 20, John admitted that there was still outstanding money from Mackiernan's salary, unpaid, but still no word on the insurance. The CIA was dragging its feet on a pension, on back salary, and on insurance, while the State Department pension was a joke.

Pegge wrote directly to the director of the CIA. John panicked and intercepted the letter. By March 16 she finally had an answer. The CIA director wrote her a letter washing his hands of any association with Mackiernan. There was no pension from the CIA for the widow of the first agent ever killed during a covert mission. Nothing.

Eight days before the first anniversary of Mackiernan's death, she prepared to leave for India for two years, a widow forced to leave her children so she could earn a living. She had one last meeting with John.

Again they sat in a car parked on a dark tree-lined Washington street. The Capitol loomed in the darkness beyond. They had made her find them in secret. They had dealt with her in secret. And now they had come to their secret understanding of the truth. The Company was finished with Mackiernan's widow—just as it was now finished with Tibet.

John had plans for their last night. He made them plain when he grabbed her, and couldn't seem to hear the word "No" when she said it. As he grabbed her, she knew at last that he had never been her friend. He had never been trying to help her. He had been there to oversee the interests of the CIA and nothing more.

It was all a setup. Now that they were through with her, John thought to pick up what he could on the side. A year after her husband's death the CIA had refused her any pension, or insurance, and now Mackiernan's handler was trying to seduce her.

Finally, John heard the muffled word from her, " No."

Driving back to her house in silence Pegge may have recalled what John had said to her the first time that they'd met.

"We are not concerned with morals—only security."

TIHWA-URUMCHI, SINKIANG-XINJIANG PROVINCE
THE PEOPLE'S REPUBLIC OF CHINA
APRIL 29, 1951

Osman Bator came up out of the dark hole, blinking. He stretched out after being cramped, stood up to his full height. The Chinese soldiers around him, dressed in blue cotton suits, were shorter than he, and his head stood above the ring of men that encircled him. The chains on his legs clanked against the wooden floor.

In the doorway of the prison, he stood erect and looked out toward the snow peak of Bogdo Shan, which Pegge and Doug Mackiernan had called "their Heavenly Mountain." Gleaming white, it floated in a blue sky above the walls of the town, down at the end of a long parallel line of poplars that lined the road.

One year after Mackiernan's death, Osman held his head up and began to walk toward the distant mountain.

When they tortured him, it seemed after a while that there was no point not to tell them what he had done. So he did. He told them about the gold that Mackiernan had given him, and the help he had given the White Russians, and he told them something about Mackiernan's work. Whatever he knew. Of course, Mackiernan knew his business and knew it was dangerous for Osman to know much, so Osman might not have had much to give up. Under torture, he told them whatever he had known. He signed the confession. Mackiernan was gone, it did not matter.

He walked to the spot of execution through the streets and lanes of Tihwa. One witness says that he walked to his execution like a young groom going to his wedding. His body and his clothes told the story of what the Chinese had done to him and all could plainly see it. Yet they could see also his head held high even as the order was given to fire.

The Chinese executed Osman Bator as a bandit for his crimes against the people and because he worked with the American spy Douglas Mackiernan.

According to someone who stood nearby as the Chinese lifted their guns, Osman's last words were: "I am not a bandit. What I did was to help my people to establish an independent country."

When China announced the execution and the link between Osman Bator and Douglas Mackiernan the United States heatedly denied it.

In the 1970s when President Richard M. Nixon first reestablished relations with Communist China, America had an urgent priority. The United States wanted China to establish a joint Sino-U.S. atomic intelligence listening post in China to keep a watch on the Soviets' missle testing in Inner Asia and their atomic testing at Semipalatinsk.

The detection equipment was sunk in the ground outside Tihwa, perhaps near the first U.S. atomic detection equipment that Mackiernan had buried there all those years ago. Once again a stream of data about Russian atomic explosions began its journey back to the U.S.— but now the United States shared the intelligence with China.

EPILOGUE
ZVANSOV, BESSAC, MACKIERNAN, AND TIBET

After Frank Bessac left in September 1950, Vasili Zvansov was stuck in New Delhi for ten months. Mackiernan had promised him that he would be given a visa to the United States. Worse, Zvansov had been there when Mackiernan told the White Russians who had remained behind with Osman Bator that they, too, would eventually be rewarded with U.S. visas, but Mackiernan was dead and no one could prove what he had or had not said. His feelings of despair grew worse when the news about the massacre at Barkol reached him; then the news of Osman's execution; and then finally word of the thousands of Kazak who died trying to make it across Tibet to Kashmir. Only a few hundred made it out alive. Over the months, these depressing pieces of news reached Zvansov one after another. They formed an ugly backdrop as he tried to deal with his own situation, stuck in India.

Unbeknownst to Zvansov, the State Department had asked Bessac what he knew about Mackiernan's commitments to the Russians. They had also asked for an assessment of Zvansov's suitability as a U.S. citizen. For reasons that are not clear now, even to Bessac, he told the State Department that he did not think Zvansov would make a very good U.S. citizen. He was also asked what he knew about Mackiernan's commitments to the White Russians, but Mackiernan had never said anything to him about them.

Zvansov did not understand why he was left in India, since he did not know what Bessac had said—if that was the reason why the United States did not immediately evacuate Zvansov to America. Zvansov did not find out about Bessac's assessment of him until 1999. When he did, he was generous in his reaction.

"In those days, I could make mistake, you could make a mistake—even bigger than that. It was a time when no matter what you did, you got in trouble."

So Zvansov sat in New Delhi and wondered how he had landed in such trouble.

"Imagine how I felt when Bessac left me. I had lost all my friends—shot dead—with only Bessac left. Then after we arrived in India, which is a strange place for anyone, he left me there and went home. I felt very bad, we lost our blood, we traveled like brothers and then I come to this hot place, so strange India was, and Frank left me."

The U.S. embassy in India debriefed Zvansov, and then provided him with a bunk in a small cottage, a job as a mechanic, and an English teacher. Bessac eventually wrote to the State Department and told them that he thought Zvansov *would* make a fine U.S. citizen.

In the summer of 1951, the U.S. embassy encouraged Zvansov to apply for a U.S. visa. Within weeks, he flew into Oakland Airport and was met by two men upon his arrival there. Zvansov says that they were from the CIA. They took him into a small room and had a few words to say to him.

"They told me that I should keep my mouth shut about everything. 'We know everything we need to know and you should not say anything to anyone about what happened during your travels. Just don't talk.'

"They did not even mention Douglas's name."

With that over, Zvansov drove down the road that leads out of the airport—today called Hegenberger Boulevard in honor of Mackiernan's old boss—into a free life in America. He found work, became a U.S. citizen, met a lovely wife, had children, lived a full life, and today enjoys his retirement in Hawaii immensely.

Zvansov knows how easy it would have been for his story to end otherwise. He followed the fate of the approximately one hundred and fifty members of his old Outfit, the Eskadrone, closely.

When units of the Chinese People's Liberation Army surrounded Lake Barkol in the spring of 1951, the Eskadrone split into two groups. Perhaps fifty followed the advice of Vasili Burigin (the White Russian to whom Mackiernan had given gold at Barkol) and fled to the mountains above the lake. They peered down as the Lake Barkol massacre unfolded, and then fled south toward Tibet. It is unclear how many left for Tibet in Burigin's party. Many died on their way from starvation, and during running battles with the PLA. Eventually, twenty-three men, women, and children reached India. The United States, in 1951, persuaded the Indian government to allow them to enter Sikkim, and finally India, where they were eventually given U.S. visas and settled in the United States.

How many of the Eskadrone—who stayed on with Osman after Burigin left—died during the Lake Barkol massacre is unknown. Some escaped with Osman when he fled the lake. Eleven of those were shot when Osman was captured. Eventually the rest were allowed to leave China. They made their way via various third countries to America.

Zvansov felt much better when he heard at least some of the Eskadrone had made it safely to America; until then Mackiernan's promises gnawed at him.

He believes that Ivan X, the sole survivor of Mackiernan's 1949 raid on the Russian uranium mine in Sinkiang, died in America in 1996. Today, the children and grandchildren of these Cold Warrior immigrants now number in the hundreds—like Zvansov, all the survivors thrived in America.

The first generation was watched after their resettlement in America, and at least a few of these new American citizens were recruited to work for the CIA, a last gift from Douglas Mackiernan. Zvansov says that he rebuffed several CIA attempts to recruit him; he had no interest in being air-dropped back into the U.S.S.R. Others in his position apparently took the offer and became quite valuable to the CIA.

There was one Russian who probably did not make it out of Tihwa. She was in Tihwa when Pegge arrived there in 1947. She appears to have been there when Mackiernan left in 1949. Mackiernan paid the rent on a house several years in advance just before leaving, and perhaps it was for her. Zvansov speaks wistfully about her.

"Doug Mackiernan's Russian girl was pretty, and certainly not Kazak —a Russian for sure. She was left in Urumchi." Her fate is unknown.

For the first few months after Frank Bessac's return to America, he suffered what may have been post-traumatic stress flashbacks. On some nights he clawed his way back from a nightmare, drenched in sweat, the images of what he had lived through fading as he stared into the dark room. He wondered if his actions in Lhasa had hastened the Chinese invasion. There was no answer to the question. It cropped up with every headline he saw about Tibet.

"I felt guilty about the invasion . . . and I am sure I heard people in D.C. say, 'Had we made a mistake?' But of course the Chinese were going to come in anyway . . . there were no answers. . . . Still I sometimes thought that I precipitated that. But my intention and that of the State Department was to somehow aid the Tibetans without precipitating the invasion."

Nor did it make Bessac feel any better when he heard that Prince De—a direct descendant of Genghis Khan—had been imprisoned in Mongolia by its Communist rulers. It would be years before he heard the conclusion to that sad tale, so similar to that of Osman Bator.

Under pressure from their Soviet masters and the Chinese, the Mongol rulers of the People's Republic of Mongolia arrested Prince De after he had fled there from China. On September 18, 1950, he was extradited back to China, where he was jailed as a criminal. One of the crimes he confessed to—apparently under torture—was that he had worked for the American intelligence agent Frank Bessac. That is certainly a distortion of their relationship. Prince De's real crime was the same as Osman's and the same as the Dalai Lama's: he said that neither his people, nor his land, were Chinese.

The Inner Asian battle was far simpler than McCarthyite supporters in America or the Chinese ever understood. It had nothing to do with Communism, or anti-Communism, as Prince De made clear in his last free statement before imprisonment. "What is the difference between the policy of the Communists for regional minorities and the Kuomintang policy of local autonomy? At any rate, they are all Chinese. To the Mongols, they are all the same."

Prince De spent the rest of his life in a Chinese prison and died there on May 23, 1966. When the prince was born, the population of Inner Mongolia was fewer than 10 percent Chinese. Today Mongolians compose only 12 percent of the population of the Inner Mongolian Autonomous Region.

The Mongol survivors of the Chinese march of colonization in Inner Mongolia say that during the Cultural Revolution, both the wearing of Mongol clothes and the teaching of Mongolian were forbidden. They estimate between twenty and fifty thousand Mongols were killed—some for simply uttering the name Genghis Khan. One hundred and twenty thousand Mongols were maimed and nearly eight hundred thousand were jailed.

Inner Mongolia—one-eighth of the modern Chinese empire—has larger coal reserves, larger forests, and larger grazing lands than any other Chinese province. Four of the six largest gold mines in China are located in Inner Mongolia. It produces more steel than any other Chinese province, and today 90 percent of the workers in the coal and steel industries of Inner Mongolia are Chinese, not Mongolian.

The final solution that has been achieved in Inner Mongolia, and half achieved in Xinjiang, is now being repeated in Tibet. During Bessac's years of wandering, he followed this Chinese march from its inception in Inner Mongolia on through Sinkiang and into Tibet. Though he has lived in the United States since his amazing journey, his life has been devoted to the study of Asia. He completed his Ph.D. at Berkeley in 1963, and by 1965 he was a professor of anthropology at the University of Montana. He never let the inevitable advance of his glaucoma—toward blindness—thwart his study of Asia. He served as chairman of the Department of Anthropology from 1978 to 1985 and today is professor emeritus. In the 1970s, Bessac was adviser to a student writing his dissertation about covert U.S. aid to the Tibetans during the 1950s. The Dalai Lama stayed on in Tibet from 1950 to 1959, under the new Chinese administration, because the Chinese had promised Tibet real autonomy. During that period, the Dalai Lama tried to take Chinese promises at face value; without any Western support there was no other choice.

Bessac's student argued that CIA support to the anti-Chinese guerrilla movement after the 1950 invasion led to the destruction of the Dalai Lama's autonomous government. Bessac had no idea—nor did anyone besides a few people in the CIA until 2002—that the United States had dropped arms to the Tibetans *before* that invasion. His student argued that the American support *after* the invasion—never enough to evict the Chinese from Tibet—had made it impossible for the Dalai Lama to create a stable government. Bessac was not sure that he accepted his student's viewpoint. He was certain the Chinese were planning their next steps, no matter what the Tibetan freedom fighters or the Dalai Lama did. In any event, the Tibetan people rose in revolt against the Chinese occupation in 1959. The repression was brutal—an estimated fifty to ninety thousand Tibetans died in the wake of the revolt. When it was over, the Dalai Lama began his life of exile, and China took the next steps in its colonization campaign. Bessac's student argued that CIA aid to Tibetan rebels in Tibet from 1950 to 1958 may have sped up this sequence of events—just as covert aid prior to the invasion may have precipitated the invasion in the first place.

In exile during the 1960s, Tibetan fighters again received covert CIA support, but once more it was too little to do any harm to the Chinese. As Gyalo Thondup, the Dalai Lama's elder brother, says, "It was just enough to make the Chinese mad." One fact links covert aid that the CIA supplied to the Tibetans—whether it was supplied in the weeks before the 1950 invasion, while the guerrillas were still in Tibet, or once they retreated to bases in Mustang, Nepal. It was always too little too late, and it was always driven primarily by American intelligence needs. It is an unlikely coincidence that atomic intelligence was uncovered by Mackiernan in 1949, who then went on to "try to help" the Tibetans, and that when America "tried to help" the Tibetans in the 1960s it again turned up invaluable atomic intelligence. America's atomic intelligence interests are the secret bookends on either side of the true story of America's covert relations with the Tibetans. Naturally the agents in the field never viewed their work this cynically, but those who sent them there may have.

The Dalai Lama says that such aid was a reflection of U.S. anti-Communist policies, "rather than genuine support for the restoration of Tibetan independence." In fact, intelligence gathered by the Tibetan guerrillas in Mustang gave the United States six months' advance warning about the Chinese development of their first atomic bomb during the 1960s. As soon as the United States established diplomatic relations with China in the 1970s, CIA support for the Tibetans was cut off. Simultaneously, the United States began to collect atomic intelligence from Urumchi/Tihwa again.

In 1989 Bessac retired but continued to advise students—and to pay keen attention to America's evolving relations with China and Tibet.

During the 1990s he noticed support for Tibet was conditioned by people's relationship with China. A new U.S. China lobby was again emerging that argued Tibetan history based not on facts but on what their Chinese patrons wanted to hear.

By the 1996 election this erupted into a full-scale political scandal. The FBI alerted California Senator Dianne Feinstein that some of her campaign contributions were coming directly from the Chinese government. They did not point out that her husband was overseeing hundreds of millions of dollars of U.S. investments in China—though the press would note that in passing. The money was returned, and Feinstein did not commit any crime, but suddenly the American public was aware that the Chinese government was spending money in America to influence the course of American politics. By the time the annual review over China's trading privileges in the United States was dropped in June 2000, American corporations were spending millions of dollars to lobby for the legislation that China wanted in America.

It was an odd circle closing for Frank Bessac. Chiang Kai-shek had started the game of trying to influence American politics by contributing to American politicians' campaigns—and using American corporations working in China as their lobbyist to the U.S. government. Now the Communist Party is up to the same old trick, but today no one calls Boeing, Coca-Cola, and Nike Communist stooges. The bet, in 2002, is that American corporations can help transform China into the democracy we would like it to be. American certainty about this modern conviction is frightening to anyone who has carefully studied the past.

In 1945 America's convictions made it blind to Tibetan Kazak and Mongolian nationalism. America's certainty that it could install Chiang Kai-shek on the Chinese throne after the war made the Chinese people's dissatisfaction with his corruption invisible to the Americans. Some Americans seeing only Chiang's corruption convinced themselves that Mao Tse-tung had to be better. Other Americans called them Communists for failing to support Chiang. Throughout it all, Americans sought a way to shape the fate of China and ignored the nationalism of the other Asian peoples who lived on the verge of China. How could they be important to America as it battled for China?

The Tibetan government returned Douglas Mackiernan's head— and those of Stephan and Leonid—to Shegar-Hunglung. They were rejoined with what remained of their skeletons, after the sky burial, and buried on the edge of the Changthang. Mackiernan's body is the only American corpse buried anywhere within a radius of one thousand miles. His remains have never been returned to the United States, though Pegge Mackiernan urged this in the 1950s and even now would still like to see the remains recovered. Mackiernan never came home. Vasili Zvansov's Russian-style crosses were pounded into the Tibetan earth above each mound. The Tibetan government took a photograph of the site and sent it to the United States, but the photo and a letter of condolence were never passed on to Mackiernan's widow as they had asked.

Instead, during much of 1950 and 1951, the U.S. State Department built a legal case against the Tibetans. They wanted to sue the Tibetans for wrongful death and thought the Tibetan government should pay the Mackiernan widow $50,000—while it was paying her $22 a month and the CIA decided it owed her not a cent. Eventually, the State Department realized how it would look to the Tibetans if the first U.S. letter to Tibet after the Chinese invasion was a demand for $50,000.

The plan was dropped. No one ever raised the idea that if any wrongful death suit needed to be brought it was against the State Department and the CIA for allowing Mackiernan to enter Tibet before the United States had received Tibetan permission for him to do so.

The Mackiernan family heard little about this. The government asked them not to talk about Mackiernan's death. The journalists who came to the Green Lantern were met with stony silence. Though Douglas was gone, his gift to his brothers—World Weather Corporation and its contracts with the federal government—survived for a few years after his death and made a good deal of money for the family. In about 1953 some folks from the government came and inspected the receivers at World Weather. They went over them closely enough that it may have allowed them to duplicate Mackiernan's installation. Shortly after that, the government contract was withdrawn. Without federal contracts World Weather collapsed, since it had been forbidden to seek other clients. The Mackiernan brothers left the Green Lantern and sought other work.

Gail Mackiernan, Douglas's first-born child with his first wife, was eight years old in 1950. Like her half brother and sister Mike and Mary, she was essentially abandoned by the CIA and the State Department. Luckily a senator from Maine stepped in and pushed a bill through congress granting $15,000 to the support and education of Gail—few kids get their own act of Congress before they are twelve. She remembers going to her grandparents' place in the summer of 1950 and in the summers that followed. Her father's Buddha statues from Tibet, and the Tibetan Buddhist paintings above them, were unforgettable icons of her lost father. She remembers asking Grammy Mackiernan about them. "Dougie got those in Tibet," was all the old woman would say. Such brief comments were all Gail heard about Tibet—bright shards turned up for an instant and then covered over again.

Gail remembers standing in the backyard holding Grammy's hand as the Newfoundland dogs howled and slavered on their chains. Grammy squeezed her hand when she said, "Dougie said that dog reminded him of the Tibetan mastiffs he saw there that were chained out in front of the houses to guard them."

The mysterious Buddhas gathering dust in the dark library, and the fragmentary stories from Grammy Mackiernan about her father, created an unalterable impression upon Gail, one that she recalls today, fifty years later, with great certainty.

"Doug was definitely involved in arming the people of Inner Asia. It was clear . . . that he was going to Tibet to do something similar, that was his mission. But he had been doing that already with Osman Bator. The United States at that time wanted to arm the people like Osman and the Tibetans, in case, somehow, they could be of use to the United States in containing the newly emerging Chinese Communist state. All this was just something I always knew about my father, since it was something that was talked about, if only rarely, at home.

"I think whatever letters once existed to prove this have been destroyed."

Douglas Mackiernan's trust in his mother's discretion was well founded. Before she died she burned all of his letters from China.

There was another family conviction as well. The Buddhas that Gail saw in the Mackiernan house were not the ones that Frank Bessac shipped back to Pegge Mackiernan in 1950. The family says that they were brought out from Tibet by Mackiernan after his *first* trip there. No one in the family knows when that trip took place, but they are all convinced it happened.

Stuart Mackiernan says, "Yeah, I think he was in Tibet. He brought back things from Tibet, the paintings and statue. . . . He said they were Tibetan artifacts that he brought back from Tibet. He said that, absolutely. . . . It was an accepted fact in the family that Dougie went to Tibet sometime before he was killed. He admitted he was in Tibet, but he wasn't talking about what he did there."

If these scattered shards are evidence that Douglas Mackiernan went to Tibet sometime between 1945 and 1947, then there remains even now another layer to the Mackiernan story. There is one set of facts that could possibly link Mackiernan and once again, uranium, to Tibet—before 1949. The OSS sent a mission to Tibet in 1942, lead by the grandson of the Russian novelist, Ilya Tolstoy. The mission walked into Tibet from India, and then walked on, across Eastern Tibet to China in 1942. Tolstoy was based in Kunming for the duration of the war, where Mackiernan also spent a great deal of time. In 1945 Tolstoy developed a consuming passion in uranium, and made trips to remote areas of China: he may have made a trip to Tihwa that same year. Tihwa was small enough, and the American's there few enough, that Tolstoy would certainly have met Mackiernan if he went there. If Mackiernan did make an earlier trip to Tibet some link with the work of Tolstoy—a native Russian speaker—would be fertile ground to explore for an explanation of these mysteries.

In his autobiography, *Freedom in Exile,* the Dalai Lama writes, "Tibet contains one of the world's richest deposits of uranium." That was unknown in 1950, though it was a matter of interest to the U.S. Army. During the 1949 review of Tibetan policy, the U.S. Army stated that Tibet was so remote that only if such valuable metals were found in Tibet would the country have strategic value to the United States. It is possible that Mackiernan had some use for his Geiger counter as he crossed the Changthang, though Bessac and Zvansov saw nothing to indicate it.

It is not clear how much gold Mackiernan had with him when he died, nor what happened to it after his death. Mackiernan family members say that the State Department did come round to ask about a large amount of money that had gone missing when Mackiernan died. Bessac believes that he may have sold Mackiernan's gold in Lhasa or New Delhi, and given the resulting cash to the State Department, though he does not remember after all these years. State Department records show no indication that they received any gold from Bessac, or cash, and those records document only the money that Mackiernan owed them. These same records state that during his debriefing Bessac gave an accounting for 100 ounces of gold, which to his knowledge, Mackiernan used during their trek. These records make no mention of the larger sums of CIA gold Mackiernan had had. "John," Mackiernan's CIA handler, told Pegge that he probably buried that trove somewhere in Inner Asia.

After the wave of publicity about Mackiernan died down in 1950, there was not a single printed reference to Mackiernan's links to the CIA until 1996. Bessac and Zvansov kept their silence, Pegge searched for the truth about her dead husband, and the CIA's version of history was unchallenged. Then the CIA began to perform an annual memorial ceremony for fallen covert agents. In 1974 it commissioned an Honor Wall. A slab of marble was installed in the vast echoing lobby of the Langley, Virginia, headquarters. On it were inscribed these words: "In honor of those members of the Central Intelligence Agency who gave their lives in the services of their country." Rows of nameless stars were inscribed below—by 2001 it reached only 79 when Johnny Michael Spann's name was added. More and more people in the Outfit whispered that the first star was for a guy called Mac, who had been shot dead on the border of Tibet and Sinkiang.

The directors of the CIA, sometime during the 1960s, became aware that Pegge Mackiernan had not been treated well by their predecessors. Perhaps her ill treatment looked particularly bad once they realized she was the widow of the First Star. They took steps to make amends, and there was some reconciliation. The CIA began to make annual payments toward the education of the Mackiernan twins, though Gail seems to have been forgotten. By then Pegge had married John Hlavacek, a noted journalist, and the family bounced around the world.

In 1986, when the CIA began to hold an annual memorial service in front of the Honor Wall, Pegge and John Hlavacek were invited to attend. Pegge was given pride of place at the annual events, perhaps as a means of apologizing for the earlier callousness. None of the rest of the Mackiernan family was invited to the ceremonies. In June 2000 when Pegge's daughter Mary Mackiernan was invited she mentioned to the CIA that several of Douglas Mackiernan's brothers were alive and had expressed an interest in attending the ceremony to which they had never been invited. The CIA explained that it did not have their addresses or phone numbers. Mary shook her head in the disbelief that they did not seem to know how to use a telephone book. The resulting invitations came too late for Duncan Mackiernan, as he had died six months earlier. Angus had died several years before that.

In June 2000, fourteen Mackiernan family members were invited to the annual memorial ceremony—more than ever before. The CIA asked them not to speak about it, and they were warned not to bring a camera or tape recorder to the event. The CIA dealt with them much as it had dealt with Pegge in 1950. The family was also told that if they were asked if any of the Mackiernan family had attended the ceremony, the CIA would deny it. The family was led to believe that it was their duty to keep silent, if only out of gratitude for being invited to the ceremony. Despite this, Douglas D. Mackiernan—whose father, Duncan, had so recently died—decided he wanted to speak on the record about his afternoon at the CIA ceremony.

Douglas Donald Mackiernan was born in the summer of 1950, near the time that the news from Tibet reached his father, Duncan Mackiernan. The newborn was named after his slain uncle only a few months after Douglas S. Mackiernan died—and today he says he is proud to be named after a great American.

Reserved seating was prepared for the Mackiernan clan, quite near the podium and the Honor Wall. Douglas D. Mackiernan had read an early version of *Into Tibet*. When a CIA official, introducing the director, referred to the "two Chinese" who died at the shoot-out on the border of Tibet he knew better. He nudged a family member and said, "They were Russians with Doug, not Chinese."

The director of the CIA, George Tenet, did a better job with his facts, or at least with the ones he chose to speak about. He told the story of the shoot-out on the border but didn't say a word about Stalin's first atomic bomb. He talked about the sacrifice that Douglas S. Mackiernan had made, but said nothing about how bungling by the State Department and the CIA probably caused it. Nor did he talk about why Douglas Mackiernan was sent to Tibet—he spoke only about an escape. An accidental shooting on the border of Tibet. Nor did Tenet mention the agreement Mackiernan had made at Timurlik, with Qali Beg, in the winter of 1949, so that Kazak intelligence couriers could pass through Tibet. Nor would Tenet want to mention the hundreds of U.S. citizens living peacefully in the United States today, descendants of the White Russians whom Mackiernan had found so useful for U.S. intelligence projects.

George Tenet kept his remarks brief, and wiped away an honest tear or two, as he spoke about the courage that stands behind the First Star on the wall. Tenet tried to bring solace to the family members. "I know what they would be thinking if they were here right now. They were great patriots and put the love of their country and their home, the CIA, first. They would be very proud of the CIA today, and to be stars on this great wall. . . . They chose to give their lives for the greatest cause." That is certainly true. A few family members knew enough to wonder if the value of Mackiernan's real personal courage, and sacrifice, was not eviscerated by cowardice among policy makers in the U.S. government.

At one point Tenet brought up the First Star. "Today, unfortunately, we cannot publicly release the name under the First Star, but to you and our CIA family we want to recognize Douglas 'Mac' Mackiernan and his family."

Tenet referred to "Mac"—as though he were member of the same family—and called him the first CIA agent ever to die in the line of duty. He urged the families to have the courage to bear their grief in silence. He seemed to imply that the deaths of their loved ones served the national security interests of the United States of America. There is no doubt that this was once the case. Nor is there doubt that the true story about Mackiernan's death needed to be kept secret for a few decades. But is that still true, now, more than fifty years later?

Douglas D. Mackiernan is not so sure. His doubts grew as the CIA photographer moved the Mackiernan clan farther away from the Honor Wall, so that none of the stars on the Honor Wall would show in the background of the picture. The background had to be white so that the CIA could deny that the Mackiernans had ever been at CIA headquarters.

Mackiernan's doubt intensified when their guide pointed them toward the souvenir shop, after the ceremony, and said, "You can buy anything you want—after all, you can buy those CIA T-shirts anywhere in D.C., so its deniable."

He was amused by the inscription on the lobby wall: "The truth shall set you free." His doubts grew yet further as he spoke with Nicholas Dujmovic, the CIA employee who wrote the agency's secret in-house biography about Douglas S. Mackiernan.

Douglas D. Mackiernan listened to Dujmovic say that "the real story is much more fascinating than the public one." He watched Dujmovic's face closely for signs of hubris when he said, "I regret that I am unable to share that with you."

Mackiernan listened to Dujmovic when he requested from the family any letters, or photographs, so that he could include them in the classified, inspirational museum exhibition that the CIA maintains about the life, work, and death of Douglas S. Mackiernan—presumably a place for new recruits to go, to touch their roots, to inspire them. Douglas D. Mackiernan could hardly believe it when Dujmovic explained that no, the family could not see the museum—but it sure would be nice if the family could add something to the secret CIA exhibition.

By the end of the day, Douglas D. Mackiernan was convinced that any national security reason for secrecy about his uncle had long passed. He considers himself, like his uncle, a patriot and would gladly go along with secrecy—even now, fifty years later—if that truly served the national interests of the United States. As Mackiernan walked out of the multimillion-dollar glass and marble CIA headquarters, he wondered exactly who or what the secrecy was now protecting.

"Douglas S. Mackiernan's relatives were never told the entire truth about his death and were never given the true purpose and reasons for his mission. They were instructed that revealing even what they were told was against the national interest and could be harmful to existing operations. The Mackiernan family's patriotism led them to honor this request for silence.

"Today, the secrecy that survives protects flawed U.S. policies of the past, based on inaccurate facts, and the blunders and faults of CIA administrators of fifty years ago. America's failure to support independence for Sinkiang, Tibet, and Inner Mongolia was not because of any historical ties between the people of these countries and China. The financial and logistical difficulties and the political repercussions domestically and internationally of supporting these areas were the compelling reasons. I see no basis for continuing the fiction that it was history, not other more practical reasons, which led the United States to accept China's occupation of those countries.

"If the United States supported these people as they resisted the Chinese takeover, then that is what happened and there is no need to deny it now. If the United States failed to notify Tibet in time to obtain safe passage for the Mackiernan party in spite of plenty of opportunity, as it now appears, then the CIA or responsible parties should admit the error. The possibility exists that this failure to notify the Tibetans was not an accident. I believe that at the least it was the result of bureaucratic procrastination on the issue of supporting Tibet. It also appears, for reasons as yet unexplained, that my uncle operated long after his cover was blown—and that the impact of that decision on Tibet was heavy.

"Continuing to deny what really happened is wrong. It is not the CIA's place to rewrite history. If the people and government of the United States cannot acknowledge their mistakes then we are bound to repeat them."

NOTES

PREFACE

xiii   Tibetan guerrilla gives U.S. intelligence that allows six months' advance
         warning on China's first atomic bomb. Laird reported this fact for *Newsweek:*
         "When Heaven Shed Blood," by Melinda Liu. April 19, 1999, international
         edition. Laird reporting for, pp. 36–39. "A Secret War on the Roof of the
         World," by Melinda Liu, August 16, 1999, U.S. edition. Laird reporting for,
         pp. 34–35. Melinda's own reporting turned up several other sources who
         confirmed this report.

xiv   *Life* story was false: FB, author interview.

         America involved Tibet in atomic intelligence: NARA 793B.56/9-150 NND
         981749, released to author on September 14, 1999, after a Freedom of Infor-
         mation Act request made three years earlier. See enclosure #2. FB asked the
         Tibetan cabinet to allow DSM intelligence couriers to pass through Tibet.
         Since DSM was involved in atomic intelligence this may have involved Tibet
         in U.S. atomic intelligence, at least in the eyes of the Chinese.

xv   "first CIA undercover agent ever killed": Even though the CIA refuses to
         publicly confirm this, they have invited members of the Mackiernan family
         to an annual memorial service, in June 2000, where this fact has been con-
         firmed by director of the CIA. MM, PL, DDM, author interviews.

xvi   "disrupt modern Sino-U.S. relations": Unnamed CIA source, currently
         employed, author interview.

         CIA employee letter says story cannot be revealed: copy of letter, on CIA
         letterhead, in author's possession.

PART ONE: WHY THEY WENT

3   Shegar-Hunglung, the shoot-out: NARA RG 59, 793B.00/9-2150. Also DSM
         death certificate, issued in New Delhi by State Department, October 23, 1950.
         The date of the shoot-out varies from April 27 to April 29, in different docu-
         ments. April 29 is probably correct. The shoot-out is told in this chapter accord-
         ing to documents that FB wrote for the State Department a few months later,
         which have been preserved in the National Archives, and FB, author interviews.

8   Estimate by General Marshal to Truman that 250,000 Americans would have
         died in U.S. invasion of Japan: McCullough, 1992, p. 437.

9   "atomic monopoly would last longer than it did": Ziegler, p. 19.

10   SSU HQ, March 5, 1946: The description of this party is based on interviews with Frank Bessac, and e-mails from both Frank and Susanne Bessac.

"a Chinese dance melody": Yue Lai Xiang, e-mail from Frank and Susanne Bessac, April 29, 2000.

11   His parents named him Francis Bagnall Bessac, but FB used "Frank" on all official records. See FB's security investigation report, 1956, collection of FB and NARA records.

FB in the army: His honorable discharge, at the rank of Tec 4, says that his effective date of separation was March 31, 1946, in Shanghai. See Enlisted Record and Report of Separation Honorable Discharge, collection of FB.

FB College of the Pacific, Chinese language training, flew over Hump: FB, author interview. The Chinese course specifically, see Certificate of Completion of Chinese training, from Cornell, dated, with FB. Also discharge papers of FB.

FB was assigned as OSS-SI agent to Chinese paratrooper mission; it was most likely a suicide mission because he would be left behind enemy lines, and though Chinese could blend in and escape an American would not be able to so easily hide in Japanese occupied China: FB, author interview.

FB's sense of honor made him stay on in China at end of World War II: FB and Susanne Bessac, author interviews, e-mails.

"intelligence reports on the Chinese army": FB confirmed to author that he wrote the SSU field reports by Source: Oregon, and others. Many of these are about Inner Mongolia. OSS agent John Bottorff also confirms that FB was the primary intelligence agent for all things about Inner Mongolia circa 1946. One example of an FB/Oregon report, at NARA is SSU #A-66668, dated March 4, 1946, entitled "Organization of Communist Military Districts." This document is twenty pages long and lists every high-ranking officer in the Chinese Communist armies of the day.

"studied by American diplomats in Washington and Moscow": NARA 893.00 MONGOLIA/10—1845, Letter from the U.S. embassy, Moscow, of October 18, 1945, cites the FB SSU reports No: A-68899, May 3, 1946, and others, discussing political developments in Inner Mongolia.

"two American agents who spoke Chinese": John Bottorff, the other Chinese-speaking agent in Peking, author interview.

SSU Peking outstanding intelligence unit in China: unpublished memo from H. Ben Smith, chief of SSU, Peking, dated June 14, 1946, collection of FB.

12   Mei-ling and the party : FB, author interview, also e-mail from FB. The name of this young woman is invented—though FB says the woman is alive in the United States today. The date of this party is not certain. It happened sometime before FB went to Inner Mongolia. Nor is it certain that FB actually read Lattimore this night. However, he was reading Lattimore that spring, and this party happened. These two events have been conflated to create this opening chapter. This is one of the rare instances where author has taken this liberty. However, FB was moved by exactly these ideas of

Lattimore's, that spring of 1946, and it is from this time that his involvement with these ideas begins.

FB's Chinese name: As written on FB's Security investigation report, 1956, document with FB.

FB says Chiang a dictator: FB letter of December 1, 1945, to his father, unpublished, collection of FB.

13 Switch U.S. support to Communists: FB now feels these were the half-baked ideas of an idealistic young man, but this is what he felt in 1945 when he wrote the letter to his father.

Washington had no idea of disaster brewing in China: FB letter of December 1, 1945, to his father, unpublished, collection of FB.

FB wanted to take UNRRA job: FB letter of December 1, 1945, to his father, unpublished, collection of FB.

FB reading about the lives of Chinese: FB letter of December 1, 1945, to his father, unpublished, collection of FB.

"The general line of the Great Wall": *Inner Asian Frontiers of China,* by Owen Lattimore, originally published by the American Geographical Society, 1940. Author citing from Oxford University Press reprint, Hong Kong, 1988, pp. 22–24.

14 Many differences . . . Great Wall: Ibid., Lattimore, p. 206.

"The Great Wall . . . is a boundary": Ibid., Lattimore, pp. 238–42.

"Many Chinese still view the Manchu as a Chinese dynasty": Even brilliant American thinkers, of Chinese origins, succumb to this propaganda. Chang, 2001, p. 193. "Manchus from the northeast breached the Great Wall, but soon they themselves became Chinese." If the Manchus became Chinese why did Mao Tse-tung cut off his pigtail, in 1912, after the anti-Manchu revolution? Mao viewed his pigtail as something imposed on Chinese (at pain of death!) by foreign invaders. Anyone who doubts that Mao, and most Chinese, viewed the Manchus as foreign invaders—even at the end of their reign over the Chinese—should consult *Red Star Over China,* by Edgar Snow, for Mao's views on this. The Manchus fled north back to Manchuria at the end of the 1912 revolution—back across the Great Wall, built to keep these foreigners out of China, and to keep Chinese inside of China. The pernicious Chinese propaganda on this subject is one of the greatest underlying errors in modern writings about Chinese history. Lattimore understood this well, even if many modern writers seem to have forgotten it.

"The strong are weak, the weak rule": Author is paraphrasing the message of the *Tao Te Ching* by Lao-tzu. While the spiritual value of this greatest of all Chinese contributions to human culture is incalculable, we would be remiss to view the *Tao Te Ching* only as a spiritual guide. There are many levels of interpretation within this twenty-five-hundred-year-old book. "Yielding to force is strength." "Therefore if a great country gives way to a smaller country, it will conquer the smaller country . . . Therefore those who would conquer must yield . . . It is fitting for a great nation to yield." "The weak can overcome the strong . . . Under heaven everyone knows this."

(Quotes from the Feng/English translation.) Yes, these are spiritual koans of great value. But they are also the people of China speaking, after centuries of bruising defeats at the hands of the people of Inner Asia. These defeats, not only the colonial humiliations at the hands of the European invaders, are the ancient roots of the sense of humiliation that plagues the Chinese nation even today. Chang, 2001, understands this humiliation very well (pp. 190–97), but like many people (of many different racial backgrounds) he fails to understand the deepest roots of this sense of outrage. This is the most dangerous fallout of Chinese propaganda on this subject.

"The Mongols and the Tibetans regarded . . . The Manchu": Lattimore, *China and the Barbarians,* 1934. In Joseph Barnes (editor), *Empire in the East,* Doubleday Doran and Company, pp. 14–15.

15 1946 morning jog: FB, author interview.

Construction of Peking city walls began 1266: "Map of Khanbalik," *Microsoft® Encarta® 98 Encyclopedia.* © 1993–1997 Microsoft Corporation.

Mao pulled down Peking walls in 1949: Sin-Ming Shaw, *Newsweek,* December 14, 1998.

16 FB notices differences between Mongols and Chinese: FB, author interview.

"How did I know they were Mongols": FB, author interview.

Mongols and Chinese created by different environments: FB, author interview, and Lattimore, 1988.

"SSU sent Bessac north through Great wall to Kalgan and Peitzemiao": NARA, Record Group 226, M-1656, FB SSU reports A-69417, A-69425 A-69221, A-69247, A-69425, and A-69428. Also FB and JB author interviews.

In Peitzemiao FB developed a lifelong commitment to non-Chinese outside The Great Wall: Ibid. and FB, author interviews.

17 "sent to US Embassies around the world": NARA 893.00 MONGOLIA/10—1845, Letter from the U.S. Embassy Moscow, of October 18, 1945, cites the FB SSU report No: A-68899, May 3, 1946 and others, discussing political developments in Inner Mongolia.

"We are not Chinese. We are Mongol": FB, author interview. FB arrived at this paraphrasing of the Mongol message after talking with dozens of people—and author is paraphrasing things FB said in many different interviews. This message also concurs with the message that Owen Lattimore tried to get across to the American public, and American policy makers, from the 1930's. See Lattimore, Inner Asian Frontiers of China, p. 234.

FB first learned about the difference between Chinese and those beyond the wall from personal experience and from Lattimore: FB, author interview.

"Neither could hold sway over the other": Lattimore, 1988, p. 512.

China inherited industrial power from West, Inner Asians did not: Lattimore, 1988, pp. 235, 512.

18 "Phonograph not played at cocktails"; DSM at cocktail party: WW and LW author interview. Wells was working in business in China at the time. It was

several years before he joined the CIA, where eventually he became a senior CIA administrator. Mr. and Mrs. Wells both attended a party where DSM was present that year, though the date is not clear. The general description of the party is based on their recollections. Mr. Wells refused to talk about whether or not DSM was a CIA employee, but he and his wife did interview about China during this period and their recollections of DSM at this point before he went back to Tihwa.

Such parties happened, and DSM went to them, before he returned to Tihwa—but author assigned this date at the convenience of the narrative. The party may not have happened during this month. This is one of the rare chapters where author has conflated accurate information from many sources into one event, the date of which is unknown.

Multiple sources for assessment of DSM: LW for handsome; PL handsome and difficult.

DSM calls world out of Inner Asia "civilization," sardonically: PL diary quotes DSM using this phrase about the world outside of Inner Asia.

DSM both frightening and appealing to women: SM, GM, PL, author interviews.

"thought they knew something": DSM thought is from PL diaries. Also from Wells interview.

Assessment of the embassy conversation, spouting newspapers: LW interview.

DSM, ever-present pipe: photographs of DSM from the period, PL collection. Also VZ, PL, author interviews.

19 Now that's an outport: LW describes this as the attitude toward Tihwa—the party took place, and DSM talked to the women from the code room, but we do not have quotes from the conversation. This is a created conversation conveying what LW thought "everyone" knew and felt and would have said at this party, which is why it is not in quotes. "Outport" is the term that embassy employees used to indicate a remote town deep inside China.

DSM spoke little unless he was very interested in subject: Assessment of DSM based on PL, author interviews, and PL diary.

DSM descriptions of Inner Asia: based on what DSM is reported to have said to people when speaking generally about Inner Asia, as mentioned in PL's diaries.

Author has no idea if DSM recalled his bigamous marriage at this party while talking with these women, but we know the marriage happened, and that it bothered him, and this is a device to introduce it. Dr. Linda Benson interviewed the British representative in Tihwa (Fox-Holmes) who was present at this wedding during World War II, at the Russian Orthodox Church in Tihwa, author interview. PL's diary also reveals that when she was there no one in Tihwa had ever heard of Doug's first marriage to Darrell. Tihwa only knew of his marriage to the "Russian woman"—author was unable to discover her name. Yet DSM was already married to his first wife, Darrell, before he arrived in Tihwa, so this wartime marriage was illegal. PL's diary shows that DSM was haunted by this decision. A discussion she records with a Catholic priest in China in the summer of 1947 shows that such wartime marriages were common, and not such a big deal in the eyes of those who lived through the war in China. Her diary also reveals that this marriage was never revealed to his family in the United States, and that in general U.S. society strongly disapproved. The diary also shows that DSM's CIA handler knew about this marriage, and that the CIA did not disapprove.

DSM's view about losing rank: Consul Paxton's letters. Yale. NARA.

DSM left MIT after freshman year because of poor grades: DSM MIT transcript states that he would not be allowed to continue after his freshman year because of poor fundamentals, unless he took remedial work. Transcript obtained by Janice Mackiernan Ianello, from MIT, 1999.

DSM told family he did not want to waste time on course work he already knew: SM, author interview.

20   His bold attitude was based on real ability: SM, author interview.

DSM worked on advanced meterology project for MIT etc.: Pan American Airways, September/October 1936, in-house newspapers, p. 3, "Hurricane Chasers to Havana."

DSM meets Goddard: SM, author interview.

DSM co-authored paper with H. T. Stetson and worked at Cosmic laboratory etc.: *On the Observation and Measurement of the Apparent Shift in Direction of the Radio Beam of an Air-Beacon and Certain Relations to Meteorological Conditions* by H. T. Stetson and D. S. Mackiernan, Jr. Transactions American Geophysical Union, 1942.

Ham radio DSM's hobby from youth: M1M, GM, SM, author interviews.

DSM breaks Russian weather code: SM, M1M, DM, GM, Janice Iannello—author interviews. This is one of many oft-repeated family myths about DSM that seems based on facts.

DSM heads U.S. Army Air Corps' Cryptoanalysis Section: Both SM and C. W. Tazewell assert this, author interviews.

21   DSM drove over Burma Road to China: Documents in the possession of the family of DM prove this; a short snorter: money from every nation the road passed through, taped together, signed by the men who traveled over it together. The amount of money was that required to buy a beer in each nation. Short snorter signed by DSM. Courtesy JMI.

DSM established weather collection base in Sinkiang during World War II: "Thor's Legions: Weather Support to the U.S. Air Force and U.S. Army, 1937–1987," pp. 117–18. This citation is courtesy of C. W. Tazewell. Tazewell also obtained a copy of the Army Air orders sending DSM to Tihwa.

"Headquarters Tenth Weather Region issued a letter subject: Historical Records of Organization," March 2, 1944, and included personnel changes chronologically with Major Mackiernan listed on February 6, 1944, as being "asgd and Jd per Radio HQ AAF, Wash., D.C."

NOTES

"Maj Douglas S. Mackiernan, Jr., is reld fr asgmt and dy Det Hq Tenth Weather Sq, APO 627; is asgd WP Hq Tenth Weather Sq, APO 492, reporting upon arrival to the CO thereof for dy. (EDCMR 14 Sep 45)" as written in Special Order Number 200; issued from HQ Tenth Weather Squadron AAF, India Burma Theater, APO 492, September 9, 1945.

U.S. bombers over Tokyo relied on DSM weather data: "Thor's Legions: Weather Support to the U.S. Air Force and U.S. Army, 1937–1987," pp. 117–18.

DSM Chronology 1945, 1946 as determined from family letters (Duncan to his future wife Vivian, and Mary—DSM mom—to Vivian). Letters courtesy Mr. and Mrs. Duncan Mackiernan, Douglas D. Mackiernan and Janice Mackiernan Ianello.

October 15, 1945—Mary
"Our oldest boy we've just found out is on a special assignment in Russian Territory, when we were hoping he was on his way home—Great thing the Air Force."

October 31, 1945—Mary
". . . It will mean another Thanksgiving without any of the boys, unless my oldest son should show up. Which seems very unlikely. Our last word from him, he was in Russian Territory.

November 2, 1945—Duncan
"Mom heard from Dougie who is still deep in China—Urumchi to be exact, apparently he'll be there some time, yet he does not seem particularly concerned about when he'll get out."

November 14, 1945—Duncan
"Dougie is still in China apparently he has come about 200 miles east of his outpost in Russia and in now at "Ft. Black"—50 miles as the piegon flies from a little Chinese Villa—Urumchi. I am not too sure of his immediate plans . . ."

November 15, 1945—Duncan
"The Chinese Civil War is Doug's reason for not leaving. He operates directly under General Wedermier (?). Officers of his rank are not discharged according to points—they simply resign. But until General Wedermier will accept Dougie's it will never reach the War Department to whom it is addressed. As Dougie puts it his mission will not be accomplished until the threat of Russian Intervention in the Chinese Civil war has died out. Of course he may be relived of his position and replaced but that's up to his General and the War Department too."

December 17, 1945—Duncan
"I've a new address for Dougie, he is now in Tihwa China—and has been declared essential—he hopes to be out in April (1946)."

March 7, 1946—Duncan
"Mom has no word from Dougie since a letter dated December 23 (1945)—now the latest letters she has written are being returned—marked no such address—Maybe he's coming home—I wish he would as the tension between

295

this country and Russia is great enough to start unscheduled clashes in China or Mongolia, which is where we think he is. Everything is very "secret" according to the last letter, whatever he means by that. . ."

March 15, 1946—Duncan

"Angus has a cable gram from Douglas from Shanghai"

March 16, 1946—Duncan

"Dougie's cable to Angus just gave a new address C/O Morrison Mansions Shanghai, China . . . I think he will be leaving China in April."

March 1946–May 1947, DSM works in Nanking, except for brief trip to U.S. He flies into Tampa during this trip, sporting a machine gun under his trench coat and giving broad hints to his brothers about his covert intelligence work in China.

22   "There was this whole alphabet soup period": FB, author interview.

"The facilities of the Department of State still offer some good covers for field agents . . .": RG 59, Intelligence Files, Bureau of Administration, Office of Security, 1942–1951, Lot File No 79 137, Box one. Memo dated September 4, 1945, on Foreign Activity Correlation letterhead, Department of State, see p. 9.

23   February 7, 1947, Leighton asks for DSM to join State go to Tihwa: NARA, RG 59, 125.937D3/2-747.

CIG becomes CIA informally May 1947, formally September 1947: The CIA Under Harry Truman, History Staff, CIA, 1994, p. 129.

DSM applies to State May 5, leaves for Tihwa May 12: NARA RG 59, 125.937D2/6-1547, Ambassador Stuart to Department of State.

24   State Department orders embassies to report on uranium transactions: NARA:893.6359/1-646.

Finding enough uranium, not the atomic science, was secret of atomic bombs: Ziegler, pp. 21–31.

25   January 25, 1946 Stalin tells Kurchatov pay any price to have atomic bomb: Holloway, pp. 147–148.

Osman Bator's nomads migrate back to Koktogai, May 1946: This event happened as stated, at about this date. Osman described this to DSM during their first meeting in 1947. NARA RG 59, 893.6359/6–3047—On-the-Spot Investigation of Peitaishan Incident, by DSM, dated June 30, 1947.

Description of nomadic life is based on Lattimore and others. Also, FB and VZ, author interviews.

26   "We will pay you ten meters of cloth for forty pounds of this rock": Osman told DSM and DSM reported this in the Peitaishan Incident Report. NARA RG 59, 893.6359/6-3047. Tense has been changed. The exact circumstances of Osman seeing the prospecting the first time is invented—he learned, this but exactly how, we do not know. This is one of the few times in the book when a scene is invented.

27   The Chinese came to the Altai in the 1930s and mined gold: This is a paraphrasing and summary of things Osman told DSM at Peitaishan in 1947. Not a quotation. NARA RG 59, 893.6359/6-3047.

Chingil River Ford, "nomad's nightmare": This event happened as stated, at about this date. Osman described this to DSM during their first meeting in 1947. NARA RG 59, 893.6359/6-3047—On-the-Spot Investigation of Peitaishan Incident, by DSM, dated June 30, 1947.

29   Leave the herds to their fate: This summary describes what happened as reported by Osman to DSM. NARA RG 59, 893.6359/6-3047—On-the-Spot Investigation of Peitaishan Incident, by DSM, dated June 30, 1947. This is not a quotation from Osman, but something he is likely to have said, based on what he told DSM, at a later date. Thus it is not in quotes.

"I believe that it must be the policy of the United States to support free peoples . . .": McCullough, p. 548.

30   "I had the impression of America . . . as the Champion of Freedom": HHDL, author interview.

DSM and Edwin Martin drive to Tihwa: Foreign Service Journal, September 1985; letter to the editor from Edwin W. Martin, ambassador, retired. Martin died, at the age of seventy-four, on October 5, 1991, in Washington, D.C.

31   "Mac's resourcefulness": Ibid.

U.S.S.R. attacks Peitaishan, two soldiers killed: details from DSM's Peitaishan Incident Report, NARA RG 59, 893.6359/6-3047.

U.S. journalist links Peitaishan Incident to rumors uranium found in Altai: NARA RG 59, 893.6359/6-2747, see attachment to dispatch 840 from Nanking embassy to D.C. UP article, datelined Nanking, June 12, 1947, that begins: "Uranium deposits may be the real cause behind the Outer Mongolian penetration into northeast Sinkiang Province, Chinese press reports hinted today."

Cherezima arrived in Tihwa asking for reinforcements about June 10: October 16, 1947, caption material for Pegge Lyons/Pegge Parker photo spread, copyright News Syndicate Company, Inc., 1947. Clipping courtesy of Mary Mackiernan, RC, and Pegge and John Hlavacek.

32   Kontescheny's magic hands : EK, author interview, 1999.

"He was a very good shot, Mr. Mackiernan": Ibid.

33   DSM may have given Osman gold: EK, VZ, author interviews. These sources believe it took place but are not certain.

DSM went on a raid with Kazak at Peitaishan: EK, author interview. Modern Chinese sources also report on DSM's trip to Peitaishan. Xinjiang Historical Materials, Book 2, Urumchi, 1981, p. 136. Thanks to Aynur Caksýlýk and her father for Chinese references. They portray the same incidents from a less gallant light. They say, for example, that DSM, while out on a Kazak raid, was fired on and ran away in terror, which contradicts everything we know about DSM; he would have delighted in the contact.

"Feed them to the wolves of the forests": October 16, 1947, caption material for Pegge Lyons/Pegge Parker photo spread, copyright News Syndicate Company, Inc., 1947. Clipping courtesy of Mary Mackiernan, RC, and Pegge and John Hlavacek.

Osman would fight way back into ETR if DSM got him some aid: DSM's Peitaishan Incident Report, NARA RG 59, 893.6359/6-3047. And NARA RG 59 893.6359/8-2947; see the enclosure, Notes on the mineral "Columbyet," by DSM. Also EK, author interview, 1999.

Osman explained uranium rumors to DSM: DSM's Peitaishan Incident Report, NARA RG 59, 893.6359/6-3047.

34   One hundred rifles to Osman's rival, March 1947: Ibid.

Trucks export uranium to U.S.S.R.: VZ, EK, author interviews.

"I heard Osman was attacking the Russian trucks": EK, author interview. Also see Moseley, 1966, p. 25 and Benson, 1988, pp. 21, 153, 156, 169, 170.

DSM made electroscope: NARA RG 59 893.6359/8-2947; see the enclosure, Notes on the mineral "Columbyet," by DSM.

DSM believed Osman's samples were radioactive: In fact, Doug's field science was wrong; the AEC, after tests in Washington, said the samples were not radioactive. NARA RG 59, 893.6359/8-2947. However, this work by DSM was greatly appreciated and later on was recalled as the United States got serious in 1949 about the Koktogai mine. If the first samples were duds, that would be the reason why DSM eventually sent the White Russians back for good samples.

Consul Clubb suspected uranium in Altai, 1943: Clubb's dispatch dated July 20, 1943, cited by Paxton in NARA RG 59, 893.6359/5-2747.

DSM made report on Osman's rocks: NARA RG 59, 893.6359/8-2947; see the enclosure, Notes on the mineral "Columbyet," by DSM.

35   "The USSR might be willing to make considerable temporary ideological compromise": NARA RG 59, 893.6359/5-2747, also on Microfilm LM 184 64 of 75, Paxton to U.S. embassy Nanking, copied to State Department.

Osman's rocks sent to AEC: NARA RG 59, 893.6359/6-3047; rock samples dispatched to State, and from there to AEC.

DSM already looking for intelligence on Stalin's bomb, perhaps starting covert action against it: Author assumes this is possible because of the mention in Butterworth's message of spring 1949 about such a covert project. And because of Erwin Kontescheny's memory about Mackiernan talking with two radio stations inside the U.S.S.R. The chronology is open to question; these projects may have begun in 1949 instead of 1947.

PL and DSM meet first time in Tihwa: Conversational quotations in this chapter are from the diary of Pegge Lyons, copyrighted, and used by permission. Much of the information on which this chapter was based came from a reading of the same diary, kindly lent to the author by Pegge and John Hlavacek, through courtesy of Mary Mackiernan and Robin Clark. Additional information from PL, author interview.

36   Walter Sullivan says he'd have split a gut to go to the ETR: Diary of PL.

Barbara Stephens: NARA RG Tihwa.

Born 1919, *Harrisburg Telegraph, Washington Times Herald, Daily News Miner:* PL interview. PL Diary. E-mail from John Hlavacek.

37   Pegge Lyons worked as a PRO for the U.S. Army: Diary of PL.

"... Sinkiang, rich, rich Sinkiang with a heart of gold": Diary of PL.

DSM like a piece of gold, "a prince among men": PL, author interview.

DSM, "handsomer than Henry Fonda": PL, author interview.

38   "red hot romance": PL, author interview.

DSM giving intelligence instructions to PL before she went into ETR: PL, author interviews, also diary of PL.

"Now we are not taking Sunday school pictures or something": PL, author interview.

Smells in Osman's yurt: PL, author interview.

Osman, things atomic, "His life and his people and what's to be the fate": PL, author interview.

DSM might have talked about uranium to Lyons, though it is unlikely he talked about atomic testing; looking back, after the Russia's first atomic tests, PL probably conflated what she heard at the time with what she later learned.

Lyons went to Kulja, modern Yinning.

39   Hakim Bek Huja, "We believe big governments": PL diary.

"A-OK, you passed": PL, author interview.

40   DSM so funny: PL, author interview.

"Where is your wife," day "stabbed": PL diary.

"I can't marry you . . . can't": PL diary.

41   "Is he REALLY the one? . . . Jeepers!": PL diary.

All the assertions about what Pegge loved or liked are based on her statements in her diary.

"Mark ye well the day of July 13": PL diary.

FB given CIA recognition code, D.C., 1947: FB, author interview.

Marge Kennedy gives FB his code: FB is not certain what his code was, but thinks it was Oregon/D. There are SSU Intel Field reports, which FB did write, that seem to use this same code for FB. Author has used this assumption throughout, though there is some doubt. Also note that FL's recollection of how he used this code on FB is different from FB's recollection of how DSM used it on him.

42   "That's right, Frank. Unless you aren't working for the Outfit": FB, author interview.

43   AFOAT-1: *Spying Without Spies,* by Charles Ziegler and David Jacobson, is the definitive work on the subject of Murray Hill and the birth of the Armed Forces Special Weapons Project.

"The Soviets will continue atomic research": Ziegler, p. 89.

Military kept Foreign Atomic Intelligence Unit to itself: Ibid.

AFSWP soon renamed AFOAT-1: Ibid., p. 150.

44   Many AFOAT-1 contractors from MIT: Ibid., pp. 118–23.

Butterworth initiated Murray Hill–inspired uranium treaty talks with China: NARA, RG 59, 893.6359/6-2747. There are dozens of documents in this part of the decimal files that describe Butterworth's long-running attempt to negotiate a treaty that would guarantee the United States monopoly access to all Chinese uranium. See also, 893.6359/11-1247, 893.6359/11-2047, NARA 893.6359/3-548. It is not a pretty story. The United States wanted a monopoly but did not want it in a treaty, since that would have to be passed by the House and Senate, and was too public for Murray Hill. Butterworth was the man who started the movement to negotiate this treaty, while in China, and then worked on the continuing saga from Washington once promoted back there.

"Life without you impossible": PL diary.

46   DSM advises Hopson on selection of bomber base site: RG 341, Air Force-Plans, Project Decimal File 1942–1954 from 452 Section 8 to 452 Section 11, Box 736, Sg 581 (Ts). The primary source for this chapter is the report of Airfield Inspection in Northwest China written/released Feb 2 1948, Air Division Army Advisory Group, Nanking China, prepared by William D. Hopson, Colonel, USAF.

Hegenberger navigator on Bird of Paradise: U.S. Air Force Biography Major General Albert F. Hegenberger, 1895–1983. *http://www.af.mil/news/biographies/hegenberger_af.html*

Hegenberger named Commanding General of the Tenth Air Force: U.S. Air Force Biography Major General Albert F. Hegenberger 1895–1983; also see *www.southernheritagepress.com/Aug45.htm* and *www.geocities.com/Pentagon/9669/341bombgroup/hq_10.htm*

Hegenberger moves Tenth Air Force to Kunming: Ibid.

Hegenberger biographical material, MIT: U.S. Air Force Biography Major General Albert F. Hegenberger.

47   "Mr. Douglas S. Mackiernan, American vice-consul at Tihwa . . . passed through Nanking on 25 September 1947. . . .": RG 341, Air Force-Plans, Project Decimal File 1942–1954 from 452 Section 8 to 452 Section 11, Box 736, SG 581 (TS). The primary source for this chapter is the Report of Airfield Inspection in Northwest China, written/released Feb 2 1948, Air Division Army Advisory Group, Nanking China, prepared by William D. Hopson, Colonel, USAF.

FB journey Shanghai to Peking, September 1947: Description of the journey, as well as Bessac's thoughts and feelings during it, FB, author interview. Also letter by FB, to his mother, dated October 3, 1947, which Bessac kindly allowed the author to read.

"learned what being undercover meant": The *Lodi News-Sentinel* of July 31, 1950 reports on its front page that Bessac had left government service by 1947; i.e., the newspaper is reporting Bessac's cover story. At what point Bessac began to speak openly about the fact that he returned to China in 1947 as an undercover agent for the CIA is unclear. When author first interviewed FB he did not reveal this. Only after several interviews did FB reveal that he was sent back undercover—and then, as FB says, quit in fall of 1947.

military transport as before: Military Travel Orders, collection of FB. Also, FB, author interview.

FB met three guys, etc.: All such descriptions in this chapter are based on a reading of FB's letter to his mother, dated October 3, 1947. Letter copyright FB. FB kindly let the author read this letter. Also, FB, author interview.

48 Chinese passengers down in steerage: This and all such descriptions in this chapter are based on a reading of FB's letter to his mother, dated October 3, 1947. Letter copyright FB. Bessac kindly let the author read this letter. Also, FB, author interview.

Life was terrible: FB, author interview.

Prices had doubled: Spence, 1990, p. 501.

49 Youthful ranting: FB, author interview.

Discomfort growing . . . undercover . . . CIA: FB, author interview.

USS *Polk*, October 4,1947: This journey, descriptions of it, and feelings of Pegge and Doug in this chapter are based on a reading of the unpublished diary of Margaret Hlavacek for the years 1946–1951. PL diary.

"wanted to take a break . . . time off from the CIA": PL, author interview.

51 Peking, China, October 15, 1947: This chapter is based on FB, author interviews. This is a description of a typical day in FB's life at this time. He did the same thing every day, and so based on research author has assigned this date as being most likely.

FB's Peking house: FB, author interview. The descriptions in this chapter, about FB's house and courtyard, are based on a reading of FB's letter to his parents, dated March 27, 1947.

No longer jogged: FB, author interview.

52 Mandarin's Examination Hall: Thanks to Claudia Cellini for taking a photograph of this site as it is today, and sending it to me via e-mail. FB says that he took his morning walks next door to this shrine; perhaps he means the ten-acre park around the shrine.

Mandarin scholar: FB, author interview.

General disapproval of U.S. policies: FB letter to his parents, dated March 27, 1947.

53 Crag Hotel, DSM and PL: My source for the feelings and events in this chapter is the diary of PL. The Kipling quotes are as written in the diary, as is the quote from *The Straits Echo*. The conversational quotes are also from PL diary.

55 FB and Prince De: This meeting between FB and Prince De took place sometime in October or November 1947. The exact date is unknown. FB, author interview.

Prince De was a direct descendent of Genghis Khan: Demchugdongrob, 1902–1966, commonly known as De Wang by Mongols, and Prince De by Chinese. Some American sources of the time call him Prince Deh. Jagchid, 1999, p. 1.

Descendants of Genghis Khan always ruled Mongols: Ibid., p. xvi.

The Outfit sent FB to interview Prince De: FB, author interview. Also see the FB SSU field intelligence reports at NARA, previously cited.

Prince De devoted his life: Jagchid, 1999, preface.

56 FB says today: FB, author interview.

Prince De's Western-style white shirt and black pants: FB, author interview.

"I have quit the service of my government": FB, author interview.

Yes, as you say. Still": This section of the conversation is not in quotes because FB does not have an exact memory of what the prince said to him that fall. He thinks the prince said something like this, and this statement concurs with things the prince is known to have thought and said about this time. See Jagchid, 1999.

"I have seen Mongols": FB, author interview. There are no written records about FB's meetings with Prince De in fall of 1947. He met him several times that fall. FB recalls mentioning this Mongol habit to the prince. It is not clear if they had this conversation before or after FB resigned from the CIA.

57 Former CIA agent, says Bessac not allowed to quit CIA: FL, author interview.

"I'm gonna set you up, Pop": SM, author interview.

58 "Right pop?": Most such quotes from DSM in the chapter are from SM, author interview.

Dougie decided what we were worth": DM, interview conducted by Janice Iannello, for author.

59 AFOAT-1 contracts signed spring 1948: Ziegler, p. 122.

Theoretically to get divorced from his first wife, Darrell: DSM may have stopped off in France to work on the CIA covert operation that penetrated the French Communist Party that winter. EK, author interview; SM, author interview.

Pegge's thoughts, "doubts about marrying Doug": PL diary.

60 "I wish you were coming with me, babydoll": PL diary.

"He always had mysterious comings and goings": PL, author interview.

Mackiernan at Eniwetok?: The dates match. Ziegler, p. 132.

Zebra atomic test date: Ibid.

61 Lattimore DSM dinner, "no way to communicate that democracy": author transposes an earlier political comment, by DSM, recorded by Pegge in her diary, within the Lattimore evening. Though DSM's political belief is recorded it is not known if he said just this, that very night, with Owen. Author has assumed he would have.

Lattimore warned that if the United States did not support Asian nationalism the Asians would turn to the U.S.S.R.: Newman, 1992, p. 130.

European colonialists argued that the United States should support return of colonialists to Asia: Newman, 1992, p. 130. This argument was the precursor to the modern debate wherein Kissinger's pragmatists claim it is sentimental, and economically unsound, for the United States to ever allow its foreign policy to be based on any concern with human rights in modern China and other dictatorships.

Lattimore, "stop pushing into Communism people whom the Russians them-selves couldn't lead into Communism": Newman, 1992, p. 148.

62   "His plans with the State Department": PL diary.

DSM told Stuart and Pegge different stories: This analysis based on author interviews with SM and PL, and PL diary.

"You're not to worry about things like that": PL, author interview.

64   Yates ordered to build and install AFOAT-1 equipment in Air Force planes in Alaska: General Mundell, author interview.

The commanding general of the Weather Service was Brig. Gen. Donald N. Yates: USAF publication, *The Roswell Report: Fact Versus Fiction in the New Mexico Desert;* see summary of this in *Synopsis of Balloon Research Findings* by 1st Lt James McAndrew, 1995.

Yates and DSM old friends: SM, C. W. Tazewell, author interviews.

Mackiernan and General Yates establish parts of the same system: This is deductive reasoning by author. That reasoning is based on the documents and interviews cited in this chapter.

Stuart Mackiernan met General Yates at Andrews Air Force Base: SM, author interview.

65   DSM's scientific skills of use to CIA: SM, author interview. Also, diary of PL.

66   "sewing gold bars into Dougie's coat": SM author interview.

DSM " melted gold": DM, interview conducted by Janice Iannello, for author.

67   Building Geiger counters, taking them to China: SM, author interview.

"He was a wonderful agent.": GM, author interview.

68   U.S. generals want to stop arming Chiang: RG 218 entry- Geographic File 1948-50 Box no 13452 China (4-3-45) Sec. 7 Pt 1-3.

In a memo for the Executive Secretary of the NSC, dated February 2, 1949, regarding current position of the US respecting aid to China, it was noted that "recent recommendations from the Directory of U.S. Military Advisory Group China, should be brought to the attention of the NSC. . . Because of the continued deterioration of the military and political position of the Na-tionalist Government in China the Director of the of the USMAGC, in his message of January 26, 1949 . . . recommending that, pending clarification of the situation in China, no military aid supplies be shipped." General Barr also sent a message through State channels to D.C., in which he amplified his feeling that military aid had to be stopped: "Our government not only has to consider the possibility of war munitions eventually falling into the hands of the Chinese Communists, but also must consider the possibility of their disposition by unscrupulous personnel of National Government in the event of its complete. . . collapse. In my opinion, under this condition, there is a strong likelihood that any munitions not immediately susceptible to Communist control would be loaded into Chinese vessels now in Formosan harbors and moved out with disposition by sale in countries engaged internal dissent and located adjacent to or south of China." [Barr means Ho Chi Minh in Vietnam] "There would be little or no consideration given to allegiance or intents of the purchaser. In view of the foregoing, I recommend that export license be withheld pending clarification of military and political situation. I further recommend that pending clarification of the situation in China, no miliary aid supplies be shipped."

Chiang Kai-shek corruption known by U.S. generals: McCullough, p. 742.

69   AFOAT-1 caused Roswell UFO?: 1995 Air Force publication *The Roswell Report: Fact Versus Fiction in the New Mexico Desert. Synopsis of Balloon Research Findings,* 1st Lt James McAndrew.

Hegenberger Eniwetok tests of detection equipment: Ziegler, pp. 84–102.

70   Sonic detectors locate atomic explosion within range of a hundred miles: Ziegler, p. 210.

71   "Regarding Hegenberger Mission: all equipment on hand": NARA RG 59, 101.61/3-1049. The document is missing from the files at the National Archives—under circumstances that indicate it was removed during a security purge of State Department files. Yet the key fragment of the message is saved in the summary of the message in the Decimal File, Source Cards, 1945–49. See Tihwa Source Cards, March 10, 1949.

Witness helped DSM bury atomic detection equipment: VZ, author interview.

Mackiernan family receiving data from Tihwa, not weather data: SM, author interview.

72   DSM Personnel Efficiency Report: Manuscripts and Archives, Yale University Library—John Hall Paxton Papers. Though the State Department will not allow access to these files on DSM, Paxton kept a carbon copy, which is at Yale. Foreign Service Operation Memo, dated March 28, 1949.

"He has seemed more content since his recent marriage": Ibid.

73   DSM fails to carry out promises: Manuscripts and Archives, Yale University Library—John Hall Paxton Papers. Paxton to Robert W. Linden, unpublished letter, November 6, 1948.

"He inspires confidence to a greater extent": Ibid.

74   Reports from as far back as 1943 were pulled about uranium: This is determined by looking at when State Department documents were read by a person. Archived messages were stamped, with office, name, and date, when they were retrieved from message files. On top of this we have the meeting memo, NARA RG 59, 893.6359/4-2249, so we can deduce this. Stamped documents include, RG 59, 893.6359/2-449, 893.50 recovery/2–449, 893.6359/12-2448, 893.6359/6-3047, 893.6359/5-2747.

Mr. Sprouse said Chiang would ask for money if the United States wanted to stop uranium exports from Sinkiang: NARA RG 59, 893.6359/4-2249, attached memo of conversation.

Truman says Chiang a thief: Merle Miller, 1974, p. 289.

75   "In order to acquire further intelligence on the reported uranium deposits": NARA RG 59, 893.6359/4-2249, attached memo of conversation.

Arneson, special assistant to the undersecretary of state for intelligence: State Department Telephone Directory, 1950.

"Dept and AEC want uranium samples": NARA RG 59, 893.6359/4-2249.

76   The Raid on the Uranium Mine: RG 59, 891.411/8-251 Decimal File, 1950-54, U.S. Consul Calcutta, William G. Gibson to Dept. of State, July 29, 1951; Subject: Arrival of 23 Russian Refugees from China via Tibet. Also, VZ, author interview.

77   Some of White Russian refugees from Semipalatinsk: Ibid.

Ivan X: VZ, author interview.

Ivan X wife in the United States: VZ, author interview.

78   "I was born in 1923" : VZ, author interview.

VZ was Eskadrone quartermaster: VZ, author interview.

U.S.S.R. promised ETR rebels they would be boss in ETR: VZ, author interview.

79   VZ began to work with DSM: This date does not concur exactly with dates from DSM story as told by other sources, such as PL diary. VZ admits he is not certain exactly when he started working with Mackiernan. If it was in 1947 then that poses the question of what he did between September 1947 and December 1948, while DSM was not there. VZ has little recollection about this period.

"I met General Ma": Apparently this is one of the famous Ma family, Omar Ma, but not the warlord, Ma Pu-fang himself.

VZ began working with DSM in 1948: VZ, author interview. VZ gave different dates for the start of his work with DSM in different interviews—1947 and 1948.

80   VZ did not know about Russian bomb until India: Quotations from different interviews have been assembled here, and VZ approved the resulting quote. VZ, author interviews.

Burying equipment to detect atomic bomb: VZ, author interview.

81   "The length of time the Soviet Union needed to develop the atomic bomb": *Stalin and the Bomb,* David Holloway, p. 223.

81–84   The assembly and explosion of Joe-1, description of test site, people there, their thoughts, difficulty of obtaining uranium, weather, tank going to site after explosion etc.: Holloway, 1994, pp. 214–218.

85   State Department asked by other agencies what it would feel if U.S. could know whether Russians had tested bomb eleven days before Russian test: NARA, Policy Planing Staff, Department of State, August 16, 1949, *Political Implications of Detonation of Atomic Bomb by the U.S.S.R.*

History states Truman had no advance warning of Stalin's bomb: McCullough, 1992.

"General Yates knew from some intelligence source that he did not reveal to me that the U.S.S.R. was about to explode an atomic bomb": USAF General Lewis N. Mundell, retired, author interview. Mundell worked under Yates in the USAF's Air Weather section. He was the head of the Alaskan Air Force base where the planes, which picked up radioactive traces of Russia's first atomic explosion, were based.

Existence of "secret history of DSM written by CIA in 1998": Confirmed by current employee of the CIA, author interview.

"Bomb was raised into tower": *Stalin and the Bomb,* Holloway, p. 215.

87 Russian scientists to be shot if bomb fails: Ibid., p. 218.

Hundreds of messages from DSM to State Department missing: NARA RG 59, Decimal File, Source Cards, 1945–1950. See Tihwa cards marked "Filed in Telegraph Branch," May through August 1949. Though FOIA'd these documents have not turned up. Also note that Ziegler, p. 30, asserts that all documents about U.S. intelligence in the U.S.S.R. for 1949–1950 remain classified.

DSM to Butterworth, will operate Hegenberger TR equipment, August 10, 1949: NARA RG 59, 125.937D/8-1049. Author assumes that since the Hegenberger name is so uncommon, and since Hegenberger ran AFOAT-1, that the Hegenberger equipment referred to was that used to detect atomic explosions. Also note March reference to arrival of Hegenberger equipment—*Spying Without Spies* shows that the Hegenberger equipment was installed in early 1949; this date match also substantiates author assumption.

DSM checked the sonic detectors, called TR device: Author assumes TR device was the sonic detectors. This assumption is based on these facts: DSM calls the Hegenberger equipment the TR device; Hegenberger was in charge of atomic detection. Ziegler reports sonic device had to be installed less than a thousand miles from the Russian test site. Only Tihwa fits all these parameters.

DSM may have received data from monitor equipment, or agents, in the U.S.S.R.: EK, author interview, says DSM had radio contact with agents in the U.S.S.R. VZ, author interview, says that DSM sent agents into U.S.S.R. on at least one occasion. SM, author interview, says that they received data from monitoring stations inside the U.S.S.R. DSM letters to family say he was in U.S.S.R. in 1945. Ziegler, p. 30, says that documents relating to U.S. intelligence in Russia, 1945–49, remain classified, but that D. Lilienthal said "we did send covert operations into Russia."

88 Discovery of Joe-1 by Air Force Air Weather methods: Ziegler, pp. 203–10.

89 Sonic data gave exact size, time, and location of Joe-1: Ibid., p. 210.

Hegenberger, Oak Leaf Cluster, Legion of Merit, for AFOAT-1 work: National Aeronautics Hall of Fame web site.

First printed mention of DSM as CIA agent in 1996: Smith, 1996, citing Laird as source, p. 278.

CIA will not confirm or deny DSM as CIA agent: CIA Public Relations staff, author interview.

90 Still "considered national security secrets": CIA letter, on CIA letterhead, in author's possession.

"The U.S. system for monitoring the first Soviet atomic test": Charles Ziegler, author interview.

PART TWO: THE JOURNEY TO TIBET

94 "The Tibetan government did nothing: GT, author interview.

Tibetan minister smoking opium: GT and Tenzin Gyatso, HHDL, author interviews.

"The great powers helped to maintain our ignorance": GT, author interview.

95 "We say China is a country vast in territory": Mao Tse-tung, *On the Ten Major Relationships,* Foreign Languages Press, 1977, cited by Smith, 1996.

Henderson said, ". . . recognition of Chinese suzerainty over Tibet had been principally to strengthen the Government of China.": RG 59- General records of the Department of State, Entry 1305. Box 11 NND 897209 Records relating to South Asia, 1947–59 Lot file No 57 D 373 & Lot File No 57 D 421, Subject Files of the Officer in Charge of India-Nepal-Ceylon-Pakistan-Afghanistan Affairs 1944–1956. July 6, 1949, NEA—Mr. McGhee to SOA—Mr. Mathews. Proposed Mission to Tibet.

"If Tibet possesses the stamina to withstand Communist infiltration . . .": RG 59- General records of the Department of State, Entry 1305. Box 11 NND 897209 Records relating to South Asia, 1947–59 Lot file No 57 D 373 & Lot File No 57 D 421, Subject Files of the Officer in Charge of India-Nepal-Ceylon-Pakistan-Afghanistan Affairs 1944–1956. July 6, 1949, NEA—Mr. McGhee to SOA—Mr. Mathews. Proposed Mission to Tibet.

96 "To secure first-hand information . . ." : RG 59- General records of the Department of State, Entry 1305. Box 11 NND 897209 Records relating to South Asia, 1947–59 Lot file No 57 D 373 & Lot File No 57 D 421, Subject Files of the Officer in Charge of India-Nepal-Ceylon-Pakistan-Afghanistan Affairs 1944–1956, from Mr. Sprouse to Miss Bacon US Policy Toward Tibet. April 12, 1949.

97 Dingyuanying, description of conference: FB, author interview. Also Jagchid, 1999, pp. 392–422. These two sources disagree on major points. Author has threaded his own way through their disagreements following his own understanding of what transpired. There is room for an alternative interpretation here.

Every political option discussed at Dingyuanying: FB, author interview. Also, Jagchid, Ibid.

FB was asked to speak: FB, author interview.

FB felt like Lafayette: FB, author interview.

98 Chinese might have executed FB: FB, author interview.

FB's Fulbright came through in fall of 1948, first mentioned summer 1948: NARA, RG 59, 811.42793 SE/7-2348, from U.S. Embassy Nanking, to Exhange of Persons Division, State, Despatch No 317, p. 5. July 23, 1948: "The USEFC's endorsement of Mr. Bessac was originally and continues to be, conditional. . . . USEFC has not had an opportunity to examine his undergraduate record which was to be sent direct to the Board of Foreign Scholarships. Mr. Bessac was endorsed on the basis of a satisfactory record in China and his emphasis on Mongolian studies, a field little developed among American sinologues." Of the six China candidates FB was ranked four of six. By November 1948 (NARA RG 59, 811.42793 SE/11-1648) Bessac in Nanking "awaiting transportation" to "Northwest China for Mongol field study." November 12, 1948 (811.42793 SE/11-1148), USEFC has suspended departure of grantees from United States because of Chinese civil war. By November 24, 1948 (811.42793 SE/11-2348), FB is still in Nanking "considering ECA post Inner Mongolia"—FB says now he was considering position with UNRRA, and that he was in Shanghai. There is some confusion here. About Fulbright, also, FB, author interview. FL raised the possibility, during author interviews, that FB's Fulbright selection was manipulated by the CIA so that the position could be used as deep cover. FB heatedly denies this. Conflict between sources.

FB nearly gave up Fulbright to go to work for UNRRA: FB, author interview.

FB exchanged Fulbright scholarship money for gold bars: FB, author interview.

Did FB go blind?: Leilani Wells, author interview.

99   Jagchid does not agree: Jagchid agrees that FB met Prince De in Peking just after his trip to Inner Mongolia. He says that in 1946 FB was the Peking agent of an American naval intelligence office—when in fact FB was working for SSU and CIG. But the basic fact—that FB was a U.S. intelligence officer—he has right. His book asserts repeatedly that FB was still a U.S. intelligence agent in 1949; of course it is possible Jagchid was misinformed. However, one of Bessac's best friends in China, John Bottoroff, was under the same impression. Speaking about Bessac, after he left Peking and went to Chengdu: "My feeling was that Frank stayed on with the agency." JB, author interview.

The Last Mongol Prince: The Life and Times of Demchugdongrob, 1902–1966, Sechin Jagchid, Center for East Asian Studies, Western Washington University, 1999. Professor Edward Kaplan was one of the editors of this book. When the author pointed out to Professor Kaplan that Mr. Jagchid's comments were in direct opposition to those of FB, and asked for his help to interview Mr. Jagchid, Kaplan said that he believed Jagchid would prefer to stand on what he had written in his book rather than be interviewed. He said that Mr. Jagchid's advanced age made it impossible for him to be interviewed. Thus author has quoted Mr. Jagchid's book. FB said in interviews that Jagchid was simply mistaken in his recollections.

Raymond Meitz US intelligence agent, promises De aid: Jagchid, p. 403.

Radio operators to connect Prince De and US intelligence: Ibid.

UNRRA equipment to be given to Prince De: Ibid.

100 "In all probability the fight against Communism": O. C. Badger to Joint Chiefs of Staff, NARA RG 218, Entry Geographic File, Box 15, Records of the U.S. Joint Chiefs of Staff, Geographic file, 1948–1950, 452 China (4-3-US) Sec. 7 Pt. 4-7, Box no. 15.

Badger knew about MAP in Congress: Ibid.

State knew Nationalists supporting Republicans, "hard intelligence": Blum, p. 67.

McCarran, "State Department peddles the Communistic": Ibid., pp. 66–67.

101 MAP, "general area of China": NARA RG 218 Records of the US JCS, Geographic File, 1948–50, Box no. 15, Enclosure to JCS 1868/107, and JCS 1721/37 and JMAC (Joint Munitions Allocation committee) 70/11, enclosure b.

JCS recommended the United Studies use some of the MAP money to aid the Inner Asians, and assigned the CIA that job: NARA RG 341 entry 335 box 737, JCS letter to Sec Def.

Perhaps a million Mongols killed, millions of Chinese have settled in Inner Mongolia: Hong Kong Cheng Ming, by Bahe (U.S.A.): "Turbulent Fifty Years of Inner Mongolia."

De planned to drive toward Tibet then walk to Lhasa: Jagchid, p. 407.

Jagchid told wavering supporters about UNRRA trucks: Jagchid, p. 406.

102 FB was U.S. intelligence officer when arrived Dingyuanying: Jagchid, p. 410.

Loss of UNRRA fatal blow to De: Jagchid, pp. 410, 421.

Latrash says FB was a CIA agent using Fulbright cover: FL, author interview.

103 I was not a spy!: FB, author interview. FB denied he ever worked for the CIA when he was first interviewed. It was only after repeated interviews that FB finally admitted that he did work for the CIA. He also said on one occasion that if there was anything he did not want the interviewer to know, the interviewer would never know. He repeatedly, over many years, kept information about DSM from the author. In every case when author then turned up that information, it appeared that FB's sense of honor to a fallen comrade had kept him from sharing the information. His Vita from 1993 avoids mentioning his work for the CIA. It says only that from 1945 to 1947 he worked for the OSS. Of course the OSS died in 1945, and the CIA was born in 1947. During the Vietnam intellectual wars on U.S. campuses, it would have been far easier for Professor Bessac to have OSS on his Vita than CIA. FB was subjected to unconscionable harassment during the Vietnam War era by antiwar demonstrators. His self-protection on this subject was born in the heat of a difficult time. It is also possible that FB is absolutely correct, despite the evidence presented by two other sources. The author has gone to great lengths to present the facts as he uncovered them; readers will have to make their own judgment on this difficult subject. It is author's opinion that Frank Bessac is an unsung American hero of the first rank.

103–106   Hami to Tihwa, flight description, landing in Tihwa, greeted by DSM, lunch etc: author interview FB and VZ.

106   Leonid Shutov: NARA RG 59, 893B.181/1-950.

"You can call me Mac": The conversations in this chapter and the description of the consulate layout are created based on long interviews with FB, EK, VZ, PL, as well as maps of the consulate and dozens of documents written by JHP as he left the consulate, from RG 59 at NARA. I have arranged all of this information into what I believe is an accurate narration of the first meeting between DSM and FB.

108   Stephan Yanuishkin: NARA RG 59, 893B.181/1-950.

109   Conversation in quotes between FB and DSM—burning the papers and the CIA code/recognition conversation: FB, author interview.

South-facing windows, description of consulate: State Department descriptions, NARA RG 59.

A contract agent, if needed: Frank Bessac, 1998, "Winter at Timurlik," an unpublished manuscript. Also, FB, author interviews.

DSM uses CIA code on FB, Tihwa: FB, author interview. Bessac insists today that the coding did not make him a contract agent, it just meant it was safe for DSM to work with him. That interpretation conflicts with the statements by other sources: FL and Jagchid.

110   FB has trouble slipping back into reins: This supposition about Mac's thinking is based on FL's reactions to FB when the latter met him; it seems logical two agents would have had the same response to FB. FB insists that he was *not* at DSM's command after being coded, that the coding just vaguely made him available to DSM if needed.

DSM quotes about going to meet Osman, and his conversation with FB after the CIA coding: Author interview FB. From all that Bessac told me, and from State Department documents, as well as interviews with VZ, I have attempted to reconstruct what DSM probably said to FB that day. I still have doubt about exactly what was said during this conversation, but to the best of my knowledge this is what happened.

111   "And Doug said to me, 'Don't worry'": VZ, author interview.

112   VZ thought FB was working for CIA: VZ, author interview.

"Consulate Tihwa, officially closed": NARA RG 59, Decimal File, Source cards, 1945–1949, see Tihwa Cards, From Tihwa to State, dated September 27, 1949. Also RG 59 893.00 Sinkiang/8-3149.

International Supply Corporation buying weapons with U.S. funds for CAT fly to Ma Pu-fang in Tihwa: NARA RG 319 Army Intelligence Document File ID# 548364, March 1949. First consignment January 1949 included 2,000 carbines, 314 cases of ammunition. One shipment a day for months. Author assumes if ISC owned by CAT and CAT owned by CIA then ISC also owned by CIA. Also since Tihwa had only three native English speakers before arrival of Bessac, DSM would have known Simmons. Since many reports indicate Mackiernan was supplying weapons to the Kazaks the evidence that

ISC had a Tihwa office creates a circumstantial proof that ISC was the avenue for those weapons.

"Bessac wrote in 1950 that Simmons had . . .": NARA RG 59125.937D/10-3150.

CAT owned by CIA from winter of 1949–1950: *http://grunt.space.swri.edu/aam2.htm,* Remarks of Dr. William Leary, Professor of History, University of Geogia, Athens, for Memorial Dedication of the McDermott Library and its Air America Oral History project. Also: *http:www.air-america.org/about/history.htm.*

113   FB realizes how serious shooting Jeep is, becoming an enemy of China: FB, author interview.

"Yep, that's the White Russians": FB, author interview.

114   DSM gives FB machine gun: FB, author interview.

"We go to Tibet": VZ, author interview.

Size of gold bar for Burigin: VZ, author interview.

Ivan X and the other White Russians were among those who Douglas brought gold for: VZ, SM, author interviews.

115   DSM promised visas to the United States for the Eskadrone: VZ, author interview.

"Maybe ten kilos of gold, at most": VZ, author interview.

116   "They keep asking for guns": FB, author interview

"CAT and ISC busy with weapons deliveries all over northwest China": NARA RG 319 Army Intelligence Document File, ID # 548364, March 1949. There are other documents at NARA that indicate there were dozens of U.S. pilots based in Lanchow during the summer of 1949 who were busy flying something out of there. A visiting U.S. missionary was stunned at what a large operation it was. When Ma Pu-fang collapsed CAT and Ma Pu-fang retreated to Taiwan and Hong Kong—from where Air America would eventually emerge.

Date for departure from Barkol: NARA RG 59, 793B.00/9–2150, Journey Log kept by DSM and FB. "Do I need to know where we are going?" "Tibet": FB, author interview.

117   VZ watched DSM hand gold to Osman: VZ, author interview.

"Most of the talking was about how to fight Communists": VZ, author interview.

A CIA employee, writing unpublished letter: Author declines to reveal source of letter. Letter in author's possession.

"These . . . matters are still considered national security secrets": Letter on CIA letterhead, in author's possession.

DSM letter, "There is the rumor that": PL, quoted by permission.

118   "played a major role in assembling forces under Osman": *New York Times,* June 5, 1950.

DSM probably told Osman: This is author assumption based on all research, and from events that will unfold; see *National Geographic,* November 1954.

"Mackiernan assumed Nationalists in Sinkaing would retreat to Tibet": NARA, RG 319, ID # 663941, Box # 4277. From the document and what is known about Mackierman's work author assumes DSM would have known about this plan—in fact he was probably involved in developing, but that is more speculative.

JCS committee had precise ideas about how to spend MAP money: RG 218 Records of the U.S. JCS, Geographic File, 1948–50, Box no. 15, at NARA. Also see RG 341, Air Force Plans, project Decimal file, 1942–54, from 452 Section 12 China to 452 Section 14, Box no. 737. Also, RG 341, Entry 335, Box 737.

119   "those special operations which will most effectively interfere with Communist control of China" and following quotes: NARA RG 218 Records of the U.S. JCS, Geographic File, 1948–50, Box no 15. Also see RG 341, Air Force Plans, project Decimal file, 1942–54, from 452 Section 12 China to 452 Section 14, Box no. 73, RG 341, Entry 335, Box 737.

$30 million for covert ops in China, Taiwan, and Tibet, JCS: Blum, p. 202.

120   Truman, "these people" "fundamentally antagonistic" to U.S.S.R.: NARA RG 59, General Records of the Office of the Executive Secretariat, Memorandums of Conversations with the President, 1949–52, Lot File Number 65D238, Box 1. The Stack location is 250/46/03/04.

President, State, and JCS all ask CIA prepare covert arms for Inner Asia: Blum, pp. 162–63.

121   Half of Mao's weapons were U.S.-made in fall 1949, reasonable supposition: April 21, 1999, e-mail from Professor Ellis Joffe.

"arms here, opium there, bribery and propaganda," Rusk's ideas on use of MAP-303: Blum, p. 155.

Pegge Mackiernan enjoyed the view from her new house: PL diary.

122   "Women paid for moment of passion": inner thoughts of PL, PL diary.

123   August 26 collect telegram from State Department: PL diary.

DSM "home for Christmas!!!": PL diary.

124   "The DSM party traveled at night": NARA RG 59, 793B.00/9-2150, Journey Log kept by DSM and FB. Also FB and VZ, author interviews.

125   FB falls from horse, knocked unconscious: FB, "Winter at Timurlik." Also FB and VZ, author interviews.

DSM was not impressed at FB unconscious: FB, author interview; he says, in fact, that DSM got quite angry.

Kuruk Gol river, camp at eight hundred feet: NARA RG 59, 793B.00/9-2150, Journey Log kept by DSM and FB. This log is detailed enough that it allows the curious to follow the route quite closely, if a detailed map of this part of Sinkiang is at hand, such as MS Encarta. The place names mentioned in the log do match those on MS Encarta—just enough so that you can map the route.

Black-sand desert: FB, author interview.

VZ remembers stalking a desert antelope: VZ, author interview.

126   DSM saw himself as nineteenth-century explorer: FB, author interview.

DSM had frequent radio contact with the CIA: FB, VZ, author interviews. Also, radio days are mentioned in NARA RG 59, 793B.00/9-2150, Journey Log kept by DSM and FB. These radio messages were received by a CIA employee in Turkey who then sent them on to the CIA in Washington, D.C. FB knew the operator before he died. The CIA and the State Department are unable to locate these messages, and/or refuse to declassify them.

DSM handler, "John": The name John comes from Pegge Lyons's diary, where she says it is a pseudonym. She was given this name by FB, she says, though FB has no memory of that today. FB also says the messages went to the CIA. From some State Department messages it appears that CIA got the messages and then passed some of them to State.

DSM's original diary seems to have disappeared; however, a transcript of it, or at least parts of it, is in the National Archives. It remained classified TOP SECRET until the 1990s. NARA RG 59, 793B.00/9-2150, Journey Log kept by DSM and FB.

Bursak (fried bread): DSM liked this fried bread; FB, VZ author interviews, and NARA RG 59, 793B.00/9-2150, Journey Log kept by DSM and FB.

127   DSM radio messages went to Butterworth: NARA RG 59, 793B.00/9-2150, Journey Log kept by DSM and FB. But also note that the Hegenberger message from Tihwa was sent to Butterworth. And it was Butterworth who was talking with Pegge about Mackiernan's location this same month.

The State Department has refused to declassify the many radio messages that DSM sent to the CIA and the State Department after he left Tihwa. State says it handed them to the National Archives, which says they were never received. However, since Pegge received her information about Mackiernan from Butterworth, and since the Hegenberger messages went through Butterworth, it is a safe assumption that Butterworth received the DSM messages via the CIA.

128   DSM atomic message of August 10, 1949, routed through Butterworth: NARA RG 59, 125.937D/8-1049. Also see chapter on Semipalatinsk, on p. 80.

Butterworth initiated the uranium treaty with China: NARA RG 59, 893.6359/6-—2747; see the memorandum attached called "Subject: Information on Deposits of Radioactive Minerals in China." Butterworth sent the U.S. consul to talk with Dr. Wong in June 1947 and those meetings were the beginning of the U-2 treaty talks. NARA RG 59, 893.6359/6-2747— Butterworth to the secretary of state suggests Sino-U.S. uranium cooperation and initiates it. Author assumes that since this work eventually involved the AEC the Murray Hill effort was also involved.

Butterworth's China service showed he was one of the most able members of Foreign Service: *Present At the Creation,* Acheson, p. 145.

Butterworth helped edit the China White Paper: *Present At the Creation,* Acheson, p. 302. This exposure brought China lobby venom on his head: Ibid., p. 431.

Chiang a crook, stole $750 million, some used for China lobby: Merle Miller, 1974, p. 289.

If the United States recognized Tibet as independent, the China lobby would present that as proof of Commies in State: This interpretation has other supporters. Knaus, p. 40.

"to see Tibet accorded diplomatic recognition by the west": Thomas, Jr., 1950, pp. 238–45.

129   British told Tibetans not to provoke Chinese by asserting independence: Smith, 1996, p. 266.

Butterworth examined letters from Tibetans and wrote replies, shared with British: NARA, RG 59, 893.00 Tibet/ 11-449.

November 2, 1949
Mr. Mautsetung, Chairman
Chinese Communist Government
Peiping
    Tibet is a peculiar country where the Buddhist religion is widely flourishing and which is predestined to be ruled by the Living Buddha of Mercy or Chenresig [the Dalai Lama]. . . . Tibet has . . . been an Independent Country . . . never taken over by any Foreign Country; and Tibet also defended her own territories from Foreign invasions and always remained a religious nation.
    . . . We would like to have an assurance that no Chinese troops would cross the Tibetan frontier from the Sino-Tibetan border, or any such Military action. . . . Please issue strict orders to . . . Military Officers stationed on the Sino-Tibetan border in accordance with the above request . . ."

Goldstein, 1989, p. 624, citing British Foreign Office documents: F0371/763 17, copy of letter from the Tibetan Foreign Affairs Bureau, Lhasa, to Mao Tse-tung, dated November 2, 1949.
    On November 4—before Mao could have seen the letter—the Tibetan Foreign Bureau sent a copy of it to the British Foreign Secretary and the U.S. Secretary of State, with an appeal for military aid.

We enclose herewith the true copy of the letter which our Government has sent to the leader of Chinese Communist Government, thinking that he may duly consider the matter. But in case the Chinese communist leader ignores our letter, and takes an aggressive attitude and send his troops toward Tibet, then the Government of Tibet will be obligated to defend her own country by all possible means. Therefore the Government of Tibet would earnestly desire to request every possible help from your Government.
We would be most grateful if you would please consider extensive aid inrespect of requirements for Civil and military purposes, and kindly let us have a favorable reply at your earliest possible opportunity.
From, The Tibetan Foreign Bureau, Lhasa.

Some in State felt small amount of arms might allow Tibetans to hold off Chinese, and then the United States would recognize Tibetans: RG 59-General records of the Department of State, Entry 1305. Box 11, NND 897209 Records relating to South Asia, 1947–59, Lot file No. 57 D 373 and Lot File No. 57 D 421, Subject Files of the Officer in Charge of India-

Nepal-Ceylon-Pakistan-Afghanistan Affairs 1944–1956. Policy Review of Status of Tibet, Sprouse.

"We are sending a special mission to the United States," Tibet wants to join UN: FRUS, 1949, vol. IX, 1087, as cited by Smith, 1999, pp. 267–69.

130   "Any Tibetan effort to obtain United Nations membership at this time would be unsuccessful": RG 59- General records of the Department of State, Entry 1305. Box 11, NND 897209 Records relating to South Asia, 1947–59 Lot file No. 57 D 373 and Lot File No. 57 D 421, Subject Files of the Officer in Charge of India-Nepal-Ceylon-Pakistan-Afghanistan Affairs 1944–1956: December 28, 1949. Department of State, Memorandum of Conversation, Subject: "U.S. Government's Reply to the Tibetan Appeal for Assistance in Obtaining Membership in UN."

131   "In the winter of 1949 and 1950, when something could have been done": Tenzin Gyatso, Dalai Lama, *The Spirit of Tibet: Universal Heritage Selected Speeches and Writings of HH the DL,* editor A. A. Shiromany, 1995, p. 75.

       "At the same time the Americans had no courage to formally recognize Tibet . . . someone comes to talk": HHDL, author interview.

132   Acheson knew DSM going to Tibet: NARA RG 59, Records of the Executive Secretariat (Dean Acheson), Lot 53D444 (Box 19), Secretary's Press Conferences (Background Material) 1950 folder no. 2, undated note prepared by Dean Rusk and Connors, for Acheson: "If asked about the whereabouts of Vice Consul Douglas S. Mackiernan who was the last person to leave Tihwa, Sinkiang Province, it is recommended that you reply that you are not prepared to comment at this time. *Background for the Secretary:* The background on this subject will be supplied directly to your office." Author assumes this proves Acheson was fully briefed on DSM.

133   "The Soviet Union is detaching the northern provinces of China": *Vital Speeches of the Day,* "Acheson Press Club Speech."

134   Sinkiang Governor Burhan's reply to Acheson speech, Shanghai paper, accusing DSM of being spy: NARA RG 59, 793.61/2–350, Shanghai to State Department.

135   "January 30 I was suddenly informed . . . Doug S. Mackiernan was a spy: PL diary.

       PL listens radio reports DSM a spy: PL diary and author interview.

136   PL suspected DSM an agent, but not confirmed: PL, author interview.

       "On the Chinese side they called these Americans spies": HHDL, author interview, 1994.

       Tony Freeman is Fulton Freeman, Chinese Affairs, State Department employee.

       "Am safe and well. Expect to return in the Spring": PL diary.

137   UP and AP clippings from collection of Gail Mackiernan.

138   U.S. AIDE ACCUSES AS SPY BY PEIPING: *New York Times,* January 30, 1950.

141   "We can no longer afford to state," Rusk briefing notes for Acheson

on Tibet: Rg 59, Lot 53D444 Executive Secretariat, Press Briefing Notes, 1950.

142 "The theme of the speech was rather simple": *A Conspiracy so Immense,* Oshinsky, pp. 108–09.

143 "The air was so charged with fear," Herb Block: McCullough, p. 756.

144 "Mr. Thomas . . . referred to his earlier conversation": RG 59- General records of the Department of State, Entry 1305. Box 11, NND 897209 Records relating to South Asia, 1947–59, Lot file No. 57 D 373 and Lot File No. 57 D 421, Subject Files of the Officer in Charge of India-Nepal-Ceylon-Pakistan-Afghanistan Affairs 1944–1956. February 17, 1950, Memorandum of Conversation, Subject: Tibet, Participants: The Secretary of State (Acheson), Mr. Lowell Thomas.

145 Inadvisable to send any U.S. official to Tibet: NARA, RG 59, 793b.02/1-2050.

Winter at Timurlik all events descriptions: NARA RG 59, 793B.00/9-2150 DSM FB Journey Log. Also author interviews, FB, VZ. Also FB *Winter at Timurlik,* 1998.

146 Mongol raiders killed two people: FB, author interview.

147 "They want us to supply them with weapons. . . . exactly like Osman": FB, author interview.

"I asked why and he said it was a complicated thing": VZ, author interview.

DSM CIA messages missing: The CIA refuses all comment on DSM, and when asked about these messages the Public Relations department says only "No Comment." One CIA employee has raised the idea that these messages have been destroyed. Another CIA employee suggests that they are still intact, but that the CIA has decided not to declassify them at this time. It is easy to prove that DSM was in contact with Washington. DSM mentions his radio contacts in his Journey Log, and both FB and VZ say that DSM had contact several times a week. It has proved impossible to obtain the messages themselves.

Dr. Linda Benson, author of Osman Bator biography: Benson, 1988.

148 Benson certain DSM involved in U.S. effort to arm Inner Asians, 1949: LB, author interview.

"One can always be made pregnant": FB, "Winter in Timurlik."

149 90 percent of Chinese oil in Sinkiang: Benson, 1988.

150 45 ounces of gold for meat-eating camels: NARA RG 59, 125.937D/10-1750 and 10-3150 and FB, VZ author interviews.

Qali Beg: Milton Clark's spelling from *National Geographic,* 1954. Benson uses "Ali Beg Hakim," 1988, p. 181. Clark's period spelling is used throughout.

151 "That's the best thing anyone has ever said": FB, "Winter in Timurlik."

Planned Nationalist military withdrawal to Tibet: NARA, RG 319, ID # 663941, Box no. 4277. Page 2, Chao His-kuang, Deputy Commander of Nationalist forces in Sinkiang, ". . . intended to retreat to Tibet with his forces in case of defeat of the Nationalist armies." The plans for the retreat were worked out by author of the intelligence report. Also see page 3, "Sinkiang is very rich in natural resources. . . . The Soviet Union has started to mine uranium there." Also see page 4, where it clearly states that once the Communists took over Sinkiang they unutilized prior Nationalist logistics steps to hasten their invasion of Tibet. DSM was in regular contact with the Nationalist forces based in Tihwa—including Chao His-kuang. It is unlikely that DSM's plan to pass through Tibet was not connected, in some way, to similar Nationalist plans to retreat there. All of this was undone by typical Nationalist malfeasance—the troops handed over to the Communists without a shot.

152   "What Doug wanted to do": FB, author interview.

"It's clear that in 1949 the United States wanted to arm people": Linda Benson, author interview.

153   "The Communists would go to great lengths": NARA RG 59, 793B.00/7-1350.

154   "possible evidence of political unreliability": RG 59, Records of the policy planning staff, 1947–1953, Working Papers, Entry 64D563, Box 58, Letter from George Kennan to Undersecretary of State Webb, March 30, 1950.

"It was never to be expected that covert operations could be . . . conducted": Ibid.

"Washington was on Mars": FL, author interview. FL does not believe it was specifically McCarthyism that was causing this confusion in Washington. He attributes it to unresolved bureaucratic confusion.

155   Agents in field not receiving policy guidance: FL, author interview.

State not guiding covert ops effectively: FL, author interview.

Acheson removed Butterworth because of attacks on China policy: Acheson, 1987, p. 431.

Acheson protecting himself by removing Butterworth: Chace, p. 260, and Blum, p. 189.

Acheson knew Rusk had good relations with Republicans: Chace, p. 260.

Rusk helped Acheson deflect Republican attacks by offering he take over Butterworth position: Blum, p. 189.

Butterworth policies 180 degrees opposite Rusk's: Chace pp. 265–66. Blum. Both authors cite documents to support the idea that Butterworth was removed to deflect Republican criticism of Acheson's China policy, and of Acheson's staffing choices. The chief attacker of course—and the source of the power Republicans had to make these changes—was McCarthy and Acheson's fear of him.

156   State and CIA believed that they understood the risks they were taking with Tibet's existence: Since DSM was a CIA agent, discussion between CIA and State about his actions was mandated by law. No documents about such discussions have been declassified. Also, FB got the impression upon his return to Washington that people at the CIA understood the risk but still felt it was worth taking. The irony for the Tibetans was that the United States was willing to take risks with Tibet's existence but would not let the Tibet-

ans take such risks themselves. When the Tibetans wanted to apply to the UN they were refused permission to do so because it might hasten a Chinese invasion. U.S. policy was being applied only when it was to U.S. interests to do so.

Two weeks for courier from Lhasa to Shegar-Hunglung: Nepalese source cited in NARA 793B.00/8-750, *Latest News from Tibet.*

"the top espionage agent in the United States, the boss of Alger Hiss": Newman, pp. 214–15.

157 McCarthy calls Lattimore "top Russian Spy . . . willing to stand or fall on this one": Ibid.

"the Senator has stated that he will stand or fall on my case": Newman, p. 255.

Tydings says nothing in Lattimore's FBI file "to show that you were Communist": Newman, p. 256.

Lattimore says McCarthy is Nationalist "stooge": Newman, p. 287.

158 Lattimore's support for Inner Asians, and Tibetans, partly led to his persecution: Newman, p. 354.

Description of camp life during trip across Changthang: FB and VZ, author interviews. The conversations about when they first meet Tibetans are from same. Some descriptions of the Changthang are from Laird's treks in western Tibet; some are from VZ and FB.

159 Scurvy, bleeding gums, loose teeth: VZ, FB, author interviews.

Kazak grave mounds as trail markers: VZ, author interview.

160 Joke from VZ, as he recalled it told by DSM, at some point on trek to Tibet: VZ, author interview.

162 Sven Hedin, last Westerner to cross Changthang before 1950: George Schaller, personal communication.

163 Wild yaks stood their ground, made caravan go around: VZ, FB, author interviews.

VZ shoots yak for leather for soles, vultures eat: VZ, FB, author interviews.

164 DSM did not share much from radio with FB: FB, author interview.

"Washington says we should take care": FB, author interview.

"You can head off this way toward the west with Stephan," DSM tried to part company with FB: FB, author interview.

165 VZ noticed Mackiernan changed, "A few days before the Tibetan border": VZ, author interview.

DSM thoughts of suicide, "Doug pulled out a pistol, stalked off": PL diary, Entry of October 4, 1950.

166 Massacre at Lake Barkol: *National Geographic,* November 1954.

169 "Well we've communicated with the Tibetans and they know we're coming": FB, author interview.

"He implied that he had a mission in Lhasa": FB, author interview.

170 DSM, "It's our first Tibetans": FB, author interview.

"Douglas knew I was five years in that turmoil with Kazak": VZ, author interview.

"No, you got to listen to me. . . put up our tents": VZ, author interview.

171   "We didn't know, but one or both of us could be shot": FB, author interview.

The shoot-out begins; "VZ unloaded a crate of guns": VZ, author interviews. This description of the shoot-out is told from VZ's viewpoint. The description at the beginning of the book is based on FB's viewpoint. There are minor discrepancies about clothing and other details.

172   "Mr. Bessac is going to die today": VZ, author interview.

176   FB's captors took his glasses: Harrer, p. 131, "Spectacles are disapproved of as 'un-Tibetan.' No official was allowed to use them and even wearing them in the house was discouraged. Our Minister had received special permission from the Dalai Lama to wear them in the office."

"I should have died": FB, author interview. PL diary.

Tibetans shove biscuit in DSM's mouth: NARA, RG 59, 793B.00/9-2150, Journey Log by DSM and FB. Also FB, author interview.

178   "They . . . learned about Mackiernan's death from a doctor in Lhasa": NARA, RG 59, Decimal File 1950–54, 891.411/8-251, American Consul in Calcutta, William G. Gibson, to Dept. of State, July 29, 1951, Subject: Arrival of 23 Russian Refugees from China via Tibet.

"I was convinced that this was one more miracle by Mr. Mackiernan": EK, author interview.

179   "Listen, compared to what people are doing . . . to the open sky": MM, author interview.

"Unfortunately, America seems to be Pakistan's friend . . .": *New York Times,* October 2, 2001, in "Pakistan a Shaky Ally," by Barry Bearak.

PART THREE: THROUGH TIBET AND HOME AGAIN

183   'Nomads and Grenades' and 'The Arrow Letter', as well as all chapters down to Lhasa; descriptions, events, conversations: NARA RG 59, 793B.00/9-2150 DSM FB Journey Log. Also author interviews, FB, VZ.

Captives led to ditch at nomad camp: NARA, RG 59, 793B.00/9-2150, Journey Log by DSM and FB, the April 29 entry. Also, FB, author interview.

186   Nyingje: This means something like "poor thing"—it expresses pity.

The arrow letter: The physical details of the Arrow Letter are described by Harrer, 1992, p. 164. Also, FB, VZ, author interviews.

187   Peking claims 5,000 Kazak killed at Barkol: Courtesy C. W. Tazwell, from his Mackiernan web site. Encl. #1 to SECRET Desp. #1101, May 11, 1950, American Embassy, New Delhi, India (Declassified: Authority 968105), Press Item datelined Hongkong May 2, 1950 (said to be from Peiping Radio Broadcast).

188   Kazak's Bones: Aynur Caksýlýk, e-mail to author, May 15, 2000.

Shentsa Dzong, May 6: NARA, RG 59, 793B.00/9-2150, Journey Log by DSM and FB. Also, FB, VZ, author interviews.

189   Herbal treatment of VZ in Shentsa Dzong: Treatment in general, VZ, author interview. The detail about the tiger-skin bag comes from author's experience in Mustang, where the herbalist for the Raja of Mustang kept his herbs in such bags.

190   FB offered woman in Shentsa Dzong: FB, author interview.

191   Flogging at Shentsa Dzong: NARA RG 59 793B.00/9-2150 Journey Log by DSM and FB.

"Army officer who had gone to Shegar-Hunglung returned": NARA RG 59 793B.00/9-2150 Journey Log by DSM and FB.

193   Gossip about shoot-out spreads: Nepalese source cited in NARA 793B.00/ 8–750, *Latest News from Tibet.*

Trip to Lhasa, doctor arrives, penicillin, heads discovered: VZ, author interview, is the primary source.

194   The doctor arrives: VZ and FB do not concur on the chronology of events here. This chapter is based on VZ's version of events. FB wrote that the heads went back to Shegar-Hunglung from Shentsa Dzong. VZ is quite certain that is not so.

Take heads to Lhasa: VZ, author interview. FB's recollection of these events, and what he wrote in government documents, is different from this version by VZ. FB recalls that the heads were returned to Shegar-Hunglung from Shentsa Dzong. The author found VZ's version more compelling, and FB never could recall finding the heads, or seeing them transported back; VZ recalled finding the heads and said that he found them after the party had left Shentsa Dzong on their way to Lhasa.

FB and VZ warned not to talk about beheading of DSM: VZ, FB, author interviews.

196   "Marching through Georgia," song names: FB author interview. General description: VZ, author interview.

U.S. request for DSM to cross Tibet reached Lhasa April 5: Nepalese source cited in NARA 793B.00/8-750, *Latest News From Tibet.* Home guard had orders to shoot on sight: ibid.

Looting common with nomads: Harrer, p. 236.

197   Thondup's father-in-law went to same school with Marshal Chu-deh: GT, author interview

Regency sent no reply to Chu-deh messages from GT: GT, author interview.

198   GT says Regency threw away chance for negotiated peace: GT, author interview.

PLA occupied Kangding: Smith, p. 275.

PLA trained in minority nationalities policy: Ibid.

Chinese promised Khampas own state: Ibid.

Chinese brothers would leave: Ibid.

PLA supplies being air-dropped in Kham: Ibid.

Nationalist agents in GT's Hong Kong house: GT, author interview.

GT basically kidnapped: GT, author interview.

199   May 21, 1950, press release, Taiwan: Shakya, 1999.

May 1950 U.S. aid to Taiwan resumes: Smith, 1996, pp. 274–75.

Date of arrival in Lhasa: NARA RG 59 793B.00/9-2150 Journey Log by DSM and FB.

"God, these people are prosperous": FB, author interview.

200   Tse Gung, and aide-de-camp, Driesur Gnu (changed to Nu to avoid confusion): NARA, 611.93b/9-2150, FB's statement made by Mr. Frank Bessac describing his relations with the Tibetan Foreign Bureau . . . for the telegraph master name, the name of Tsegung is from 793b.00/9-2150—the journal entry for arrival in Lhasa.

FB gives conflicting reports on exactly when he met Harrer: In NARA RG 59 611.93b/9-2150, he says Harrer met him the day before he rode into Lhasa, but in NARA RG 59 793b.00/9-2150—the journal entry for arrival in Lhasa—he says so only on the day they arrive. Harrer does not say which day it was and leaves it open.

"thinking that it might be some comfort to the young American to have a white man": Harrer, p. 233.

"We met the young man in a pouring rain . . . the Government could not be blamed": Ibid., p. 238.

201   Thirty thousand people in Lhasa, 1950: Population estimate from Tibet Information Network, March 22, 2000.

Lhasa only one square kilometer, 1950: Lhasa City, 1:12,500, Centre for occupied Tibet Studies, copyright, 1995, Amnye Machen Institute. Also see Tibetan Old Building and Urban Development in Lhasa, 1948–1985–1998, by Lhasa Archive Project, published in Berlin in 1998 by Verlag Freie Kultur Aktion.

Jokhang, "Holiest shrine in all Tibet": HHDL, *Freedom in Exile,* p. 45.

202   Jokhang built under instruction of Nepalese princess to house her statue: Ibid., and Lhasa Old City, Tibet Heritage Fund, THF, 1999, and Stein, etc.

203   Lhasa developed urban architectural style, in a country traditionally without cities: Ibid.

Potala 400 feet above Lhasa plain: G.P.S. Reading G.M.

Potala constructed between 1645 and 1705: *Cultural History of Tibet,* Richardson and Snellgrove, p. 199.

The Mongols helped put Fifth Dalai Lama on throne of Tibet in 1642, two years before the Manchu added the Ming throne to their empire: Richardson and Snellgrove, p. 288.

No airplanes, automobiles, etc., in Tibet, 1949: Thomas Jr., p. 20.

204   Football banned, English hospital banned, etc.: pp. 131, 133, 137, 149, 192.

"Well, perhaps," replied one official: Thomas Jr., p. 19.

Kublai Khan annual sacrifice of Chinese in lake: *The Mongols and Tibet.*

First Manchu emperor received HHDL as equal, 'Preceptors to the Emperor' during Manchu: HHDL, author interview. Also Richardson and Snellgrove pp. 82–84.

205   "I'm a lost Fulbright student.": FB, author interview.

Tride Lingka: NARA, 611.93b/9-2150; the name of the house is given on page one of FB's statement made by Mr. Frank Bessac describing his relations with the Tibetan Foreign Bureau—Bessac uses an alternative spelling, but it is the same building.

Lowell Thomas stayed at Tride Lingka: Thomas Jr., p. 170.

206   Mr. Latrash's Lhasa "assets": FL, author interview.

CIA told FL that DSM was career CIA agent, FB was contract agent under Fulbright cover: FL, author interview.

"My function would be to go up there and get Bessac. . .": FL, author interview.

207   "got their thumb out of their ass": FL, author interview.

Dalai Lama saw airfield being cleared by CIA, did not know what it was: Knaus, p. 50. Also HHDL author interview.

"I knew every day who was being tortured . . . in the dungeons at the Potala": FL, author interview.

Some of FL's sources for his intelligence out of Lhasa were Tibetan government and military: FL, author interview.

"There was no task force . . . Tibet just fell between the cracks": FL, author interview.

208   "I'm not going to get into sources and methods": FL, author interview.

"There's some times when you have to do things. We just did it. . . and then we said, "It's done": FL, author interview.

CIA said that quality of FL intelligence was higher than any other out of Tibet, did not order him to stop: FL, author interview.

209   "put policy and the clandestine engine together": FL, author interview.

U.S. agent—FB—passed through Tibet, was not sent. "Yes, it happened. And during his stay in Lhasa he had some consultation with Tibetan officials": HHDL, author interview.

210   "You see we considered him as . . . something official": HHDL, author interview, 1994.

DSM should not have died: FB, author interview.

211   "heart bellowed": PL diary.

212   "the Dalai Lama has to bless you if you are going to stay on his territory": VZ, author interview.

Bodhisattva *Chenrezig:* This is the academically correct English transliteration of this Tibetan word.

"Chinese could not be trusted" was FB message to Tibetans: NARA, 611.93b/9-2150, statement made by Mr. Frank Bessac describing his relations with the Tibetan Foreign Bureau. Also FB, author interview.

Dalai Lama looked forward to moving to Jewel Park: HHDL, author interview.

213   How FB and VZ got to Jewel Park: FB and VZ, author interviews.

214   VZ and FB coached on how to bow to Dalai Lama: VZ, author interview.

Dalai Lama put one hand on VZ's head: VZ, author interview.

Dalai Lama places both hands on FB's head: FB, author interview.

Lowell Thomas seventh American to meet HHDL: Thomas Jr., p. 21.

"Useless": HHDL, author interview.

Tibet's focus on religion at this time, to an unreasonable degree, was one of the reasons Tibet fell to the Chinese: HHDL, author interview.

215   90 percent of New Lhasa is Chinese: Rapid urbanization in Lhasa has led to a seven-fold increase in population in the city over the past 40 years, from 30,000 in 1959 to an estimated 200,000 today, with more than 60% of this total estimated to be Chinese: Tibet Information Network, March 22, 2000.

Tibetan commander in chief at dinner with FB: See NARA 611.93b/9-2150, declassified 1994, entitled "statement by Frank Bessac describing the relation between Mr. Bessac and the Tibetan Foreign Bureau."

216   Tibetan nobles frustrated by lack of foreign support as invasion looms: Nepalese source cited in NARA 793B.00/8-750, *Latest News from Tibet*.

217   "were both convinced that no good . . . contact Beijing": Shakya, p. 30.

Visas accidentally issued by ill-informed British consular staff then Tibetans prevented from boarding plane: Shakya, pp. 28–29. Also, Goldstein, p. 656.

"We can hardly wash our hands of Tibet . . .": Goldstein, p. 647.

Communist China believed foreigners purposely thwarted attempts at peaceful negotiation: Shakya, p. 43.

"We have heard that you have deputed your representatives": Nepalese source cited in NARA 793B.00/8-750, *Latest News from Tibet*.

"Our people of the province of Tibet": Ibid.

218   Radio transceiver found in Lhasa: Ibid. Also, this incident is mentioned by Shakya and by Smith.

219   Pema and Lhamo offered to Bessac and Zvansov: author interviews FB, VZ.

"Sometimes it happened that a pretty young servant girl was offered": Harrer, p. 175.

June 16, 1950, FB visits Richardson, Foreign Ministry on same day: All of these events happened and were described to the author during author interviews with FB. However, the exact dates of these events is not clear and they are conflated into a single day in this narrative. All evidence indicates it was about June 16. FB does not recall the details of his talks with the Tibetans—these were retrieved from State Department documents in the National Archives. The description of Lhasa, and the walk, rely on the author's own travels, as well as published accounts, and FB, author interview.

220   FB on *kora* slips away from minders: FB, author interview.

Gyalo Thondup, brother of Dalai Lama, today thinks of Richardson in 1940s as Britain's hand behind the curtain: GT, author interview.

Servants in red livery: Harrer, p. 128.

221   "Tibet and China shall abide by the frontiers of which they are now in occupation": HHDL, *Freedom in Exile,* p. 46-52. Also, see *Lhasa Old City.*

FB in the Jokhang, lights butterlamps, listens to monks: FB, author interview.

Jowo encrusted, description of temple: Author's own trips to Lhasa and interviews with Tibetans there.

222   FB sees DSM in death in Jokhang, traumatic stress flashback: FB was having such episodes frequently, but the author has conflated that general occurrence into this visit to the Jokhang. FB does not say such an episode happened in the Jokhang.

223   Serfs, noble and monastic land holdings, "subject of furious debate": No fact about Tibet, as it was before the Chinese invasion, is more colored by the political motivations of modern observers than a discussion about serfdom in Tibet. The Chinese created most of the available statistical data about serfdom in Tibet most often cited by western academics. It was created after their invasion. An invasion, which they justified in advance by saying that most Tibetans were enslaved by the monasteries and nobles, whom they claimed owned nearly all the land. Clearly this data—which is about all that we have available—was deformed at birth by political motivations.

On the other hand those who are outraged at China's invasion of Tibet have sometimes gone out of their way to say that serfdom in Tibet was not so bad. They argue this case not based on the merits of serfdom, but because China always cites serfdom in Tibet as an excuse for its invasion. The facts about what percentage of Tibetans were serfs, and what were the conditions of their lives, has thus become a political football. In this discussion few point out that a vast number of Chinese and Indians were effectively 'serfs' in 1950: bonded in some way to large landholders. Feudalism died in Asia only after WWII, and lingers in some pockets even now. One wonders if the dozens of young virgins procured for an aging Mao's bed (according to one of his doctors) saw themselves as comrades, for example.

China's claim that it invaded Tibet to liberate the serfs is a political canard of the most odious type: it used popular resentment against serfdom to help it conqueror a weaker neighbor. Serfdom in Tibet—no matter how odious it may have been—was no more a 'reason' for China to invade Tibet in 1950, than serfdom in China was a reason for Japan to invade and colonize China in the 1930's. With that prelude, here are the Chinese statistics.

62 percent of all arable land was held in 'manorial estates': 32 percent in religious estates and 25 percent in noble estates. Goldstein, 1989. But who

owned the rest? To further complicate these matters one estimate says that 48 percent of the entire population of Tibet lived as nomads—whose obligations to the feudal nobility is subject to a complicated debate. *A Portrait of Lost Tibet,* Tung, 1980.

Chinese figures assert that 60 percent of the population of Tibet were 'serfs'—of many types (Grunfeld, 1996, p. 14). Nearly half of this number, 30 percent of all Tibetans, were not attached to any noble's estate but paid a 'human lease' fee. (Grunfeld, 1996 and Goldstein, 1989) Was this a tax? Were only 30 percent of the population really serfs, who were tied to the land? What percentage of the population were 'freemen'? No one has clear answers to these questions and everyone who tries to answer them relies to some degree on statistics created by China in an attempt to justify its invasion of Tibet.

Nomads escaped serfdom but paid some tax: See Norbu.

Surkhang Lhawang Topgyal, name of officer: Tsering Shakya, personal communication. FB spelling in NARA documents is difficult to decipher.

Surkhang dressed in silk with pigtail and turquoise: Photo of Surkhang in Thomas, Jr.

Corner house, *Surkhang: Lhasa Old City,* vol II, a clear lamp I . . .

224   Liushar Thupten Tharpa, name of monastic Foreign Office secretary: Tsering Shakya, personal communication. Name of this officer is difficult to decipher from FB spelling in NARA documents.

Tibetan moves rejected for their "own good" because of the "precipitate invasion" argument: NARA RG 59 793b.01/1-650 Original Tibetan letter to President Truman and Sec State Acheson dated December 22, 1949, see translation attached to above file . . . Note that Harry Truman's office referred his letter to Sec State on January 6, 1950, and Acheson replied to Tibetans via Delhi embassy, on January 12, 1950, in NARA RG 59 793.02/1-1250.

Dalai Lama says Tibetans wanted to talk about arms supply: HHDL, author interview.

FB report declassified only in 1994: NARA, RG 59, 611.93b/9-2150 statement by Frank Bessac on his relations with the Tibetan Foreign Bureau. See declassification date on the above.

"They asked me for advice concerning the possibility of relationships between the Government of Tibet and the Government of the United States of America": Ibid.

The Tibetans said that earlier the US had refused to allow them to send a mission to the America: Ibid.

225   Officials who refused to allow FL into Lhasa under rescue cover also knew FL was CIA: FL, author interviews. FL says his sources of information were high officials in the Tibetan government and military; author assumes these same people might have been involved in decision to refuse permission for FL to visit Lhasa.

"I agreed with the Tibetans in their action": NARA, Civilian Records, State Department, 611.93b/9-2150-statement by Frank Bessac on his relations with the Tibetan Foreign Bureau.

The CIA or the State Department, or both, wanted to change that policy":
There had to have been State/CIA discussions about this, but if so those
documents remain classified.

FL issued only State Department orders to Lhasa: FL, author interview.

"I deemed it necessary that first the Governments of Tibet and the United
States of America": NARA, RG 59, 611.93b/9-2150- statement by Frank
Bessac on his relations with the Tibetan Foreign Bureau.

226   "I also stated that the American Government could hardly be expected . . .
newspaper reporter": Ibid.

FB "urged" Tibetans to allow Kazak intelligence couriers from Sinkiang to
pass through Tibet to India: Ibid.

Tibetans approve of FB's plan but have to ask regent, Cabinet, and National
Assembly: Ibid.

227   Nedbailoff: Harrer, p. 197.

228   Nedbailoff, "a real artist": VZ, author interview.

VZ thought Harrer was an intelligence agent for someone: VZ, author
interview.

229   VZ recalled DSM promise of a U.S. visa: VZ, author interview.

The Flogging: Life, November 13, 1950, story by FB.

230   Harrer showed FB to assembly hall: FB, author interview.

FB thought meeting in Potala was of Kashag, but it could have been of the
National Assembly.

Tibetans knew that to request U.S. weapons could hasten Chinese invasion:
FB, author interview.

231   FB recalls that he argued in the Potala, in front of the Kashag, why Tibet
should request U.S. aid: FB, author interview, videotaped, June 1998. The
Dalai Lama says that if this happened it was the National Assembly that
Bessac addressed, not the Kashag: author interview.

"I was just trying to do something for Tibetans as I'd tried to do with the
Mongols and with the Kazak": FB, author interview, June 1998.

"I got them to accept an American there, an official covert military adviser":
FB, author interview, August 1998.

FL assumed there were Chinese spies in the Kashag: FL, author interview.

"You want a document from the Dalai Lama, one guy?": FL, author
interview.

232   FL says FB "screwed up the United States government": FL, author
interview.

"In response to Shakabpa's direct question . . . [the ambassador] stated":
Goldstein, p. 665, citing USFR, 611.93b/6-1850

233   Last Days in Lhasa: The various events described in this chapter occurred as
described, i.e., Harrer dropped off the map and FB got the letter from the
Foreign Office. FB, author interviews. Also NARA RG 59, 793B.56/9-150, Enc
2 to Desp 496, New Delhi, September 1, 1950. But neither VZ nor FB recalls

the date of their departure from Lhasa—it happened between July 10 and July 25. The author has conflated all these happenings into a created scene of FB smoking on the roof, one of very few such created scenes in the book.

234   Harrer knew that if the Chinese knew he had sent the U.S. maps he would be considered a spy: NARA, RG 59,793b.022/9-2150, Letter by FB, classified, SECRET Office Memorandum to CA Mr. Stuart on October 20 ,1950, Subject: Maps of the Kyigrong Valley, Tibet.

No one outside U.S. government knew who supplied them: Ibid.

"Here, you might need this if World War Three breaks out": FB, author interview, and NARA RG 59, 611.93b/9-2150- statement by Frank Bessac on his relations with the Tibetan Foreign Bureau.

235   "What you have told us during our last meeting here was reported to His Highness the Regent of Tibet": Foreign Bureau, confidential note, undated: NARA RG 59, 793B.56/9-150 NND 981749, released to author on September 14, 1999, after FOIA made three years earlier. TOP SECRET, Enc # 2 to Desp 496, New Delhi, September 1, 1950.

"What Doug had wanted to do was to allow the People of East Turkestan and Tibet": FB, author interview, on September 16, 1999—just after the document was released by FOIA. NARA, RG 59, 793B.56/9-150 NND 981749, released to author on September 14, 1999, after FOIA made three years earlier. TOP SECRET, Enc # 2 to Desp 496, New Delhi, September 1, 1950.

236   Tibetan Foreign Office says it is stalling Chinese negotiations, hoping to get arms, intend to fight: NARA RG 59, 611.93b/9-2150- statement by Frank Bessac on his relations with the Tibetan Foreign Bureau.

Dorje Drakden: Spelling as in HHDL, *Freedom in Exile,* p. 44.

237   "They thought it would be important that I come" to state oracle: FB, author interview.

Description of the oracle: FB, author interviews.

By August 1950 Chinese had begun to believe Tibetans were stalling negotiations with them in order to try to arm themselves: Smith and Shakya both assert this in their books.

238   Swimming suits: See Shakya.

"Shit on the picnic": Shakya, p. 44. Shakya's English translation revised for colloquial English impact.

State Department assumed that DSM's trip to Tibet would be cited by the Chinese for propaganda purposes, no matter when it was revealed: NARA RG 59, 793B.00/7-1350, Delhi to Sec. State.

239   State Department sought to hide DSM's death amidst the uproar over Korean War: NARA RG 59, 793b.00/6-2850—Sec. State to Delhi.

State Department cover story to be issued: NARA, RG 59 793b.00/7-1350 Sec. State to Delhi.

U.S. CONSUL FLEEING CHINA, SLAIN BY TIBETANS ON WATCH FOR BANDITS: *New York Times,* July 30, 1950, front page.

240   FRANK BESSAC, LODIAN, ESCAPES COMMUNIST CHINA THROUGH TIBET: *Lodi* (California) *News-Sentinel,* July 31, 1950.

241   ". . . if Tibet intended to resist Communist aggression and needed help U.S. Government was prepared to assist in procuring material and would finance such aid": Goldstein, p. 670, and USFR 693.93B/8-750.

U.S. consul in Calcutta discouraged Shakabpa's reasonable request about airlift: Goldstein, p. 671, and USFR 693.93B/8-750.

FL intelligence went to CIA in Washington; he was forbidden to share with State Department in India, directly: FL, author interviews.

242   August 15, 1950, earthquake fifth-largest in record history, thousands died: Craig, p. 142.

"Perhaps there is a scientific explanation" for earthquake: HHDL, *Freedom in Exile,* p. 55.

243   Telegrams sent back and forth from India to Tibet about meeting date for FB at border: NARA Rg 84, Entry Calcutta, India 1950–52, Calcutta Consulate General, Classified General Records, 1950–52 350-350.2. Multiple telegrams July and August, 1950, Box 23.

FL and Forman met FB at Tibetan border on August 19 : NARA 793b.00/8-2550, New Delhi to Sec. State; however, this exact date is debatable—perhaps August 21.

Trees, crickets—FB had not heard in a year: FB, author interviews.

244   FL got messages from Lhasa about FB, who is he?: FL, author interview.

FL impressions of FB: FL, author interviews.

FL agrees to ship DSM effects to Pegge: NARA, RG 59, 793B.00/8-3050, Delhi embassy to State about Bessac Press Conference in Delhi. Also FB, author interview.

FL codes FB in Calcutta, FB says, "I need more recognition": FL, author interview. FB agrees FL coded him, details vary: FB, author interview.

245   CIA told FL to start his debriefing of FB with finances—this and all other details in this chapter: FL, author interview.

"Do you have any information"; FB, "No, I don't"; FB fails to mention DSM travel log: FL, author interview.

246   DSM "decided to leave Sinkiang and advised me to accompany him . . . held any official positions in the American Government": NARA, RG 59 511.933/8-3150.

Tibetan military aid request reached Dean Rusk on September 12, 1950: NARA, 793B.56/9-150 NND 981749, released to author on September 14, 1999, after FOIA three years earlier.

Knaus says Dean Rusk was "calling the shots on U.S. policy in Tibet": *Orphans of the Cold War: America and The Tibetan Struggle for Survival,* John Kenneth Knaus, 1999, p. 88.

Rusk kept President Truman and Secretary of State Acheson fully briefed: Ibid.

247   By September 19, 1950, Dean Rusk had already had discussions with the CIA about the covert military aid to Tibet: NARA, 793B.56/9-150, NND 981749.

Author obtained this doc on September 14, 1999 after a long three-year FOIA battle. It's part of NND 981749 (doc n9), as is the document FB brought out requesting aid from Tibetan Government (n11).

TOP SECRET, 1 of 5 copies
September 19 1950
TO: S/S Mr. McWilliams
FROM: FE Mr. Rusk

The subject of military assistance to Tibet, which is of primary interest to FE, NEA and S/P for Departmental action, is also of interest to an outside agency which would assist in the procurement and furnishing of such materiel. At a recent meeting between representatives of that above offices and the outside agency it was decided that, as an extra measure of protection for this delicate operation, distribution of telegrams on the subject should be restricted, through the use of an indicator, only to the immediately concerned offices. The indicators are TOTIB to New Delhi and TIBTO to the Department. DC/T informs us that, under normal procedures an absolute restriction to certain offices will not be made.

In view of the extreme necessity for secrecy on this subject, it would be greatly appreciated if you would issue necessary instructions to the end that distribution of telegrams bearing the above indicators be restricted S/S (for distribution to S/P), G, NEA and FE. Mr. Krentz o S/P has talked with Mr. Ohly of S/MDA who agrees that his office need not be on the distribution.

Note there is another document, N10, that replies to this request for secrecy by Rusk. It's dated September 25, 1950, and is copied to Mr. Rusk. It appears to be from the S/S to DC/T, Mr. Pfeiffer. The letter agrees with Rusk and asks it be done the way Rusk requests.

I understand that FE has discussed with your office the establishment of a new series between the Department and New Delhi covering procurement and furnishing of military assistance to Tibet, such a series to be identified by the indicator TOTIB to New Delhi and TIBTO to the Department.

This procedure has been approved by Mr. McWilliams . . . and it is requested . . . the system be established immediately and that all messages in the new series be restricted in the distribution to FE for action or origin and S/S, G and NEA for info.

This proves that Dean Rusk directed policy regarding covert aid to Tibet in fall 1950, weeks before the Chinese invaded, and it also supports FB's assertion that in fall 1950, when he got back to the States, CIA was preparing to ship arms to Tibet that winter.

The United States decided in September 1950 to ship weapons to Tibet despite Indian lack of cooperation: Ibid. The FOIA'd Rusk document about codes for Tibet arms shipment indicates that the arms transfers were to begin soon, and yet according to all known sources India was still opposed to the passage of arms through India to Tibet, which means there was no other way to get the weapons to Tibet except by circumventing that. FL, below, says that in the weeks before the invasion, suddenly the United States wanted to drop weapons into Tibet, directly. Thus there are two pieces of information that point in this direction.

"If you are going to do anything, you've got the airfield now . . . It's not going to be stolen off planes": FL, author interview.

248 United States decides, too late, to arm Tibetans; now plans aircraft carrier: FL, author interview.

"Now they were too late": FL, author interview.

United States did begin to air-drop military aid to Tibet just before invasion: FL, author interview.

Dalai Lama says U.S. weapons may have reached Tibet before invasion: HHDL, author interview, 2000.

Mrs. Douglas Mackiernan goes to Washington: Author interview, PL. PL Diary.

249 CIA had moved to Virginia offices by 1950: FB, author interview.

Marge Kennedy with CIA still, and some old OSS friends of FB now in R&A at CIA: FB, author interview.

"You must come over. So much to talk about," CIA to FB: FB, author interview.

250 Everyone wants FB's intelligence firsthand; FB darts around D.C.; Americans so ready to save Tibet: FB, author interview.

CIA was "certainly going to try to arm the Tibetans that winter": FB, author interview.

CIA working with many Tibetans to arm them: FB, author interview.

CIA sincere about Tibetan independence: FB, author interview.

Tibetan miliary mission arrives in New Delhi for talks with United States on October 4, 1950: Goldstein, p. 678.

"Tibet must accept that it is part of China": Ibid., p. 676.

251 Clubb, uranium, 1943: Clubb's despatch #20, July 28, 1943, is cited by Paxton in NARA 893.6359/5-2747.

"As far as I understood it": FB author interview.

FB says U.S. policy in October 1950 was to get aid to Tibetans so they could "repulse the Chinese invasion, and be recognized as a sovereign independent nation": FB, author interview.

If you supported Tibet "you were a colonialist" dismembering China: FB, author interview.

252 People in State now "wanted to help the Tibetans defend themselves": FB, author interview.

"Acheson didn't buy it anymore . . . yellow on Chinese maps or not": FB, author interview.

Superior Service Award by Department of State, October 18, 1950: Letter from the State Department's Honor Awards Board, John Finlator, dated

October 4, 1950, inviting Margaret Lyons Mackiernan to the ceremony on Constitution Avenue. Collection of PL; photocopy kindly given to the author by MM and RC.

253 "Oh yes, the medal . . . on a red ribbon": PL diary, quoted by permission.

"I went into shock . . . McCarthy from Appleton, Wisconsin?": FB, author interview.

254 "I think our friend McCarthy will eventually get all that is coming to him": Truman quoted in McCullough, p. 769.

"I remember the conclusion": FB, author interview.

255 "When it came to Vietnam": McNamara, pp. 32–33.

Shakya (p. 43) says the invasion started on October 7; Goldstein (p. 690) says it began on October 5.

256 PLA cuts off retreat route for Tibetan army: See Shakya and Smith.

Deng Xiaoping among top three commanders of PLA's Southwest Military Region: Shakya, p. 43.

Letter to FB by PL written October 15, 1950; letter with FB. Author allowed to read photocopy, quoted by permission of PL.

257 5,738 Tibetan troops liquidated: Shakya, p. 45—only 180 killed? The rest were disarmed and sent home?

FB looks slender, clothing: Compare pictures of FB in the *Stockton Record* of October 31, 1950, with pictures of FB in Tibet.

258 "Doug sought death—" FB explained, "and meeting you probably prolonged his life or effort for life . . .": All the quotes from FB are from the PL diary, entry of October 19, 1950. FB disagrees with these quotes, says he did not say them.

259 "I tried to cover up for Doug": FB author interview.

FB says he did not tell PL many hurtful things, divorced from her, etc.: FB, author interview.

Tony Freeman: PL diary entry of October 19, though the Freeman meeting happened on the 20th.

260 "May I see you before I go home?": This chapter and the quotes from PL diary.

261 FB gives PL DSM's handler's name: PL diary; FB confirms, author interview.

Pegge's security clearance was not complete: PL diary. The entire story of Pegge and "John" is based exclusively on a reading of Pegge Lyons's diary, kindly lent to the author.

262 "We needed his technical skill": PL diary.

263 "I will not. I am an American"; FB does not kowtow: *Life* magazine, November 13, 1950.

264 "nothing, nothing": The caps and underlining are exactly as in PL diary.

"That's the way most of these invasions are in these crazy places": FL, author interviews. FL saw a few during his years with CIA.

265   "And here I had the engines and he had all these dreams": FL, author interviews.

       Betrayed by these people: The Dalai Lama, author interview, July 2000.

       "Then eventually, we returned to Lhasa": The Dalai Lama, author interview, July 2000.

266   "Hey, this is history": current CIA employee, author interview, name withheld at request of source.

       "should developments warrant consideration could be given to recognition of Tibet": Shakya, pp. 60–61, citing U.S. government documents.

267   Britain did not want to challenge any colonial rights: Shakya, p. 58.

268   Deng Xiaoping wrote terms under which Tibet joined China: Shakya, p. 46.

       "Now that the PLA has entered Tibet . . . Tibet will not be changed.": Ibid.

       "Tibet has been part of China since ancient times": March 22, 2000 (Tibet TV, Lhasa) World Tibet News, March 23, 2000.

269   Chinese are now a majority even in Tibetan towns as small as thirty thousand: These numbers are difficult to believe; however the 30,000 number is for the town of Tsetang and the population estimate was made by a reliable primary source. Similar trends are blatantly obvious in all Tibetan towns and cities. China blandly denies these facts.

270   CIA paid Mackiernan $8,344 a year: PL diary.

271   The other vice consul at Tihwa (Robert Dreesen) told PL it was CIA not State that ordered DSM to stay in Tihwa: PL diary.

270–272 Winter of the Cold War, All Pegge and John quotations: PL diary.

274   "I am not a bandit. What I did was to help my people to establish an independent country": Linda Benson, 1988. She is citing from a 1981 interview with Arslan Tosun, a relative of Osman's.

       Sino-U.S. listening post established outside Tihwa to watch U.S.S.R. atomic and missle tests: "U.S. Listening Post Jeoparidzed in China," *Air Force Times,* June 19, 1980.

275   FB today not sure why he at first recommended against citizenship for VZ: FB, author interview.

       "I could make mistake, you could make mistake": VZ, author interview.

       "Imagine how I felt when Bessac left me": VZ, author interview.

       Bessac wrote State and said VZ would make fine citizen: FB, author interview.

276   Eskadrone flight through Tibet to India, twenty-three survived: RG 59, 891.411/8-251 Decimal File 1950–54, U.S. Consul Calcutta, William G. Gibson, to Dept. of State, July 29, 1951, Subject: Arrival of 23 Russian Refugees from China via Tibet. Also, VZ, author interview.

       Eleven Eskadrone with Osman shot, the rest left China, arrived in United States via third countries: VZ, author interview.

277   "Doug Mackiernan's Russian girl was pretty" : VZ, author interview.

"I felt guilty about the invasion": FB, author interview.

278 Prince De confessed to working for U.S. agent FB: Jagchid, p. 439.

"At any rate, they are all Chinese. To the Mongols, they are all the same": Jagchid, p. 424.

Mongolians only 12 percent of Inner Mongolia today: Jagchid, Introduction.

800,000 Mongols jailed: Bahe, "Turbulent Fifty Years of Inner Mongolia." See also, "Xanadu Remains Closed, Controversial," *South China Morning Post,* May 31, 1996.

90 percent of workers in steel and coal industries in Inner Mongolia are Chinese: Article by Bahe, "Turbulent Fifty Years of Inner Mongolia."

280 "rather than genuine support for the restoration of Tibetan independence.": HHDL, *Freedom in Exile,* p. 211.

Mustang-based guerrillas gave United States six months' advance warning on China's first atomic bomb: Nepalese General Aditya Shumsher, author interview. See same reported in *Newsweek,* April 19, 1999.

282 Government may have duplicated World Weather equipment just before contract with government was canceled: DDM, author interview, citing his father, Duncan Mackiernan.

"Dougie got those in Tibet"; "Dougie said that dog": GM, author interview.

284 "Tibet contains one of the world's richest deposits of uranium": HHDL, *Freedom in Exile,* p. 261.

"Unless rare minerals are found in Tibet, the Army does not regard Tibet as of strategical significance": NARA, RG 59, Entry 1305. Box 11, NND 897209 Records relating to South Asia, 1947–59, Lot file No. 57 D 373 and Lot File No 57 D 421, Subject Files of the Officer in Charge of India-Nepal-Ceylon-Pakistan-Afghanistan Affairs 1944–1956. Mr. Sprouse. U.S. Policy Toward Tibet. April 4, 1949.

Mackiernan family members say U.S. government asked about missing gold after DSM death: Malcolm Mackiernan, author interview.

DSM buried gold somewhere in Inner Asia, says "John": PL diary.

1996 first printed reference to DSM and FB as CIA employees: Smith, p. 278, in a footnote. Smith notes that he heard this from author, after author's first interview with FB. When Smith's book was published, even that brief footnote provoked a phone call from CIA asking Smith about this comment.

286 "I know what they would be thinking if they were here right now": George Tenet, as quoted by DDM, author interview.

BIBLIOGRAPHY

AUTHOR'S INTERVIEWS

Linda Benson, Michigan • Frank Bessac, Montana • Karen Boatman, California • John Bottorff, California • Aynur Caksýlýk, Turkey • Anonymous CIA Employees • CIA Public Relations Staff • Tenzin Gyatso, His Holiness the Fourteenth Dalai Lama of Tibet, Dharamsala, India • Greg Hirkin, Washington, D.C. • Margaret (Lyons Mackiernan) Hlavacek, Oklahoma and California • Phillip Ho, Gauhati, India • Erwin Kontescheny, New Jersey • Fredrick Latrash, Florida • Ambassador James Lilly, Washington, D.C. • Douglas D. Mackiernan, North Carolina • Duncan Mackiernan, Florida • Gail Mackiernan, Washington, D.C. • Malcolm Mackiernan, Virginia • Mary Mackiernan, California • Stuart Mackiernan, Massachusetts • General Lewis L. Mundell • C. W. Tazewell, Virginia • Gyalo Thondup, New Delhi, India • Ah Tinley, Kathmandu, Nepal • William and Leilani Wells, Washington, D.C. • Baba Yeshe, Kathmandu, Nepal • Charles Ziegler, Massachusetts • Vasili Zvansov, Hawaii and California

Most interviews were done in person. A few were done over the telephone. There were many follow-ups by e-mail. The above sources are cited in the source notes with their names or their initials, whenever the audio- or videotaped interview transcripts are quoted or paraphrased to substantiate facts in the narrative. LB-Linda Benson, FB-Frank Bessac; KB-Karen Boatman; JB-John Bottorff; AC-Aynur Caksýlýk; Unnamed CIA employees, CIA Public Relations Staff; HHDL-Tenzin Gyatso, His Holiness the fourteenth Dalai Lama of Tibet; GH-Greg Hirkin; PL-Pegge (Lyons Mackiernan) Hlavacek; PH-Phillip Ho; EK-Erwin Kontescheny; FL-Frederick Latrash; JL-James Lilly; DDM-Douglas D. Mackiernan; DM-Duncan Mackiernan; GM-Gail Mackiernan; JMI-Janice Mackiernan Ianniello; M1M-Malcolm Mackiernan; MM-Mary Mackiernan; SM-Stuart Mackiernan; LLM-General Lewis L. Mundell; CWT-C. W. Tazewell; GT-Gyalo Thondup; AT-Ah Tinley; LW-Leilani Wells; WW-William Wells; BY-Baba Yeshe; CZ-Charles Ziegler; VZ-Vasili Zvansov. Robin Clark, spouse of Mary Mackiernan, is cited in the notes as RC—he played a major role in document access.

UNPUBLISHED SOURCES

ARCHIVAL

National Archives, Washington, D.C., and College Park, Maryland—Military Reference Branch RG 218, Records of the U.S. Joint Chiefs of Staff, Geographic file, 1948–50, China, RG 226, RG 341 Air Force Plans, Project Decimal File, 1942–1954, RG 330

Entry 199 Defense Relations with CIA, RG 330 ENTRY 341 • Civilian Records • General Records of the Department of State specifically: 793b.00, 691.93b, 125.9375 to 937Dc, 393.1114, 661.90d, 811.42793 • Audio Visual RG 226, Item 5, Inside Tibet, 1943, 16mm motion picture, 39 minutes. OSS trip to Tibet by Tolstoy and Brooks. Also newsreel footage on most personalities in this book: Mao, Chiang, Owen Lattimore, Joe McCarthy, Acheson, and Truman • Manuscripts and Archives of Yale University Library—John Hall Paxton Papers • Harry S. Truman Library, Independence, Missouri—Papers of Harry S. Truman, President's Personal File, Official File, White House Permanent File, Post Presidential Files • Papers of Dean Acheson

NONARCHIVAL

Letters, photographs, and other documents from Frank Bessac • Letters, photographs, clipping file, and diaries lent from Margaret Lyons Mackiernan Hlavacek • Letters, photographs, and newspaper clipping file from Frederick Latrash • Letters, photographs, and newspaper clippings from family of Duncan Mackiernan.

PUBLISHED SOURCES

OFFICIAL PUBLICATIONS

Foreign Relations of the United States, 1943–1951. Washington, D.C.: Government Printing Office.

The CIA Under Harry Truman. Warner, Michael, editor, CIA History Staff. Washington, D.C., 1994.

Thor's Legions: Weather Support to the U.S. Air Force and U.S. Army, 1937–1987.

Foreign Service Journal, September 1985, letter to the editor from Edwin W. Martin.

The Roswell Report: Fact Versus Fiction in the New Mexico Desert, see summary of this in *Synopsis of Balloon Research Findings* by First Lt. James McAndrew, 1995 USAF publication.

The Mongols and Tibet. A Historical Assesment of Relations between the Mongol Empire and Tibet, the Department of Information, Central Tibetan Administration, Dharamsala, India, 1996.

BOOKS

Acheson, Dean. *Present at the Creation. My Years in the State Department.* New York: Norton, 1969.

Ahmad, Zahiruddin. *Sino-Tibetan Relations in the Seventeenth Century.* Serie Orientale Roma, XL. Roma: Instituto Italiano Per Il Medio Ed Estremo Oriente, 1970.

———. *A History of Tibet* by Fifth Dalai Lama of Tibet. Translated by Zahiruddin Ahmad. Bloomington: Indiana University Research Institute for Inner Asian Studies, 1995.

Bamford, James. *The Puzzle Palace: Inside the National Security Agency, America's Most Secret Intelligence Organization.* New York: Houghton Mifflin, 1982.

Barnett, A. Doak. *China's Far Northwest: Four Decades of Change.* Westview Press, San Francisco/Oxford.

Bawden, C. R. *The Modern History of Mongolia.* London: Kegan Paul International.

Beldon, Jack. *China Shakes the World.* New York: Monthly Review Press, 1970.

Benson, Linda. *The Ili Rebellin: The Moslem Challenge to Chinese Authority in Xinjiang 1944–1949.* M. E. Sharpe, 1990.

Bernstein, Richard, and Ross H. Munro. *The Coming Conflict with China.* New York: Vintage, 1998.

Blum, Robert M. *Drawing the Line. The Origin of the American Containment Policy in East Asia.* New York: W. W. Norton, 1982.

Caldwell, Oliver J. *A Secret War: Americans in China, 1944–1945.* Carbondale: Southern Illinois University Press, 1972.

Chace, James. *Acheson.* New York: Simon & Schuster, 1998.

Chang, Gordon R. *The Coming Collapse of China.* New York: Random House, 2001.

Chen, Jack, *Sinkiang Story.* New York: Macmillan, 1977.

Craig, Mary. *Kundun: A Biography of the Family of the Dalai Lama.* Washington, D.C: Counterpoint, 1997.

Conze, Edward, et al. *Buddhist Texts Through the Ages.* New York: Harper Torchbooks, 1964.

Dunlop, Richard. *Behind Japanese Lines. With the OSS in Burma.* New York: Rand McNally, 1979.

Epstein, Israel. *Tibet Transformed.* Beijing: New World Press, 1983.

Fairbank, John King, and Merle Goldman. *China, A New History.* Cambridge: Belknap Press, 1992.

Fariello, Griffin. *Red Scare: Memories of the American Inquisition.* New York: Avon Books, 1995.

Fleming, Peter. *Bayonets to Lhasa.* Hong Kong: Oxford University Press, 1984.

———. *News From Tartary.* London: Jonathan Cape, 1936.

Ford, Robert. *Captured in Tibet.* Oxford: Oxford University Press, 1990.

Goldstein, Melvyn. *A History of Modern Tibet, 1913–1951.* Berkeley: University of California Press, 1989.

———. *The Snow Lion and the Dragon: China, Tibet and the Dalai Lama.* Berkeley: University of California Press, 1997.

———. *Nomads of Western Tibet: The Survival of a Way of Life.* Hong Kong: Odyssey, 1990.

Grose, Peter. *Operation Rollback, America's Secret War Behind the Iron Curtain.* Boston: Houghton Mifflin, 2000.

Grunfeld, Tom. *The Making of Modern Tibet.* New York: M. E. Sharpe, 1996.

Gyatso, Tenzin (His Holiness the Fourteenth Dalai Lama of Tibet). *Freedom in Exile: Autobiography of the Dalai Lama of Tibet.* London: Hodder & Stoughton, 1990.

———. *The Spirit of Tibet: Universal Heritage. Selected Speeches and Writings of HH the Dalai Lama XIV.* editor A. A. Shiromany. New Delhi: Allied Publishers Ltd., 1995.

Gup, Ted. *The Book of Honor: Covert Lives and Classified Deaths at the CIA.* New York: Doubleday, 2000.

Harrer, Heinrich. *Lost Lhasa: Heinrich Harrer's Tibet.* New York: Harry N. Abrams, Inc., 1992.

———. *Seven Years in Tibet.* New York: Flamingo, 1997.

Haynes, John E. *Red Scare or Red Menace? American Communism and Anticommunism in the Cold War Era.* Chicago: Ivan R. Dee, 1996.

Hogan, Michael J. *A Cross of Iron: Harry S. Truman and the Origins of the National Security State, 1945–1954.* Cambridge: Cambridge University Press, 1998.

Holloway, David. *Stalin and the Bomb: The Soviet Union and Atomic Energy 1939–1956.* New Haven: Yale University Press, 1994.

Jagchid, Sechin. *The Last Mongol Prince.* Western Washington University, 1999.

Knaus, John Kenneth. *Orphans of the Cold War: America and the Tibetan Struggle for Survival.* New York: Public Affairs, 1999.

Lattimore, Owen. *China and the Barbarians.* In Joseph Barnes (ed.) *Empire in the East.* New York: Doubleday, Doran & Co., 1934.

———. *Inner Asian Frontiers of China.* Hong Kong: Oxford University Press, 1988.

McCarthy, Roger E. *Tears of the Lotus: Accounts of Tibetan Resistance to the Chinese Invasion, 1950–1962.* London: McFarland & Company, Inc., 1997.

McCullough, David. *Truman.* New York: Touchstone, 1992.

McNamara, Robert S. *In Retrospect: The Tragedy and Lessons of Vietnam.* New York: Vintage Books, 1995.

Miller, Merle. *Plain Speaking: An Oral Biography of Harry S. Truman.* New York: Berkley Publishing, 1974.

Moseley, George. *A Sino-Soviet Cultural Frontier: the Ili Kazakh Autonomous Chou.* Cambridge: East Asian Research Center, Harvard, Harvard University Press, 1966.

Nazaroff, Paul. *Hunted Through Central Asia. On the Run from Lenin's Secret Police.* Oxford: Oxford University Press, 1993.

Norbu, Namkhai. *Journey Among the Tibetan Nomads: An Account of a Remote Civilization.* Dharamsala: Library of Tibetan Works and Archives, 1997.

Norbu, Jamyang. *Warriors of Tibet. The Story of Aten and the Khampas' Fight for the Freedom of their Country.* London: Wisdom Publications, 1986.

Oshinsky, David M. *A Conspiracy So Immense: The World of Joe McCarthy.* New York: The Free Press, 1983.

Pach, Jr., Chester J. *Arming the Free World: The Origins of the United States Military Assistance Program, 1945–1950.* Chapel Hill: The University of North Carolina Press, 1991.

Prejelvasky, N. *Mongolia, The Tangut Country and the Solitudes of Northern Tibet, 1876.* New Delhi (reissued): Asian Educational Services, 1991.

Price, Eva Jane. *China Journal 1989–1900: An American Missionary Family during the Boxer Rebellion.* New York: Collier Books, 1989.

Rawicz, Slovomir. *The Long Walk: The True Story of a Trek to Freedom.* New York: The Lyons Press, 1997.

Reeves, Thomas C. *The Life and Times of Joe McCarthy: A Biography.* New York: Stein and Day, 1982.

Schaller, George. *Wildlife of the Tibetan Steppe.* University of Chicago Press, 1998.

Schaller, Michael. *The United States and China in the Twentieth Century.* New York: Oxford University Press, 1979.

Schell, Orville. *Virtual Tibet: Searching for Shangri-la from the Himalayas to Hollywood.* New York: Metropolitan Books, 2000.

Schultz, Duane. *The Maverick War: Chennault and the Flying Tigers.* New York: St. Martin's Press, 1987.

Schurmann, Franz, and Orville Schell. *Republican Reader: Nationalism, War, and the Rise of Communism, 1911–1949.* New York: Vintage Books, 1967.

Shakabpa, Tsepon W. D. *Tibet: A Political History.* New Haven: Yale University Press, 1967.

Shakya, Tsering. *The Dragon in the Land of Snows.* London: Pimlico, 1999.

Short, Philip. *Mao: A Life.* New York: Henry Holt, 2000.

Smith, Nicol. *Burma Road.* Garden City: Garden City Publishing Co. Inc., 1942.

Smith, Jr., Warren W. *Tibetan Nation: A History of Tibetan Nationalism and Sino-Tibetan Relations.* New York: Westview Press, 1996.

Snellgrove, David and Hugh Richardson. *A Cultural History of Tibet.* London: George Weidenfeld and Nicolson Ltd., 1968.

Snow, Edgar. *Red Star Over China.* New York: Grove Press, 1968.

Spence, Jonathan D. *The Search for Modern China.* New York: W. W. Norton, 1990.

Stein, R. A. *Tibetan Civilization.* London: Faber and Faber, 1972.

Stoler, Mark A. *George C. Marshall: Soldier-Statesman of the American Century.* New York: Twayne Publishers, 1989.

Strasser, Roland. *The Mongolian Horde.* New York: Jonathan Cape and Harrison Smith, 1930.

Thomas, Jr., Lowell. *Out of This Word: Across the Himalayas to Forbidden Tibet.* New York: Greystone Press, 1950.

Tsu, Lao. *Tao Te Ching.* Translated by Gia-Fu Feng and Jane English. New York: Vintage, 1989.

Tucci, Guiseppe. *Tibetan Painted Scrolls.* Rome: La Libreia dello Stato, 1949.

Tuchman, Barbara W. *Stillwell and the American Experience in China 1911–1945.* New York: Macmillan, 1970.

Tung, Rosemary Jones. *A Portrait of Lost Tibet: Photographs by Ilya Tolstoy and Brooke Dolan.* Ithaca: Snow Lion Publications, 1980.

Vitalai, Roberto. *Early Temples of Central Tibet.* London: Serindia, 1989.

Warner, Roger. *Back Fire: The CIA's Secret War in Laos and its Link to the War in Vietnam.* New York: Simon and Schuster, 1995.

Whelan, Russell. *The Flying Tigers. The Story of The American Volunteer Group.* New York: Viking Press, 1943.

Wu, Harry, with George Vecsey. *Troublemaker: One Man's Crusade Against China's Cruelty.* London: Chatto and Windus, 1996.

Ziegler, Charles, and David Jacobson. *Spying Without Spies: Origins of America's Secret Nuclear Surveillance System.* Westport: Praeger, 1995.

ARTICLES

Allen, Thomas B. "Xingjiang." *National Geographic,* March 1996.

Bahe, "Turbulent Fifty Years of Inner Mongolia." Hong Kong, Cheng Ming.

Benson, Linda. "Osman Batur: the Kazak's Golden Legend," in L. Benson and I. Svanberg, eds., *The Kazaks of China: Essays on an Ethnic Minority.* Uppsala, Sweden: Studia Multiethnica Upsaliensia, 1988, pp. 141–188.

Bessac, Frank. "This Was the Trek to Tragedy." *Life,* November 13, 1950.

———. "Winter in Timurlik, 1949–1950: Life in a Kazak Nomad Encampment," Unpublished ms. 1998.

———. *Revolution And Government In Inner Mongolia: 1945–1950.* Papers of the

Michigan Academy of Science, Arts, and Letters, Vol. I., (1964 Meeting) *Impressions of Inner Mongolia, 1945–1950.* Studies on Mongolia, Proceedings of the First North American Conference on Mongolian Studies.

Byers, Mel and Verne Morse. "Detour: Tibet Journal," *The Christian Standard,* Issue No. 40, October 7, 1950.

Clark, Milton J. "How the Kazakhs Fled to Freedom." *National Geographic,* November 1954.

Clifton, Tony. "Tibet: Shards of a Nation." May 31, 1999.

Colton, F. Barrows. "Weather Fights and Works for Man." *National Geographic,* December 1943.

Lattimore, Owen. "The Desert Road to Turkestan." *National Geographic,* June 1929.

———. "New Road To Asia." *National Geographic,* December 1944.

———. "China Opens Her Wild West." *National Geographic,* 1944.

———. "Byroads and Backwoods of Manchuria." *National Geographic,*

Liu, Melinda. "Tibet: China's Kosovo." *Newsweek,* April 19, 1999.

———. "When Heaven Shed Blood," *Newsweek,* April 19, 1999.

Lungta, Vol 7. *The Institution of The Dalai Lamas.* Dharamsala, India.

———, Vol 8. *The Amnye Machen Range. Ancestors of the Tibetans.* Dharamsala, India.

———, Vol 10. *The Lives of the Panchen Lamas.* Dharamsala, India, Winter 1996.

Mackiernan, D. S. and H. T. Stetson, *On the Observation and Measurement of the Apparent Shift in Direction of the Radio Beam of an Air-Beacon and Certain Relations to Meteorological Conditions,* Transactions American Geophysical Union, 1942.

Martynov, A. S. "On the Status of the Fifth Dalai Lama. An attempt at the interpretation of his diploma and title." Budapest: Proceedings of the Csoma De Koros Memorial, 1976.

Okada, Hidehiro. "The Third Dalai Lama and Altan Khan of the Tumed." Tokyo.

Paxton, J. Hall and Milton Lehman. "I Escaped Over the Roof of the World," *The Saturday Evening Post,* April 29, 1950.

Paxton, J. Hall. "Flight From China," *U.S. Camera,* Spring 1950.

Petech, L. *China and Tibet In The Early XVIIIth Century. History of the establishment of the Chinese Protectorate in Tibet.* Leiden: E. J. Brill, 1972.

Powell, John B. "Today on the China Coast." *National Geographic,* February 1945.

Richardson, H. E. "The Fifth Dalai Lama's Decree Appointing Sangys-Rgyas Rgya-Mtsho as Regent." London: Bulletin of the School of Oriental and African Studies, 1980.

Shaw, Sin-Ming. "Opinon Column." *Newsweek,* December 14, 1998.

Tolstoy, Ilia. "Across Tibet from India to China." *National Geographic,* 1943.

NEWSPAPERS

Air Force Times, June 19, 1980, "U.S. Listening Posts Jeopardized in China," by Balman Jr., Sid.

New York Times, July 30, 1950, front page. And other dates for DSM.

New York Times, January 30, 1950, "U.S. Aide Accused As Spy By Peiping", p. 1. "Washington Not Worried At Lack of News Of U.S. Diplomat Accused by China Reds", inside page. January 31, 1950, Page 3. February 1, 1950, Page 2. June 5, 1950, inside page, "Kazakhs Crushed Chinese, Reds Say." July 29, 1950, page 3, Mackiernans death announced. July 30, 1950, Page 1. August 6, 1950, Bessac survives. October 19, 1950, page 27 Mackiernan honored at State Department.

Lodi (California) *News-Sentinel,* April 31, 1950.

Pan American Air Ways, September/October 1936, in-house newpaper. page 3. "Hurricane Chasers to Havana."

South China Morning Post, May 31, 1996. "Xanadu Remains Closed, Controversial."

The Sunday News, New York, October 19, 1947. Photo Feature: Sinkiang Tinder Box of Asia, by Pegge Parker (Margaret Hlavacek).

The Washington Post, November 10, 1950. "Bessac Says Tibetans Slew M'Kiernan as He Raised His Hands."

REFERENCE

The Columbia Encyclopedia, fifth edition. Columbia University Press, 1993.

Lhasa Old City, Vol II, *A Clear Lamp Illuminating the Significance and Origin of Historic Buildings and Monuments in Lhasa Barkor Street,* Tibet Heritage Fund, THF, 1999– Pimpin de Azevedo, Andre Alexander, Nyima Tashi, John Harrison, Nyima Tsering, Kertsin Grothmann, Zara Thiessen, John Niewoehner, Lhundrup Dorje, Yangdrol. With the support of the German Society for Technical Cooperation (GTZ).

Tibetan Old Building and Urban Development in Lhasa, 1948–1985–1998, Lhasa Archive Project, published in Berlin in 1998 by Verlag Freie Kultur Aktion.

Lhasa City, 1:12,500, Centre for Occupied Tibet Studies, Amnye Machen Institute, 1995.

WEB SITES

The best online source for news and information about Tibet.
Search their archives for any published news story about Tibet in recent years.
Canada Tibet Committee
http://www.tibet.ca/english/

Students for a Free Tibet
http://www.tibet.org/sft/tibet.htm

If you need a quick overview of Tibetan History, this is it.
International Committee of Lawyers for Tibet.
http://www.tibeticlt.org/reports/chron.html

C. W. Tazewell site with much information about Douglas S. Mackiernan.
The only site now devoted entirely to DSM. Tazewell knew DSM.
http://www.geocities.com/Athens/Parthenon/7933/dsm.html

Some things on DSM. He is a grand old man for these folks.
Index to National Weather Association Newsletters and Archives.
http://users.visi.net/~cwt/nwa-indx.html

DSM and Hegenberger's WWII Outfit.
491st Bomb Squadron—H. Q. Tenth Air Force, CBI.
http://pages.prodigy.com/jing_bao/hq_10.htm

U.S. Air Force Biography Major General Albert F. Hegenberger 1895–1983.
http://www.af.mil/news/biographies/hegenberger_af.html
Other USAF sites of use.
www.southernheritagepress.com/Aug45.htm
www.geocities.com/Pentagon/9669/341bombgroup/hq_10.htm
Also see National Aeronautics Hall of Fame web site.

A good place to start looking at what China has done in Inner Mongolia.
Turbulent Rule Over Mongolia, Resistance Efforts Discussed.
http://www.taklamakan.org/smongol-l/archive/bahe1.html

Excellent presentation of Chinese vision of Tibet,
Or: how China twists history.
The Historical Status of China's Tibet.
http://www.tibet-china.org/historical_status/english/

Eastern Turkistan Information Center.
http://www.uygur.com/english.htm

UIGHUR-L Members Link Page.
http://www.taklamakan.org/uighur-l/member.html

DSM contributed to the foundation of this field and some of the little information about
him comes from tracking leads in this area.
Index to National Weather Association Newsletters and Archives.
http://users.visi.net/~cwt/nwa-indx.html

Central Asian Studies World Wide.
http://www.fas.harvard.edu/~casww/

U.S. Army Military History Institute.
http://carlisle-www.army.mil/usamhi/

U.S. Department of State Reading Room.
http://foia.state.gov/cgi-bin/cqcgi.exe/@dos.env

State Department's, Foreign Relations of the United States—Volumes Online.
http://www.state.gov/www/about_state/history/frusonline.html

Air Force History site.
http://www.au.af.mil/au/afhra/link.htm

List of CIA's Deputy Chiefs of Intelligence (DCIs) through Helms.
http://intellit.muskingum.edu/intellsite/ciadcis_folder/ciadcisthruhelms.html

Air America and the CIA
http://grunt.space.swri.edu/aam2.htm
http://www.air-america.org/about/history.htm

NUCMC Home Page.
http://lcweb.loc.gov/coll/nucmc/

A CIA site.
Center for the Study of Intelligence.
http://www.odci.gov/csi/index.html

The Atomic Archive.
http://www.atomicarchive.com/main.html

Trinity Atomic Web Site and HEW Archive.
http://www.enviroweb.org/enviroissues/nuketesting/

MILNET—Military Open Source Encyclopedia.
http://www.onestep.com:80/milnet/

The Soviet Nuclear Weapons Program.
http://www.enviroweb.org/enviroissues/nuketesting/hew/Russia/Sovwpnprog.html

Selected Works of Mao Tse-tung.
http://www.blythe.org/mlm/mao/mao_sw.htm

The National Security Archive Homepage.
http://www.seas.gwu.edu/nsarchive/

Stefan Landsberger's Chinese Propaganda Poster Pages.
http://www.iisg.nl/~landsberger/zd.html

China WWW VL—Internet Guide for China Studies (ANU/Heidelberg University).
http://sun.sino.uni-heidelberg.de/igcs/

To see how little of use is being released on Tibet, check here.
Central Intelligence Agency—Electronic Document Release Center.
http://www.foia.ucia.gov/

The fact that Frederick Latrash worked for the CIA has been a matter of public record
for many years.
See *http://www.hartford-hwp.com/archieves/42a/129.html* for a list of 20 published works
that touch on his activities.

LATRASH, FREDERICK WALDO

Agee, P. Wolf, L. Dirty Work. 1978 (49 543–4)
Assn. Former Intelligence Officers. Membership Directory. 1984
Counter Spy. Jordan. 1977 (2)
Counter Spy 1975-W (23)
Counter Spy 1975-SU (44)
Counter Spy 1976-12 (27)
Covert Action Information Bulletin 1980-#7 (32)
Eveland, W. C. Ropes of Sand. 1980 (183–4)
Frazier, H. Uncloaking the CIA. 1978 (60 130)

Freed, D. Death in Washington. 1980 (76)

Geheim Magazine (Germany) 1986-#3 (28)

Mader, J. Who's Who in CIA. 1968

NACLA. Latin America and Empire Report 1973-10 (15)

NACLA. Latin America and Emprie Report 1974-08 (8)

Neuberger, G. Opperskalski, M. CIA in Mittelamerika. 1983 (199) Parvus
Company. Brochure. 1987 (5)

Ray, E. Dirty Work 2. 1979 (407-8)

State Dept. Biographic Register. 1973

Tarasov, K., Zubenko, V. The CIA in Latin America. 1984 (121)

Top Secret (Germany) 1992-W (25)

ACKNOWLEDGMENTS

MANY INDIVIDUALS, AND institutions assisted me in so many ways as I worked on this project. I am grateful to all of you—both named and unnamed. I hope this book is some repayment for the offerings you made to this stranger.

This book could not have been written without the help of many Tibetans who gave of their time generously. I owe His Holiness the Dalai Lama sincere thanks for his time, and his clear vision. I also thank Gyalo Thondup, Ngari Rinpoche, the late Anne Thondup, Tsering Tashi, Tenzin Geyche Tethong, Lhakdor Jordhen, Kelsang Gyaltsen, the staff at Kashmir Cottage, the staff at Chonar House, Baba Yeshe, and Lobsang and Ah Tinley. All the staff at the Library of Tibetan Works and Archives was tremendously helpful and have my sincere thanks. I especially thank Lobsang Shastri and Pema Yeshi, both of whom are devoted librarians. May Lord Buddha watch over the people of Tibet.

Much of the primary research for this book was done at the National Archives in College Park, Maryland. The men and women working at NARA are unsung heroes and guardians of history. This is as true for the men and women who push the carts through the miles of stacks as it is for the research staff who helped me locate the needle in their haystack that I was searching for. I salute all employees at NARA for doing a wonderful job and without the sufficient support you deserve. In particular I thank Mary Ronan, Ed McCarter, Kathy Vinson, Michael Hussey, Wilbert Mahoney, Pauline Testerman, and John Taylor. Tim Nenninger, that last document was important, thank you. To Martin McGann—model archivist and researcher—I extend my deepest gratitude.

Mary Mackiernan and her mother, Pegge (Lyons Mackiernan) Hlavacek, her stepfather, John Hlavacek, and her husband, Robin Clark, allowed me a degree of entree into their lives and memories that I had no right to ask for. Without Mary's faith in the story I wanted to tell about her father—and the lengths to which she went to support me as I told that story as I saw fit—Douglas Mackiernan's story would have lacked all emotional depth. Without Pegge's diaries, this story would have been much poorer. My sincere thanks to all of you for your gifts.

Duncan Mackiernan, Stuart Mackiernan, and Malcolm Mackiernan have my gratitude for entrusting me with their memories of their brother. Janice Mackiernan Ianniello was a valuable ally as I researched her mysterious uncle's story. Thank you in particular for the interview with your father. Thanks also to Meredith Mackiernan and Tom Mackiernan. Gail Mackiernan also earned my special thanks for her assistance and trust. To Douglas D. Mackiernan (and your family), my thanks for your honesty and bravery—seems to run in your family.

Frank Bessac participated in more than fifty hours of on-the-record interviews and spent many more hours responding to follow-up questions. He helped me understand the smallest details of his life in China, Inner Mongolia, and Tibet between 1945 and 1950—as well as the larger political events that intersected with his life. Thank you.

Both Vasili Zvansov and Erwin Kontescheny were extremely generous and helpful to a stranger, despite the long hours of intense questioning. I thank both of you, and your sons, Alex Zvansov (and Wendy Sisson) and Leonid Kontescheny, for trusting me and sharing your memories with me. America owes men and women like Zvansov and Kontescheny a great debt. These people were willing to risk their lives for the ideals of this nation even before they became citizens—you are true Americans.

General Lewis L. Mundell, C. W. Tazewell, Frederick Latrash, John Bottorff, Ambassador James Lilly, William Wells, and Leilani Wells were generous with their time and knowledge and I thank them for agreeing to be interviewed. Charles Ziegler and David Jacobson's book, *Spying Without Spies,* was incredibly useful to me, as were the interviews with Ziegler: thank you for assistance and allowing me to stand on your shoulders. Thank you to Aynur Caksýlýk and Jaksylyk Samituly for translating and sharing documents I would otherwise never have seen—I look forward to our meeting. Natalie Burigin, thank you for trying—I understand. Thank you to Karen Back Boatman and Phillip Ho—your story will be told. I am sorry it did not make it into this book. Learning about your story helped me find this one.

Dr. Linda Benson, professor of modern Chinese history at Oakland University in Rochester, Michigan, gave of her time and knowledge graciously, simply because we were interested in similar subjects. Thank you.

I owe special thanks to many professionals and institutions who provided invaluable information, assistance, or guidance: David Rothenberg, Katy Frank, Patricia Roberts, Stefan Landsberger, Robert Gray, Sloane Crosley, Orville Schell, Frances Howland, Robbie Barnett, Mark Bryant, Melinda Liu, Gregory Walker, Nancy Hinton, Rick Hertzberg, Tom Grunfeld, Tsering Shakya, Warren Smith, Melvyn Goldstein, Elliot Sperling, Ed Victor, James Fisher, Matthew Kapstein, Ronald Schwartz, Cathy Bernotas, Chuck Hansen, Kushwant Singh, Steve Wolan, Julia Moore, Scott Moyers, Kevin Lavin, Jeff Long, Ted and Kuniko Thomas, David Queen, Abdulrakhim Aitbayev, Rakhim Aitbayev, Ellis Joffe, George Schaller, Dan Miller, Tony Clifton, Steve Walden, John Dolphin, Phillip Capper, Mikio Kaminaga, Hirouki Yokokura, Irene Kirkpatrick, Edward Kaplan, Henry Schwarz, Randy Sowell, Mitch Wood, Isabel Hilton, Gay Browning, Scott Grogin, Richard Rutowski, Alton Walpole, Mark Magidson, Richard Green, Janet Yang, Danny Halstead, Kevin Ross, Sean Daniels, Raymond Teichman, Jack Churchward, Karl Greenfield, Kate Saunders, Kyra Borre, Philip Clay, Dennis Cusack, Michael Telson, Karl Waldron, Scott Armstong, Oyunbilig, Michael Hanson, Michael Telson, Writers Guild of America, Steven Aftergood at the Project on Government Secrecy, Federation of American Scientists,

Authors Guild, Ed Bolton, Robert Colburn and Mary Ann Hoffman at IEEE History Center, Abdujelil at East Turkestan Information Center, Phil Hogle and ASA Online History, Katherine Gold at the Center for the Study of Global Change, Zhanashyr, Ainur Sydykova at USIS, Almaty, Cwynar Christopher at AFHRA, Harold Young of Barnett and Young Investigations, Glenn LaFantasie, the Naval Historical Center in Washington, D.C., Lt. Jeff Davis, Deputy Public Affairs Officer U.S. Seventh Fleet, Master Sergeant Jim Biggerstaff, superintendent, products and production, Air Force News Service (and Steve Richards, Anna Sutherland, and Stephen Richards also at AFN), FDR Library, Lillian Wilbur at the Air Weather History Office, Randy Sowell at the Truman Library, University of Washington, Greg Hirkin and the Smithsonian Air and Space Museum, Louis Alexander, Elizabeth Andrews, Jean Connolly and Lawrence Bacow at MIT, Frank Phillips, president MIT Class of '37, and Danelle Moon at the Manuscripts and Archives of Yale University Library. I am indebted to many people at the U.S. State Department—both alive and deceased. In particular I thank John Hall and Vincoe Paxton, Harriet Schwar and William Slany.

Morgan Entrekin is a courageous and committed publisher. My personal experience has proven to me that such qualities are rare in the American publishing industry. Heartfelt thanks to Matthew Guma for believing in this story and driving me toward the ability to tell it. Your editing skills, tact, trustworthiness, and perceptiveness were all offered with a remarkable generosity of spirit. My sincere thanks to Gail Hochman who rescued this book when that seemed impossible, and then placed it instantly: I know I did not make it any easier for you. Robert Youdelman has my thanks for his tact and force and for his assistance in the rescue of this book. Daniel Maurer, you came in at the end of the long journey and made arrival seem easy, thank you. Thank you also to Neil Olson. Swain Wolf, thank you for your early and critical assistance. Peter Matthiessen and Oliver Stone both offered me useful education about the narrative path: thank you for putting up with me. Bob Shacochis and Catfish, thank you for your friendship, your knowledge so graciously shared, your hand-holding, and your counsel during hard times.

A special thanks to the late General Aditya Shumsher Rana, A.D.C. to His Majesty King Birendra—may Lord Pashupatinath watch over you. You were right and I did not believe you till you were gone. My humble thanks to the Raja and Rani and people of Mustang, for your hospitality to a stranger. May Lord Buddha watch over the people of Mustang and Solu Khumbu.

I wish that I could publicly thank the people in the CIA who deserve it. I cannot—but you know who you are.

My friends helped me survive this book. Thank you for your friendship: Claire Ritter, Adam Clayman, Thapkhey Lama, Ian Baker, Nick Gregory, Heather Stoddard, Helen Douglas, Chrissy Gregory, Kim Lau Hansen, Lee Birch, George Monagan and Annie Martel, Keith and Meryl Dowman, Carroll Dunham, Thomas Kelly, Sam Chapin, Stobbie Fairfield, Jeff Greenwald, Hugh Moss, Linda Fullford, Molly Bingham, Hamid Sardar, Claudia Cellini, Julian West, Jim and Jane Singer, Sigmund Kvaloy, Nick Seeley, Charles Gay and Pam Ross, Maura Moynihan, Maynard Seaman, Jeremy Pine, Ian and Lois Alsop, the late James Pryor, Thomas Burke, Patrick Gauvain, Jack Corman, Andy Rogers, Johnny Birt, Mike Kefford, Vittorio Chiaudano, Francesco Papalia, Diane Summers, David and Shawn Schenstead, Barend Toet and Kate Russell, Ellen Livingston, Susan Becker, Alexandra Morrow, Morris and Erin Kittleman, Gordon Campbell, Toni Collette, Jonathan Rhys Meyers, Erin Potts, Brian and Carlene Keller, Peter Blessing, Greatneck, Peter and Tanya, David and Louise Allardice, Videah Shrestha, Emil Wendel, Thomas Schrom, the late Jim Traverso, Martin Lama, Toni Neubauer, Victor Chan, Warangkhana, Charles Lambe, Gary McCue and Kathy Butler, Josh Baren, David Breashears, Francis Klatzel, Maraleen Manos-Jones, Hugh Downs, Pico Iyer, Dale and Christopher Davis, John Stewart, David and Christine Wiley, David and Suzi Kleinman, Dan and Jill Richter, Peter Bendry, David Hurst, Steve Brothers, Stuart Hawkins, Jenny Dubin, Mary Ellen and Jerry, Nancy Jo Johnson, John Fredericks, Eric Valle, Charles Henri Ford, Ira Cohen, Don Seckler, Billy Hamilton, Frank Ward, Gary Del Valle, Bill Abbott, Bob A., Susan R., Kerry Moran, Mike M., Matthieu Ricard, Robert Kelly, Jeff Bornemeier, Moke Mokotoff, Ganden Thurman, Bob Thurman, Barry Bryant, Tsutomu and Nel Shimda,

Juyo and Harry Masuno, Julia Chang Bloch, Frank Douglas, Kafle, Meen, Jay Furman, Shanti and Jagdish Rana, Jerri, Michael and David Silpa, Gyelbu, Pimba, Krishna, Bharat, Janaki, Ken Crawford, and, last but not least, Bosworth Dewey and The Gang at the now defunct Ratso Palace.

Michael Victor worked for weeks to help me transcribe some of the interview tapes. He also worked with me, without any prayer of compensation, when I was first trying to understand the story I had uncovered. When I began the last lap toward a finished book, Mike was also there again, editing, prodding, questioning, and supporting my work with unflinching devotion. Mike, you have been a true friend. Thank you.

My family was of direct support to me as I worked on this book and I am grateful to: Earl and Bonnie Fenner, Tommy Laird and Lois Wilson-Laird, Terry and Jeff, Timothy Laird, Jason McCrary, Alfred and Vicki Laird, Charles Laird, Albert Laird, Imogene Laird, Jerry Laird, Leroy Laird, Heather Laird, Michael and Elizabeth Laird, Alledia and Kevin Tubbs, Mary Ann and Steve Collara and Jimmy— as well as Lee and Lynn Fowler.

The following were essential products or services during the research and writing of this book: Switchboard.com, Google.com, Microsoft Encarta World Atlas, MSWord, Dell Computer Corporation, Eva Airlines, Thai Airlines, United Airlines, Avis, Wanderers' Mail, Hardy's Nottage Hill SE Australian Wine, Starbucks, Pete's Coffee, Jitendra, and Beltronix.

Jann Fenner, my best friend and wife, bore the weight of this book and without her daily support and patience I could not have completed it. Further, she believed in what I was doing and knew why, even when I forgot. Thank you.

I extend my sincere gratitude to all of you for your contributions to my education. If I have offended any of you in my eagerness to discover and write this story, please forgive me. Despite the generosity of so many, I assume full responsibility for my interpretation of the facts as I have been allowed to know them.

Thomas Laird—laird100@yahoo.com

INDEX